Morocco

Perfect places to stay, eat & explore

Contents

Rural Idylls

Cities

Coast

Small Gems

Mountains

Into the Desert

Morocco

0   50   100km

ATLANTIC

OCEAN

WESTERN SAHARA

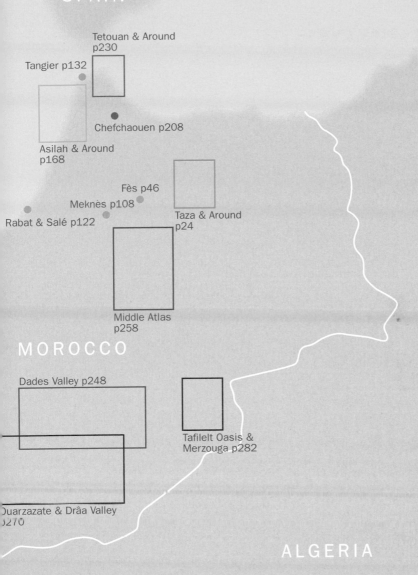

SPAIN

Tetouan & Around
p230

Tangier p132

Chefchaouen p208

Asilah & Around
p168

Fès p46

Meknès p108

Taza & Around
p24

Rabat & Salé p122

Middle Atlas
p258

MOROCCO

Dades Valley p248

Tafilelt Oasis &
Merzouga p282

Ouarzazate & Drâa Valley
p270

ALGERIA

Published by Time Out Guides Ltd, a wholly owned subsidiary of Time Out Group Ltd.
Time Out and the Time Out logo are trademarks of Time Out Group Ltd.

© **Time Out Group Ltd 2008**

10 9 8 7 6 5 4 3 2 1

This edition first published in Great Britain in 2008 by Ebury Publishing
A Random House Group Company
20 Vauxhall Bridge Road, London SW1V 2SA

Random House Australia Pty Limited 20 Alfred Street, Milsons Point, Sydney, New South Wales 2061, Australia
Random House New Zealand Limited 18 Poland Road, Glenfield, Auckland 10, New Zealand
Random House South Africa (Pty) Limited Isle of Houghton, Corner Boundary, Road & Carse O'Gowrie,
Houghton 2198, South Africa

Random House UK Limited Reg. No. 954009

Distributed in USA by Publishers Group West
1700 Fourth Street, Berkeley, California 94710

Distributed in Canada by Publishers Group Canada
250A Carlton Street, Toronto, Ontario M5A 2L1

For further distribution details, see www.timeout.com

ISBN: 978-1-84670-093-4

A CIP catalogue record for this book is available from the British Library

Printed and bound by Firmengruppe APPL, aprinta druck, Wemding, Germany

The Random House Group Limited supports The Forest Stewardship Council (FSC), the leading international forest
certification organisation. All our titles that are printed on Greenpeace approved FSC certified paper carry the FSC
logo. Our paper procurement policy can be found at http://www.rbooks.co.uk/environment.

Time Out carbon-offsets all its flights with Trees for Cities (www.treesforcities.org).

Introduction

Welcome to *Time Out Morocco: Perfect places to stay, eat & explore*, one in a new series of guidebooks that picks out the very best of a country. We've chosen 20 of Morocco's most inspiring destinations, with the most compelling sights and landscapes, and singled out the most appealing hotels, shops and places to eat.

The phenomenal growth of Marrakech as a tourist hub – largely through the conversion of old Medina houses into boutique hotels – has been the big story of the last two decades. Marrakech is a wonderful destination (featured in this book, of course), but now we want to bring you more – the best of the whole country, with all the major cities and our pick of rural and coastal areas. Our out-of-town chapters don't aim to cover an entire region: instead, we focus on areas rich with interest. Our aim is to introduce the amazing diversity of Morocco, a country with snow-capped mountain peaks, green valleys, desert sands and Atlantic swells.

If the physical environment of Morocco has more than its fair share of beauty and drama, the built environment is equally entrancing and diverse. Some towns have a local colour: Marrakech is known as the red city (it's more ochre really); Chefchaouen is blue. The past is written on the peaks and valleys of the Atlas Mountains in the form of abandoned earth-coloured kasbahs, or fortified palaces; and it's very much present in the green-tiled roofs and intricate multicoloured mosaic tiling of medieval Fès. The restoration drive, now spreading throughout the country, is responsible for some of Morocco's loveliest hotels, combining traditional aesthetics, artisanship and materials with modern comforts, as well as ensuring the future of historical monuments.

A word about the listings. The £ symbols indicate the price bracket of a venue: £=budget, ££=moderate, £££=expensive and ££££=luxury. Most hotels accept Visa and MasterCard credit cards, but it's wise to check first as this isn't always the case, particularly with budget establishments. Budget restaurants are unlikely to take credit cards. Many restaurants and hotels are hidden away deep in the mountains or countryside. In these cases we've indicated a location relative to a nearby town or village, but do check venues' websites for detailed directions.

All our listings are double-checked, but businesses do sometimes close or change their hours and prices. While every effort has been made to ensure accuracy, the publishers cannot accept responsibility for any errors this guide may contain.

Contributors

Claire Boobbyer is a freelance writer, photographer and editor. She first photographed Marrakech in 2003, and fell in love with the colours, carpets and riads. She returned to the imperial cities and the Middle Atlas for this guide.

Sam Le Quesne is a travel writer and guidebook editor who has spent the last ten years visiting and writing about Europe, North Africa and America. He first visited Morocco on a three-month trip in 2000 and has never missed an opportunity to return. He researched this book by car, bus, mountain bike, quad, camel and surfboard.

Jonathan Perugia is a London-based travel, commercial and documentary photographer, who has photographed over 35 books for *Time Out* and other publishers in cities all over the world, This was the first of what he hopes will be many wonderful journeys in Morocco.

Suzanne Porter is a photographer and writer. After several jobs in Morocco she realised she liked it so much that she bought a house there. She now lives in a crumbling little riad in the heart of the Marrakech medina, where dodging donkeys and snake charmers is all in a day's work.

Dave Rimmer is a travel writer, guidebook editor, music journalist and author, who divides his time between Berlin and London. Since 2001 he has visited Morocco many times, taking every opportunity to explore more of the country.

Gavin Thomas is a freelance travel writer specialising in Asia and the Arab world. He first visited Ouarzazate in 1999, and dreams of one day being able to drive (or ride a camel) south along the old route from Zagora to Timbuktu.

Emma Woodhouse is a lifestyle journalist and founder of a publishing agency. She has written for and edited travel and in-flight magazines on four continents and travelled to over 20 countries. She loves Morocco for its contrasts.

Contributions by chapter

Ameln Valley & Tafraoute Sam Le Quesne. **Taza & Around** Claire Boobbyer. **Casablanca** Emma Woodhouse. **Fès** Claire Boobbyer. **Marrakech** Dave Rimmer; *Marrakech's party people* Ros Sales. **Meknès** Claire Boobbyer. **Agadir to Sidi Ifni** Sam Le Quesne. **Asilah & Around** Sam Le Quesne. **Essaouira** Dave Rimmer. **Rabat & Salé** Claire Boobbyer. **Tangier** Sam Le Quesne. **El-Jadida, Oualidia & Azemmour** Emma Woodhouse. **Chefchaouen** Sam Le Quesne. **Taroudant** Sam Le Quesne. **Tetouan & Around** Sam Le Quesne. **Toubkal Atlas** Dave Rimmer. **Dades Valley** Dave Rimmer, Gavin Thomas, Edoardo Albert. **Middle Atlas: Azrou, Ifrane, Midelt & Around** Claire Boobbyer. **Quarzazate & Drâa Valley** Gavin Thomas. **Tafilelt Oasis & Merzouga** Dave Rimmer, Suzanne Porter, Edoardo Albert; *Queen of the south* Dave Rimmer.

Time Out
Travel Guides

Worldwide

All our guides are written by a team of **local experts** with a unique and stylish insider perspective. We offer essential tips, trusted advice and honest reviews for everything you need to know in the city.

Over 50 destinations available at all good bookshops and at timeout.com/shop

Time Out Guides

Featured Places

DAR AZAWAD
Le Riad au désert — M'Hamid, Maroc

www.darazawad.com

DAR AZAWAD   "the house of hot winds"

In the Draa Valley, where the road stops & the great Saharan desert dunes start, Vincent Jaquet created Dar Azawad an oasis of peace in perfect harmony with its fascinating natural environment. Here, among the Saharoui Nomadic people, proud of their tradition & their legendary hospitality Dar Azawad is built in the in the purest local Moroccan tradition, in the heart of the Palmgrove.

Dar Azawad's gardens, pools, hamam, jacuzzi, massages with argan oil, desert sand rooms and cuisine will make your trip at the edge of the desert unforgettable.

Location: near M'Hamid el Ghrizlane, 80 km from Zagora & 250 km from Ouarzazate.

LES BIVOUACS D'AZAWAD
at the dunes of Ch'Gaga

Dar Azawad's tented camps are set 60 km from M'Hamid el Ghrizlane, amongst the most stunning dunes in Southern Morocco.
Discover the adventure from in these tents, both authentic and luxurious.
Be charmed by the songs of Sahara nomads, under a sky of millions of stars amongst the infinity of the desert.

Transfers to and from Marrakech, by private chartered plane or by 4WD car.

vincent@darazawad.com
www.darazawad.com
00212 (0) 24 848730
00212 (0) 61 247018

Time Out Guides Limited
Universal House
251 Tottenham Court Road
London W1T 7AB
Tel + 44 (0)20 7813 3000
Fax + 44 (0)20 7813 6001
Email guides@timeout.com
www.timeout.com

Editorial
Editor Ros Sales
Listings Checker Amina Agueznay
Proofreader Jo Willacy
Indexer Holly Pick

Managing Director Peter Fiennes
Financial Director Gareth Garner
Editorial Director Ruth Jarvis
Deputy Series Editor Dominic Earle
Editorial Manager Holly Pick
Assistant Management Accountant Ija Krasnikova

Design
Art Director Scott Moore
Art Editor Pinelope Kourmouzoglou
Senior Designer Henry Elphick
Graphic Designers Gemma Doyle, Kei Ishimaru
Ad Designer Jodi Sher

Picture Desk
Picture Editor Jael Marschner
Deputy Picture Editor Katie Morris
Picture Researcher Gemma Walters
Picture Desk Assistant Marzena Zoladz

Advertising
Commercial Director Mark Phillips
International Advertising Manager Kasimir Berger
International Sales Executive Charlie Sokol
Advertising Sales (Morocco) Aniko Boehler
Advertising Assistant Kate Staddon

Marketing
Marketing Manager Yvonne Poon
Sales & Marketing Director, North America Lisa Levinson
Senior Publishing Brand Manager Luthfa Begum
Marketing Designers Anthony Huggins, Nicola Wilson

Production
Group Production Director Mark Lamond
Production Manager Brendan McKeown
Production Controller Damian Bennett
Production Coordinator Julie Pallot

Time Out Group
Chairman Tony Elliott
Group General Manager/Director Nichola Coulthard
Time Out Communications Ltd MD David Pepper
Time Out International Ltd MD Cathy Runciman
Group IT Director Simon Chappell
Head of Marketing Catherine Demajo

Maps Kei Ishimaru. Marrakech maps by JS Graphics (john@jsgraphics.co.uk), based on material supplied by Jean-Louis Dorveaux.

Back cover photography by Olivia Rutherford and Elan Fleisher.

Photography by pages 3, 16, 21, 22, 32, 35, 36, 39, 40, 43, 44, 134, 137, 140, 143, 144, 147, 150, 168, 171, 175, 176, 179, 180, 182, 184, 187, 191, 192, 198, 203, 204, 206, 207, 208, 213, 214, 217, 218, 230, 235 Jonathan Perugia; pages 21, 134, 149, 224 Sam Le Quesne; 3, 24, 28, 46, 49, 51, 52, 55, 57, 58, 60, 62, 110, 115, 116, 119, 120, 121, 122, 124, 128, 131, 132, 172, 236, 237, 243, 258, 261, 262, 265, 266, 276 Claire Boobbyer; 30, 31, 64, 71, 81, 82, 87, 89, 90, 93, 94, 99, 182, 188, 192, 196, 238, 248, 268, 267, 282 Olivia Rutherford; 3, 14, 15, 74, 152, 153, 154, 157, 158, 162, 166, 220, 222, 226, 228, 238, 245, 247, 248, 251, 252, 255, 256, 270, 279, 282, 288, Suzanne Porter; 71, 270, 276, 280, Elan Fleisher; 195, 287 Dave Rimmer.

The following images were provided by the featured establishments/artists: pages 97, 160, 179

The editor would like to thank Abdella Lahrizi, Rahmouni Aziz and Youssef Maamri.

Rural Idylls

Clockwise from top left: Tafraoute; Souk de Babouches, Tafraoute; Hotel Salama; Souk de Babouches, Tafraoute; Aït Mansour; Chez Messaoud; painted rocks.

Ameln Valley & Tafraoute

Ringed by cloud-capped peaks, riven with deep valleys and gorges, the landscape that surrounds Tafraoute bears the scars of the earth's formation. The drama, the sheer, barren scale of what's here seems somehow too big for human habitation. But, from the lush oases cradled in the Aït Mansour gorges to the thriving town of Tafraoute and its satellite villages, this is a region that is very much lived in. Not just lived in, in fact, but enjoyed and made to prosper thanks to its abundant natural resources and, in no small part, to the curiosity of visitors drawn here by a sense of adventure or a desire to surround themselves with some peaceful, quiet and empty space.

While trekkers and sundry scalers of the Anti Atlas have known about the relaxed, high-altitude town of Tafraoute for decades, it is much more than a base camp for the expeditionary-minded. It is a peaceful pocket of civilisation whose spectacular surroundings make it seem somehow cosier, that little bit more welcoming than your average Moroccan town. And furled around it are the ancient villages of the Ameln Valley, their dwellings shored up against the sheer stone of the valley walls (many seemingly a hair's breadth away from subsidence, with all manner of elaborate props allowing their façades to continue to cheat gravity).

Just a short drive, up and over a skyscraping mountain road, are the plunging rose-tinted gorges of Aït Mansour. Here, the transformation in scenery is simply amazing. Where a few minutes ago there was nothing but arid mountain roads, suddenly the horizon disappears behind rock faces vaulting up to the heavens, dense groves of palms and streams huddling at their feet.

Explore

Tafraoute is in the midst of the stunning Ameln Valley, which is dotted with tiny villages. To the south are the dramatic gorges of Aït Mansour.

TAFRAOUTE

The town is simply laid out and compact (it can comfortably be walked end to end in 20 minutes), with one main square (the bare, unlovely place El-Massira, also known as place Mohammed V) and a couple of sweet little permanent markets. The most interesting of these is the Souq de Babouches (slipper market), which consists of a few interconnected alleyways of leather goods stalls, redolent with the tang of hides and ringing with the sounds of artisans beating, nailing and stitching them into shape. At the top (southern end) of this market, around the entrance to Hôtel Salama (*see p20*), is where the town's few hustlers congregate to make half-hearted attempts at luring tourists to one of a few tacky souvenir shops or sub-standard restaurants.

The most famous of Tafraoute's sights are to be found a short(ish) walk to the south of town. Chief among these are the **Painted Rocks**, a group of boulders decorated by Belgian artist Jean Vérane (who has produced similar works in Texas, Corsica and Egypt). Stranded in the middle of an arid, scrubby landscape, the rocks (painted mostly in sky blue tones, some in earthy reds) are striking, even after 25 years, when much of their colour has been bleached out by the sun.

The route to the rocks takes you via the picturesque village of **Tazekka**, whose mud-red buildings are almost lost to the eye against their background of wind-smoothed boulders, piled high against the horizon. It is here that a prehistoric 'gazelle' rock carving can be found (look for the indistinct original, rather than the much more clearly discernible recent addition), and, a short distance away, also en route to the rocks (overshadowing the village of Aguerd Oudad), the famous **Châpeau de Napoléon**. This latter, an enormous rock in the shape of a tricorn hat, is perhaps the least impressive sight in these parts, simply because wind erosion and the flukes of natural geometry have created innumerable fascinating rock formations in this area – it's just that this one happens to have a name. Unlike, for instance, others that we spotted: 'man with long neck and pipe' (just to the north of the Painted Rocks) or 'glass with swizzle stick' (on the road to Tazekka).

These trips can be made on foot but are best negotiated on mountain bike (known as *VTT*) or on quads, both of which can be hired at Tafraout Quad (*see p23*). Serious stone monkeys and trekkers planning more ambitious trips will want to have a word with Houssine Larousse at Coin des Nomades, an excellent climbing centre next to the Hôtel Salama (*see p20*).

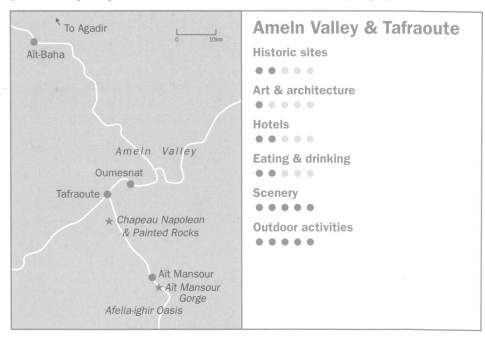

To Agadir

Aït-Baha

0   10km

Ameln Valley

Oumesnat

Tafraoute ●

★ *Chapeau Napoleon & Painted Rocks*

● *Aït Mansour*
★ *Aït Mansour Gorge*
Afella-ighir Oasis

Ameln Valley & Tafraoute

Historic sites
● ● ● ● ●

Art & architecture
● ● ● ● ●

Hotels
● ● ● ● ●

Eating & drinking
● ● ● ● ●

Scenery
● ● ● ● ●

Outdoor activities
● ● ● ● ●

AMELN VALLEY

Among the small villages that cling to the hills on either side of the Ameln Valley, the most popular, and by far the most accessible, is **Oumesnat**. A once ramshackle roadway leading up to the village has recently been completely resurfaced and is now smooth enough to play billiards on – hence the increased traffic in daytrippers and mobile-homers.

But despite these gestures at modernisation, the valley remains an essentially isolated, parochial place (to see just how life was lived a century ago, pay a visit to the Musée de la Maison Traditionelle; *see below*). And it's all the more charming for it. To get there (on foot or by bike), take the main road north out of Tafraoute and turn off on to the dirt track on the right hand side of the road when you reach the low-rise, pinkish ONEP building. From here, continue all the way along the track, past the old Jewish mausoleum (a domed blue and white structure with a star of David above its doorway) until you rejoin the main road (now running east to west). Opposite you is the new road to Oumesnat.

"Tandilt is the very essence of the place that time forgot."

Heading out of Oumesnat on to the circuit of footpaths, beware of the various pipes and conduits that surface likes giant worms in the dirt beneath the loose, gravelly track. The walk back to Tafraoute is not one you'd want to undertake with a sprained ankle. But persevere, as **Tandilt**, the neighbouring village (to the west) is well worth a visit. Half in ruins and yet still very much inhabited, Tandilt is the very essence of the place that time forgot. Magnificent views appear at odd corners of its overgrown streets as sightlines of the mountains suddenly open up – or else as an unexpectedly immaculate house with verdant walled garden and bright stained glass windows hoves into view.

On a practical note, many of the footpaths that connect the Ameln's villages are unreliable and often prove to be impassable or dead ends. It's best, then, to stick to the main road and take its signposted turnings to the various access points along the valley.

Musée de la Maison Traditionelle
Oumesnat *Centre d'Oumesnat (066 91 77 68). Open 9am-6pm daily. Admission free (small donation expected).*
Despite being blind and of eminently pensionable age, the charismatic Mr Abdesalame continues to guide visitors around his makeshift museum. Simply put, it is an unreconstructed Berber dwelling, whose rudimentary interior has been left intact from the early part of the last century: the kitchen, with its open chimney and mud walls, is still stocked with ancient bellows, earthenware pots and wooden utensils; the living quarters (for the family and for the cattle) remain as they were; the roof still has its drying pegs, where porcupine skins dangle in the sun until they are ready to be made into quills. But what makes a visit here really worthwhile is that this is the house where Mr Abdesalame was born, and where he grew up, making this a uniquely personal tour. He will show you, for instance, what looks like an ancient lacrosse racket dangling from the ceiling, but was in fact his infant cradle. He will tell you (in French) stories from his childhood – how he and his brothers slept out on the roof in the heat of the summer, counting the stars until they fell asleep. Enchanting stuff and, true to Berber tradition, this is history straight from the horse's mouth.

AIT MANSOUR

About 30 kilometres south of Tafraoute, the jaw-dropping gorges of Aït Mansour have to be seen to be believed. The route there (the winding, high-altitude mountain road via the village of Tisrirte) is certainly too long to walk, which leaves several options. The most popular of these is to hire a *grand taxi* to take you to the village of Aït Mansour, deep in the gorges, and continue from there on foot to explore the Afella Ighir oasis to the south. The most fun, however, is to be had by hiring quads from Tafraout Quadbikes (*see p23*) and making the journey there on your own.

By crossing the *oued* (small river) at Aït Mansour, you officially enter the green-fringed oasis of Ifella Aghir, where towering palms sway at the roadside, and the way underfoot suddenly transforms from smooth tarmac to rough track. Continue (on foot or by quad) as far as the precipitous village of **Gdourt**, where the uneven roofs of packed-earth houses huddle around the bright white beacon of the mosque's minaret.

On the way, you will notice that many of the palms' trunks are burnt and blackened; this is not a result of the heat or natural fire. Years ago, when an infestation of locusts threatened the crops, locals burnt huge pyres to chase them away – a tactic that, in time, succeeded and restored the fortunes of the area. For more stories like this, stop for refreshments and a chat at the charming Chez Messaoud (*see p20*) along the way.

Eat

Unsurprisingly for a region renowned for its almond harvest, this ingredient features in many of the local dishes, especially tagines and salads. Foodies, then, should lick their lips, those with nut allergies should seal theirs.

Café Atlas
Tafraoute *Place Al Massira (072 196349). Open 8am-10pm daily. £. Moroccan.*

Facing the Étoile d'Agadir (*see below*) across the town's main square, the Atlas does pretty much the same job as its opposite number, mainly to fill a mealtime gap and slake the morning thirst for coffee and the need for a refreshing juice when the afternoon sun gets too hot to handle. It may not exactly perform its duties with style, but it gets the job done: brochettes are fresh, ditto the tagines (which are priced according to weight), and the lighter snacks (kefta sarnies and the like) are a good bet for a quick lunch. The lip-smacking fruit juices and decent coffee are also reasons to come here – as is the presence of a well-fed and contented café cat (a heartening exception to the scrawny, mewling norm).

Chez Messaoud
Aït Mansour *Douar Tizghit (028 801245). Open 11am-6pm daily. £. Moroccan.*

A sight for trail-sore eyes, Chez Messaoud appears rather unexpectedly at the end of a corridor of palm-lined piste and broken asphalt. Other than a small RV park and a couple of modest local houses, there is little sign of life on this remote strip of the Aït Mansour gorge, and so it's a welcome surprise to discover not just a restaurant here, but a pretty decent one, to boot. The place consists of little more than a small shop stall (selling chocolate bars and various nick-nacks) and, behind that, a handful of tables in a scrubby garden. But the food, which is ferried across from the busy kitchen in the house on the other side of the track, is hard to fault. Piping hot tagines, freshly squeezed orange juice and mountains of couscous are cheap, cheerfully served and provide filling fuel for the next leg of the journey.

Chez Sabir
Tafraoute *41 Route d'Amelne, opposite the hospital (066 41 99 68). Open 11am-2.30pm, 6.30-11pm daily. ££. Moroccan.*

Foodies will want to seek out this pretty and accomplished restaurant, sequestered down a small sidestreet (next to the Café de Paris) a few paces away from the bustle of place Moulay Rachid. Its intimate dining room has the feel of a well-kept secret, with smart paintwork and elegant seating enlivened by a quirky eye for detail – a fragment of an ancient door, for example, hangs where a picture might be. The man in charge is Abdel, who works tirelessly in his gleaming kitchen to produce high-quality traditional dishes. His speciality couscous (vegetable, lamb or chicken) comes highly recommended, while excellent tagines and interesting soups (pea and avocado, say) are good winter warmers to restore the tissues of trail-weary trekkers. Salads, brochettes and a variety of other dishes are also on offer, depending on what's fresh at the market – call ahead to book a table and Abdel will tell you what's on the menu.

L'Etoile d'Agadir
Tafraoute *Next to Post Office, place Al Massira (028 800268). Open 8am-10pm daily. £. Moroccan.*

Looking out on to the innocuous salmon-coloured façades of an essentially characterless square, the Etoile is not exactly a destination restaurant but it is, by and large, the most popular of the town's cheap eats. Why? Partly because the no-nonsense menu delivers on its modest promises of tagines, salads, brochettes and all the other bog-standard Moroccan stuff, partly because it has the occasional glimmer of live entertainment, and partly because it's in a convenient location on the town's main square. Not a show-stopper, then, but it's fast, convenient and perfectly palatable.

Restaurant Le Tanger
Tafraoute *Rue El-Jeish El-Melaki (028 800190). Open noon-3pm, 6-10pm daily. £. Moroccan.*

It doesn't look much from the outside (or, put another way, it looks like what it is: a budget hotel) but the restaurant at Le Tanger is, in fact, one of the better cateries in town. As long as you avoid any dishes that are obviously a concession to the town's tourists ('spaguitti', for example) , you will end up having a decent meal here, for little more than a few quid. Tagines are the pick of the menu (the almond and prune version, in particular) but the omelettes are also good and the juices refreshingly fortifying (notably the *jus de bananes*). The dining room has the bleak functionality of a retirement home refectory, so bring a partner or a book.

Stay

Hôtel Les Amandiers
Tafraoute *BP 10, Centre de Tafraoute (028 80 00 08/ www.hotel-lesamandiers.com). £.*

From its location, atop a small hill on the southern edge of the town, Les Amandiers overlooks Tafraoute's mosaic rooftops and has uninterrupted views of the mountains beyond. The rooms and public spaces have the curious distinction of being at once homely (wood panelling, 1970s lounge chairs, dining room furniture from the same era) and weirdly functionalist, thanks to a blocky layout and spartan aesthetic that makes the place look like something designed with East European Olympians in mind, back when tracksuits were tighter and sideburns bushier. Still, it's a relaxing and pleasant base, with a typical cross-section of guests ranging from amateur walercolourists to tight-knit cliques of climbers. In short, this remains the most expensive (and, let's be fair) best hotel in town. Just don't expect anything too fancy. Tafraoute doesn't do fancy.

Hôtel Salama
Tafraoute *Opposite Souq de Babouches (028 80 00 26/ www.hotelsalama.com). £.*

With a smart lobby, clued-up staff and tidy, bright guest rooms, the Salama is a good option for those who don't want to dirty their hands with the town's budget hotels nor shell out the few extra dirhams for a room at Les Amandiers (*see above*). The reception area is especially cosy in winter, thanks to its log fire and sofas, but summer visitors will have to content themselves with the rather prosaic roof terrace, whose views of concrete rooftops bristling with satellite dishes won't be making it on to any postcards. Also, the Salama's highly convenient location,

Clockwise from top left:
Aït Mansour; painted
rocks; Gdourt; Ameln
Valley; Aït Mansour;
Ameln Valley.

Chez Messaoud (top);
Yamina (bottom).

right in the heart of the town, hard by the mosque, is a bit of a double-edged sword (at this range, the muezzin's call has all the mystery and charm of a Metallica soundcheck). Still, there's plenty of good, strong coffee in the hotel's pleasant terrace café.

Tizourgane Kasbah

14km N of Tafraoute *Souk Khemis des Ida Ougnidif (061 94 13 50/www.tizourgane-kasbah.com). £.*
You will see it from the road, some way out of town on the 105: a sturdily defiant hilltop kasbah, fortified, ancient, surrounded by a basin of arable land at the foot of the mountains. And you won't believe your eyes. It looks like something out of *Lord of the Rings*. And yet this is where the softly spoken Jamal was born, it is where he and his families sought refuge for centuries against marauders and warlords, and it is the same kasbah that had all but fallen into abandon and ruin, until, that is, Jamal decided to quit his job in Agadir and come back to make something of the place. It was a long, gruelling project, with years spent sleeping under a leaky roof, but finally it is finished, much of it Jamal's own work. And the result is one of the most extraordinary guesthouses in Morocco. Beyond the thick walls and mighty gates are ancient, narrow streets, their original painted doorways still intact; blustery, deserted ramparts with staggering views; gorgeous little guest rooms entwined around secret staircases; a cushion-strewn salon illuminated by firelight; a roof terrace at the ceiling of the world, circled by hawks, enveloped by a blazing canopy of stars. A once in a lifetime experience.

La Maison Traditionelle

Ameln Valley *Centre d'Oumesnat (066 917768). £.*
A pretty, secluded guesthouse in the heart of the Ameln Valley (follow the signs for 'Maison d'Hôte' at Oumesnat), the Maison Traditionelle provides an updated, fully plumbed and nicely furnished glimpse of life in a typical Moroccan rural community. Surrounded by palm groves and almond thickets, the tastefully furnished rooms have amazing views of the lush vegetation for which this valley is renowned (especially in spring, when the blossom swirls into great drifts along the paths and fields). Treks into the surrounding hills and mountains can be organised here, or you can just content yourself with enjoying nature from the comfort of the pretty roof terrace. The switched-on and dynamic Rachid, his two brothers and their sister (a talented cook) take care of the daily running of the guesthouse, but for the real low-down on what peasant life around these parts used to be like, you'll need to pay a visit to their father at the fascinating museum next door (*see p19*).

Yamina

Ameln Valley *Off the Route d'Agadir, Tandelt (070 52 38 83). £.*
More sophisticated than the other *maisons d'hôte* around these parts, Yamina offers something a little more than the simple charms of a spruced-up Berber house nestled among the mountains. There is a certain style, flair even, in the way the place has been furnished, with whitewashed walls (to match white-painted furniture) and the occasional splash of colour (wooden beams, say, painted a pastel pink) artfully combining to create a distinctly contemporary vibe. There are similar nods to modern design in the choice of furniture or in the way that the simple lean-to eating areas have been put together on the terraces. There are only a few rooms (with a maximum capacity of ten) so it's wise to call ahead, especially given the relatively remote location (a good half-hour's walk out of Tafraoute in the Ameln Valley village of Tandelt – follow signs from the main road, then head for the white and yellow minaret of the village mosque).

Factfile

When to go

The Ameln Valley, best known (and, indeed, named after) the innumerable almond groves that stretch along its floor, is at its most spectacular in spring, when its fields and pathways are decorated with delicate blossom. Otherwise, the altitude means that winters are certainly chilly and the surrounding mountains inaccessible to all but the most experienced climbers and trekkers.

Getting there

Buses and grands taxis leave from Rue Al Jeish Al Malaki in Tafraoute. Various bus companies have kiosks and offices along this road.

Drivers can take Route 104 east from Tiznit or Route 105 south from Agadir. Both are very scenic roads (besides the great views, keep the camera handy for the sight of mountain goats grazing in the argan trees). Both are also very tortuous and very high, so take it slow.

Getting around

You can get around Tafraoute on foot but you'll need transport to stray much further afield. Hire bikes (pedal powered or motorised) from Tafraout Quadbikes (Avenue Mohamed V, route Hôtel Les Amandiers, 070 409 384/ www.tafraout-quadbikes.com).

Tourist office

Office du Tourisme (ONMT), Place Prince Héritier, Agadir (028 846 377/www.visitmorocco.com). Open 9am-12.30pm, 2-6pm Mon-Fri.

Internet

Cyber Tafraoute (Route de Hôtel Les Amandiers, no phone). Open 9am-9pm daily.

Clockwise from top:
Parc National du Tazekka
(2); Medina, Taza (2);
Gouffre du Friouato.

Taza & Around

Built as a fortress, with forbidding defensive walls dating from the 12th century, Taza straddles the wide slash between the grey flanks of the Rif mountains and the first verdant slopes of the Middle Atlas. For many centuries its strategic position meant that everyone wanted a piece of it. Successive dynasties fortified it, used it as a garrison town and a base for conquering sorties. Today, it is a rather isolated provincial town – with stunning views of not one but two mountain ranges.

The isolation becomes apparent as you head out of Fès. The approach to Taza climbs steeply through rolling hills of brown and velvety green. Rows of olive trees and bean plants cling tenaciously to rubble-strewn earth. Nearby is the wilderness of Jbel Tazekka National Park, a nature reserve that is part forested hills and part red gorge, and home to the largest cave system in North Africa. From its peaks there are stunning views of the Rif to the north and the Middle Atlas and snowy Jbel Bouiblane to the south. In the forest are waterfalls, and Barbary sheep and deer make their home here.

Foreign visitors are pioneers here: this green, wild Morocco has yet to make it on to many itineraries. But those who find their way here will discover a pristine natural beauty in lieu of tourist-pleasing facilities.

Explore

Looking at Taza today, it's hard to imagine it being fought over by waves of occupiers from the 12th century Almohads to the French in the 20th century. Twenty-first century Taza is a quiet provincial town.

Jbel Tazekka is to the south-west. It's a hilly landscape of 13,700 hectares covered with great swathes of green oaks. The Gouffre du Friouato cave system extends 245 metres into the earth; the flat expanse of the Dayat Chiker lake bed, dry for much of the year, is another dramatic feature.

TAZA

The town of Taza is made made up of two distinct parts: Upper Taza is the Medina, with some three and a half kilometres of fortifications; Lower Taza is the Ville Nouvelle. Around two kilometres separates the New Town centre from the Medina.

To enter the Medina, climb the many wide stone steps facing the main road leading to the Ville Nouvelle, which lead up to, and skirt around, the 12th-century Almohad city walls. Entering the Medina at Bab (Gate) Jemaa, to the left is place Ahrrache, leading into place Moulay Hassan, with maroon café awnings around the square and the ivory-toned minaret of the Moulay Hassan mosque. Bab Guebor and the Governor's House are past the square on the left. From here, swing right along rue El-Haj and the southern wall of the Medina, lined with acacia trees, before heading back into the Medina through Bab Titi. Steer to the left, and after 500 metres you will come to Bab Er-Rih, the Gate of the Wind, on the northern side of the Medina. From here there are sweeping views to the slopes of the lower Rif.

From Bab Er-Rih walk west, along the Medina perimeter, towards the Almohad Sarasine Tower for a good view of the town's honey-brown outer ramparts, much of them crumbling. As you walk, there are stunning views along the valley. Returning to Bab Er-Rih, turn your back on the gate and walk straight ahead up the road. You will shortly come across a narrow alley marked Zenquat Zaouia Derqaoua on the left. This will lead you to the Grand Mosque, founded in 1135, with nine entrances. One of the country's oldest Almohad structures, it's inaccessible to non-Muslims.

Head south through the souk before coming to the mechouar (assembly place) and then head towards the Andalusian mosque, which dates from the 12th century. Behind the mosque are the ruins of the Palais Bou Hamra. Bou Hamra was pretender to the throne in the early years of the 20th century. Claiming descendency from the Prophet Mohamed, this eccentric but charismatic figure wandered around performing 'miracles', and had himself proclaimed as Sultan. It's indicative of the fiercely independent spirit of the mountain people of this period, and of Taza's strategic position, that he controlled much of

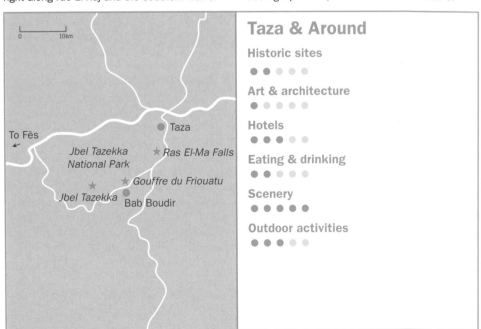

Taza & Around

Historic sites
● ● ● ○ ○

Art & architecture
● ● ○ ○ ○

Hotels
● ● ● ○ ○

Eating & drinking
● ● ○ ○ ○

Scenery
● ● ● ● ●

Outdoor activities
● ● ● ○ ○

eastern Morocco from this palace for some years. He was captured by Sultan Moulay Hafid, brought to Fès in a small cage, fed to the lions (who refused to eat him) and eventually killed in 1912.

PARC NATIONAL DU TAZEKKA

Climbing out of Taza on Route 5411, the most incredible view of the Rif and, behind you, the Atlas mountains unfolds.

There are stepped falls at **Ras El-Ma** (head of the spring), some 14 kilometres from Taza. Shepherds bring their flocks down from the hills to drink here. Just beyond is Ras El-Ma village, which has a reservoir full of trout. The café just before the reservoir on the left (unsigned except for an Arabic Coca Cola sign beside the white arch) has fabulous views.

Climbing higher, you pass almond trees and shrubby green oaks before arriving at the first viewpoint. From here there is a panorama of the surrounding area: Taza, in the flat valley below, and the Rif mountains some 40 kilometres away.

The official park entrance is at the village of Sidi Majbeur. Beyond the village is a picnic area with a kiosk that opens during the summer months. Inside the park, green signs mark walks, with lengths, estimated times, and degree of difficulty. The starting points are marked by a red arrow painted on to stone or a red/green dot.

The park, initially 680 hectares, was created in 1950 with a mission to protect the Tazekka cedar. It was extended to 13,700 hectares in 2004. Forest covers 70 per cent of the park area, and trees include the Atlas cedar (Cedrus Atlantica), the green oak or holm oak (Quercus Rotundifolia), the Portuguese oak (Quercus Faginea), and the cork oak (Quercus Suber).

Climbing higher, the oaks metamorphose from shrub to proper tree. Keep on the road for Bab Bouidir, and Dayat Chiker will come into view on your left. This vast, flat expanse of rubble-strewn and cereal-field laden land is actually a seasonal lake, but recent water shortages mean it has been empty for longer periods.

Opposite Dayat Chiker is the entrance to the **Gouffre du Friouato**, limestone caves said to be the deepest in North Africa (open 6am-sunset daily; 5dh entrance). Over 500 steps take visitors into the bowels of the earth – a depth of nearly 250 metres. It costs 200dh to hire a guide who will take you three kilometres inside the caves. Torches and suitable clothing are available. Drinks and snacks are sold on site. One kilometre beyond the cave entrance and 1.5km south off the main road is the Gîte d'Etape Aïn Bechar (067 25 44 21; 30dh a night per person; meals, 40dh) on Dayat Chiker. Jassabe, the owner, has one room for six to eight people.

Bab Bouidir is the next village along, with camping facilities (no phone; open summer only, parking 5dh per metre). Just past the village is

the park information centre. Inside are detailed information boards on the park's flora and fauna, in French and Arabic only.

On the road to Bab Azhar, stop for the second lookout point, which has wonderful views of the 3,172-metre Bouiblane, with snow streaking down its brown-black, brooding slopes.

Just past this lookout point is a nine-kilometre unmarked track to the right, which leads up to **Jbel Tazekka**. A 4x4 will make it (as will a Berber 4x4, otherwise known as a donkey). From the summit (1,998 metres), surrounded by green, temperate forest, the view of the dry and denuded Rif beyond is a stark contrast.

Back on the main road, the gnarled branches of cork trees begin to emerge. Moss grows on some of the trunks, lending a velvet sheen to the bark. Cork from here is exported to Spain for house insulation, bottles and sandals and is harvested every ten years by hand.

Just before the second picnic area is the Vallée des Cerfs, the deer reserve (Barbary deer, which had disappeared from the park, were reintroduced in 1994; in 2002 there were 44 animals) and a magical cork tree glade where the grass appears a luminous green.

After passing through the gate out of the national park, the road pushes through the red craggy river gorge of the Oued Zireg. The turning to Aïn-Sahla is along here on the left.

The route detailed above can also be done in reverse, turning south off the Fès-Taza road at the Sidi-Aballah turn-off (this is also the auberge Aïn-sahla turn off), 35 kilometres before Taza. The entire circuit is 76 kilometres.

Parc National du Tazekka

055 28 00 96/drefne@eauxetforets.gov.ma/ www.tazekka.com. Abdelaziz Rahmouni (035 28 00 96/ azizandy2000@yahoo.fr) of the Direction des Eaux et Forêts can provide written information.

Eat

Taza and tourism is a marriage not yet consummated, and there are no restaurants catering to the whim of the discerning foodie. That said, you won't go hungry.

Café La Jaconde

Ville Nouvelle *Zanquat Oujda (035 28 24 74). Open 6am-10pm daily. Café. £.*
This popular café serves pastries and creamy cakes coated with apple, strawberry or chocolate flakes from the best pâtisserie in town, Pâtisserie du Palais. Customers can order a cake, and then sip mint tea from pretty duck eggy blue and burnt orange tea glasses. La Jaconde also does a line in juices, in flavours including almond, avocado, apple and banana. In summer there's ice-cream too.

Auberge Aïn-sahla.

Grand Hotel Dauphiné Restaurant

Ville Nouvelle *Place de L'Independence (035 67 35 67). Open noon-3pm, 6-10pm daily. £. International.*
This cavernous hotel dining room offers standards of the omelette, brochette, escalope, pasta and spaghetti bolognese variety. Portions are generous: a beef brochette came with peas, rice, beans and a large chunk of mashed potato. Another bonus is that beer, wine and spirits are available.

Restaurant Pizzeria du Jardin

Ville Nouvelle *44 rue Sultane Abou El Hassane (035 28 19 62). Open noon-midnight daily. Moroccan/International. £.*
This great-value, simply furnished restaurant turns out a tasty pizza, with a good range of toppings. There's also a long menu of meat and fish tagines, fried fish, omelettes, chicken and cheese paninis, brochettes, and couscous on Fridays.

Restaurant La Tour Eiffel

Ville Nouvelle *Route de Fès, Route No.6 (035 67 15 62). International. ££.*
Another functional hotel restaurant. The menu is oddly ambitious: there are some 15 fish dishes, including exotica like sea bass grilled with fennel and *filet de St-Pierre* with green peppers, as well as paella, grilled sole and fish brochettes. Meat dishes are the likes of veal escalope and lamb chops grilled with thyme. There's also a tourist menu of salad, fried fish or grilled meat and crème caramel.

Stay

The Auberge is the best place to stay in the area. Although hotels in Taza town are serviceable, they don't have charm or style.

Auberge Aïn-sahla

Bouchfaa, 37km W of Taza *BP 59 Oued Amlil-Bouchfaa, 35250, Taza (061 89 35 87/www.ain sahla.com). ££.*

Aïn-sahla is owned and run by Aomar Ouardiri, who devoted ten years to building this haven on a hillside. Aomar wants guests to have a share of his quality of life: watching the sun set over the mountains; pottering about the gardens of olives, figs, oranges, roses, lemon trees, apple trees, and strawberry bushes before congregating around the outdoor barbecue or indoor fireplace. Among the 25 rooms scattered across a series of terraces are troglodyte rooms with little bathrooms through a connecting arch. You can also stay under a Bedouin tent, and there are more conventional rooms too. Woodburning stoves provide heat in winter. There's a hammam and sauna on site and a pool for summer. The funky restaurant serves traditional Moroccan food; it's BYO alcohol. Aomar can organise tours from here to the park by horse or on foot.

To reach the Auberge, take the turning at Sidi-Abdallah, 37km before Taza on the road from Fès. The turning is marked by a yellow national park sign and a sign saying Bab Azhar. Drive 14km towards the national park.

Grand Hotel Dauphiné

Ville Nouvelle *Place de L'Independence (035 67 35 67). £.*
With occasional flashes of art deco flair, this dusty pink and cream hotel, while not grand, has an excellent location at the heart of the Ville Nouvelle. There are 26 standard bedrooms with ensuite bathrooms; if you're thinking of visiting outside the summer months, bear in mind that there's no heating. It's a busy hotel, and doesn't accept telephone reservations.

Hotel La Tour Eiffel

Ville Nouvelle *Route de Fès, Route No.6 (035 67 15 62/ tourazhar@hotmail.com). £.*
The location isn't convenient, but the Tour Eiffel is the most comfortable place to stay in town. There are some 30 rooms with air-conditioning and TV and decent-sized ensuite bathrooms with showers; ask for the rooms with incredible views of the Medina and Atlas mountains. It's extremely quiet and the staff bend over backwards to help. The on-site restaurant has a reasonable menu but the breakfasts need some work.

Factfile

When to go

Winters are cold but a drive around the national park in the snow is beautiful. Most of the region's snow falls in December, January and February, but it can snow any time between October and April. In spring, between March and June, flowers flourish and rain pumps life back into the trees. Temperatures are comfortable in summer. Spring, summer and the beginning of October are best for birdwatching.

Getting there & around

Taza can be reached from Fès on three trains a day (2 hours 10 minutes).

A taxi from Fès to Taza officially costs 500dh. You will need your own transport to complete the circuit, or you can hire an entire *grand taxi* from Taza for around 500dh.

Tourist information

There is no tourist information. Aziz Rahmouni (*see p27*) can help with information about the national park.

Internet

Cyber Friouato Net, Rue de Fès Oujda, close to Café La Jaconde, Taza (035 67 29 02). Open 24hrs daily.

Cities

Clockwise from top left:
Hôtel Volubulis; port;
Hassan II Mosque;
Sacré Coeur; place
des Nations Unies;
Central Market.

Casablanca

Preconceptions of Casablanca are often wrong. Glamorous visions of Humphrey Bogart and intrigue in the kasbah bear little relation to this thoroughly modern metropolis. In many ways Casa, as everyone calls it, is more Marseille than Maghreb. This is the country's economic powerhouse; the principal port, centre of finance, industry, commerce, media and manufacturing. Its imposing sprawl is home to more than three million inhabitants, and as the shanty towns on the outskirts attest, more are arriving every day. Not all of them make it out of the *bidonvilles*, of course, but the city remains a magnet of opportunity, its energy and verve unmatched in the Maghreb.

Detailed town planning and other large infrastructure projects by the French in the early 20th century have shaped the modern city. In 1912 Morocco's Résident Général, Hubert Lyautey, declared that Rabat would be Morocco's Washington DC, and Casablanca its New York. The resulting economic and property boom left a legacy of myriad 20th-century architectural styles, particularly art deco and its colonial spin-off, Mauresque. There are deco gems everywhere, not all of them well preserved.

In Casablanca today, residential boulevards that wouldn't look out of place in Beverly Hills, along with chic French restaurants and chi-chi beach clubs, play host to Morocco's wealthiest and most westernised people. And while the city's seafront is dominated by the immensity of the Hassan II Mosque, Casablanca is also home to North Africa's largest Jewish population, consisting mainly of well-off, middle-class Moroccans.

Explore

It was the conquering Portuguese who turned a pre-existing settlement into a fortress and called it 'Casa Branca' (White House). The Lisbon earthquake of 1755 flattened the town and the Portuguese deserted it. Sultan Sidi Mohammed Ben Abdellah reclaimed the area in 1770 and began reconstruction, building the Medina to the east of the ruined port: the surviving walls and Grand Mosque date from this period. Only the name of the Portuguese settlement survived, mutating into its Spanish version when European merchants began establishing themselves in the area after 1830. Increasing European influence, and French rule from 1907 to 1956, left behind a café culture and a distinctly European-style infrastructure.

Though daunting at first, orientation is actually easy in Casablanca. The central points of reference are Place des Nations Unies, adjacent to the Old Medina, and Place Mohammed V to the south. Streets of Mauresque architecture, cafés and hotels radiate from these hubs. Jump in a taxi for La Corniche or the Quartier Habous.

VILLE NOUVELLE

Place des Nations Unies is an empty expanse, complete with concrete underpasses and dominated by the Hyatt Regency. But this is where the Medina meets the New City, and from here Casa's main avenues reach out in all directions. Boulevard Mohammed V, heading eastwards, was once the city's grandest shopping street, but these days is pleasantly down at heel. Reasons to walk this way include an assortment of Mauresque and deco buildings, and the bustle

Casablanca

Historic sites
● ● ● ● ●

Art & architecture
● ● ● ● ●

Hotels
● ● ● ● ●

Eating & drinking
● ● ● ● ●

Nightlife
● ● ● ● ●

Shopping
● ● ● ● ●

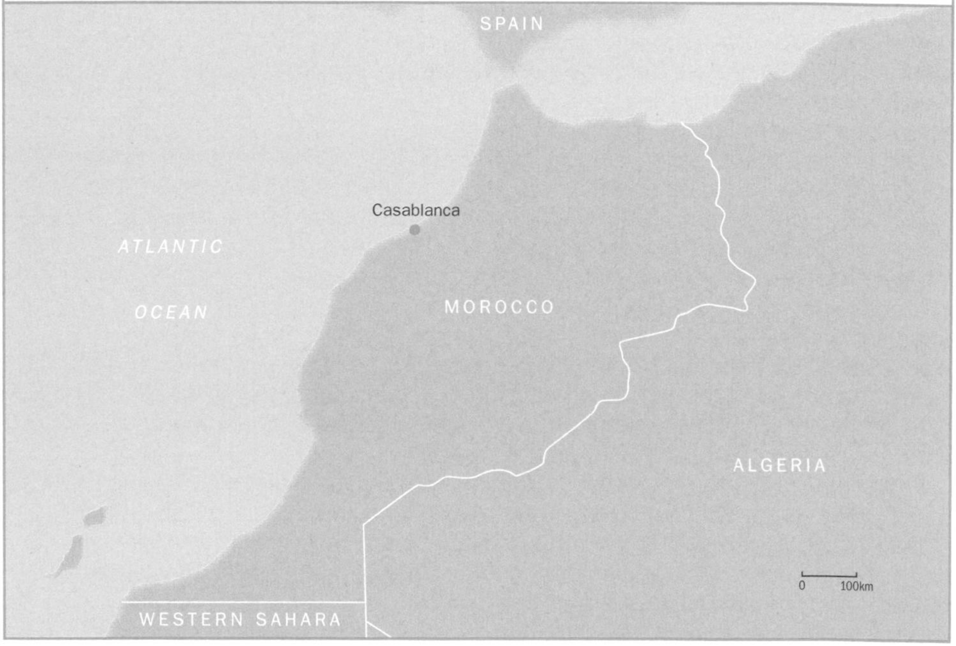

SPAIN

Casablanca

ATLANTIC

OCEAN

MOROCCO

ALGERIA

0   100km

WESTERN SAHARA

Top: Centre Ville.
Bottom: Sacré Coeur
(left); Medina (right).

Hassan II Mosque

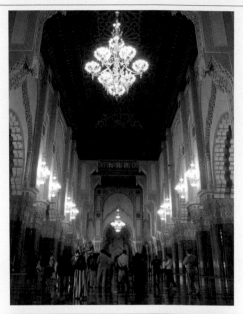

Monumental, triumphal and colossal, Casablanca's landmark mosque was commissioned by King Hassan II for a rumoured excess of £500 million and – amazingly – funded by voluntary public subscription (with, it has to be said, alleged pressure on those less than eager to 'volunteer' their contributions). The mosque was completed in 1993. Its cloud-kissing minaret is the highest in the world at 200 metres. Fifty-seven Murano glass chandeliers hold 50 elaborate bulbs each. Inside there's space for 25,000 worshippers; 80,000 more can pray in the courtyard. An ablution hall has 41 fountains. Built on a promontory over the Atlantic, its dramatic setting references a Quranic quote: 'God's throne is on the water.' A seemingly endless glass floor gives a view of the waters below; above, the entire roof slides back electronically.

The design – by French architect Michel Pinceau – is Moorish, and blends traditional Moroccan decoration with very modern technology and design (in addition to the retractable roof, there are heated floors and flaps in the floor for individual shoe storage compartments).

It took 6,000 Moroccan artisans working with indigenous methods and materials five years to create the intricate tiled mosaics and painted wood ceilings, using crystallised granite from Agadir, cedar wood from the Atlas mountains and three-colour marble from southern Morocco. The ablution hall is plastered with traditional yet practical tadelakt, the same finish beloved of new-generation riads everywhere – a powdered limestone plaster that is then polished with flat stones, sealed with a glaze of egg white and polished again with Moroccan black soap to create a silky yet waterproof effect.

The immensity of scale, the uncanny views of sea and sky through distant arches, even the presence of the sparrows swooping down into the mosque through the open roof: this building is designed to engender a sense of awe – and it succeeds. It is also the only working mosque in Morocco that admits non-Muslims, with tours held between the five daily prayer times. Scarves aren't compulsory for women but both sexes should dress modestly, with clothing that covers knees, shoulders and midriffs.

022 03 34/36. Guided tours 120dh, 30dh children. Sept-June 9am, 10am and 11am, 2pm daily. July, Aug 2pm, 3pm daily.

and fresh produce of the Marché Central. More art deco can be found in streets to the south, between Mohammed V and avenue Lalla Yacout. The area east of rue Chaouia offers a westernised retail experience remote from any souk. This is the heart of the commercial downtown.

In the other direction is the Parc de la Ligue Arabe, with a French-style layout. On its western side is the striking, skeletal **Cathédrale de Sacré Coeur**. A neo-gothic masterpiece in gleaming white concrete by Paul Tournon, with art deco and Mauresque influences, it towers above the palm trees that flank its entrance. After independence it was used as a school, cultural centre and theatre. It is currently closed, but if the guard lets you have a peep inside you will be rewarded with an ethereal, almost fairy ale-like interior.

The two towers of the 28-storey **Twin Center** are nearby, on the corner of boulevards Mohamed Zerktouni and Al-Massira Al-Khadra. But the city's most famous landmark is the gargantuan **Hassan II Mosque**, on the city's northern shore.

Musée de Judaisme Marocain
Ville Nouvelle *18 rue Chasseur Jules Gros, Oasis (022 99 49 40/www.casajewishmuseum.com). Open 10am-6pm Mon-Fri. Admission 20dh. Guided tour 30dh.* Casablanca has the largest Jewish population in North Africa, and this modern, well-curated museum is devoted to the history, religion and culture of Judaism in a Moroccan context, with exhibits covering daily life (jewellery, clothes and so on) as well as religious objects, ranging from old Torah to historical marriage contracts. There is also a library and photographic collection.. The museum functions as a cultural centre and occasional concerts and other performances take place here.

ANCIENNE MEDINA
On the north side of Place des Nations Unies is the entrance to the Medina. Lining the Atlantic coast for a kilometre, the Old Medina was originally surrounded by ramparts, known as the Sqala, parts of which still exist. Most of its buildings date from the 19th century, however. The early part of the route into the Medina from Place des Nations Unies is unappealing. But walk ten minutes past stalls selling pirated DVDs and awful oil paintings of desert scenes and you will come to quieter – mainly residential – alleyways, broader than their equivalent in Fès or Marrakech. The vibe here is pleasantly neighbourly, with cafés with outdoor TVs for the men, women gathering to chat and share tasks, and thriving local businesses like barber shops and grocers.

QUARTIER HABOUS
Where the Old Medina wins points for idiosyncrasy, the new Medina gets by on charm and a Provençal-inspired layout set around communal squares. About a kilometre, or a short taxi ride, south-east of town, the Quartier Habous

lies beyond the Palais Royale and was built by the French in the 1930s in response to a housing shortage. Neat and picturesque, the Quartier Habous is like a Western 'garden city' version of a Moorish quarter. Its souk sells much better craftwork than you will find in the Old Medina.

Across the railway bridge by the market at rue des Ait Yafalman you will find rue Taroudan. Here, fortune tellers ply their trade, and this is the place to buy hedgehogs, crows, chameleons and more for use in magic: a reminder that Casablanca is not always as European as it looks.

AIN DIAB, LA CORNICHE
The coastal road west from the Hassan II Mosque leads into the oceanside suburb of Ain Diab. Sunday sunsets are best spent strolling the promenade on the beachfront here, where the city's residents come to see and be seen, hang out and meet for ice-cream at the beachside cafés and beach clubs. If you are coming in from the city centre, the El-Hank promenade appears on the right. Clusters of loved-up couples sit along the mile-long stretch, admiring the sleek cruise liners, the El-Hank lighthouse and Hassan II Mosque in the distance.

Most of the beach clubs here have bars and pools more suitable for swimming than the rolling Atlantic, and sell day tickets.

Eat

As you would expect of a city this size, there are restaurants serving food from many corners of the globe in Casablanca. But this city is best known for its seafood. In addition to the places listed below, you can find great seafood (at knock-down prices) at the stalls behind the Marché Central.

La Bavaroise
Ville Nouvelle *Rue Allal ben Abdellah 133, Marché Central (022 31 17 60/www.bavaroise.ma). Open noon-2.30pm, 7.30-10.30pm Mon-Fri; 7.30-10.30pm Sat. £££. French.* Swanky yet intimate, this split-level classic French brasserie pulls off working lunches and romantic dinners with equal finesse. Steak, foie gras, oysters, serious cheeses and dense crème brûlée leave you feeling decadent at decent prices. The wine list is extensive.

La Bodega
Ville Nouvelle *Rue Allal ben Abdellah 129, Marché Central (022 54 18 42). Open noon-2.30pm, 7.30pm-late Mon-Sat. ££. Spanish.* Next door to La Bavaroise (*see above*) and owned by the same group, this Spanish restaurant and bar does dining upstairs and partying downstairs. The walls are covered in signs, posters and beer ads, and a sprightly young team serves up jugs of sangria and great-value regional tapas

sampler menus. There is also a crowd-pleasing selection of pasta dishes, burgers and Mexican food. Cosy booths and kid-friendly fare make it a good place for families during the day. In the evening revellers load up on croquettes and tortilla before heading downstairs for live music and Mojito-fuelled dancing.

La Fibule
Ain Diab *Boulevard de la Corniche (El-Hank) (022 36 06 41). Open noon-3.30pm, 7.30pm-midnight daily. £££. Moroccan.*
An interior as peach, chintzy and cavernous as a Dubai hotel ballroom is remedied by tableside windows overlooking the restaurant's own floodlit and dramatically rocky bit of shore. In the evenings, a lute player and candlelight accompany high-end tagines, pastillas and couscous. The Fez-wearing waiters are friendly and welcoming. A good place to stop for dinner on the way back into town from La Corniche.

Maure at La Sqala
Ancienne Medina *Avenue des Almohades (022 26 09 60). Open 8am-midnight Tue-Sun. ££. Moroccan.*
In pretty much idyllic surroundings in a garden in the shade of the Sqala, the 18th-century ramparts overlooking the fishing port, this bright and breezy restaurant, with doors and tiled seating in bright, luminous blues and greens, makes a great place to stop for lunch. Food is a mixture of standard Moroccan dishes – piquant salads, tagines and the like – along with a few international staples.

"Enjoy big, honest portions of harira soup, stewed aubergine, fried fish, paella and pasta."

Mystic Garden
Ain Diab *Boulevard de la Corniche (El-Hank) 33 (022 79 88 77). Open 8.30pm-late daily. £££. French/international.*
All neutral tones and minimalist lines, Mystic Garden is where the young and fashionable come to dine and party. Food is primarily French, with a few international dishes like Thai green curry thrown in. Tables surround a raised platform, where a jazz band often plays in the evenings. Things get lively after dinner, and the party really gets going around midnight. By then the bar area and garden have filled up with cocktail-sipping and hip-swaying revellers.

Port de Peche
Ville Nouvelle *Port de Peche, Port (022 31 85 61). Open noon-2.30pm, 7.30-10.45pm daily. ££. Seafood.*
This dark wood, maritime-themed second-floor restaurant overlooks the port, but most people come here for the buzz inside rather than the views outside. It's a much-loved city institution. Wrinkled, bow-tied retainers – who've served thousands of bowls of fish soup in their time – approach

their task with military precision, seating boisterous customers, throwing down fresh paper tablecloths and weaving around carrying bowls of garlic prawns, platters of whole grilled fish and piles of calamari. All orders come with bread, parsley mayonnaise, more-ish fried potatoes and green beans. There's a range of Moroccan wines.

Rick's Café
Medina *Boulevard Sour Jedid 248, place du Jardin Public (022 27 42 07/08/www.rickscafe.ma). £££. International.*
Kathy Kriger – former commercial attaché for the American Embassy, known affectionately as 'Madame Rick' – set herself a difficult mission: to recreate the Rick's Bar of *Casablanca* fame in the heart of the city of that name, while steering clear of cheesy theming and memorabilia. To this end, she scoured Morocco for true-to-the-film fittings and set about creating a space with just the right, slightly louche, colonial look. Set in a lovely three-storey Mauresque building with inner courtyard at the edge of the Medina, Rick's Bar brings the 1940s *Casablanca* look to life, with hand-picked furniture and *objets d'art*, dramatic lighting and sultry acoustics that carry the sounds of Edith Piaf or a jazz jam session around the courtyard. Visitors come to enjoy an international food menu, or to sip cocktails in an upstairs lounge where the film plays silently on a discreet screen built into a wall. Kathy occupies her own corner of the bar, and – just like Rick – plays an active role as host.

Rouget de L'Isle
Ville Nouvelle *Rue Rouget de L'Isle 16, Centre Ville (022 29 47 40). Open noon-2.30pm, 7.30-10.30pm Mon-Fri; 7.30-10.30pm Sat. ££££. French.*
Rouget de L'Isle is an expat favourite, serving grown-up, traditional, fine French cooking – the likes of *mignon de boeuf*, roast pigeon and sole poached *à la dieppoise* – in a stylish 1930s art deco villa, filled with *objets d'art*. A varied wine list matches the classic menu and sophisticated decor. Diners can eat in the comfortable dining room, or outside on the terrace in fine weather.

Snack Amine
Ville Nouvelle *Rue Chaouia 32, Marché Central (022 54 1331). Open 11am-11.30pm daily. £. Moroccan.*
Across the street from the Marché Central flower market, this sizeable, spotless and fuss-free canteen is a Casa institution. Grab a seat outside, facing the bouquets, to enjoy big, honest portions of harira soup and stewed aubergine, salads, fried fish, paella and pasta. Two doors down, Snack Yamine offers a similar but more limited menu late into the night for the post-party crowd.

La Taverne du Dauphin
Ville Nouvelle *Boulevard Houphouet Boigny 115, Centre Ville (022 22 12 00). Open noon-midnight Mon-Sat. ££. Seafood.*
By far the best option for seafood in the city centre, this charming restaurant opened in 1935 and is currently run by an owner from Marseille. It's just a stone's throw from the Hyatt/Hôtel Excelsior roundabout, oozes character and has more choice than most of its ilk: oysters from Oualidia,

Quartier Habous.

Top: Chez Paul. Middle: Rick's Café. Bottom: Pâtisserie Benis Habous.

cuttlefish in ink, mussels, squid, lobster, salads and more. In the back bar locals who work at nearby hotels and markets tuck into olives and plates of fried whitebait, washed down with bottles of Casablanca beer.

Thai Gardens
Ville Nouvelle *Avenue de la Côte d'Emeraude, Centre Ville (022 79 75 79). Open noon-3pm, 7pm-1am daily. ££. Thai.*
This dark wood and plum Thai restaurant attracts some of Casa's most fashionable young diners. They are attracted by the quality of the food – it's probably the best Asian food in the city – and by the sleek, chic decor. Downstairs is the G-Sound bar and DJ lounge, also popular with Casa's young hipsters. Food is also available in the bar (small Thai plates, sushi, the odd modern European dish) – along with good cocktails.

Villa Zevaco
Ville Nouvelle *Corner of boulevard Moulay Rachid & boulevard d'Anfa (022 23 66 00). Open 7am-10pm daily. £££.*
The dining terrace is huge, the linen is white, the women are blinged-up, the suits are razor-sharp. But when the sun is shining on your smoked duck salad and sparkling water, and you're on the terrace of a classic 1949 modernist villa designed by Morocco's most progressive architect, Jean-Francois Zevaco, eating from a menu featuring superlative salads, fresh ravioli and high-end brasserie fare, life can seem pretty good. There is also a patîsserie run by French chain Chez Paul on the premises, and, the management say, this will be joined by an haute cuisine restaurant in autumn 2008.

Shop

Casablanca may be Morocco's biggest city but it's no shopping mecca. The area around the Twin Center, specifically rue Aziz Bellal and Centre Ben Omar, has the best range of womenswear. A few casual menswear shops are also on this street. Rue Al-Massira, across from the Twin Center, is home to Zara, Mango, Massimo Dutti, Lanvin and high-end boutiques.

The city has yet to embrace the notion of upmarket adaptations of traditional indigenous styles – in clothing, interiors, and so on – that has become popular in Marrakech.

QUARTIER HABOUS
The New Medina is a manageable, hassle-free and tat-free souk, with a good variety of local crafts available. There are rows of hanging Berber rugs in one section; another is home to antique shops selling just about everything, from art deco statuettes to old European oil paintings, African statues, heavy silk and gold-threaded antique djellabas, brass urns and leather ottomans. While you're in the market it would be a crime to miss

the gazelle horns from **Pâtisserie Benis Habous** on rue Fklh El-Gabbas (022 30 30 25). The family-run pâtisserie opened in 1938.

Arts

Casablanca has cinemas, cultural centres and art galleries. Listings can sometimes be found at hotel reception desks or in the local papers. The **Complex Cultural Sidi Belyout** at 28 Rue Léon l'Africain (022 30 37 60), behind the CTM bus station, showcases Moroccan music, drama and dance. The **Centre Culturel Français** on Boulevard Mohammed Zerktouni (022 25 9077) has an extensive programme of concerts, exhibitions and films, especially during the winter months.

Arte à Beaute au 9
Ville Nouvelle *Rue d'Irfane, Hay Salam 9, Maarif (022 94 73 97). Opening times vary.*
Co-owned by a Frenchman who also runs L'Oum Errebia, a hotel and gallery in the coastal town of Azzemour (*see p168*), this gallery showcases Morocco's most talked-about contemporary artists and sculptors.

Villa Des Arts
Ville Nouvelle *Boulevard Brahim Roudani 30, Maarif (022 29 50 87). Open 9am-7pm Wed-Sun.*
Opened in 1999 by Swiss curator Sylvia Frei Belhassan, this gallery – set in a 1934 villa with large garden near Sacre Coeur cathedral – shows mixed media, photography and abstract art by Moroccan and European artists, with 800 permanent pieces on show.

Nightlife

Most Casablanca nightlife happens on the Corniche, and at the larger high-end hotels in the city centre. Clubs tend to get going around 11pm and stay busy until 3am or 4am. Outside of La Corniche and city-centre hotels, bars tend to be men-only strongholds.

Amstrong Legend
Ain Diab *Boulevard de la Corniche 41 (022 79 76 56/ www.amstronglegend.com). Open 8pm-late Tue-Sat. £££.*
Part of the Azur Hotel complex, Amstrong Legend is small on space but big on merriment, and the 20-year-old Casa stalwart has a loyal fan base who crowd the dancefloor when the band comes on stage to belt out Top 40 hits and pop classics. Resident bands change every few months and hail from across the globe. There is no sign on the club's door, and the fact that an 'r' seems to be missing from its name only adds credence to artistic director Kevin Jordan's claim that Casablanca's nightlife scene is 'semi-broken, but oh so much fun'.

Black House

Ville Nouvelle *Hyatt Regency, place des Nations Unies (022 43 12 34). Open 9pm-late daily. £££.*

A far-off galaxy meets Studio 54 in the Hyatt's glitzy club, named, we presume, after its all-black interior, which is set off by a ceiling covered in glowing stars. Tables are on tiered platforms in the circular room, facing a laser-lit dancefloor complete with video screens. Tables are reserved most nights of the week for the flashy bottle-service spenders, but most of the fun happens on the dancefloor, where revellers get their groove on to hip hop and Arabic music.

Le Dawliz

Ain Diab *Boulevard de la Corniche 6 (022 39 69 43). Open 9pm-late daily. ££.*

New on the scene and part of Le Dawliz hotel, DJs in this Corniche club spin techno well into the early hours. It's a good place to start an evening before heading further down the coast and stopping in at Mystic Garden (*see p38*), or heading next door to Le Balcon.

Kazbar

Ville Nouvelle *Rue Najib Mahioud 7, Gauthier (022 20 47 47). Open 7.30pm-1am Tue-Thur, Sun; late Fri, Sat. £££.*

Designed by Portuguese architect Miguel Cancio Martins, also responsible for Paris's Buddha Bar and the Raffles bar in Singapore, Kazbar is a trendy place for wealthy young Casablancans to dine and dance. Depending on the night, DJs or live bands get the crowd going amid the sexy black tables and fittings. It's a good idea to book for dinner at weekends.

Le Petit Roche

Ain Diab *Boulevard de la Corniche (022 236 2626). Open 8pm-late daily. ££.*

This first-floor lounge bar next to the El-Hank lighthouse has low-slung seating, and drinking and dancing into the early hours. And if you're in the mood for pondering cultural contrasts, there are some great views of the Hassan II Mosque across the bay.

Stay

Casablanca is a very different city from Marrakech or Fès. Hotels tend to be either five-star chains like the Hyatt and Le Meridien Mansour, or lacklustre inns featuring plastic flowers, ancient sofas and TV-watching guards. But that's not quite the end of the story. Some deco buildings have become interesting and characterful mid-range hotels. And there are even a few tender shoots of a boutique aesthetic emerging, with the appearance of hotels like Jnane Sherazade.

Azur

Aïn Diab *Boulevard de la Corniche 41 (022 79 74 93/ www.hotelazurcasablanca.com). £££.*

Forty-five of the 58 rooms in this Corniche hotel overlook the bay, and there are some great views from higher floors.

The modern building is set back from the beach, has a large pool, comfortable rooms decorated in generic hotel style and most of the amenities one would expect of a four-star, including a pleasant bar called Aladdin. It is also host to the Amstrong Legend club (*see p41*).

Le Dawliz

Ain Diab *Boulevard de la Corniche 6 (022 39 69 43). ££.*

One of Casablanca's new breed of independent mid-range hotels, and – along with the Azur (*see above*) – one of the few hotels on the Corniche, Le Dawliz has 43 spacious rooms, most with sea-view terraces. A stone's throw from some excellent restaurants and clubs, including its own, the hotel has more amenities than most at this price range. Rooms have a TV and mini bar and there is a swimming pool, spa, gym and sauna.

Excelsior

Ville Nouvelle *Rue El-Amraoui Brahim, place des Nations Unies 2 (022 20 02 63). ££.*

The glamour has largely gone from what was Casablanca's premiere hotel back in the 1920s. These days it's a mixed bag: parts of it are newly renovated, while in others the carpet looks as if it was laid in 1915 for the hotel's opening. So it's a good idea to insist on a renovated room. It's also worth taking a moment to poke around the other floors via the spiral staircase and imagine the place in its glory days. The exterior is the most elaborate example of French colonial architecture in the city.

Hôtel Central

Ancienne Medina *Place Ahmad El-Bidaoui 20 (022 22 00 25/022 26 25 25). ££.*

One of a couple of small hotels located inside the walls of the Old Medina and probably the only one worth staying at. The best rooms are the ones with terraces overlooking the port and the little square in front of the hotel. If you can't get one of these, there is always the sunny roof terrace. Rooms are airy and Mediterranean, with solid colours, white bed linen, satellite TV and tiled floors. An international mix of young travellers convenes for breakfast in an elaborately designed Moorish dining room with free Wi-Fi. Scenes from the 2001 film *Spy Game*, starring Brad Pitt, were filmed from the roof. With this kind of clientele it might be worth coming down for breakfast.

Hôtel Maamoura

Ville Nouvelle *Rue Ibnou Batouta 59, Centre Ville (212 22 45 29 67/68/www.hotelmaamoura.com). ££.*

Functional, clean and comfortable, the well-managed Maamoura also has the benefit of a city-centre location, in the heart of the Mauresque architecture district. There's attention to detail here: there's Wi-Fi for guests; showers are of the power variety, and breakfast includes freshly squeezed orange juice. Decor is typical hotel creams and browns, with a few Moorish touches like the lacy stucco work and multi-coloured Moroccan lamp in the lobby.

Hôtel Les Saisons

Ville Nouvelle *Rue El-Oraibi Jilali 19, Centre Ville (022 49 09 01/www.splendia.com). ££.*

Top: Corniche. Bottom: Amstrong Legend.

Top: Hôtel Central.
Bottom: Hôtel Transatlantique.

This well-maintained three star – part of the Splendia chain – is one of the best in its price range. Rooms are well-appointed, air-conditioned and spacious, though there are no surprises when it comes to decor, which is pretty international. The multilingual staff are helpful, and facilities include a small fitness centre.

Hôtel Transatlantique
Ville Nouvelle *Rue Chaouia 79, Centre Ville (212 22 29 45 51/29 52 04). ££.*
This newly restored 1922 building, a highlight of the art deco district, is as embellished with period detail as they come, and resonates with history. Edith Piaf and champion boxer Marcel Cerdain had an affair here in the 1940s and the singer's possessions, including a handbag and accordion, sit in a glass cabinet. The Salle Morocaine features intricate Mauresque stucco work and stained-glass windows, it's an atmospheric place to drink mint tea, or there's bellydancing here at 8pm Thursday to Saturday. Rooms are clean and well-appointed, and the restaurant is open 24 hours.

Hôtel Volubulis
Ville Nouvelle *Rue Abedelkrim Diouri 20-22, Centre Ville (212 27 27 71/ 27 27 72). ££.*

The Mauresque façade of the Volubilis – with wrought iron details and the sign written in a fabulous art deco typeface in cool shades of beige and sage – evoke a time when this hotel was all the rage. Built in 1916 and recently taken over by the management of the adjacent Hôtel Transatlantique, which is accessible by a courtyard, the guest rooms have been given a lick of paint and fresh sheets. If you look closely, you will notice two stars of David on either side of the hotel's sign – a reminder of the city's Jewish heritage.

Jnane Sherazade
Ville Nouvelle *Rue de Belgrade 8, Ben Slimane (022 82 17 65/022 82 44 44/www.jnanesherazade.com). £££.*
A white, detached villa has been transformed into a smart new town *maison d'hôte*. Grey marble and deco-style curved ironwork banisters dominate the entrance hall and main stairway. The six bedrooms and two suites are all spacious and comfortably furnished, with Moroccan touches in the form of tiled floors and bathrooms. The staff are flexible with extra beds for children, and one room has disabled access. The large garden is a big asset for a city hotel, and a new hammam and sauna are other attractions.

Factfile

When to go
Late April to mid June is the most pleasant time to visit Casablanca. The sun shines during the day and evenings are breezy rather than cold. Mid June to late August can be hot, though not unbearably so, and evenings remain cool enough for comfort. You'll need a jacket during the winter months between November and February.

Getting there
There are direct flights from major European cities and New York to Casablanca's Mohammed V airport, located around 25 kilometres south of the city. From the airport *grands taxis* cost around 230dh to the centre of town.

The train system in Morocco is reliable and well-organised; trains arrive at Casablanca's two stations, Casa Port and Casa Voyageur. Fares and timetables are available in French and English on www.oncf.ma, the national rail service's website. Buses from Marrakech and other destinations arrive at the CTM bus station on rue Léon l'Africain, behind the Hotel Farah.

Getting around
From Place des Nations Unies, the Ancienne Medina, cafés, and streets of Moorish art deco buildings are all accessible on foot. Hop in a taxi to get to Ain Diab and La Corniche, Hassan II Mosque, Twin Center, Habous (the New Medina) and the port. Drivers can generally be trusted

to turn the meter on, but it doesn't do any harm to have a quick look to check that it's in use.

There's no shortage of the little red *petits taxis*. People are in the habit of sharing, so don't be put off if a taxi stops for you with a passenger already on board. The driver will ask your destination, and if you and the passenger are going the same way invite you to share the trip; he can press a button on his meter to keep the fares separate.

Street names are prone to cause confusion. Drivers sometimes refer to the Place des Nations Unies, beside the Old Medina, as Houphouet Boigny, the name of the street that links it to Casa-Port station.

Tourist information
Syndicat d'Initiative Boulevard Mohammed V, 98 (022 22 15 24). Open 8.30am-noon, 3-6.30pm Mon-Fri; 8.30am-noon, 3-5pm Sat.

You might find it easier to ask reception in your hotel for information, or one of the four- or five-star hotels on the streets radiating from Place Mohammed V or Place des Nations Unies. Many hotels provide free maps and brochures.

Internet
Casablanca is fairly well served by internet cafés. Gig@Net at 140 Boulevard Mohammed Zerktouni (022 48 48 10) is open 24 hours a day. Many three-, four- and five-star hotels also offer free Wi-Fi.

Clockwise from top left: souks (4); Royal Palace; camel meat stall, souks; *zelije* detail.

Fès

For many travellers, Fès still represents the 'real Morocco': a medieval, labyrinthine Medina, distinctive Arabesque architecture, a total assault on the senses. Heading down the steep incline of Talaa Kebira in the Fès El-Bali district, you are pulled along by a whirlpool of people, goods and overburdened donkeys, towards the holy heart of the Medina, where the cavalcade of sights and smells, and the density of men, women and beasts rises as you approach the core religious sites of the mausoleum of Moulay Idriss II and the Karaouiyine Mosque. Non-Muslims can only glimpse these, but enough of the city is open to all for everyone and anyone to appreciate the glory of the best preserved medieval city in the Arab world.

Developed from the ninth century, Fès became a major centre of religion, culture and learning at a time when the Islamic world led intellectually. Its monuments reflect this status, with numerous *mcrdersas* (religious schools) alongside historic mosques. As well as many distinguished scholars from around the Arab world, it is said that Pope Silvester II (946-1003) studied at Karaouiyine University, the world's first, picking up the latest in mathematical knowledge to take back home.

Fès may be an extraordinary monument to the past, but it's also a living and working city. Around 200,000 Fassi still live within the walls of the medieval Medina area of Fès El-Bali. Many of them work here too, in commerce or trades eschewing modern production methods, producing outstanding decorative arts. To explore this warren of narrow passages, teeming souks, huddled housing, archaic industry and venerable mosques is to find oneself in a space where elements of the Middle Ages never came to an end.

Explore

It's almost impossible to get a sense of the whole city from ground level, but a circuit by taxi of the outer ramparts – around 15 kilometres – provides some kind of overview. Another can be found from the Borj Sud or the Merenid Tombs in the surrounding hills, where there are views over Fès El-Bali that help make sense of the layout.

Fès is made up of three distinct areas: to the north is Fès El-Bali (Old Fès), the core of the Medina; Fès El-Jedid (New Fès), housing the Royal Palace and Jewish quarter (Mellah) is to the south-west; further south-west, outside the city walls, is the Ville Nouvelle. Half the fun of exploring the Medina is in getting lost. However, if this doesn't appeal, you may want to hire an official guide through your hotel. *Faux guides*, although fewer in number than in days of old, still hang out near the entrance to the Medina at Bab Boujloud, touting for business. Official guides, who will have an ID card, are a much better bet (though they too will probably want to take you shopping).

FES EL-BALI

The largest working medieval city in the Islamic world is said to contain 9,400 streets (or alleys), 365 mosques, 80,000 shops, 80 fountains and 80 *fundouks* (merchants' hostels, with accommodation for men and stabling for beasts). Each of its 187 quarters are equipped with a mosque, Quranic school, fountain, hammam and communal bread oven. Even the widest streets are too narrow for cars.

Seen from above, it is a dusty white city of cube-shaped, flat-roofed buildings – today with

Fès

Historic sites
● ● ● ● ●

Art & architecture
● ● ● ● ●

Hotels
● ● ● ● ○

Eating & drinking
● ● ● ○ ○

Nightlife
● ○ ○ ○ ○

Shopping
● ● ● ● ●

Tanneries.

THE SHORTLIST

WHAT'S NEW | WHAT'S ON | WHAT'S BEST

Amsterdam
2009

Barcelona
2009

Berlin

Cyprus

Dubai

Dublin

Dubrovnik

Edinburgh

Florence

Las Vegas

London
2009

Malta

Manchester

Marrakech

Mexico City

New York
2009

Nice & Cannes

Paris

Prague
2009

Rome
2009

San Francisco

Sydney

Tokyo

Venice

- **Pocket-sized guides**
- **What's on, month by month**
- **Full colour fold-out maps**

TIME OUT GUIDES
WRITTEN BY
LOCAL EXPERTS
timeout.com/shop

How to make a Fassi feast

the almonds out of their skin, crushed walnuts, sliced up oranges and onions, rolled dates in desiccated coconut and chopped olives and parsley. It was organised chaos and at the end of it, we somehow managed to pull off delicious *briouates* – chopped olives, paprika and parsley enfolded in soft cheese wrapped in filo pastry, sprinkled with cumin; a Moroccan ratatouille of aubergine, green pepper, artichoke with orange, lemon and garlic; chicken cooked with lemon; and deliciously indulgent date and coconut balls.

Lahcen, who comes from a small village in the High Atlas, has been cooking professionally for some years. The son of a farmer and shepherd, he learned to cook when his parents sent him to school in another town at the tender age of ten, and he was left to cater for himself. He later took cooking lessons in Erfoud. 'The class was entirely women and they wondered what I was doing there,' he remembers. He went on to work as a chef, cooking in some of Fès's top restaurants. *Lahcen Beqqi (015 86 61 44/www.fes cooking.com) 300dh per person for groups of two or more for one-day classes. Longer cooking courses are also offered.*

'Do you eat everything?' The question was particularly apt, considering that it was asked by cooking tutor Lahcen Beqqi, while passing a stall selling camel legs, camel hooves and bulls' penises in the souk area of Fès El-Bali.

We went for a chicken instead. After watching the picking, killing and plucking of our bird we emerged from the bloody meat stalls into the light. The smell of spices and the mounds of semolina were much more enticing. We picked our way through stalls of wild radish, soaking chick peas, fennel, mini celery, enormous tomatoes, fat juicy oranges and cricket-ball-sized purple-skinned onions. Lahcen taught us how to choose artichokes (by their pointedness) and aubergines (by the darkness of their colour). A basketful of vegetables cost us just 15dh – about £1. Finally, we grabbed some filo pastry (ready made, we weren't *that* dedicated) and *khobz* – the ubiquitous Moroccan flatbread.

We went to work in the kitchen of a riad in an operation that was nothing short of military, with strategic planning ensuring we would have multiple dishes ready at the same time for a lavish lunch. To this end, we grated tomatoes, cut artichoke hearts, cubed aubergine, pinched

Souks.

a forest of satellite dishes and antennae sprouting from the roofs. At ground level, it is a place of exquisite decorative artwork, covering panels, columns, doors and domes. Bamboo screens and wooden trellises shelter and cool the alleys of the souks. In each quarter, blacksmiths, coppersmiths and dyers use their skills in traditional artisanship.

One of 14 gates (singular bab), beautiful blue-tiled **Bab Boujloud** is a main entrance to the Medina. From here, to the left, the main street running downhill is **Talaa Kebira** (the big slope); on the right is **Talaa Sghira** (the little slope). Talaa Kebira leads eventually to the main souk area. The road changes its name to rue es-Cherabliyin (slipper makers' street). The Cherabliyin Mosque is on the right. Cobblers and slipper-makers are found just beyond here. Next are stalls trading the gold-tooled leather bookbinding known everywhere as 'Moroccan'. The Souk El-Attarin houses the spice sellers. Note that the **Medersa El-Attarine** is being restored and will be closed until 2010.

Off to the right are the carpenters' and henna souks. Place Nejjarine (Carpenters' Square) is also home to the **Nejjarine Fountain**, with beautiful mosaic tiling. Also to the right off Souk El-Attarin (also accessible from place Nejjarine) is the **Zaouia Moulay Idriss II**. Built originally as a mosque, the Zaouia became a place of pilgrimage after the discovery here of what were said to be the remains of Moulay Idriss II in 1308. A cult was born and the mosque was turned into a shrine, and one of the holiest buildings in the city. Wooden beams mark the limits of the shrine's zone of sanctuary – once non-Muslims were allowed no further. These days you can duck under these and walk around the outside. A glimpse of the legendary founder of Fès's tomb, draped in embroidered velvet and surrounded by candles, praying women and – strange though it may seem – offerings of clocks, can be had from the women's entrance.

The main alley, meanwhile, now known as Souk El-Attarin, leads into place Es Cafforino, where coppersmiths hammer away producing kettles and cooking pots. The firing of the pots produces a noise like a brass band firing up. The really huge ones, for weddings and festivals, are for rent rather than sale. The square has fig trees, a fountain and the entrance to the **Seffarine Medersa**, Morocco's first, founded in 1271. It's still in use by Islamic students.

Also here is Fès's holiest monument, the **Karaouiyine Mosque & Library** (entry for Muslims only). Founded in 857 by Fatima El-Fihri, it was improved and enlarged in the 10th and the 12th century, and also functioned as the world's first university. It's typical of Fès that you can be right outside its biggest and culturally most important monument yet not necessarily even notice that

it's there. Though large enough for 20,000 people to pray inside, and still leave room for one of the Islamic world's most significant libraries (it contains 30,000 books and 2,000 manuscripts), it's so snugly embedded among shops and houses that it's impossible to discern from outside. Only occasional glimpses of the interior are afforded by whichever of its enormous 14 cedar doors happen to be open as you pass – ten of them if it's a Friday. Its exterior can also be seen from gates on Talaa Kebira and place Es-Seffarine. At Bab Wouroud there's a good view of the Saadian ablution fountain. At the north-east corner of the mosque is the well-preserved Tetouani Fundouk, dating from the 14th century.

Medersa Bou Inania

Talaa Kebira. Open 8am-5pm daily. Admission 10dh.
Not far from Bab Boujloud, Bou Inania is the largest and finest medersa in Fès, its lofty, patterned interior and intricately decorated courtyard demonstrating the sublimely sophisticated craftsmanship of 14th-century Fès. Built between 1350 and 1356 by the Merenids, the large central courtyard, with an ablutions fountain in the middle, is covered in decoration, including wood carving, stucco work and *zelije* (mosaic tiling). Inside are fine horseshoe arches, imposing *mashrabeya* (carved wood) screens and delicate *muqarna* (an assembly of highly stylised little niches of stucco or wood carving, stacked in tiers for decorative effect). Its minaret is a web of interlaced lobes in Islamic green, best viewed from Café Clock (*see p56*). Across Talaa Kebira are the remnants of a water clock. How this bizarre construction worked remains a mystery.

Musée Dar Batha

Rue Zerktouni, off place de L'Istiqlal (035 63 41 16). Open 8am-4.30pm Mon, Wed-Sun. Admission 10dh.
South of Bou Inania and reachable from Talaa Seghira, this 19th-century palace boasts a fabulously lush garden that is worth the visit alone. Surrounded by galleries, it is dominated by a giant green oak tree. Orange trees, aspidistra, buddleia, and jacaranda abound; some of the trees are labelled. The exhibits of Moroccan arts and craft include a cushion fragment decorated with embroidery, beautiful calligraphy, mannequins dressed in ornate wedding gowns, Gnaoui instruments, engraved bronzeware, 18th- and 19th-century perfume lances, Berber jewellery, tapestries, and a wonderfully intricate marquetry Quran box, in ivory and bronze and dating from the 16th century. Labels are in French and Arabic only. No photography.

Musée Maroc Belghazi

19 derb El-Ghorba (055 74 11 78/http://museebelghazi. marocoriental.com). Open 9.30am-5.45pm daily. Admission 40dh.
South of place Nejjarine, the Belghazi is a private ethnographic museum set in a riad and run by the formidable Dr Mohamed Belghazi, who may show you around if it isn't too busy. The exhibits are set around the courtyard of the 17th-century house and include gold and silver jewellery from the 17th to 19th centuries, 18th- and 19th-century arms,

embroidered camelhair bags, camel whips, Quran boxes, 18th-century silk belts and 18th- to 20th- century Fès ceramics. Manuscripts, engraved stamps, ink wells, musical instruments and sugar hackers are also displayed.

Museé Nejjarine des Arts et Métiers du Bois

Place Nejjarine. Open 10-5pm daily. Admission 20dh.
Next to the fountain in the place Nejjarine (*see p53*), this three-storey, 51-room *fundouk* was erected by Moulay Ismail in 1711 and restored in 1990. Its interior reveals handsome wooden slatted balconies and in its rooms contain exhibits of carpentry craftsmanship: woodwork utensils, oil presses, bellows, hammam tubs, marriage beds, friezes, musical instruments, Quran tablets, and an interesting collection of combs and kohl pots. Climb to the roof for a restorative mint tea at the café and great views over the Medina. Labels are in French and Arabic only. No photography.

Palais Glaoui

1 Derb El-Hamia, Ziat (067 36 68 28). Open by appointment. Donations appreciated.
Dar Glaoui, a rambling palace in the Ziat quarter, south of Talaa Seghira, was built in the late 19th century and belonged to the Glaoui family who once ruled southern Morocco. The family of Abdelkhalek Boukhars, who currently runs the palace as a sight, has been here for 100 years; currently a plan is underway to restore the building. Some of the interior decoration is exquisite: there's a riot of *zelije* tiling, acres of stucco and tall ceilings. The Andalusian room has windows overlooking a garden, an unusual architectural feature in a style of architecture where the focus is normally on the interior. Dominated by a fountain, the harem area was home to 100 women; now it is unfortunately colonised by pigeons. Look for the colourful doors painted with flowers and leaves around the central dry oblong pool. Abdelkhalek may also show you the extraordinary 100-year-old bathroom with a green marble sink.

DYERS' SOUK & TANNERIES

The lane from the south-east of place Es-Seffarine (*see p53)* drops down to the Souk des Teinturiers, or Dyers' Souk. You'll see swatches of fabric stretched overhead to dry and workers stirring cauldrons, their arms coloured to the elbow in the hue of the day. Men dyeing wool, rolled around their arms, bend over cans dipping and sloshing. The wool is wrung by twisting between two batons. The colours are created by seeds and minerals crushed in a small riverside mill, and small gullies of water rush through the quarter, harnessed to various purposes in a living display of medieval technology.

Even more medieval are the tanneries, or Chaoura, downriver. Follow rue El-Mechattine from the north-east corner of place Seffarine and the odour will soon confirm you are heading in the right direction. The best place to see the tanneries is from the terrace of Terrasse de Tannerie (10 hay Labilda Chouara). Clamber

stairs and pass through stacks of bags, wallets, and *babouches* before reaching the terrace. Shopkeepers will give you an explanation and won't pressurise you too much into buying. The tanneries, a series of honeycomb vats, date from the 11th century and are worked by 60 families. The sheep, goat and camel hides are dunked in water, salt, limestone and pigeon droppings, which contain ammonia, by barefoot dyers. The hides are then transferred to a washer and spinner before being immersed in pools of liquid colour for two weeks. Whipped out, they are then hung on the roofs or strung along the walls to dry for two days.

FÈS EL-ANDALOUS

The Andalous Mosque is at the heart of the Andalusian quarter, settled by Muslim Andalusians after Idriss II, the founder of Fès, called upon them to settle in the city. Lying in the eastern section of Fès El-Bali, it is reached over the Oued Fès river via the Bein El-Moudoun bridge, south of the tanneries. The vast main north gate, dating from the early 13th century, is striking. Little can be seen of the inside of the mosque, founded at the same time as the Karaouiyine (*see p53*) by Meryem, sister of Karaouiyine founder Fatima El-Fihri.

The **Medersa Sahrij** (open 8am-sunset daily, admission 10dh), close to the mosque, was built between 1321-23 by Merenid Sultan Abu El-Hassan. It's built around a large, rectangular central pool (*sahrij*) after which the *medersa* is named.

FÈS EL-JEDID

Fès El-Jedid (meaning New Fès) was built by the Merenids in the 13th century – so it's hardly new any more. Half of the area is taken up by the inaccessible **Royal Palace**, also known as Dar El-Makhzen. The imposing main gate on the place des Alaouites, with its bronze doors, hides the 82 hectares of palace grounds.

Fès El-Jedid can be entered through 13th-century **Bab Semarine**. The rue des Merenides then leads west towards place des Alaouites. Along the route, you first come to the **Mellah**, then the **Jewish Cemetery** (open 7.30am-7.30pm daily) to the south. The Mellah – or Jewish quarter – is a warren of tiny alleys and covered passages. Its houses have windows with ironwork grilles and balconies overlooking the street – a very different style from that of Fès El-Bali. Once Morocco's largest Mellah, all save a handful of an original population of around 17,000 emigrated to Israel during the 1950s and '60s. Some historic synagogues remain, mostly in alleys off rue des Mercnides. **Synagogue Rabbi Shlomo Ibn Danan**, built in the 17th century, has been restored and is free to enter (open 7.30am-7pm Mon-Thur, Sun).

Restoration renaissance

When Fès was declared a UNESCO World Heritage Site in 1980, much of the old city was in a state of decay. The Moroccan government, with UNESCO, began a massive project for the restoration of mosques, *medersas*, *fundouks* and other buildings, and a renewal of Medina infrastructure. Meanwhile, private properties began to be acquired by owners with an interest in the stewardship and preservation of the city's medieval heritage.

Fès Medina Morocco deals with visitors interested in the restoration process. Clients are housed in restored houses and visit properties currently undergoing work, along with artisans' workshops. Hafid El-Amrani, an employee with the company, bought his own house, in the Ras Jnan neighbourhood, in 2003 for €7,000. An abandoned ruin, it was structurally precarious. He estimates (title deeds are often elusive) the house to be 400 years old. He has since spent €1,200 and hopes to finish it for another €8,000. He estimates that, on completion, the house would sell for €60,000-€80,000 but, unlike many other restorers in the Medina, Hafid wanted the place for a home rather than to make a profit.

'I bought the house because it was cheap and I was about to get married and had nowhere to live,' he explained. When he showed his fiancée their new marital home, she told him, with some degree of understatement, that it 'needed a lot of work'.

The house's support columns had to be rebuilt using lime, cement and bricks. Electricity and plumbing had to go in and a wall is being removed to create a balcony. Special liquids are being used to clean the painted woodwork. Up on the roof – a sun trap with sweeping views of the surrounding area – workmen have covered the roof with a sand, lime and rubble mix known as *afira*, after which unglazed tile known as *hresh* will be laid.

In the next neighbourhood, Laayoune, we tour a 300-year-old home in need of serious foundation and sewage attention. The house was bought by a British buyer for €30,000. So far the owner has spent €70,000 on it and is hoping to complete with just another €10,000. It already has a confection of decorative plaster work and very attractive cedar wood lining the *halka* (skylight). A chimney has been installed; the next step is a marble and a *zelije* mosaic tiled floor.

Sadly, Fès's less upright citizens are also reaping rewards from the restoration process. Lori Wood, founder of Fès Medina Morocco,

explained: 'Doors and windows are being stolen from Medina houses and sold to tourists, leaving these houses irreparably damaged. We are encouraging people not to buy objects that have been "salvaged" from these buildings. These items are hot commodities; they are extremely tempting and precious. If only we could change the common perception that it is ethical to buy these things, we would go a long way toward protecting the architectural treasures in the Medina of Fès.' One long-term expat finally tracked down his stolen doors to Rabat, where he had to buy them back.

But difficulties aside, its hard to overstate the case for how much Fés's medieval heart has benefitted from both private and public restoration. Apart from the obvious benefits to the built environment, the interest in preserving the city's heritage is doing a great job of reviving traditional building methods and keeping Fassi decorative arts alive.

Fès Medina Morocco *(www.fesmedina.com) offers restoration tours exclusively to those renting traditional houses through the company. A three-hour tour costs 600dh for two people.*

You can also enter Fès El-Jedid from Bab Boujeloud. The avenue des Francais then leads west towards the enclosed square of the Petit Mechouar. To your left are the peaceful **Boujloud Gardens**, open to all, cut through by ornamental watercourses. This area was a no-man's land until developed by Moulay Hassan in the 19th century. From the Mechouar, head south along the grande rue de Fès El-Jedid to reach the Mellah.

AROUND FÈS

BORJ NORD, BORJ SUD & THE MERÉNID TOMBS

Saadian Sultan Ahmed El-Mansour built the **Borj Sud** on the hills to the south of the city in the 16th century. From here there are incredible views of the Rif to the north-east and the Atlas to the south-east. At the time of writing a new museum of architecture was being created here. The **Borj Nord**, on the northern hills outside the city, also built during Sultan Ahmed El-Mansour's reign, houses the Armaments Museum (035 64 75 66, open 8.30am-noon, 2.30- 6pm Tue-Sun, admission 10dh). Close by are the ruined **Merenid tombs** belonging to the 14th-century sultans of this dynasty. This is a good place from which to view the sunset; make sure you climb down before it gets completely dark.

Eat

As one might expect, the tagine is pretty ubiquitous on the Fès dining scene, though these days a few restaurants offer a bit of variety. Another popular dish is *bessara*, a bean and olive soup sold at small canteens in the Medina. Ladled out into bowls from huge cauldrons, and served with a hunk of bread, it makes a filling lunch, and usually costs a mere 4.50dh. Moroccan pastries are another favourite, and you'll find them piled high in the souks: *chbakiya* are round pastries of flour, honey and sesame seeds; *briwat bloz* are sticky brown triangles of almond paste and pastry.

L'Ambre

Fès El-Bali *Riad Fes, derb Ben Slimane, Zerbtana (035 94 76 10/www.riadfes.com). Open noon-10pm daily. £££. Moroccan.*
Small and intimate, stylish and romantic, L'Ambre sits in an old part of Riad Fes (*see p60*), up a flight of steps from the bar. The look is a kind of contemporary oriental, and one table is lined up against a tiny window from which you can peer down into one of the Medina alleys. The set menu includes some less common or more inventive variations on the Moroccan theme, and the food is wonderful. Tagine m'khader, for example – lamb or beef in a ginger sauce – was full of subtle flavour, as was a tagine of lamb and

apricots. Desserts include sweet briouates with honey. Service is extremely attentive. Alcohol is served. The Riad Fes also serves dinner in more full-on Moorish surroundings in its L'Oriental and Salon Oriental dining rooms.

Café Clock

Fès El-Bali *7 derb El-Magana, Talaa Kebira (035 63 78 55/www.cafeclock.com). Open 9am-8.30pm daily. ££. Moroccan/international.*
Brit Mike Richardson, a former maître d' at the Wolseley, has created a warm, inviting space in the Medina house he has restored. Café Clock has plenty of attractions, in addition to the food, to keep you coming back: a roof terrace with unrivalled views of the superb green Medersa Bou Inania minaret, a small library and WiFi. It also hosts Clock Culture, a programme of music, conversation and art. Food is eclectic, with influences from Morocco and further afield. The Fès Platter is a smorgasbord of onion bread, dates, nuts, warm and gooey aubergine purée, curried cauliflower, and goat's cheese samosas. This can be followed by dishes as diverse as fishcakes, couscous boohaloo – a chicken, apricot, raisin, caramelised onion and almond dish, or camel burger with salad and chips. Pastry chef Tariq's lemon tart is the talk of the quarter but the marble cake with hot chocolate and walnut sauce is a serious competitor.

Dar Roumana

Fès El-Bali *30 derb El-Amer, Zkak Roumane (035 74 16 37/www.darroumana.com). Dinner served 8pm Tue-Sat. Reservations required for non-residents. ££. French.*
This riad is a magical place to dine, with the central courtyard candlelit and the fountain illuminated. There are just four tables. Sebastian, a flamenco guitarist, may treat you to a few tunes while you enjoy a glass of wine, while his wife, and Dar Roumana's owner, Jennifer, a Cordon Bleu-trained chef, puts the finishing touches to some truly great food. The menu changes with the seasons. Hope for the lightest, most delicate goat's cheese soufflé, followed by chicken marinated in sherry accompanied by mashed potato, asparagus tips and saffron. Pudding might be a very rich chocolate mousse with a touch of cinnamon and honey served up in a large glass dish.

Médina Café

Medina *6 derb Mernissi, Bab Boujloud (035 63 34 30). Open 10am-11pm daily. ££. Moroccan.*
Just up from Bab Boujloud, this small two-storeyed café is more elegant and spacious than the nearby Kasbah. It's perfect for a quick meal as service is prompt and you can escape lengthy sessions with a set menu if you are short of time (though set menus are also available). From the roof terrace, there's a view of the blue tilework of Bab Boujloud. If it's raining, the downstairs seating area is inviting, with multicoloured cushions and tiny brass lamps suspended from the ceiling. Moroccan dishes include *briouates* (pastry parcels) of meat, cheese or seafood, and pigeon or fish *pastillas*. The ultra-clean loo is an added bonus.

Palais La Medina

Fès El-Bali *8 derb Chami, Bourajjoue, Racif (035 71 14 37/www.palaismedina.com). Open noon-3pm, 8.30-11pm daily. £££.*

Zaouia of Moulay Idriss II.

Escaping the 'show restaurant' in the Medina is difficult. So you might as well embrace the fun, sit back and enjoy the spectacle. Every night the Palais La Medina puts on an energetic and lengthy performance of drumming, dancing, singing, sorcerer's tricks, a fire-eating belly dancer and a faux Moroccan wedding with volunteer guests adorned in the ceremonial wear. Set in a large house, guests dine on the ground floor under the impressive inverted coffin-shaped ceiling or on the first floor, peering over the balcony at the stage. There are seven set menus, and the quality is good: the cheapest comes with a salad or harira soup, chicken tagine, fruit, tea and biscuits. The most expensive features *mechoui* (roast lamb) with Atlas herbs. Alcohol is served.

Restaurant Laanibra

Fès El-Bali 61 Aïn Lkhuil (055 74 10 09). Open Sept-May noon-4.30pm daily; June, July, Aug noon-4.30pm, 8-11pm. £. Moroccan.

In the heart of the Medina, Restaurant Laanibra is set in a small, 14th-century palace. Diners eat in a central courtyard, surrounded by tiled and stuccoed columns, or in adjoining salons. Service is very friendly. While you wait, the waiter will explain that Laanibra is the word for a mini musk burner, derived from the word Lambra for a large one; there's a bulbous example in the centre of the restaurant. Six set menus offer traditional Moroccan dishes: everything from a chicken and lemon tagine, to meatballs with tomato sauce cooked with Atlas herbs, to a delicate and filling *pastilla* made the traditional way, with pigeon.

Les 3 Sources

Ville Nouvelle Km4, Route d'Immouzer (035 60 65 32). Open noon-3pm, 7pm-1am Mon-Thur, Sun; noon-3pm, 7pm-2am Fri, Sat. Closed Ramadan & Eid Al-Adha. £££. International.

The 3 Sources would look more at home in the Scottish Highlands than the outskirts of Fès. On entering the large dining room – outside the summer months – you'll encounter a roaring open fire; there's a stuffed wild boar's head above the fireplace in the next-door bar. Despite the small hike to get here, this place is busy and popular with monied Fassi. Food is pretty international, with a French bent. The place is particularly known for its fish, such as dorade and pavé de salmon. Meat dishes range from the filtos of lamb chops with *herbes de l'atlas* to a good lamb tagine with egg and herbs. Service is exceptional, and the restaurant will arrange free pick-up and return to your hotel. Alcohol is served.

Shop

Fès is shopping heaven. Everything and anything can be found in the city's souks: dates, nougat, beef jerky in pots; herbs, all kinds of potions including Moroccan 'Viagra'; gold jewellery, silver, brassware, leather and, of course, carpets. The most exciting thing is that you can buy brass, say, in the very same alley where craftsmen are at work creating more of the same kind of pieces. That's not to say that shopping in Fès without

its challenges: Fassi traders are tough negotiators and the shopping experience can be heavier here than elsewhere. The best way to approach it is to have an idea of what you should be paying for a particular purchase – you can get an idea from the fixed-price shops in avenue Mohamed V in the Ville Nouvelle. Also bear in mind that if you enter a shop with a guide he will get commission on anything you buy, and that cost will be passed on to you.

While you're shopping in the Medina, it's worthwhile having a look in the old *fundouks* (merchants' hostels) that are now used as craft workshops for activities such as weaving.

Art Naji

Ville Nouvelle 20 Quartier Industriel, Ain Nokbi (035 66 91 66/www.artnaji.net). Open 8am-6pm daily.

Fès is well known for its ceramic quarter, which is outside the Medina, around two kilometres from Bab Boujloud. This factory and showroom will give you a decent tour where you can watch men throw pots, dishes being painted and mosaic tables made. The two vast showrooms display plates, tagines, pots, soap dishes, vases, tiles, garden pots, bowls and table tops in Fès blue with a starting price of 20dh; you'll get a 30 per cent discount if you come without a guide. Prices are cheaper in the Medina, but then you don't get the variety there that you do here.

Made in M

Fès El-Bali 246 Talaa Kebira (011 05 48 63) Open 9.30am-1.30pm, 3-7pm Sat-Thur. No credit cards.

Fès's first chi-chi shop is run by a member of the Sefrioui family, owners of the Riad Fes. Stylishly arranged on its glass shelves are candles, 2,000dh leather bags, passport holders, men's washbags, perfumes, candlesticks and a few modern ceramics and mugs. Most of these hard-to-resist products can't be found anywhere else in the Medina.

Au Petit Bazar de Bon Accueil

Fès El-Bali 35 Talaa Sghira (035 63 37 64/ m.benabdejlil@menara.mu). Open 8.30am-8pm Mon-Thur, Sat, Sun; 8.30am-1pm Fri.

Mohammed Benabdejlil runs a treasure trove here and the more you probe, the more will be revealed. But, be warned, Mohammed 'won't sell to just anyone'. Clamber upstairs for the more exciting stuff: antique perfume lances, old cameras, men's embroidered leather bags, old babouches, ceramics, wooden doors, statues, pots, instruments, old books and kaftans. He also harbours a few unusual Berber garments as well as some lovely antique Berber cushion covers.

Nightlife

Bar Al Mandar

Fès El-Bali Sofitel Palais Jamaï, Bab Guissa (035 63 43 31/www.sofitel.com). Open noon-11pm daily.

An old-fashioned, traditional hotel bar with live piano music every night, the Al Mandar overlooks the hotel pool through large glass windows and there's easy access to the terrace and its wonderful Medina views. Choose from wines, spirits, eight beers, and alcoholic and non-alcoholic cocktails. The Al-Mandar signature cocktail is orange, armagnac, grenadine and champagne; the Jamaï is a heady mix of champagne, gin, strawberry liqueur and orange juice. Women will feel very comfortable here.

Camping Fès

Camping International de Fès, route de Sefrou (055 61 80 61). 9am-1am daily. Closed Ramadan.
This down to earth but not quite spit and sawdust venue plays host to Arabic singers and belly dancers. Alcohol is served from behind the skull and cross-boned bar. It's where the locals come to wind down and listen to live raï, *chaabi* and Amazigh (Berber) music. It's lively; some get up for a twirl on the dance floor, and it's a good place to meet Fassi having a good time. It's a 20-minute taxi ride from the Medina and you may have to wait a while for a return taxi ride. In summer, it gets insanely busy.

Riad Fes

Fès El-Bali *Derb ben Slimane, Zerbtana (035 94 76 10/www.riadfes.com). Open 7am-10.30pm daily.*
The long, sleek bar opposite the sublime courtyard pool is where the young and the beautiful (and the foreign) hang out within the elegant surrounds of Riad Fes. Customers can perch on bar stools or sit on modish seating cubes around low tables beneath the illuminated carved stuccowork of the Riad's arches. The mixologists can get to work on the Blue Fez, a vodka, lemon juice and Curaçao concoction. Or perhaps you fancy a delicious Brandy Medina, whose ingredients include brandy, vermouth and crystallised cherries.

Stay

The loveliest places to stay in Fès are converted houses in the Medina, generally based around an inner courtyard. Fès's guesthouses (known as riads) get booked up well in advance, especially over the popular holiday periods and during festivals. All guesthouses have staff who will meet you at the nearest car access point on the borders of the Medina, guide you to your riad and carry your luggage if you arrange in advance.

Dar Roumana

Fès El-Bali *30 derb El-Amer, Zkak Roumane (035 74 16 37/www.darroumana.com). ££.*
Much care and attention, and a real commitment to restoration, has been lavished on this house. The commitment has paid off in the shape of a beautiful property. It makes a real retreat at the Medina's outer edge, and owners Jennifer and Sebastian offer one of the warmest welcomes in Fès. The painted wooden ceiling in the entrance hall gives a taste of what is to come. The interior courtyard is a visual feast of stucco work, intricate *zelije* mosaic tiling, a central fountain and enormous carved wooden doors. Rooms are painted in neutrals, but here, too, floors are

beautifully tiled; bathrooms are spacious. A filling breakfast can be taken in the courtyard or up on the roof terrace.

Dar Seffarine

Fès El-Bali *14 derb Sbaa Louyate, Seffarine (071 11 35 28/www.darseffarine.com). ££.*
Stunningly beautiful large doors, decorated with a red and blue star motif bordered by flowers, feature in this ancient house close to the Karaouiyine Mosque in the Medina. Owners Alaa, from Iraq, and Kate, from Norway, have achieved something different here through judicious use of salvaged objects: a painted wooden panel makes a handsome headboard, handmade chairs have been created from old beams, a cylindrical sink unit perks up a bathroom and a carved wooden divider from the Mellah screens a bed from the rest of the room. Dar Seffarine also benefits from light – unusually, some of the rooms have external windows. The top suite has a gorgeous domed ceiling and friezes of calligraphy and flowers. The terrace has wonderful views of the Karaouiyine Mosque and you can spy the huge door of the El-Andalous Mosque from the white-cushioned seating area. Breakfast is eaten communally and dinners are provided on request. Chats across the tables make this a very friendly place.

Riad Al Bartal

Fès El-Bali *21 rue Sournas, Ziat (035 63 70 53/ www.riadalbartal.com). ££.*
An extremely warm welcome awaits you at this lovingly cared-for house. It begins at the enormous carved wood doors that lead into the interior courtyard. Off here is the salon, where newly arrived guests are offered mint tea and biscuits. There's also a large library here, with books on history, art, travel and photography. Inside, in the potted-plant-dotted courtyard, columns covered with intricate blue and white *zelije* tiling and topped by stucco support the first floor balcony; from there creepers and flowering plants tumble downwards. Vases on the tables are generously stuffed with flowers. Rooms are artfully decorated with huge beds, Berber carpets on the walls, lamps and unusual furniture. Food is good too – the delicate slices of aubergine-wrapped cheese deserves wider publicity – and service is impeccable.

Riad Fes

Fès El-Bali *Derb ben Slimane, Zerbtana (035 94 76 10/www.riadfes.com). £££.*
Riad Fes is a complex of buildings restored to a very impressive standard, which pivots around a main courtyard with superlative stucco work. Its terrace has one of the best views in the Medina and its long bar is the most stylish and popular in town. The main building dates from 900; later 17th- and 18th-century buildings house the restaurant and Prince's Quarter. The Sefriouis, a family of architects, began to restore the buildings in 1999. Decoration in the rooms ranges from sleek beige, grey and white tones in the roomy modern areas to a more traditional look, with leatherwork chairs and a mix of modern and older fittings in older parts. There are two restaurants (*see p59*), a bar (*see p60*), a small outdoor pool and a hammam. Definitely more of a hotel than a riad, but friendly staff ensure the place has a personal touch.

Salad Niçois
Tagine of Art
Pea + Bro
Tuna Melt

CAFÉ CLOCK

Clockwise from top left:
Dar Roumana (2); Café
Clock (2); Les 3 Sources;
L'Ambre; Café Clock; Dar
Roumana.

Clockwise from top left:
Riad Al Bartal (3); Riad
Fès; Sofitel Palais Jamai;
Riad Al Bartal.

Riad Maison Bleue

Fès El-Bali *33 derb El-Miter, Talaa El-Kebira, Ain Azliten (035 74 18 73/www.maisonbleue.com). ££££.*
The sister property of the original Maison Bleue, the Riad Maison Bleue is dominated by a courtyard pool surrounded by orange trees. It also has a terrace with great views of the Borj Nord and the Merenid Tombs. The riad, with 12 suites, is made up of a series of buildings. Furnishings and accessories are individually chosen and sometimes antique. The Hnya suite, for example, features dark wood furniture, a desk inlaid with mother of pearl, a beautiful carved headboard and an old mustard yellow kaftan hanging on the wall. It also has the unusual advantage of a spa. The main Maison Bleue doesn't have the chi-chi elegance or style kudos of some of the other riads in Fès, but its location is unbeatable.

Riad9

Fès El-Bali *9 derb Lamsside, Souiket ben Safi, Zkak El-Ma (035 63 40 45/www.riad9com). £££.*
This three-roomed house has been beautifully styled, with white walls and touches of celadon green, stained glass, mosaic floor tiling, judicious lighting and carefully chosen furnishings and accessories. The result is glossy magazine looks, a zen-like sense of calm in most of the house, and a sense of fun in bits of it: the pièce de résistance is a huge suite with a vast painted ceiling and a bathroom featuring barber chairs, stacks of evergreen towels and piles of old travel trunks. Breakfast, served by the friendly housekeeper, Atika, is taken in the courtyard in the Japanese sunken dining area; the beetroot blended fruit juice is a winner. This is a house for animal lovers: there are Japanese koi carp in the courtyard pond, an aviary of birds, some tortoises and the star of the household, Tache, the cat.

Riad Tizwa

Fès El-Bali *15 derb Guebbas (2nd no.15), Batha (035 63 78 74/www.riadtizwa.com). ££.*
Tizwa is Berber for beehive and a nod to British owner Richard Bee's surname. Nine bedrooms, ranging from extremely spacious to weeny but cute are set around the central courtyard. Some boast cactus silk bedspreads, their own dressing room and separate loos; two are warmed in winter with open fires. The atmosphere here is pleasantly relaxing and informal. A leisurely breakfast (Moroccan or continental) on the terrace or in the salon can be taken at any time of day, and an early morning delivery of coffee in a thermos flask (complete with tassel) is a thoughtful detail, as are the fluffy white bathrobes with red tassled hoods. Karima, the charming housekeeper, is always ready to help. Tizwa is close to the Batha hub, with good access.

Sofitel Palais Jamaï

Fès El-Bali *Bab Guissa (035 63 43 31/ www.sofitel.com). £££.*
At the northern edge of Fès El-Bali, Sofitel's Palais Jamaï has unsurpassable views over the city: it would be a shame not to have a room with a Medina view. The majority of the 142 rooms are in a new building; the old 19th-century palace, designed in Arab-Moorish tradition and once home to the Grand Vizier Jamaï, houses five Moroccan-style suites. This is the place to stay if you want something differerent from the riad experience, and the hotel's appeal lies in its wide range of facilities: the lush Andalucian gardens bulging with bougainvillea and butterflies; the inviting sky-blue heated pool; the spa with hammam, Jacuzzi and sauna, and the three restaurants (including Al-Fassia, which offers expensive Moroccan food in sumptuous surrounds). Note that rooms with a garden or ramparts view cost less than those overlooking the Medina.

Factfile

When to go

Fès is a good destination to visit all year round although it can get unbearably hot in July and August. All the hotels and guesthouses we list have heating, although this is not always the case. It can get pretty chilly, and warm clothes are a necessity for the winter months.

Getting there & around

Royal Air Maroc (www.royalairmaroc.com) flies to Fès from London Heathrow via Casablanca. Ryanair (www.ryanair.com) flies to Fès from Girona, Marseille and Frankfurt. Atlas Blue (www.atlas-blue.com) flies from Lyon and Marseille. Fès-Saïss Airport (035 62 48 00/www.onda.ma) is a 25-minute taxi ride (150dh) from the Medina.
By rail, Fès can be reached from Marrakech, Rabat and Meknès on the same line (www.oncf.ma).

The official fee for a taxi from Casablanca to Fès is 1,200dh; from Rabat, 800dh; from Meknès, 400dh; from Marrakech, 2,000dh.

Tourist information

Delégation Régionale du Tourisme, place Mohammed V, Ville Nouvelle (035 62 34 60; open Mon-Fri 8.30am-4.30pm) can help with only the most basic of enquiries.
Official guide rates: half a day for a national guide 150dh, full day 250dh. For a local guide: 120dh for a half day, 150dh full day.
Youssef Maamri (070 89 31 38/g-youssef@live.fr) is an English-speaking national tour guide who has access to a car for trips outside the city.
The Conseil Régional du Tourisme de Fès has a website, www.visitfes.org, in French.

Internet

There are internet cafés throughout the city.

Clockwise from top left:
Ben Youssef Medersa;
Bab Es-Salam Market;
Riad El-Cadi; Agdal
Gardens; Amandine (2);
Dar Zemora; Badii Palace.

PATISSERIE
Amandine

Marrakech

Founded at the confluence of ancient trade routes, Marrakech has always been rooted in the twin activities of hospitality and trade. A fortified settlement in a vast oasis, the most southerly outpost of Mediterranean civilisation, it was a place to stock up your caravan before heading across the desert, or to kick back and dispose of your goods after trekking back over the mountains. Trans-Saharan trade might have petered out long ago but, in its booming 21st-century incarnation, Marrakech is still about the same two things: chilling out and shopping.

The piecemeal refurbishment of the medieval Medina in the 1990s, largely through the phenomenon of the 'riad' hotel – literally hundreds of old courtyard houses have been bought up and converted into boutique hotels – led to the current growth spurt of Morocco's southern capital, and the revival of a traditional, local aesthetic. Renovations have reinvigorated the city's artisan culture of mosaic work, stonemasonry, wood carving and plasterwork. And, as European designers absorb the potential of local craft skills, new design ideas gleaned from the incomers sweep through the entrepreneurial and manufacturing hub of the souk like wildfire.

In Marrakech, all roads lead to the fantastical Jemaa El Fna. The city may be exploding at the outskirts, but at its centre still pulses the nightly carnival of the square. The punishing pace of change may have bewildered many Marrakchis, but as long as the uniquely Moroccan life of Marrakech's principal public space is not completely drowned by the rising tide of tourists, the red city has a bit of magic in her yet.

Explore

Marrakech is generally thought of as having three parts: the old **Medina**, which includes Jemaa El Fna and the Koutoubia Mosque, the colonial-era new town, comprising **Guéliz** and **Hivernage**, and the **Palmeraie**, the palm oasis that's now a kind of luxury suburb full of opulent private homes and golf hotels. As the city booms, whole new urban quarters are going up, including a massive 'Zone Touristique' hotel and holiday apartment district to the south. But most of what matters is in the alleys of the Medina and the avenues of Guéliz.

The square, towering minaret of the Koutoubia Mosque is Marrakech's main landmark. At over 800 years old, it's also one of the city's oldest structures. While the mosque and its minaret are unquestionably the heart of Marrakech, the soul lies 200 metres to the west in the amorphous form of Jemaa El Fna, the city's thronging market square and forum almost since its foundation. On the other side of avenue Bab Jedid from the Koutoubia Gardens lie the Mamounia Gardens, part of the legendary, currently closed, Mamounia Hotel.

JEMAA EL FNA & AROUND

It's the main open space in Marrakech, but to call Jemaa El Fna a public square is misleading. Uncontained, disorderly, untameable by council or committee, Jemaa El Fna is nothing less than bedlam. It's an urban clearing, as irregular in shape as an accident of nature, and thronged day and night with a carnival of local life – from dentists to snake-charmers to musicians, and totally at odds with its name, which roughly translates as 'Assembly of the Dead'.

Marrakech

Historic sites	Eating & drinking
● ● ● ● ●	● ● ● ● ●
Art & architecture	Nightlife
● ● ● ● ○	● ● ● ● ○
Hotels	Shopping
● ● ● ● ●	● ● ● ● ●

SPAIN

ATLANTIC

OCEAN

MOROCCO

Marrakech

ALGERIA

0   100km

WESTERN SAHARA

JNANE TAMSNA

24 bedrooms 5 pools 1 tennis court 9 acres of gardens.
Spectacular views. Table d'hôtes. Organic produces from the garden.
Cooking class, yoga, reflexology, massages.
Ideal for house parties and special events.

"There is no hotel garden like it in Marrakech: it has the feeling of farmland
dotted with swimming pools."   **- House & Garden May 2008**

www.jnane.com • email:meryanne@jnane.com

Also known simply as 'La Place', Jemaa El Fna was laid out as a parade ground by the Almoravids in front of their royal fortress (Dar El-Hajar). When the succeeding Almohads built a new palace to the south, the open ground passed to the public and became what it remains today – a place for gathering, trading, eating, entertainment and the occasional riot. The name refers to its former role as a venue for executions, when decapitated heads were put up on spikes for public display.

In the 1970s, the municipality attempted to impose order on this decidedly unsquare square with a scheme to turn it into a car park. This was opposed and defeated. Since then, thanks in part to the lobbying efforts of Spanish writer Juan Goytisolo (who has lived just off the square since the late '70s), Jemaa El Fna has been recognised by UNESCO as part of mankind's cultural heritage and its preservation is secured. There's still some tidying-up impulse at work, however. The design of the orange-juice carts has been regularised in a faux traditional style and the whole square has been paved over – a blessing in wet weather.

"The snake-charmers are early starters, with their black, rubbery reptiles laid out in front or sheltered under large drums."

During the early part of the day the square is relatively quiet. The orange-laden carts of the juice-sellers line the perimeter, wagon-train fashion, but otherwise there's only a scattering of figures, seated on boxes or rugs, shaded under large shabby umbrellas. The snake-charmers are early starters with their black, rubbery reptiles laid out in front or sheltered under large drums (be careful what you kick). For a few dirhams visitors can have a photograph taken with a large snake draped over their shoulders; for a few more dirhams they can have it removed. Gaudily clad water-sellers wander around offering to pose for dirhams. Other figures may be dentists (teeth pulled on the spot), scribes (letters written to order), herbalists (good for whatever ails you) or beggars (to whom Moroccans give generously). Overlooking all, the prime morning spot for unhurried businessmen and traders is the patio of the landmark Café de France, on the square for the last 50 years.

The action tends to wilt beneath the heat of the afternoon sun, when snake-charmers, dancers and acrobats can barely manage to stir themselves for camera-carrying tourists. It's not until dusk that things really kick off.

As the light fades, ranks of makeshift kitchens set up with tables, benches and hissing flames, constituting one great open-air restaurant where adventurous eaters can snack on anything from snails to sheep's heads.

Beside the avenues of food stalls, the rest of the square takes on the air of a circus. Visiting Berber farmers from the surrounding plains and villages join Medina locals in crowding around the assorted performers. These typically include troupes of cartoon-costumed acrobats, musicians and their prowling transvestite dancers, storytellers and magicians, and boxing bouts between underage boys who can hardly lift their hands in the heavy leather gloves. The tourists and visitors who provided the raison d'être for the afternoon entertainers are now negligible in this far more surreal evening scene.

Approaching midnight the food stalls begin to pack up, the performers wind down, and the crowds thin. Only the musicians remain, purveyors of seedy mysticisms, attended by wild-eyed devotees giddy on repetitive rhythms, helped along by hash. At the same time, the place becomes one great gay cruising ground, busy with tight-shirted, tight-trousered teens, sharp and cynical beyond their years.

The best way to experience the buzz, at any time of the day, is to be in among it all (watch your wallet and bags), but several of the peripheral cafés and restaurants have upper terraces with fine ringside seating. But whether you choose stealthy observation from the terraces or a headlong plunge into the mêlée, the Jemaa El Fna always remains somewhat elusive. 'All the guidebooks lie', writes Juan Goytisolo, 'there's no way of getting a firm grasp on it'.

KOUTOUBIA MOSQUE

The minaret of the Koutoubia Mosque, Marrakech's most famous symbol – in the Koutoubia Gardens, off avenue Mohamed V – is visible from near and far. It is not really that high (77 metres), but thanks to local topography and a local ordinance that forbids any other building in the Medina to be higher than a palm tree, it towers majestically over its surroundings. Two previous mosques have stood here: the first, constructed by the Almoravid dynasty, was demolished by the Almohads, who built their own on the site in 1147. This building, torn down because it was incorrectly aligned with Mecca, was rebuilt as the present mosque, and its minaret was finally completed more than half a century later under the patronage of the Almohad Caliph Yacoub El-Mansour.

The name Koutoubia is derived from *koutoubiyyin* – Arabic for booksellers – since a booksellers' market once filled the surrounding streets. The mosque's exterior is of red stone, but it's thought to have originally been covered with plaster. The tower is 13 metres wide. Six rooms, one above the other, constitute the interior; leading around them is a ramp by way of which the muezzin could reach the balcony – it was supposed to be wide enough for him to ride a horse up there.

The Koutoubia was built in a traditional Almohad style and the minaret is topped with four copper globes; according to legend, these were originally made of gold. It is also said that in times past only blind muezzins were employed because a sighted person could have peered into the royal harem from the minaret.

The Koutoubia Mosque is still an active place of worship and non-Muslims may not enter. But it's possible to get a good view of the exterior by walking around either side, clockwise between the main entrance and the wall that encloses the grounds of the French Consulate, or anti-clockwise along the top of the Almohad ruins. Either route leads into the rose-filled Koutoubia Gardens, which spread south and west of the mosque.

MAMOUNIA GARDENS

The world-famous Mamounia Hotel (avenue Bab Jedid, 024 38 86 00, www.mamounia.com), south-west of Jemaa El Fna, takes its name from its gardens, the Arset El-Mamoun, which predate the hotel by more than a century. They were established in the 18th century by Crown Prince Moulay Mamoun on land gifted to him by his father the sultan. The gardens were later annexed by the French and in 1923 a 100-room hotel built on the site. Happily, the gardens remain. They're designed in a traditional style, on an axis, with walkways, flowerbeds, orange groves and olive trees and attended by 40 gardeners who, twice a year, plant 60,000 new annuals. At the time of writing the hotel and gardens are closed for renovation. Press-time gossip said the Mamounia may reopen in March 2009; the hotel's press people were saying nothing.

NORTH MEDINA & SOUKS

The area of the Medina north of the Jemaa El Fna is commercial – at least in its more central areas – with a fibrous network of souks, plus three of the city's moderately interesting monuments: the Musée de Marrakech, Koubba El-Badiyin and Ben Youssef Medersa.

SOUKS

Beginning on the north edge of Jemaa El Fna, the souks comprise alleyway upon alleyway of tiny retail cubicles. In the most heavily touristed areas, the huge number of shops is offset by the fact that most seem to offer the same old slippers, plates and embroidered robes. These areas are where you are most likely to get pestered, but it's all a lot quieter than it used to be. The authorities twigged that foreigners dislike full-on hassle and souk shopkeepers are models of good behaviour compared to what they were some years ago.

The further into the souks you venture the more interesting they become. The two main routes into their heart are rue Semarine and rue Mouassine; the former offers the more full-on blast of bazaar, the latter is a more sedate path leading to choice boutiques.

Entrance to the **rue Semarine** (aka Souk Semarine) is via an elaborate arch one block north of Jemaa El Fna – reached via either the spice market or the egg market, both pungent experiences, but only one of them pleasant. Semarine is a relatively orderly street, broad and straight with overhead trellising dappling the paving with light and shadow. Every section of the souk has its own speciality and here it has traditionally been textiles, although cloth merchants have been largely supplanted by souvenir shops.

About 150 metres along, the first alley off to the east leads to a wedge-shaped open area known as the **Rahba Kedima**, or the 'old place'. The way between Semarine and the Rahba Kedima also leads to a small court, the Souk Laghzel, formerly the wool market but now a car-boot sale of a market where women come to sell meagre possessions such as a single knitted shawl or a bag of vegetables. The Rahba Kedima used to be the corn market but is now a mix of vendors selling raffia bags and baskets, woollen hats and cooked snails, spices and magic supplies.

The upper storeys on the northern side of the Rahba Kedima are usually hung with carpets and textiles, an invitation to search for the partially obscured passageway that leads through to the **Criée Berbère** (Berber Auction). These days this partially roofed, slightly gloomy section of the souk is the lair of the rug merchants, but until well into the 20th century it was used for the auction of slaves.

Back on rue Semarine, just north of the turning for the Rahba Kedima, the street forks: branching to the left is the **Souk El-Attarin**, straight on is the **Souk El-Kebir** (Great Souk). Between the two is a ladder of narrow, arrow-straight passages, little more than shoulder-width across and collectively known as the **Kissaria**. This is the heart of the souk. Stallholders here specialise in cotton, clothing, kaftans and blankets.

Just north is the dusty open plaza of the place Ben Youssef, dominated by the Ben Youssef Mosque. The original mosque went up in the

Clockwise from top left:
Jemaa El Fna; Badii
Palace; Jemaa El Fna;
Koutoubia Mosque;
Bab Es-Salam Market;
Agdal Gardens.

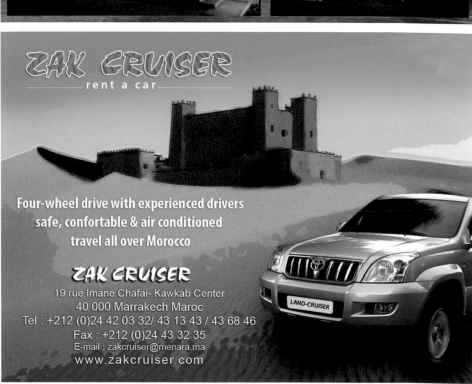

12th century and was the grandest of the age, but what stands now is a lesser 19th century incarnation. Non-Muslims may not enter. However, in the immediate vicinity of the mosque is a cluster of tourist-friendly sights, including **Musée de Marrakech**, the enchanting **Ben Youssef Medersa** and the venerable **Koubba El-Badiyin**.

Ben Youssef Medersa

Place Ben Youssef (no phone). Open 9am-6.30pm daily. Admission 30dh (60dh for museum, Koubba & Ben Youssef Medersa).

A medersa is a Quranic school, dedicated to the teaching of Islamic scripture and law. This one was founded in the 14th century, then enlarged in the 16th. It was given a further polishing up in the 1990s courtesy of the Ministry of Culture. Entrance is via a long, cool passageway leading to the great courtyard, a serene place centred on a water-filled basin. The surrounding façades are decorated with *zelije* tiling, stucco and carved cedar, all executed with restraint. At the far side is the domed prayer hall with the richest of decoration, notably around the mihrab, the arched niche that indicates the direction of Mecca. Back in the entrance vestibule, passageways and two flights of stairs lead to more than 100 tiny windowless students' chambers, clustered about small internal lightwells. Medieval as it seems, the medersa was still in use until as recently as 1962.

Koubba El-Badiyin

Place Ben Youssef (no phone). Open Apr-Sept 9am-7pm daily. Oct-Mar 9am-6pm daily. Admission 10dh (60dh for museum, Koubba & Ben Youssef Medersa).

Across from the Ben Youssef Mosque, set in its own fenced enclosure and sunk several metres below the current street level, is the Koubba El-Badiyin (it's also known as the 'Koubba Almoravide'). It looks unprepossessing but it's the only surviving structure from the era of the Almoravids, the founders of Marrakech, and as such it represents a wormhole back to the origins of Moorish building history. It dates to the reign of Ali ben Youssef (1107-43) and was probably part of the ablutions complex of the original Ben Youssef Mosque. It's worth paying the slight admission fee to descend the brickwork steps and view the underside of the dome, which is a kaleidoscopic arrangement of a floral motif within an octagon with an eight-pointed star.

Musée de Marrakech

Place Ben Youssef (024 44 18 93/www.museede marrakech.ma). Open 9am-6.30pm daily. Admission 40dh (60dh for museum, Koubba & Ben Youssef Medersa).

Inaugurated in 1997, the Musée de Marrakech is housed in a converted early 20th-century house. In the outer courtyard there's a pleasant café along with a rather boring bookshop. Within the museum exhibits rotate, but the star attraction is the building itself, particularly the tartishly tiled great central court, roofed over and hung with an enormous chandelier that looks like the mothership from *Close Encounters of the Third Kind*. The former hammam is lovely and makes a fine exhibition

space. If nothing else, the museum is a cool refuge from the heat, and the toilets are pleasant and clean.

MOUASSINE

Although it's far from immediately apparent, Mouassine is rapidly becoming the most chic of Medina quarters. West of the main souk area and north of Jemaa El Fna, it's home to a growing number of smart boutiques, interesting galleries and hip *maisons d'hôtes*.

At the centre of the quarter, north of the Mouassine Mosque (which lends its name to the quarter and was erected in the 1560s), is the Mouassine fountain with its quadruple drinking bays – three for animals and one, the most ornate, for people. It's here that the character Louis Bernard is fatally stabbed in Hitchcock's 1955 version of *The Man Who Knew Too Much* – although not so fatally that he can't stagger half a mile to Jemaa El Fna to expire in the arms of Jimmy Stewart. Beside the fountain is an arched gateway beyond which is the Souk des Teinturiers.

> ## "It's full of dark, cavern-like workshops in which firework bursts of orange sparks illuminate tableaux of grime-streaked craftsmen."

Around here are some good examples of *fundouks*. These were built as merchant hostels, providing accommodation and warehousing for caravan traders. They offered stabling and storage rooms on the ground floor, and bedrooms off the upper galleries. Most surviving *fundouks* now operate as ramshackle artisans' workshops, such as the one at No.102 rue Mouassine. This *fundouk* also featured in the film *Hideous Kinky* as the hotel where Kate Winslet and daughters lodged – at No.38 on the first floor.

DYERS' QUARTER

Between rue Mouassine and rue Semarine are some of the most fragrant and colourful souks, among them the **Souk El-Attarin**, or Spice Souk. Contrary to the name, this part of the souk no longer deals in spices. Instead its traders largely traffic in tourist tat. Almost opposite the subdued entrance to a workaday mosque is the **Souk des Babouches**, an alley devoted to slippers.

Ringing hammer blows announce the **Souk Haddadin**, accessible from the Souk El-Attarin,

Ben Youssef Medersa.

the ironworkers' quarter. It's full of dark, cavern-like workshops in which firework bursts of orange sparks illuminate tableaux of grime-streaked craftsmen, like some scene by Doré.

West of Attarin three alleys run downhill into the **Souk des Teinturiers**, which is the area of the dyers' workshops. Labourers rub dyes into cured hides (to be cut and fashioned into *babouches*) and dunk wool into vats of dark-hued liquids. This results in brightly coloured sheaves of wool that are then hung over the alleyways. It also results in the labourers having arms coloured to their elbows. You know you're nearing this part of the souk when you start seeing people with purple forearms.

THE TANNERIES

To experience Marrakech at its most medieval – and most pungent – take a taxi to the place du Moqf and walk east along rue de Bab Debbagh to the tannery district. The tanners have been here since the city was founded and their work remains a pre-industrial process, using hundreds of vats full of foul liquids to cure animal hides. First, hair and traces of flesh are removed by soaking in vats of quicklime and water. They are then washed and pressed in other vats. After that the skins are placed in a vat of water and blood, which strengthens them. One of the workers separates and wrings the skins, which are then coloured yellow by being rubbed with pomegranate powder. Olive oil is used to make them shiny and other traditional products, such as bark, saffron, henna and poppy are also used for dyeing purposes. Stretched-out skins are then left to dry in the sun beside the tanneries. The whole complex process takes about 20 days.

The hides are mostly sheep and goat although cow and camel are sometimes used for bigger items. Individual tanneries can be tricky to find but some loitering youth will always approach unaccompanied foreigners and offer his services as a guide. The tanneries fill large yards and, with rows of lozenge-shaped pools of various hues, look like giant paintboxes. However, closer up the bubbling pits are more like cesspools of floating, bubbling crud and the piled-up hides look like rancid tripe. Pity the poor labourers who wade in the noxious fluids ladling the skins from one pit to another.

The eventual products can be seen and purchased at the leather shops near the gate, but you may prefer to get the hell out of the quarter and purge yourself in the nearest hammam. Taxis can be caught outside the Bab Debbagh on the route des Ramparts ringroad.

SOUTH MEDINA

Almost since the founding of Marrakech, the South Medina has been the domain of sultans and their retinues. Today it houses the museum

palaces of the city plus the **Kasbah** and the **Mellah**, historically Marrakech's Jewish quarter. The present Royal Palace is built on the site of the earliest Almohad palaces and covers a vast area. Morocco's new king, Mohammed VI, had a much smaller residence built nearby. Neither is open to the public, but visitors are allowed to explore two 19th-century viziers' palaces, the **Bahia Palace** and the **Dar Si Said Museum**, as well as the impressive ruins of the **Badii Palace** and the ornate **Saadian Tombs** to the west.

Agdal Gardens

Path off SW corner of Méchouar Intérieur. Open usually on Fri & Sun; closed if the king is in residence at the Royal Palace. Admission free.

Essentially the huge back garden of the Royal Palace, the Agdal Gardens cover a vast 16 hectares and stretch for a couple of kilometres south of the Medina. Laid out in 1156-57 by the Almohads, they are several hundred years older than those most celebrated of Islamic gardens at the Alhambra. At the centre of the Agdal is a massive pool, the Sahraj El-Hana. The rest of the area is divided into different orchards and gardens, including an orange grove, vineyards, areas of pomegranates and figs, masses of walnut trees and palm groves. There are several ornamental pavilions, and it's possible to climb on to the roof of one of them, the Dar El-Hana, beside the pool, for an impressive view of the gardens and the High Atlas beyond.

Badii Palace

Place des Ferblantiers (no phone). Open 8.30-11.45am, 2.30-5.45pm daily. Admission 10dh; 20dh minbar pavilion.

Constructed by Sultan Ahmed El-Mansour (1578-1607), the Badii Palace is one of the two principal monuments of the Saadian era (the other is the Saadian Tombs). Today it survives only as a denuded ruin, but once it was a model of triumphal ostentation. Walls and ceilings were encrusted with gold from Timbuktu, while the inner court had a massive central pool with an island, flanked by four sunken gardens. At the centre of each of the four massive walls were four pavilions, also flanked by arrangements of pools and fountains. It took some 25 years to complete the palace and barely were the inaugural celebrations over before the ageing ruler passed away. His palace remained intact for less than a century before the Merenid sultan, Moulay Ismail, had it stripped bare and the riches carted north for his new capital at Meknès.

The palace is entered from place des Ferblantiers via a canyon-like space between two precipitous walls. The former main gate is gone, and entrance is through a hole in the fortifications. The great court is a vast empty space ringed by pockmarked walls with stork nests along the battlements. The sunken areas that were once gardens still exist, as does the great dry basin that was once the ornate central pool. On the west side are the ruins of the Pavilion of Fifty Columns, with a small area of dulled mosaic on the floor.

In the south-east corner, a gate leads through to a newly reconstructed pavilion housing the Koutoubia Mosque

Association Al Kawtar

Day Care Centre for Disabled Women

Officially registered non-profit association to give their members a safe place to spend their days and earn a living.

Providing

Medical & Technical Assistance, Education & Empowerment and a place to work together

Producing

Table & Dining cloths, Bed & Bath linen, Children's wear

Day Care & Embroidery Workshop:
Rue Jbel Lakhdar 35
Ramila, Marrakech-Medina

Boutique:
Rue Laksour 57
Ksour, Marrakech-Medina

For more information visit **www.alkawtar.org**

minbar. This was the original minbar (stepped pulpit) in the city's great mosque. It was fashioned in the early 12th century by Cordoban craftsmen, and the 1,000 decorative panels that adorn the sides supposedly took eight years to complete. Next to the minbar pavilion are the excavated remains of troglodytic chambers and passages: a small underground labyrinth opened up for visitor exploration.

One of the palace bastions remains intact at the north-eastern corner of the great central court. Steps lead up to a rooftop terrace with fine views of the site, the storks and the surrounding quarter.

Bahia Palace
Riad Zitoun El-Jedid (no phone). Open 8.45-11.45am, 2.45-5.45pm Mon-Thur, Sat, Sun; 8.45-11.30am, 3-5.45pm Fri. Admission 10dh; 5dh children.
Built principally by Bou Ahmed, a powerful vizier to the royal court in the 1890s, the Bahia Palace's shady spaces and mosaic walls make a pleasant break from the hot bustling streets outside. Entered via a long garden corridor, it's a delightful collection of paved courtyards, arcades, pavilions and reception halls with vaulted ceilings, traditional tiling, sculpted stucco and carved cedarwood doors. On Bou Ahmed's death – he was probably poisoned by the sultan's mother – the palace was completely looted by Sultan Abdel-Aziz, with caravans of donkeys hauling out all the furniture and fittings. In the 20th century it served as the living quarters of the French *résident généraux* and it's still occasionally used by the current royal family.

Dar Si Said Museum
Riad Zitoun El-Jedid (024 38 95 64). Open 9am-12.15pm, 3-6.15pm Mon, Wed-Sun. Admission 20dh.
The former home of the brother of Ba Ahmed, builder of the Bahia, now houses a large collection of crafts and woodwork. Among all the kitchen implements, weapons and musical instruments are beautiful examples of carved cedar, rescued from the city's lost dwellings. There's also one room devoted to 'rural' woodwork that includes some primitively worked and painted Berber doors. Such items are very much in vogue with collectors these days and change hands for vast sums. The exhibites are captioned in French only,

KASBAH
The traditional entrance to the Kasbah is the gorgeous **Bab Agnaou** (Gate of the Gnawa), built in 1185 during the reign of Sultan Yacoub El-Mansour. It's one of few stone structures in this otherwise mud-brick city, and has weathered so that the aged limestone now resembles heavily grained wood. Across the street from Bab Agnaou is the original southern gate to the Medina, the Bab Er Rob, now filled by a pottery shop and bypassed by traffic.

A short distance inside the Agnaou gate is the Kasbah Mosque, constructed in 1190, again during the reign of Sultan Yacoub El-Mansour (hence its alternative name of El-Mansour Mosque). It has been renovated many times

since (most recently during the reign of Hassan II, father of the current king), but the cut-brick-and-green-tile decoration on the minaret is original. The plaza in front is usually busy with tourist groups. They're not here for the mosque, which, like nearly all mosques in Morocco, they're forbidden to enter, but for what lies hidden in the lee of its southern wall: the **Saadian Tombs**.

Maison Tiskiwin
8 derb El-Bahia, off Riad Zitoun El-Jedid (024 38 91 92). Open 9am-12.30pm, 3-6pm daily. Admission 15dh; 10dh children.
On display in this private house owned by veteran Dutch anthropologist Bert Flint is his fascinating collection of crafts and decorative arts from southern Morocco and the Sahara. The exhibition is designed to show Morocco's connection to sub-Saharan Africa and is geographically laid out to take you on a virtual journey across the Sahara to Timbuktu. Exhibits include masks from as far afield as Mali and an entire Berber tent made of camel hair.

> ## "Evidence of Jewish heritage is abundant. Several houses have external balconies, which was peculiar to Morocco's Jewish population."

Saadian Tombs
Rue de Kasbah, Bab Agnaou (no phone). Open 8.30-11.45am, 2.30-5.45pm daily. Admission 10dh.
Flanking the south side of the Kasbah Mosque, the site of what is possibly Marrakech's most visited monument is an ancient walled garden, the use of which far predates the Saadian era. Dotted around the shrubbery are early mosaic graves; the identity of those interred is long lost. Attention instead focuses on the three pavilions built during the reign of Saadian sultan Ahmed El-Mansour. Despite drawing so many visitors, it's not spectacular – the modest setting reminds one of an English parish churchyard.

First on the left is the Prayer Hall, which was not intended as a mausoleum but nevertheless holds numerous graves, mainly of Alaouite princes from the 18th century. Their resting places are marked by what look like marble offcuts from a mason's yard. Next to it is the Hall of Twelve Columns, a more ornate affair with three central tombs surrounded by a dozen marble pillars. The tomb in the middle is that of Ahmed El-Mansour, flanked by those of his son and grandson. A third, stand-alone pavilion has ornate Andalucian-style entrance portals.

THE MELLAH

Hugging the eastern walls of the Badii Palace are the narrow gridded alleys of the old Jewish quarter. The name translates roughly as 'Place of Salt', a reference either to the Jews' historic monopoly on the trade in mineral salts from the Atlas Mountains, or to their job of salting the heads of decapitees before they were hoisted on spikes. Although the number of Jews in Marrakech is now negligible, evidence of Jewish heritage is abundant. Several houses in the neighbourhood have external balconies, which was peculiar to Morocco's Jewish population. Some have Hebrew letters on the metal grills above the doors and there's even an occasional Star of David.

Across the road from the Rose Garden, a green-painted arch leads through into the **Bab Es Salam Market**. Following this south and east, leads deep into the Mellah. The streets here are some of the narrowest and poorest in the Medina and in places only crude scaffolding keeps the houses from collapsing.

At the heart of the quarter is a small square, place Souweka, now disfigured by a badly sited concrete building. At No.36 along the street that runs north just beyond the square is one of the Medina's three last working synagogues (once there were 29). It occupies a large hall off the open courtyard of a well-maintained community centre. On the very eastern edge of the Mellah is the extensive Miâara Jewish cemetery; the sheer number of modestly marked graves (tens of thousands) is probably the best remaining testament to the one-time importance of Jewish life in Marrakech.

NOUVELLE VILLE

GUELIZ

North-west of the old city walls is the nouvelle ville or 'new city', a French colonial creation of the 1930s, named Guéliz (pronounced 'gileez'). Old city and new are connected by the broad, tree-lined **avenue Mohammed V** (pronounced 'M'hammed Sanc'), the main street of Guéliz. Middle-class Marrakchis and expats favour this part of town for its car-friendly streets, modern apartment blocks, decent restaurants and shops, plus most of what passes for nightlife.

Home to some interesting modernist buildings and known for its 1930s elegance, Guéliz has more recently been marred by new concrete blocks, tourist coaches and a McDonald's. Meanwhile, the rise of the riad hotel in the 1990s made the Medina the place to stay, and with an increasing number of decent restaurants there too, Guéliz has been pushed off the tourist map. But while the area is devoid of big sights, it does have a pleasant, unhurried atmosphere.

This is the part of town where you can shop at fixed price stores, or find an alcohol shop.

The 'new city' came into being shortly after December 1913 – the arrival date of city planner Henri Prost. One of his early sketches shows how he took the minaret of the Koutoubia as his focal point and from it extended two lines: one north-west to the Guéliz hills; the other south-west to the pavilion of the Menara Gardens. In the pie slice between these lines (which have since become avenue Mohammed V and avenue de la Menara) is the original nucleus of the new European city.

> ## "At the junction is an elaborate colonial building with pavement arcades, art deco lines and Moorish flourishes."

Sadly, instead of developing as the *grand rondpoint* of Prost's vision, place du 16 Novembre, the hole in the middle of Guéliz's spider-web street pattern, has been disfigured by some plug-ugly structures, including a totalitarian central post office and two mammoth apartment blocks.

At the junction of avenue Mohammed V and rue de la Liberté is an elaborate colonial building with pavement arcades, art deco lines and Moorish flourishes. It dates to 1918 and is just about the oldest surviving building in Guéliz. This was the address (30 rue de la Liberté) of the city's first tourist office. A fading gallery of ancient hand-painted scenes of Morocco decorates the hallway.

On and around **rue de la Liberté** are the new city's chicest shops. The eastern stretch, though, is the local maid market, with poorly dressed women hanging around on the chance of some cleaning work. At the street's western end, where it meets rue de Yougoslavie, is a forgotten bit of Marrakech history: a narrow alley with mulberry trees and single-storey dwellings daubed in many colours (it may be the only non-pink street in Marrakech). This is the old Spanish quarter, a reminder of the city's once significant Hispanic population.

A little further north on Mohammed V is **place Abdel Moumen**, the hub of an area of cafés, bars, restaurants and nightclubs.

Majorelle Gardens

Avenue Yacoub El-Mansour (no phone). Open 8am-5.30pm daily. Admission 30dh. Museum of Islamic Art 15dh.
Privately owned by the late Yves Saint Laurent – but open to the public – the gardens were created in the 1930s by two

generations of French artists, Jacques and Louis Majorelle. Although small in scale and out on the edge of the ville nouvelle, the glamour of the YSL connection has ensured that the gardens are usually packed beyond comfort by coachloads of visitors. The juxtaposition of colours is striking; plants sing against a backdrop of the famous Majorelle blue, offset with soft yellows and terracottas. Bamboo groves rustle in the soft breeze and great palms tower over all, sheltering huge ancient cacti. Rills lead into pools floating with water lilies and great pots overflow with succulents. For the botanically curious, everything is clearly labelled.

Jacques Majorelle's former studio has been turned into a fine little Museum of Islamic Art, recently renovated and reorganised to display a collection of traditional jewellery, fine embroidery, illuminated manuscripts, carved wooden doors and Majorelle lithographs of the High Atlas. Air-conditioned and dimly lit, the museum is a welcome refuge from the intensity of light and colour outside; exhibits have English labelling. Beside the museum is a small boutique selling books, T-shirts, leather goods, babouches, pottery and cushions. Picnics, unaccompanied children and dogs aren't allowed.

HIVERNAGE

South of Guéliz and immediately west of the city walls is Hivernage, a small, low-density neighbourhood of villas and international five-star hotels. Out this way lie the city's civic trappings such as the sports stadium, opera house, the enormous convention centre and beyond them all, the airport.

Avenue Mohammed VI (formerly known, and still often referred to, as the avenue de France) is the central artery of Hivernage. The area it bisects is a veritable showcase of colonial planning. On curving suburban streets, hidden in greenery, hotels sit next to modernist villas. In the shade of a well-groomed hedge, machine-gun toting soldiers indicate a royal in residence.

There's an attractive little colonial-era railway station, soon to be replaced by a big new station. The junction with avenue Hassan II is lorded over by the monumental Théâtre Royal & Opera House, designed by local star architect Charles Boccara. More than 14 years after it was begun the interiors have yet to be completed due to the spiralling costs.

Menara Gardens

Avenue de la Menara (no phone). Open 5am-6.30pm daily. Admission free; picnic pavilion 15dh.
Coming in to land at Marrakech Menara Airport, you may notice a large rectangular body of water to the east. This is the pool of the gardens from which the airport takes its name. The Menara Gardens were laid out by the Almohads in the 12th century. Later they fell into neglect and their present form is the result of 19th-century restoration. The green-tile-roofed picnic pavilion that overlooks the basin was added in 1869. Climb to the upper floor for a view over the water, or stroll around to the opposite side for a view of the pavilion against a backdrop of the Atlas.

Eat

Al Fassia

Guéliz *55 boulevard Zerktouni (024 43 40 60/ alfassia@menara.ma). Open noon-2.30pm, 7.30-11pm Mon, Wed-Sun. ££. Moroccan.*
One of the few posh Moroccan restaurants in town that allow diners to order à la carte, Al Fassia is also unique in being run by a women's co-operative – the chefs, waiting staff and management are all female. It recently moved from avenue Mohammed V into this quieter location, where excellent versions of Moroccan standards are served in a sober dining-room with traditional touches. We'd come here for the Moroccan salad alone, but there are also ten tagines, five couscous dishes and a couple of pastillas, all in very unladylike portions.

Alizia

Hivernage *Corner of rue Ahmed Chouhada Chawki (024 43 83 60). Open noon-3pm, 7-11pm daily. £££. International.*
This is an intimate and well-established Italian-flavoured venture popular with the old-school expat crowd. As well as pizzas, pastas, fillets and steaks, it serves wonderful fish dishes. Ask about the special of the day – a roll of plaice stuffed with salmon and spinach on a recent visit. Save room for the dessert selection, one of the best in town. There's a decent wine list too. Although the pitch is upscale, prices are reasonable and the atmosphere relaxed, especially in the bougainvillea-draped garden.

Café des Epices

Souks *75 Rahba Kedima (024 39 17 70). Open 8am-10pm daily. £. Café.*
Marrakech was crying out for a place like this: a spot in the souks to sit down in pleasant surroundings and refresh with a soft drink or light snack. In a small building overlooking the spice souk, there's a ground-floor terrace, a first-floor salon for lounging and tables on the roof. The decor is simple, the staff young and friendly, there's Wi-Fi and good music. A basic menu comprises tea and coffee, salads and sandwiches, juices and sodas. The only problem is that it's always packed.

Café du Livre

Guéliz *44 rue Tarek Ibn Ziad (024 43 21 49). Open 9.30am-9pm Mon-Sat. ££. Café.*
Sandra Zwollo's bookshop café, a key lunch spot for anglophone expats, is a comfortable first-floor space (accessed from the courtyard of the Hotel Toulousain) with (mostly second-hand) books at one end and tables at the other. Breakast is served until 11.30am, high tea from 4pm to 6pm, and an all-day menu including a handful of dishes devised by celebrity chef and erstwhile Marrakech resident, Richard Neat. Popular attractions include the excellent traditional hamburgers and the lemoniest lemon tart in North Africa.

Chez Chegrouni

Jemaa El Fna *Jemaa El Fna (no phone). Open 6am-11pm daily. £. Moroccan.*

Clockwise from top left:
Dar Moha (2); Café des
Epices, Kechmara;
Al-Fassia.

Clockwise from top:
Palais Soleiman;
Ksar Es Saoussan;
Narwama (2).

Everybody's favourite cheap restaurant in the Medina, Chegrouni has a first-floor dining-room and a rooftop terrace with a partial view of the Jemaa El Fna, as well as the ground-floor terrace – a great vantage point for people-watching. Chegrouni is clean, well run, and all the usual dishes are served briskly and with big baskets of fresh bread. The menus are in English and glasses on the tables contain paper napkins on which you scribble your order and then hand it to a waiter; it returns at the end as your bill.

"Two lanterns mark the door into a gorgeous courtyard space with creamy leather seating below a spindly chandelier."

Dar Yacout

North Medina *79 rue Ahmed Soussi, Arset Ihiri (024 38 29 29). Open 8pm-1am Tue-Sun. ££££. Moroccan.*
Yacout's fame rests more on its design and sense of performance than anything coming out of the kitchen. The building is a madcap mansion by Bill Willis, all flowering columns and candy stripes. Arriving guests are led up to the yellow crenellated roof terrace and invited to take a drink (included in the price) before being taken down and seated for dinner at great round tables inset with mother-of-pearl. On comes the food, delivered with maximum pomp by teams of costumed waiters, course after course. It's perfectly adequate stuff, but you wouldn't come here just for the couscous.

Foundouk

North Medina *55 rue du Souk des Fassi, Kat Bennahid (024 37 81 90/www.foundouk.com). Open noon-midnight Tue-Sun. £££. French-Moroccan.*
Two lanterns mark the door into a gorgeous courtyard space with creamy leather seating below a massive spindly chandelier. Softly glowing side rooms are filled with plush seating; one holds a tiny bar. There is more dining space upstairs at candlelit tables around a gallery open to the sky most of the year. The French-Moroccan food is generally good, though the menu is doggedly inflexible and not everything lives up to the surroundings. Stick to the simple stuff and leave experimentation to the expert bar staff. Drinks are ideally sipped on the roof terrace beneath the stars.

Grand Café de la Poste

Guéliz *Corner Boulevard Mansour Eddahbi & Avenue Imam Malik (024 43 30 38/www.grandcafe delaposte.com). £££. French.*
Just behind the main post office on place Novembre 16, one of the oldest buildings in Guéliz (a hotel when it opened, surrounded by trees) is now a sophisticated brasserie serving

breakfast, lunch and dinner. The charm of the terrace, cooled by misters in summer, isn't wrecked by traffic noise, and there's a generous interior with a mezzanine 'colonial' lounge. The steaks are enormous, the calamari and artichoke starter is worth a punt, and the oysters are fantastic when they have them. Great service too.

Jemaa El Fna food stalls

Jemaa El Fna *Jemaa El Fna. £. Moroccan.*
Early evening in the square sees the arrival of massed butane gas canisters, trestle tables and tilly lamps to form an array of food stalls that together form probably the world's biggest outdoor eaterie. Most stalls specialise in one particular dish, and between them they offer a great survey of Moroccan soul food.

Several places serve bowls of harira (a thick soup of lamb, lentils and chickpeas flavoured with herbs and vegetables). Similarly popular standbys are grilled brochettes, kefta (minced, spiced lamb) and merguez (spicy sausage; stall no.31 apparently sells the best in Morocco). Families perch around stalls selling boiled sheeps' heads, scooping out jellyish gloop with plastic forks. Elsewhere are deep-fried fish and eels, bowls of chickpeas drizzled with oil, and mashed potato sandwiches, while a row of stalls along the west side have great mounds of snails, cooked in a broth flavoured with thyme, pepper and lemon. Humblest of all is the stallholder selling just hard-boiled eggs.

Menus and prices hang above some stalls, but it's easy enough to just point, and prices are so low that they're hardly worth worrying about. Etiquette is basic: walk around, see something you like, squeeze in between fellow diners. Discs of bread serve instead of cutlery. For the thirsty, orange juice is fetched from one of the many juice stalls that ring the perimeter of the square.

The food is fresh and prepared in front of you. Few germs will survive the charcoal grilling or boiling oil, but plates and dishes are a different matter. The single same bucket of water is used to wash up all night, so play safe with your stomach and ask for the food to be served on paper.

Kosybar

Kasbah *47 place des Ferblantiers (no phone). Open meals noon-2.30pm, 7.30-11pm; drinks only 2.30-7.30pm Tue-Sun. £££. International.*
With funky Moroccan decor and tables on various levels, it's not unlike the Foundouk (see above) in style, but a bit smaller. The menu features fish and meat dishes, but the main culinary attraction here is a skilled sushi chef. As the place belongs to a family which owns some of Morocco's best vineyards, there's also an interesting wine list. The chief entertainment is watching the storks nesting in the walls of the Badi Palace opposite, but there's also a pianist at weekends.

Narwama

Jemaa El Fna & Koutoubia Mosque *30 rue de la Koutoubia (024 44 08 44). Open 7pm-2am or 3am daily. £££. Thai/international.*
The city's first proper Thai restaurant is a fun place, housed in the central courtyard of a palatial 19th-century residence. It's an enormous space that, with its potted palms, pastel hues

and global lounge music, feels like a Buddha Bar night in some orientalist conservatory. Some intimacy is offered in a smaller rear room with fantastic old painted ceilings and a couple of curtained diwans. Thai dishes (prepared by a team from Bangkok and mostly pretty good) are supplemented by a miscellany of Moroccan and international standards. If you're not hungry, there's a spacious bar.

Pavillion

North Medina *Derb Zaouia, Bab Doukkala (024 38 70 40). Open 7.30pm-midnight Mon, Wed-Sun. ££££. French.*
The setting is superlative: the courtyard of a splendid old house where tables cluster under the spreading boughs of a massive tree. Several small salons provide for more intimate dining. The day's menu is scrawled on a white board presented by the waiter. Offerings change regularly but expect the likes of *agneau*, *canard* and *lapin*, all exquisitely presented with seasonal veg and rich wine sauces. The staff can be supercilious, but otherwise this is a classy affair.

Rôtisserie de la Paix

Guéliz *68 rue de Yougoslavie (024 43 31 18). Open noon-3pm, 6.30-11pm Mon-Thur; noon-11pm Fri-Sun. ££. Rôtisserie.*
Flaming for decades, the 'peaceful rôtisserie' is a large garden restaurant with seating among palms and bushy vegetation. Simple and unpretentious, it's utterly lovely whether lunching under blue skies (shaded by red umbrellas) or dining after sundown when the trees twinkle with fairy lights. (In winter, dining is inside by a crackling log fire.) Most of the menu comes from the charcoal grill (kebabs, lamb chops, chicken and merguez sausage) but there are also delicacies such as quail, and a selection of seafood.

Le Tanjia

Mellah *14 Derb J'did (024 38 38 36/www.letanjia.com). Open 10am-1am daily. £££. Moroccan.*
This Moroccan à la carte venture occupies a house on the edge of the Mellah, with a comfortable candlelit bar on the ground floor, and a variety of dining spaces on the balconies and terraces above. It's named after a local speciality (a tanjia, like a tagine, is a kind of cooking pot) and there are both chicken and beef tanjias on the menu, but the real gastronomic selling-point is the mechoui, a lamb barbecue dish that in most places has to be ordered a day in advance, but here can be had on the spot.

Terrasses de l'Alhambra

Jemaa El Fna *Jemaa El Fna (no phone). Open 8am-11pm daily. ££. Café/international.*
A clean, smart, French-run café-restaurant on the east side of the main square. The ground floor and patio is a café for drinks and ice-cream; the first floor with terrace is for diners; the top-floor terrace is for non-alcoholic drinks. The menu is brief – salads, pizzas and pasta, plus a few desserts, ice-cream and milkshakes – but the food is good. If you're new to Marrakech, it's somewhere you can eat and feel confident that your stomach will hold up. Settle in air-con comfort indoors or slow roast in the open air overlooking the madness of Jemaa El Fna.

Tobsil

North Medina *22 derb Abdellah ben Hessaien, Bab Ksour (024 44 40 52). Open 7.30-11pm Mon, Wed-Sun. ££££. Moroccan.*
Rated by some as Marrakech's premier Moroccan restaurant, Tobsil has no menu. On being led to the door by a uniformed flunkey (it's otherwise impossible to find), diners are greeted by owner Christine Rio, and seated either in the courtyard or upstairs in the galleries. And then the endurance test. Aperitifs (included in the set price, as is the wine) are followed by a swarm of small vegetarian meze dishes. Then comes a pigeon pastilla, followed by a tagine, then couscous, and finally fruit and tea or coffee with an array of pastries. Everything is delicious but you need a very good appetite to manage it all.

Restaurant Toubkal

Jemaa El Fna *48 Jemaa El Fna (024 44 22 62). Open 24hrs daily. £. Moroccan.*
Big with backpackers but also popular with Marrakchis, Toubkal is the next to last stop on the restaurant chain, just above eating al fresco at the food stalls on Jemaa El Fna. The prices are the main draw. The Toubkal does some of the cheapest tagines, couscous dishes and brochettes in town. The premises are as basic as it gets, with plastic furniture and plastic tablecloths, but the wildlife is real. Chiller cabinets at the rear sell basic grocery-style provisions including yoghurt, packets of biscuits, cheese, chocolate and juice to take away.

Shopping

Akbar Delights

Souks *45 place Bab Fteuh (071 66 13 07). Open 10am-1pm, 3-7.30pm Tue-Sun.*
This upmarket French-owned boutique specialises in luxury clothing and textiles from Kashmir, with some items made to their own designs. The tiny space is crammed with embroidered tops and dresses, cotton robes, silk shawls and scarves, plus shimmery, golden shoulder bags. The only made-in-Morocco items are some extraordinary brocaded babouches. A new showroom recently opened on the rue de la Liberté in Guéliz, as some of their well-heeled customers (members of the royal family among them) may baulk at an excursion to the Medina. The new space stocks more home linens and a wider selection of clothing than you'll find in the Medina, and is open by appointment; call to arrange a visit (071 66 13 07, rue de la Liberté, Imm 42C, apartment 47, just past Atika Shoes).

Atelier Moro

Souks *114 place de Mouassine, Mouassine (024 39 16 78/060 54 35 20/ateliermoro@menara.ma). Open Summer 9am-1pm, 2-6pm Mon, Wed-Sun. Winter 9am-5pm Mon, Wed-Sun.*
This L-shaped first-floor space by the Mouassine fountain contains a cool, eclectic selection of homeware, clothes, accessories and carpets chosen by Viviana Gonzalez of Riad El Fenn. Some of the clothes are designed by Viviana

herself, but most of the stock is Moroccan, often the work of nameless artisans that would otherwise be lost in the souks. There's everything from inexpensive hand-made scissors and Tuareg cutlery to pricey rugs, lamps made from ostrich eggs and suede or Egyptian cotton tops. The door is to the west of the fountain, just right of the arch that leads into the Souk des Teinturiers. Ring for entry.

Atika
Guéliz *35 rue de la Liberté (024 43 64 09). Open 8.30am-12.30pm, 3.30-8pm Mon-Sat.*
This is where well-heeled residents and enlightened tourists flock for stylish and affordable men's and women's shoes – everything from classic loafers to natural leather sandals and stylish beige canvas mules. Prices start at 300dh and rarely go beyond 750dh. It also carries children's shoes and a small selection of handbags.

Au Fil d'Or
Souks *10 Souk Semmarine, Medina (024 44 59 19). Open 9am-1pm, 3-8pm Mon-Thur, Sat, Sun; 9am-1pm Fri.*
It's almost indistinguishable from the multitude of small stores that surround it, but Au Fil d'Or is worth checking for the finest quality *babouches* and wool *djellabas*, plus fantastic own-label hand-stitched shirts in gorgeous deep hues, and finely braided silk-lined jackets – just the thing should one be invited to the palace. Note that the bulk of the stock is kept in the cellar-like space downstairs, accessed via a trapdoor behind the counter.

Bazar du Sud
Souks *117 Souk des Tapis (024 44 30 04/ bazardusud@menara.me). Open 9am-7pm daily.*
This place has possibly the largest selection of carpets in the souk, covering all regions and styles, new and old. The owners say they have 17 buyers out at any one time scouring the country for the finest examples. Although considerable effort goes into supplying collectors and dealers worldwide, sales staff are just as happy to entertain the novice. Prices range from 2,000dh to 350,000dh. Ask for Ismail, who speaks perfect English.

Beldi
Souks *9-11 Bab Fteuh, rue Laksour (024 44 10 76). Open 9.30am-1pm, 3.30-8pm Mon-Thur, Sat, Sun.*
Toufik studied fashion in Germany and now, back in Marrakech, he and his brother Abdelhafid have transformed the family tailoring business into probably the most talked-about boutique in town. They offer both men's and women's ranges in the most beautiful colours and fabrics, fashioned with flair and an eye to Western tastes. Beautiful velvet coats lined with silk start at around 1,600dh; men's shirts in fine linen cost from 400dh. Collections change seasonally.

Boutique Bel Hadj
Souks *22-33 Fundouk Ourzazi, place Bab Fteuh (024 44 12 58). Open 9am-8pm daily.*
Take the passage to the left of the pharmacy on place Bab Fteuh, then head up the staircase on the left. Mohammed

Bari's shop is around the other side of the mezzanine, visible from the top of the stairs. Inside there's a huge collection of beads, and other pieces of jewellery, old and new. Choose your beads, and the charming Mohammed will make them up into a necklace or bracelet, as per your specifications.

Centre Artisanal
Kasbah *7 Derb Baissi Kasbah (024 38 18 53). Open 8.30am-8pm daily.*
Don't let the humble entrance fool you – this is the closest thing to a department store in Marrakech, albeit a department store selling nothing but handicrafts. It's the ultimate souvenir store, with everything from trad clothing (babouches, jellabas, kaftans) to jewellery, and home furnishings to carpets. Prices are fixed at slightly above what you would pay in the souk, but this at least does away with tiresome haggling. The stalker-like behaviour and rudeness of the sales assistants can irritate.

> ## "Au Fil d'Or is worth checking for the finest quality *babouches* and wool *djellabas*, plus fantastic own-label, hand-stitched shirts."

Chez Moulay Youssef
Souks *Souk El Kchachbia, off rue El Hadadine (024 44 34 01). Open 10am-8pm daily.*
One of our favourite shops in the souk, Moulay Youssef does beautiful, richly coloured and stripy bedspreads in sabra, cotton or raffia. There are also homeware items such as jewellery boxes, napkin rings and pillow cases, plus fashion accessories like belts and hand-embroidered bags. It isn't the easiest place to find, but if you can locate the general neighbourhood, just ask – everybody round here knows Moulay Youssef.

Chez Said
Souks *155 Souk Chkairia (024 39 09 31). Open 9.30am-7.30pm daily.*
Said specialises in fashionable leather bags, decorated with coins or beads, or just a simple metal disc on the front. Designs come in both modern and vintage styles. The leather is either au natural or dyed; when the latter, colouring is properly fixed and doesn't come off on your clothes. Said speaks English, and also sells his bags in bulk to certain well-known stores in the UK.

Haj Ahmed Oueld Lafram
Souks *51 Souk Smafa (024 44 51 27). Open 10am-6.30pm Mon-Thur, Sat, Sun.*
Most of the souk's slipper shops are much of a muchness – look into one and you've pretty much seen them all. But Haj

Clockwise from top left:
Caverne d'Ali Baba;
Boutique Bel Hadj;
Marché Couvert;
Bazaar les Palmiers.

Airline flights are one of the biggest producers of the global warming gas CO_2. But with **The CarbonNeutral Company** you can make your travel a little greener.

Go to **www.carbonneutral.com** to calculate your flight emissions then 'neutralise' them through international projects which save exactly the same amount of carbon dioxide.

Contact us at **shop@carbonneutral.com** or call into the office on **0870 199 99 88** for more details.

CarbonNeutral®flights

Riad revolutionaries

Tadelakt walls, carved stucco, colourful *zelije* tiling, rugs on the walls and floor – it sometimes seems like every riad has been designed from the same Marrakech Style handbook. The basic forms and materials are native, of course, as is the palette – the pinks and ochres of local earth, lemon yellow, the blue of cobalt skies. But for traditional Moroccan and Berber crafts and methods to result in an internationally known style required outside intervention. Enter Bill Willis, the man who ignited the Marrakech interiors explosion.

A native of Memphis, Tennessee, Willis moved to Marrakech in the 1960s and began working for clients such as Paul Getty Jr and Yves St Laurent. He developed a style based on traditional Moroccan references (arches, painted woodwork, geometric patterns in tiling), but imbued with his own slightly camp sense of humour. Look at his candy-striped, onion-domed fireplaces at Dar Yacout (*see p83*), or the palm tree columns at the Tichka Salam hotel in Guéliz.

While his particular twists are wholly modern, the techniques he employed are age-old – intricate mosaic work, wood carving, stone masonry. And because his interiors demanded local craftsmen to adapt and stretch, Willis also helped to revive the city's artisan traditions.

He worked on the Tichka with architect Charles Boccara, who also used traditional elements to convey a strong sense of place while striking an unmistakably modern pose. His interiors make stunning use of *tadelakt*, the polished wall finish traditionally employed in hammams, where heat and moisture are a problem. Surfaces are trowelled in a plaster of powdered limestone mixed with coloured dust to provide the requisite hue. The plaster is then polished hard with flat stones, sealed with a glaze of egg white, and polished again with Moroccan black soap. Boccara brought *tadelakt* out of the steam room and into style.

French-Senegalese architect Meryanne Loum-Martin also schooled herself in traditional crafts and methods, then applied the knowledge to a half-built concrete shell in the Palmeraie. The result was Dar Tamsna, the protoype boho-chic villa and the place that really introduced Marrakech to the international lifestyle press (eight pages in *Condé Nast Traveller!*). Like Willis, she reinterpreted local ingredients, but with

a beautifully restrained simplicity – an approach refined with her Jnane Tamsna (*see p95*), completed in 2002.

Meanwhile, the riad scene began to boom in the Medina. Low property prices and the abundance of local artisans encouraged designers to buy houses and go to town on them. Each started with the same traditional references, but the beauty of the whole modern Marrakech thing is how readily traditional methods lend themselves to experimentation and innovation.

Thus Björn Conerding and Ursula Haldimann took trad Moroccan into the realm of gothic fantasy with their Riad Enija (pictured, *see p98*). Christian Ferré played heavily on colour and patterning in his Riad Kaiss (*see p101*). Giovanna Cinel married Marrakech to Milan at her Riad 72 (*see p98*). And Jill Fechtmann and Jean-Michel Jobit have mixed local elements with an idiosyncratic eclecticism in their Riad Noir d'Ivoire (*see p101*). It's astonishing how many riads are now owned by designers turned hoteliers: Marrakech has become their playground.

Clockwise from top:
Chez Moulay Youssef (2);
Marché Couvert (2);
Boutique Bel Hadj.

Ahmed Oueld Lafram offers a selection of babouches in a variety of styles from all over Morocco – embroidered leather ones from Tafraoute, for example – and in a variety of materials including dyed goat fur, horse leather and python skin. They're not the cheapest, but the quality is excellent.

Miloud Art Gallery

Souks *48 Souk Charatine Talaa (024 42 67 16/070 41 76 61). Open 9am-8pm daily.*
A one-stop shop for competitively priced versions of modern Moroccan design objects. A generous space in the souks is packed with large furniture pieces and smaller, more transportable items to take back home. Armchairs and coffee tables, ceramics and textiles, pouffes and picture frames are all specially made and of good quality. With no shop front, this place can be hard to find; call to arrange a visit.

Mustapha Blaoui

Northern Medina *142-144 Bab Doukkala (024 38 52 40). Open 9am-8pm daily.*
This is the classiest, most beloved 'best of Morocco' depot in town. It's a warehouse of a place; crammed, racked, stacked and piled with floor-to-ceiling irresistibles – lanterns, dishes, pots, bowls, candlesticks, chandeliers, chests, tables and chairs… If Mustapha doesn't have it, then you don't need it. Plus, he's a real sweetheart, his staff are ultra-helpful and shipping here is a cinch.

Arts

Marrakech is bereft of theatres and music venues, and the few cinemas aren't going to be showing much you'll understand, but there's a growing commercial gallery scene.

Dar Cherifa

Souks *8 derb Charfa Lakbir, Mouassine (024 42 64 63/ www.marrakech-riads.net). Open 9am-7pm daily.*
This gorgeous townhouse is the Medina's premier exhibition space. Parts of the building date back to the 16th century and it has been lovingly restored by owner Abdelatif ben Abdellah, who's taken great pains to expose the carved beams and stucco work while leaving walls and floors bare and free of distraction. Regular exhibitions lean towards resident foreign artists, but there have also been shows by Moroccan artists Hassan Hajjaj and Milaudi Nouiga.

Galerie 127

Guéliz *127 avenue Mohammed V, 2nd floor (024 43 26 67/ galerie127mohammedV@hotmail.fr). Open 2-7pm Tue-Sat.*
When Nathalie Locatelli opened Galerie 127 in February 2006 it became the very first photo gallery in the Maghreb and only the third in Africa (the others are in Dakar and Bamako). It's an appealingly simple space – a converted apartment with tall windows and walls left unsurfaced – and got off to a good start with an opening show by Tony Catany. The king bought 30 of the photographs.

Locatelli has continued with work by other big names in contemporary photography, mostly French or France-based.

Galerie Rê

Guéliz *Résidence Al-Andalus III, angle rue de la Mosquée and Ibn Touert No.3 (024 43 22 58). Open 10am-1pm, 3-8pm Mon-Sat.*
With a background of collecting Berber textiles and running a New York gallery specialising in Egyptian art, Lucien Viola opened this serious and lavishly designed contemporary gallery for changing exhibitions by mostly 'Moroccan and Mediterranean' artists. Upstairs is a selection from established Moroccan artists such as Abdelkarim Ouazzani, Tibari Kantour and Mohammed Lagzouli. Viola's next project is to open a museum of ancient textiles in the souks.

Light Gallery

Kasbah *2 derb Chtouka (072 61 42 10/light. marrakech@gmail.com). Open 11am-1pm, 3-7pm Tue-Sat.*
Just down the derb from Les Jardins de la Medina, and founded by Marcelle Danan, Julie Caignault and Nicolas Carré, the Light Gallery kicked off in 2007 with photographs of neon and fluorescent lights by Gilles Coulon, then moved on to drawings by Swiss painter Mathias Schauwecker. It's a big, bright, modern space where they also sell a few clothes, books, and have some small photos for sale from the likes of Robert Mapplethorpe, Helmut Newton and Martin Parr.

Matisse Art Gallery

Guéliz *61 rue Yougoslavie, No.43 passage Ghandouri (024 44 83 26/www.matisse-art-gallery.com). Open 9.30am-12.30pm, 3.30-7.30pm Mon-Sat.*
A decent space devoted to solo shows by young Moroccan artists such as calligraphy painters Nouredine Chater and Nouredine Daifellah, and figurative painter Driss Jebrane. More established names are also exhibited, such as Farid Belkahia and Hassan El-Glaoui (the late son of the former 'Lord of the Atlas' was devoted to painting horses). Upstairs are some vintage Orientalist canvases.

Nightlife

Comptoir

Hivernage *Avenue Echouhada (024 43 77 02). Open 5pm-2am daily. Admission free.*
Marrakchi socialites will tell you that Comptoir is sooo over, but on the right night it's still the best party in town. From the outside it's a well-behaved little villa on a quiet residential street, but inside the place buzzes with dressed-up diners on the ground floor, while upstairs is a sizeable lounge filled each weekend night to within a whisper of health and safety violations. The crowd is a mix of good-looking locals, sharper expats and wide-eyed tourists delighted to have stumbled on the Marrakech they'd always heard about. Drinks are pricey but the nightly belly-dancers are hilarious.

Kechmara

Guéliz *3 rue de la Liberté (024 42 25 32). Open 7am-midnight Mon-Sat. Admission free.*

A café by day and restaurant by night, Kechmara also functions well as a lively and convivial bar. There's a long bar counter to the right as you enter with a tap for bière pression, back shelves lined with spirits and bar stools for perching. The menu lists long drinks and cocktails, which are also served on a spacious roof terrace.

Pacha

Zone hôtelière de l'Agdal *Boulevard Mohammed VI (061 10 28 87/www.pachamarrakech.com). Open 11.30pm-6.30am daily. Admission from 120dh; free to chill-out area with terrace.*

Pacha is an enormous complex which, apart from the club itself, also includes two restaurants – Jana and Crystal – as well as a chill-out lounge and swimming pool. The dancefloor and bars can accommodate up to 3,000 smiley souls, and guest DJs are flown in most weekends. The names include many of those you'll find elsewhere on the international Pacha circuit. The club is some 7km south of town, so getting there and back can be pricey.

Palais Jad Mahal

Hivernage *10 rue Haroun Errachid (024 44 81 35). Open bar 7am-2am; club midnight-4am daily. Admission bar free; club 100dh.*

Almost too big for its own good, this complex just outside Bab Jdid has a nice restaurant and bar with (usually) a boring live band playing vintage rock covers on the ground floor, and a voluminous club down below (separate entrance along the street, admission 100dh) that today houses a nightly 'oriental cabaret' frequented mostly by Moroccans.

Thêatro

Hivernage *Hotel Es Saadi, avenue El-Qadissia, (024 44 88 11/www.essaadi.com). Open 11.30pm-5am daily. Admission 150dh.*

Thêatro is where you'll find the hippest, best-informed locals. The venue was once a theatre; now, the stalls are filled with sofas, while the balcony is tiered with throw cushions. A series of semi-private, gauze-veiled crash crèches fill the stage, while the former orchestra pit houses a long curved bar, well stocked with chilled champagne and Red Bull. The sound system is thunderous, and psychedelic cinema projections entertain the eye – it's just a pity no one thought to leave space for a dancefloor. Look out for nights by Sound of Marrakech, as well as occasional international names such as Andy Morris.

Stay

There are hundreds of 'riads' in the Medina – guesthouse conversions of villas with courtyards – but they're all pretty small. Book early to get the place you want. On the old-school side of town, the venerable Mamounia is currently struggling to reinvent itself with endlessly postponed refurbishments. It may reopen in early 2009. Hotels in the Palmeraie are a world away from the bustle of the Medina for a maximum chill-out experience, but are inconvenient for the rest of the city without your own transport.

Casa Lalla

South Medina *16 derb Jamaa, off Riad Zitoun El-Kedim (024 42 97 57/www.casalalla.com). ££.*

This beautiful little guesthouse, with eight rooms ranged on two floors around a grand central courtyard, is elegant yet homely. Two rooms have fireplaces, some of the bathrooms are wonderful and a couple of the suites have their own mezzanine areas. A lounge area has a fireplace, a small library and a couple of tables set up for chess; for further relaxation, there's a plunge pool that you can set fizzing with bubbles and a nice green-tiled hammam. If you've heard of this place before, however, it's probably because of its former connection with Michelin-starred British chef Richard Neat. Alas, he's now in Costa Rica.

Dar Atta

North Medina *28 Derb Raouia, Rmila & 32 rue Jebel Ladkhar (024 38 62 32/www.daratta.ma). ££.*

At first sight it seems an unpromising location – a not very picturesque part of the Medina – but you can get a taxi to the door, or walk to the Jemaa El Fna in ten minutes, and once inside, this Italian-owned *maison d'hôte* is a very pleasant place. Seven stylish double rooms and three spacious suites are ranged around a sunken patio and two terraces. We liked the generally unobtrusive design – cool, without being in your face. Staff are equally discreet, drifting around in black uniforms. There's also a charming hammam and massage area and a restaurant that serves Moroccan and Italian dishes.

> ## "For further relaxation, there's a plunge pool that you can set fizzing with bubbles and a nice green-tiled hammam."

Dar les Cigognes

Kasbah *108 rue le Berima (024 38 27 40/www.lescigognes.com). £££.*

Across the street from the eastern ramparts of the Baadi Palace, Dar les Cigognes (House of Storks) comprises two 17th-century merchants' houses, converted into one elegant 11-room riad hotel. Indoor public spaces, including a library, restaurant and bar, feature arches and orientalist paintings. There is also an African-themed 'living room'. Courtyards are spectacular, with lots of comfortable nook seating. The guest rooms have a restrained kind of opulence, with deep jewel colours and luxury furnishings. A European spa is on site, in addition to the usual hammam, and the location means there are great views from the roof terrace.

Top: Dar Zemora.
Bottom: Riyad Edward.

Top: RiadEnija;
Bottom: Jnane Mogador.

Dar Fakir

South Medina *16 derb Sidi Boufail, Kennaria (024 44 11 00/darfakir@yahoo.fr). ££.*

Dar Fakir's central courtyard and surrounding salons are layered with casually strewn rugs and scattered with glittery throw cushions while incense hangs heavy in the air and tea candles serve for illumination. There's a bar counter, and every corner and recess is filled with exotic plunderings from South-east Asia and the Levant. A chilled soundtrack adds to the Buddha Bar vibe. Of the eight guestrooms, two are on the ground floor and six are upstairs; they're simply done but attractive, including *tadelakt* bathrooms.

"You emerge into a big garden with rows of orange trees and a heated swimming pool actually large enough to swim in."

Dar Karma

Kasbah *51 derb El-Mennabha (024 38 58 78/ www.dar-karma.com). £££.*

This big old house near the Royal Palace was once the home of Mohammed V's French translator. An elegant *maison d'hôte* since 2003, it retains something of a homely air, despite such mod cons as a small swimming pool and a water-mist cooling system on the roof terrace. The five bedrooms are smart but unfussy, with fine bedlinen and spacious bathrooms. Communal salons are comfortable, the hammam is very grand indeed, and the card supplied to guests bearing a map with the hotel's location and instructions for what to tell taxi drivers is an innovation other establishments would do well to imitate.

Dar Zemora

Palmeraie *72 rue El-Aandalib, Ennakhil (024 32 82 00/www.darzemora.com). £££££.*

Set in a hectare of lush gardens filled with roses and hibiscus, bougainvillea and palm trees, Dar Zemora is Marrakech's answer to the English country-house hotel – perhaps it achieves this status because it's owned by an English couple, who have remodelled this former private abode beyond all recognition. Apart from two large sitting rooms, a dining room and a library with leather armchairs, the main house contains just three rooms and two big suites. The 'Perla' suite has a colossal private terrace with plant life in pastel urns and a view over the garden's big heated pool. 'Zahara' has a smaller terrace but a better sitting room and a huge bath. Both have fireplaces, king-size four-posters and dressing rooms. In the garden there's also a two-bedroom pavillion with a kitchen and big living room.

Jardins de la Koutoubia

Jemaa El Fna & Koutoubia Mosque *16 rue de la Koutoubia (024 38 88 00/www.lesjardinsdela koutoubia.com). £££.*

If you want to be in the Medina but prefer the relative impersonality of a hotel over the intimacy of a *maison d'hôte*, then this comfortable, well-run establishment is the place for you. It's brilliantly located, just two minutes from either the Jemaa El Fna or the Koutoubia mosque and a steady stream of taxis. The *faux* traditional design may be nothing to write to the style supplements about, but the place isn't too shabby and both beds and bathrooms are big and welcoming. A huge extension has brought the total number of rooms up to around 100 and added another garden, a couple more swimming pools and a fitness centre.

Les Jardins de la Medina

Kasbah *21 derb Chtouka (024 38 18 51/ www.lesjardinsdelamedina.com). ££££.*

At the southern end of the kasbah, this former royal residence has been a luxurious 36-room hotel since 2001. From the beautiful reception area you emerge into a big garden with rows of orange trees and a heated swimming pool actually large enough to swim in. Comfortable rooms in a sort of Moroccan-international style come in three categories; most are in the middle 'superior' class – big enough to have sofas as well as beds, and all equipped with DVD players and iPod docks. A big international restaurant, a splendid hammam, a decent gym and a beauty salon round off the services.

Jnane Mogador

South Medina *116 Riad Zitoun El-Kedim (024 42 63 24/www.jnanemogador.com). £.*

Arguably offering the best value accommodation in town, the Mogador is a small riad with considerable charm and warmth. And, what's more, it's clean. The 17 rooms are simple and predominantly pink with light pine and wrought-iron furniture and *tadelakt* bathrooms. Public areas are more ornate, with fountain courtyards, stucco arches and a large roof terrace. No heating in winter, however. Advance reservations are essential as the place is permanently full.

Jnane Tamsna

Palmeraie *Douar Abiad (024 32 94 23/ www.jnane.com). ££££.*

The creation of designer Meryanne Loum-Martin and her ethnobotanist husband Dr Gary Martin, Jnane Tamsna is a 'Moorish hacienda' with seven opulent suites and 17 gorgeous rooms, set in five buildings scattered around some beautiful gardens, each with its own pool. The architecture is vernacular chic, coloured in the palest tones of primrose, peppermint and clay and enhanced by Loum-Martin's own inspired furniture. Surrounding fruit orchards, herb and vegetable gardens provide organic produce for the kitchen. A second kitchen is used for 'culinary adventure' programmes. The combination of rural tranquillity, Zen-like aesthetics and ecological initiative makes for an almost utopian (no locks on the doors!) scenario.

EARTH CAFÉ MARRAKECH

N°2, Derb Zawak, Riad Zitoun Kedim, Médina, Marrakech
Phone : 212 (o) 60544992/61289402
Email : earthcafemarrakech@yahoo.com
www.earthcafemarrakech.com

EARTH CAFÉ MARRAKECH is the 1st vegetarian, vegan organic Café-restaurant in Marrakech and Morocco, specializing in delicious, healthy gourmet vegetarian cuisine, dedicated to providing a great tasting menu at affordable prices.

AL BADII ART GALLERY

For the best of the Moroccan arts, craftsand antiques

54, Bd. My Rachid Guéliz 40.000 Marrakech Maroc
Tel. +212 (0) 24 43 16 93 - Fax +212 (0) 24 43 16 79 - E-mail albadii@riadkniza.com

Marrakech's party people

Got something to celebrate? Marrakech is tailor-made for parties, occasions and events of all sorts, with just the right combination of exoticism and convenience, and the added attraction that riads are often small enough to rent outright to accommodate groups of guests. These days – like most things connected to Marrakech – the events business is booming. Event organiser Lara Cleminson got into the business while she was working at Kasbah Agafay, a hotel outside Marrakech. She found herself fitting more and more events organisation for British companies into her working day and eventually decided to set up her own company, Koubba.

Lara believes her unique selling point is her insider knowledge. Now based back in the UK, she travels to Marrakech every six weeks. Her colleague, Laetitia Trouillet (see p293 for information on her personal shopping service) lives full-time in the city. Between them they can lay on everything from bellydancers to hot-air ballooning to Moroccan cookery lessons. A typical weekend celebration to celebrate a 40th birthday, say, might include an exploration of the Medina followed by a relaxing afternoon hammam on the first day, with guests picked up by horse-drawn caleche and taken to an exotic Moroccan restaurant for dinner in the evening. Party day could begin with some personal shopping with Laetitia (with that evening's outfit in mind, perhaps). The big night could include a spectacular show with musicians, dancers and acrobats, in addition to your Moroccan birthday feast. The following day you and your guests can wind down with a horse or camel ride out to the desert for lunch in a nomad tent. Or if you'd like to have your whole party at this lovely desert location, Koubba can arrange that too.

The company has also had success with wedding parties – Marrakech is nothing if not romantic, and the riads, kasbahs and gardens of the city and beyond can provide storybook settings for your big day. Lara can ensure that little personal touches have a special local flavour, by providing each guest with *babouches* embroidered with their initials, for example.

Working for television and film production companies is another string to the Koubba bow. Lara was fixer for the Marrakech episode of the 2008 UK series of *The Apprentice* – viewers will remember the notorious 'kosher chicken' incident. This woman definitely knows her Marrakech.

Koubba *Studio IP2 Cooper House, 2 Michael Road, London SW6 2AD (+ 44 207 751 3139/www.koubba.com).*

Ksar Char-Bagh
Palmeraie *(024 32 92 44/www.ksarcharbagh.com). ££££.*
Char-Bagh takes the Moroccan fantasy trip to extremes. A charming French couple have re-created an Alhambran palace court on a kasbah-sized scale. A moated gatehouse with six-metre-high beaten metal doors fronts an arcaded central court with pool. The extensive grounds contain herb and flower gardens, an orchard, an open-air spa and the deepest of swimming pools. Indoor amenities include a cigar salon, a house sommelier, and a chef trained under Alain Ducasse and Joël Robuchon. All this is shared by a mere handful of sumptuous suites, each with private garden or terrace, and one with its own swimming pool.

"It shuns the traditional in favour of black and white floor tiles, playful accents in pinks and purples, and furniture by Laurence Corsin."

Les Deux Tours
Palmeraie *Douar Abiad (024 32 95 27/www.les-deux tours.com). ££££.*
One of the longer established guesthouses in the Palmeraie, Les Deux Tours (named for its distinctive twin-towered gateway) is the sublime work of premier Marrakchi architect Charles Boccara. It's a walled enclave of earthen-red villas that together offer 24 chic rooms and suites in a lush garden setting. No two rooms are the same, but all feature glowing *tadelakt* walls and zelije tiling with stunning sculpturally soft bathrooms. Guests share the most attractive of outdoor pools, keyhole shaped and fringed by perfectly maintained lawns, as well as a stunning subterranean hammam.

Maison Arabe
North Medina *1 Derb Assehbe, Bab Doukkala (024 38 70 10/fwww.lamaisonarabe.com). £££.*
Maison Arabe is part of Marrakech tourism history. It began life in the 1940s as a restaurant, closed in 1983, and lay dormant for 15 years before reopening in 1998 as the city's very first *maison d'hôte*. Today, there are nine rooms and eight suites set around two leafy, flower-filled courtyards. The prevailing style is Moroccan classic with French colonial overtones. The rooms and suites are supremely comfortable, most with their own private terraces and a couple with fireplaces. The hotel pool may be a 20-minute drive away (serviced by hourly shuttles), but it's set in a lovely garden planted with olive and fig trees. Back at the hotel, the restaurant is excellent and there's a fine bar.

Nejma Lounge
North Medina *45 Derb Sidi M'hamed El Haj, Bab Doukkala (024 38 23 41/www.riad-nejmalounge.com). £.*
This notable budget option, close to Bab Doukkala, shuns the traditional in favour of black and white floor tiles, playful accents in pinks and purples, and furniture by Laurence Corsin. It's the riad as pop art. The six rooms, named for their colours, are not the biggest in town but they're nice for the price. The young French owners maintain a cool but animated atmosphere. There's a small bar off the courtyard, snacks and drinks are served all day long, and you can even imbibe from floating trays in the modest plunge pool.

Riad 72
North Medina *72 Derb Arset Aouzal, off rue Bab Doukkala (024 38 76 29/www.uovo.com). £££.*
Italian-owned, this is one sleek and good-looking place – Marrakech has it away with Milan. The result is a trad townhouse given a black, white and grey *tadelakt* makeover. The structure, space and detailing are Moroccan, the furniture and fittings imported. There are just four guest bedrooms, including a master suite that's over five metres high and crowned by an ornate octagonal fanlight. The Milanese owner and designer, Giovanna Cinel, has now also opened two other riads in the area, each with four more rooms and a similar aesthetic. The cosy Riad 12, off nearby rue Dar El-Bacha, includes a single room – a real rarity in Marrakech. Riad 2 is more grand and spacious, with an enormous suite sporting a big copper bathtub in the huge main room. All three houses have the same menu and services. Riad 72, with its superior vehicle access, remains this small chain's main rendezvous point.

Riad El Fenn
North Medina *2 Derb Moulay Abdallah ben Hezzian, Bab El Ksour (024 44 12 10/www.riadelfenn.com). ££££.*
Three historic houses have been joined to create 18 spacious rooms and suites. Clutter-free and colourful, each room is dominated by an Egyptian cotton-swathed imperial-sized bed. There's a striking split-level suite, a huge garden suite with a sunken bath in the bedroom and a steam room in the bathroom, and another with a private pool on the terrace above, accessed by a spiral staircase. Despite grand architecture and some serious modern art, the mood is relaxed, with plenty of private spaces. Top-rank facilities include two pools, a DVD screening-room, an excellent library and a 120-seater restaurant that can double as a theatre. Co-owned by Vanessa Branson (sister of Sir Richard).

Riad Enija
Souks *9 Derb Mesfioui, off rue Rahba Lakdima (024 44 09 26/www.riadenija.com). £££.*
Swedish/Swiss owners Björn Conerding and Ursula Haldimann have created an enclave of drop-dead gorgeousness at Riad Enija. Its 12 rooms and suites variously boast glorious old wooden ceilings, beds as works of art (wrought-iron gothic in one, a green muslin-wrapped four-poster in another), some striking furniture and grand

Koutoubia Mosque.

bathrooms resembling subterranean throne chambers. Central to the three adjoined houses is a Moorish courtyard garden gone wild, where maroon-uniformed staff flicker through the greenery. The service and food are both excellent, and the riad is just a few minutes' walk from Jemaa El Fna.

Riad Farnatchi

North Medina *2 Derb Farnatchi, Q'at Benahid (024 38 49 10/www.riadfarnatchi.com). ££££.*
The creation of Jonathan Wix (42 The Calls in Leeds, the Scotsman in Edinburgh and Hotel de la Tremoille in Paris), this is an intimate, top-class hotel. Eight vast and luxurious suites – arrayed off three small courtyards, one with a modest heated pool – have large sunken baths, under-floor heating, desks and armchairs and private balconies. Design is a striking update of the local aesthetic, with all furniture, except for bathroom fittings by Philippe Starck, specially manufactured in Marrakech. The place is superbly run and right in the middle of the Medina; taxis can get to within 200m.

Riad Kaiss

South Medina *65 derb Jedid, off Riad Zitoun El-Kedim (024 44 01 41/www.riasdkaiss.oom). £££.*
Renovated, owned and managed by architect Christian Ferré, the eight-room Kaiss is small but exquisite. Its Rubik's Cube layout has rooms linked by galleries, multi-level terraces and tightly twisting staris, all around a central court filled with orange, lemon and pomegranate trees. The decor is traditional Moroccan; earthy ochre walls with chalky Majorelle-blue trim, jade *zelije* tiling and frilly furniture (including four-poster beds). Guests are greeted by red rose petals sprinkled on their white linen pillows. There's a cool plunge pool on th e roof and a well-equipped fitness room too.

Magi

North Medina *79 Derb Moulay Abdelkader, off Derb Dabbachi (024 42 66 88/UK + 44 20 8834 4747/ www.riad-magi.com). ££.*
Petite, unpretentious and homely, Riad Magi has six carefully colour-coordinated rooms on two floors around its central orange-tree shaded courtyard. The first-floor blue room is particularly lovely, with its step-down bathroom. Breakfast can be taken on the roof terrace or in the courtyard (which may or may not sport tree-clinging chameleons); other meals are available by arrangement. When in town, English owner Maggie Perry holds court from her corner table, organising guests' affairs and spinning stories of local absurdity – at such times Riad Magi becomes one of the most entertaining hangouts in Marrakech.

Riad Noir d'Ivoire

North Medina *31 Derb Jedid, Bab Doukkala (024 38 09 75/www.noir-d-ivoire.com). ££££.*
Riad Noir d'Ivoire has that gratifying combination of looking spectacular while feeling supremely comfortable. Owners Jill Fechtmann and Jean-Michel Jobit have knocked together two grand houses and mixed specially commissioned Moroccan elements with assorted curiosities from sub-Saharan Africa, Europe and India. Nine rooms and suites have huge beds with sheets of Egyptian cotton, big

bathrooms and pleasingly eccentric furnishings that reflect an animal theme. There's a small swimming pool and sun loungers in one courtyard and a baby grand in the other, as well as a cosy bar, a hammam in Tiznit marble, a lounge/library, small boutique, and dining area.

Riad Samarkand

North Medina *41 Derb Sidi Lahcen, Bab Doukkala (024 38 78 80/www.riadsamarkand.com). ££££.*
Deep down a derb but in one of the Medina's more convenient quarters, this well-run, centuries-old house boasts five suites surrounding a leafier-than-usual courtyard where the abundant greenery shelters a small swimming pool. Some of the rooms have private terraces and a couple of the bathrooms are spectacular. The decor is uncluttered and restrained, incorporating much original detailing, there are no televisions or sound systems, and a feeling of peace and privacy prevails throughout. Management is charm personified.

Riad Tizwa

North Medina *26 Derb Gueraba, Dar El-Bacha (068 19 08 72/UK +44 7973 238 444/www. riadtizwa.com). ££.*
Small (five rooms) and comfortable, Tizwa has a slightly rough-around-the-edges charm that is all its own. Laid out in the usual fashion around a central tiled courtyard, rooms are white with splashes of colour, and design solutions are simple but striking. There is a hammam, a roof terrace for dining or sunbathing and each room is equipped with an iPod dock. One big advantage is that Tizwa is accessible to taxis, just a few yards down a narrow alley off rue Dar El-Bacha.

Riad W

South Medina *41 Derb Boutouil, Kennaria (065 36 79 36/www.riadw.com). ££.*
Feeling that guests would get quite enough sensory input from their forays into the Medina, Spanish owner Elsa Bauza designed her four-room riad with a philosophy of simplicity and 'quiet in the head'. The bedrooms – one huge, two big, one small – have white walls, unadorned save for a few framed textiles. Downstairs, zen-like lines are matched by some quietly retro furnishings. Up top are two roof terraces, each shared by two rooms. Below is a spacious courtyard, a plunge pool, two sitting-rooms (one with piano), and Bauza and her daughter's apartment. Breakfast is included.

Riyad Al Moussika

South Medina *62 derb Boutouil, Kennaria (024 38 90 67/www.riyad-al-moussika.ma). ££££.*
One reason Turinese owner Giovanni Robazza opened this former mansion as a guesthouse was to showcase the Cordon Bleu cooking of his son Khalid – both a big breakfast and a two-course lunch are included in the rates. This is a riad for gourmands, with a comfortable, worn-in feel. Restoration has been relatively traditional: fountains splash and birds chirp in trees, while six bedrooms are complemented by a hammam, a formal dining-room, a music room with piano, a small but interesting library, and two flower-filled roof terraces. One of three courtyards has a long, thin 'Andalucian' swimming pool. Minimum stay of three nights.

Riyad Edward

North Medina *10 derb Marestane, Zaouia El-Abbasia (024 38 97 97/024 38 48 55/www.riyadedward.com). £££.*

Up in the north of the Medina, this is a rambling conversion of two 500-year-old houses. An ancient cypress towers from the main courtyard, shading the swimming pool and marking the location from a distance. The style is unpretentious Moroccan, slightly weathered, with some original detailing and an odd scattering of art from amiable English owner Stephen Skinner's collection. His partner Beatriz Maximo, meanwhile, ensures the place is run with a feminine touch. Of the ten rooms, we favour those on the rooftops and the big square suite.

Riyad El Cadi

North Medina *87 derb Moulay Abdelkader, off derb Debbachi (024 37 86 55/www.riyadelcadi.com). £££.*

Comprising eight interconnected houses, El Cadi is a rambling maze in which getting lost is a pleasure – luckily, for it'll happen quite a lot in the first few days you're here. The 12 well-appointed suites and bedrooms, as well as the various salons, corridors, staircases and landings, also double as gallery spaces for a collection of art and artefacts gathered by late former owner Herwig Bartels. The overall feel, however, is uncluttered, cool and contemporary. Bartels's daughter Julia now runs the riad, and standards remain high.

Sherazade

South Medina *3 derb Djama, off Riad Zitoun El-Kedim (024 42 93 05/www.hotelsherazade.com). £.*

Probably the most popular budget accommodation in the Medina – perhaps because it's so much better run than most of its competitors. The desk staff speak a variety of languages, rooms come with meal menus, services and trips out of town, the place is cleaned regularly, and there's a general air of competency – which isn't always a given at this end of the market. Some rooms are better than others; those on the roof share toilets and can get overly hot in summer, while only a handful have air-conditioning.

Villa Vanille

Palmeraie *(024 31 01 23/064 40 04 65/ www.villavanille.com). £££.*

Pierre Blanc and Pia Westh set up their family home in these generous grounds, and then built a bungalow for friends. Soon they were renting it out, then building another, different bungalow. And another, and another... Almost by accident they ended up with a unique hotel. Rooms are stylish and comfortable, referencing local style without going overboard. Scattered around the huge garden are tables, chairs and hammocks, and meals can be served wherever you want. The place is great for children, with lots of space to run around and a small playground. For grown-ups there's a gym and massage room; Pia is a trained masseur. A heated 20-metre pool serves the whole family.

Factfile

When to go

The weather is perfect from March to May. Summers can be oppressively hot but it cools down again in September. Winters are mild, but can be damp and overcast. Marrakech is at its most packed over Christmas and New Year, and at its emptiest in January.

Getting there and around

Marrakech's international airport (Aéroport Marrakech Menara) is six kilometres west of the city. From the airport to the city centre is a ten-minute drive. The airport information desk (9am-9pm daily) is in the check-in area. For flight information, call 024 44 78 65 or 024 44 79 10.

Taxis wait outside the arrivals building. In a *petit taxi* the official fare to anywhere in the Medina or Guéliz is around 60dh but drivers usually demand more. Most hotels will arrange for you to be collected.

There are several trains a day from Casablanca and points north, operated by the national railway company ONCF (024 44 77 68, www.oncf.org.ma). The train station is on the western edge of Guéliz, on avenue Hassan II. The *petit taxi* fare into central Guéliz is 5dh-6dh; to the Medina 10dh-12dh.

Buses to and from Essaouira and Agadir use the small Supratours (024 43 55 25) terminus near the train station. Most other long-distance buses, including those operated by national carrier CTM (024 43 39 33), terminate at the Gare Routiere outside the Medina walls at Bab Doukkala.

Petits taxis are the best way to get around, and are officially very cheap, but make sure the driver turns on the meter or agree a price before setting off. Vehicle access is limited in the Medina, where you'll inevitably do a lot of walking.

Tourist information

ONMT, place Abdel-Moumen, Guéliz (024 43 61 31, open 8.30am-noon, 2.30-6.30pm Mon-Fri; 9am-noon, 3-6pm Sat) is of limited use. The best source of information is probably your hotel.

Internet

Most *maison d'hôtes* have Wi-Fi these days. Otherwise, there are plenty of cyber cafés in the area around place Abdel Moumen, charging around 10dh an hour, and free Wi-Fi at Café du Livre.

Jnane Bel Abbés

KAA
EL MRCHRA

ZAOUIA
EL ABESSIA

AVENUE D'EL JEDIDA

AVENUE DU 11 JANVIER

Bab El Inane
Bel Abbés

Bab El Arset
Ben Brahim

Cemetery

Shrine of Sidi
Bel Abbas

DIOUR JDAD

Bab
Taghzout

SID

Bab
Moussoufa

ARSET IHIRI

SIDI
BEN SLIMANE

RUE DE S

Gare routière

Bab
Boutouil

RUE

EL

GZA

Shrine of Sidi
Ben Slimane
El Jazouli

BAB

TAGHZOUT

RUE

ARSET
BEN CHEBLI

Bab
Doukkala

SIDI
BOU AMEUR

RUE

RIAD

EL

RIAD
LAAROUS

RUE BAB DOUKKALA

LAAROUS

Chrob ou Chouf
Fountain

BAB
DOUKKALA

Bab Doukkala
Mosque

RUE BAB DOUKKALA

RUE DAR EL- BACHA

Shrine of
Sidi Abdel Aziz

Ben Youssef
Mosque

R'MILA

RUE

FATIMA

Dar El
Bacha

Koubba
El Badiy

MOUASSINE

Hôtel de Ville

ZAHRA

Ministerio
del Gusto

Mouassine
Fountain

RUE

SEMARINE

Ensemble
Artisanal

RUE JEBEL LAKHDAR

RUE

YAMAMI

Dar Cherifa

Mouassine
Mosque

Souks

AVENUE MOHAMMED V

RUE

MOUASSINE

Arset Abdelsalam

RUE

SIDI

Swimming
Pools

RUE

ABOU

EL

ABBAS

SEBTI

Sidi Moulay
el Ksour

Bab Fteuh

Mosque

RUE FATIMA ZAHRA

RUE DE LA KOUTOUBIA

Jemaa
El Fna

RUE DES BANQUES

Mosque

Marrakech Medina — North

Cemetery

0   300 m
0   300 yds

© Copyright Time Out Group 2008

ROUTE DES REMPARTS

GHALEM

Bab El Khemis

HALEM

BAB EL KHEMIS

Bab Kechich

RUE ASSOUEL

Hôpital El Antaki

RUE DE BAB EL KHEMIS

ASSOUEL

Dar Bellarj

Medersa Ben Youssef

MOQF

PLACE DU MOQF

RUE DE BAB DEBBAGH

Bab Debbagh

Musée de Marrakech

DAR DEBBAGH

ESSEBTIYNE

Bab Lalla Aouda

ROUTE DES REMPARTS

KAAT BENAHID

Sidi Ishak Mosque

Shrine of Sidi Ben Salah

RUE ESSEBTIYNE

ARSET SIDI YOUSSEF

AYLEN

Bab Aylen

DERB DEBBACHI

RUE SIDI BOULABADA

ARSET MOULAY BOUAZZA

Cadi Ayad Mosque

ARSET EL BARAKA

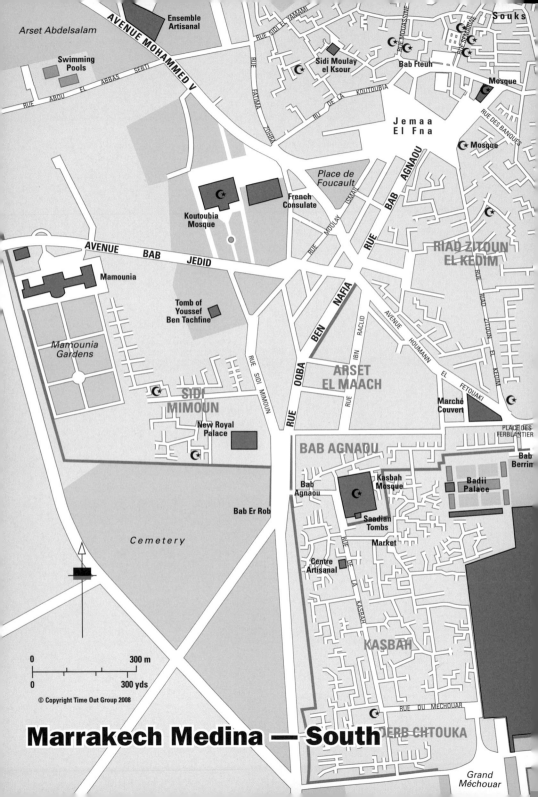

Marrakech Medina — South

Shrine of
Sidi Ben Salah

RUE ESSEBTIYNE

ARSET
SIDI YOUSSEF

AYLEN

Bab
Aylen

DERB DEBBACHI

RUE SIDI BOULABADA

Cadi Ayad
Musique

ARSET
MOULAY
BOUAZZA

ARSET
EL BARAKA

DOUAR
GRAOUA

RUE BA HMAD

CADI AYAD

JNANE
BOUSSEKRI

Dar Si Said
Museum

Moulay Idriss
Palace

RUE EL JEDID

RUE EL ZITOUN

JNANE
BEN CHEGRA

RUE EL JDID

Maison
Tiskiwin

Bab
Ghemat

Pottery
Market

RUE IMAM EL RHEZALI

Shrine of Sidi
Youssef Ben Ali

RIAD ZITOUN
EL JEDID

Bahia
Palace

Bab Es Salam
Market

MELLAH

PLACE
SOUWEKA

Jewish
Cemetery

Cemetery

BERIMA

Berima
Mosque

JNANE EL AFIA

Royal
Palace

Bab Jnane
El Afia

BAB
HMAR

Bab
Hmar

QUARTIER
SIDI YOUSSEF
BEN ALI

Méchouar
Intérieur

The best guides to enjoying London life

(but don't just take our word for it)

'A treasure trove of treats that lists the best the capital has to offer'
The People

'Armed with a tube map and this guide there is no excuse to find yourself in a duff bar again'
Evening Standard

'I'm always asked how I keep up to date with shopping and services in a city as big as London. This guide is the answer'
Red Magazine

'Get the inside track on the capital's neighbourhoods'
Independent on Sunday

'You will never again be stuck for interesting things to do and places to visit in the capital'
Independent on Sunday

Rated 'Best Restaurant Guide'
Sunday Times

Guéliz/Hivernage

To Semlalia &
Route de Casablanca

Cemetery

Majorelle
Gardens

RUE ABDELOUAHAB DERRAQ

BOULEVARD DE SAFI

AVE YACOUB EL MANSOUP

Polyclinique
du Sud

RUE IBN AICHA

BOULEVARD MOHAMMED ZERKTOUNI

AVENUE MOHAMMED

Cinema
Colisée

CTM
Office

PLACE
ABDEL
MOUMEN

RUE TAREK LA LIBERTE

RUE DE IBN ZIAD

RUE SOURYA

Gare
routière

BOULEVARD

RUE YOUGOSLAVIE

AVENUE MOHAMMED V

RUE IMAM MALEK

PLACE EL
MOURABITENE

BD MOHAMMED ZERKTOUNI

ABDELKARIM

BOULEVARD EL MANSOUR EDDAHBI

AVENUE MOHAMMED EL BEKAL

GUÉLIZ

AVENUE DES NATIONS UNIES

Boulevard MOULAY   RACHID

RUE DE MAURITANIE

Main
Post Office

PLACE DU
16 NOVEMBRE

AVENUE MOHAMMED V

RUE OUM
ERRABIA

EL MELLAKH

EL KHATTABI

AVENUE HASSAN II

RUE CADI AYAD

RUE OUED EL MAKHAZINE

Jnane
El Harti

Hôtel de
Police

AVENUE YACOUB EL MARINI

RUE MOHAMMED

Gare

Royal
Opera House

Royal
Tennis Club

Church of
St Anne

PLACE DE
LA LIBERTÉ

Supratours
Terminus

El Harti
Stadium

Kawkab
Centre

Bab
Nkob

RUE IBN EL CADI

AVENUE MOHAMMED VI

AVENUE DU PRÉSIDENT KENNEDY

AVENUE MOULAY HASSAN

AVENUE ECHOUADA

To Jénàa El rià

Palais
des Congrès

AVENUE DE PARIS

HIVERNAGE

AVENUE (DE FRANCE)

AVENUE EL DADISSIA

To Pacha & Bô-Zin

To Airport

AVENUE DE LA MENARA

To Jénàa El rià

0   400 m

0   400 yds

© Copyright Time Out Group 2008

Clockwise from top left:
Bab Mansour; Palais Didi;
Ryad Bahia; a baker
at the covered market;
Palais Didi; Volubilis
triumphal arch; olives
at the covered market.

Meknès

The city of Meknès was the creation of one of Morocco's most megalomaniac sultans, Moulay Ismail (reigned 1672-1727). Just spitting distance from the imperial city of Fès, his own imperial city was a triumphal symbol of his personal dominion over the land and its people. Everything was on a grand scale: at the centre of his new development was a complex of 12 imperial palaces, along with massive stores for grain and weapons; the city was fortified by 44 kilometres of battlements.

But its magnificence was shortlived: the great Lisbon earthquake of 1755 brought much of Moulay Ismail's work crashing down, and his son eventually moved the capital to Marrakech. Meknès's glory days were over. Today, a modest and understated city thrives amid the fascinating remnants of Moulay Ismail's grand ambition. Business is done in narrow Medina lanes and the expanding *ville nouvelle*. The main square, place El-Hedim, has been likened to a mini version of Marrakech's Jemaa El Fna, a centre for trade, performance and entertainment. Amid the ruins and the remaining 25 kilometres of walls is a small scattering of riads and restaurants, but the pace of life in this town is pleasantly slower than in major tourist centres.

Close by, in a truly spectacular setting, are the well-preserved remains and mosaics of the Roman city of Volubilis, and the neighbouring shrine town and pilgrimage centre of Moulay Idriss.

Explore

Alaouite Sultan Moulay Ismail's *grand projet* of a new imperial capital in Meknès has led to comparisons with Versailles – the similarly extravagant work of his contemporary, Louis XIV. The sultan is the stuff of legend: he is said to have used some 25,000 Christian slaves, most captured by pirates in raids on Western Europe, kept in order by his Black Guard of sub-Saharan Africans, to build the fortified imperial city complex. But the work was never finished, and following damage from the 1755 earthquake, many monuments were stripped to provide building materials for use elsewhere. The city remained a backwater. Its use as a military headquarters under the French protectorate did something to revive its fortunes, but it is a modern recognition of its historic architectural assets – and their tourist potential – that has done most to breathe new life into Meknès.

Now a UNESCO World Heritage Site, **Volubilis** was an important Roman town, probably built on the site of an earlier settlement and home to major monuments including a triumphal arch, temples, baths and civic buildings, as well as private homes and businesses. The almost-intact mosaics are perhaps the site's most striking aspect. Excavations began in 1915 and are still continuing.

THE IMPERIAL CITY

The Imperial City was entered through the enormous and majestic Bab Mansour. The most significant structure within is the Mausoleum of Moulay Ismail, one of Morocco's few holy places that is open to non-Muslims.

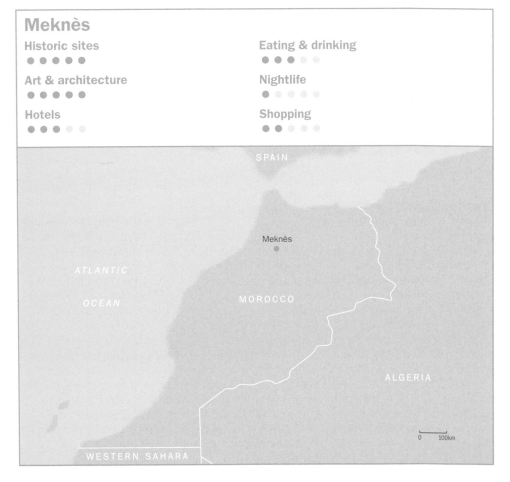

Meknès

Historic sites
● ● ● ● ●

Art & architecture
● ● ● ● ●

Hotels
● ● ● ● ●

Eating & drinking
● ● ● ● ●

Nightlife
● ● ● ● ●

Shopping
● ● ● ● ●

SPAIN

Meknès

ATLANTIC

OCEAN

MOROCCO

ALGERIA

WESTERN SAHARA

0   100km

BAB MANSOUR & PLACE EL-HEDIM

Bab Mansour is the mightiest of gates. Formal, imposing and stunning, it was built in 1686 by a Portuguese convert to Islam. A central keyhole-shaped arch is flanked by the arches of two smaller loggias. Above all three, stucco work in fleur de lys-style pattern is combined with intricately patterned *zelije* tiling. The gate is topped by a merlon (masonry with a saw-tooth effect). The loggias are supported by composite capitals made from Carrara marble from Italy.

Bab Mansour faces place El-Hedim. Hedim means 'destruction', and it is said it got this name after Moulay Ismail tore down a kasbah originally on the site. Ranged along the walls at the edge of the square are 11 small towers with green-tiled roofs. Cafés, food stalls and souvenir shops line the square. In the middle, a mini version of Marrakech's Jemaa El Fna gets going in the late afternnoon, with groups of men gathering around potion sellers with colourless liquids in small jars, laid out alongside explanatory drawings of whales and engorged penises; peanut and balloon sellers tout their wares, and a dressed up and saddled horse waits for children to clamber aboard for a photo session. The smell of oranges and grilling meat from the food stalls hangs in the air.

Koubbet Es-Soufara & the underground storage

Open 9am-noon, 3pm-sunset daily. Admission 10dh.
Passing through the gates adjacent to Bab Mansour and walking past place Lalla Aouda, a rather uninviting barren square newly laid with bricks, you will come to an awkwardly shaped public area surrounded by high walls as far as the eye can see. Following the road around to the right will bring you to the Koubbet Es-Soufara (the Ambassador's Pavilion). The green-roofed building dates from the 17th century; its front door is embellished with an enormous geometric sun. Its interior is not as elaborately decorated as many other buildings in the imperial capitals. It was here that Moulay Ismail would receive foreign diplomats, paying court to secure the release of their slaves. The huge network of underground chambers was built by Cara, a Portuguese architect, who secured his freedom on completion of the subterranean space. It was said that enough weaponry to arm 150,000 men was stored here; guides like to suggest that slaves also languished in the dark and dank crypt as the envoys discussed their fate above.

Mausoleum of Moulay Ismail

Open 9am-noon, 3pm-sunset Mon-Thur, Sun; 3pm-sunset Fri. Also closed during burial ceremonies. Admission free.
The entrance to the mausoleum is through a wooden door in a perfect horseshoe arch, decorated above with carved stonework. Either side of the principal entrance are 14 horseshoe arches in green, black and brown tiles, as well as three arched fountain pieces. Visitors pass through several courtyards before entering the sanctuary where Moulay Ismail is buried; his tomb is the largest, second from the left. His first and favourite wife, Khnata, is the last tomb on the right. Next to her is Moulay Ahmed, who succeeded his father. The first tomb on the left is Moulay Abderrahmane (the great grandson of Moulay Ismail who ruled 1822-1859). On display are four clocks given by Louis XIV to Moulay Ismail after the Sun King refused him the hand in marriage of one of his daughters. The hall facing the tomb is beautiful, with walls covered in geometric mosaic tiling and intricate stucco, with a *mihrab*, marble columns and star-design tiled courtyard with a small fountain.

> "It is said that Moulay Ismail travelled this route in a chariot pulled by his wives and eunuchs and accompanied by up to 30 black slaves."

DAR EL-KEBIRA, THE ROYAL GOLF COURSE & DAR EL-MAKHZEN

Behind the mausoleum is Dar El-Kebira, completed as a complex of 12 palaces in 1677 but virtually destroyed by the 1755 Lisbon earthquake and now a series of picturesque ruins. Opposite Dar El-Kebira is the Royal Golf Course, its entrance opposite the Koubbet Es-Soufara compound. A large door opens on to what must be one of the most spectacular settings for a golf course in the world. The greens roll out to the edges of the monumental walls that contain it, on grounds that used to be the gardens of Moulay Ismail's concubines, who were said to number 2,000.

South of the golf course is Dar El-Makhzen. This was the principal residence of Moulay Ismail and is occasionally used by the current king. Between Dar El-Kebira and Dar El-Makhzen, passing through the Bab Er-Rih, you travel along a kilometre-long passage running between imperial walls. It is said that Moulay Ismail travelled this route, and others in his imperial city, in a chariot pulled by his wives and eunuchs and accompanied by up to 30 black slaves.

The Granaries

Open 9am-noon, 3pm-sunset daily. Admission 10dh.
This enormous set of chambers and silos was built in 1690 to store enough wheat and barley to feed the country, it was said, for around 20 years. Inside the first buildings you enter were ten wells, with wheels turned by horses. Underground

canals, with water kept at a temperature of 16 degrees celsius – the optimal temperature for conservation – were also installed. The silos were almost two kilometres in length and one kilometre wide, and it is also thought that 3,000-4,000 horses were stationed here. Originally the granaries were underground but all the ceilings have collapsed leaving a series of arches and passageways. Parts of *Jewel of the Nile* and *The Last Temptation of Christ* were filmed here. South of the silos is the reservoir, El-Agdal, surrounded by jacaranda trees, built in case of siege.

THE MEDINA

Meknès's Medina lies north of the Imperial Palace complex and place El-Hedim. It is riddled with souks, but these are on a much smaller scale than those in Marrakech and Fès. At the entrance of the Medina on place El-Hedim is the Dar Jamaï, a 19th-century palace. Within the Medina are the Grand Mosque and the Medersa Bou Inania.

"Among the jewellery exhibits are gold collars inlaid with precious stones such as coral, amber and emerald."

Musée Dar Jamaï
Open 9am-5pm Mon, Wed-Sun. Admission 10dh.
Dar Jamaï, built in 1882, belonged to Mohamed ben Larbi Jamaï, grand vizier to King Moulay Hassan I (reigned 1873-1894), the same grand vizier who built the Palais Jamaï in Fès. The museum, set in rooms around the small interior courtyard garden of palm and banana trees, exhibits historical pieces demonstrating arts and crafts from the city: wooden doors, 14th-century cedar supports, epigraphs, and *mashrabeya* windows. Fabrics include 19th-century embroidered belts, 18th-century embroidery work and a sumptuous green velvet and gold *kandoura* from the late 19th century. Among the jewellery exhibits are gold collars inlaid with precious stones such as coral, amber and emerald. There are also engraved silver kohl bottles and sugar hammers. The vizier's reception room has been restored. Topped by a huge dome with a chandelier, with a sandalwood incense burner, *muqarnas* (decorative tiered stucco) and polygonal *zelije* work, you can sense the authority through wealth. Photography is not allowed.

Grand Mosque & Bou Inania Medersa
Bou Inania Medersa. Open 9am-noon, 3pm-sunset daily. Admission 10dh.
The Almoravids built the Grand Mosque in the second half of the 11th century; it was restored and enlarged in the 13th century. Close by is the Medersa Bou Inania, begun in 1336 by Abu El-Hassan, a Merenid king, and completed by his successor Abu Inan. It closed as a *medersa* in 1950 and is currently under restoration, but it remains open to the public. Surrounding the *sahn* (inner courtyard) are beautiful cedar panels, verses from the Quran inscribed in plaster work – 'Stand up for your Lord when you can do so and try to perform the prayers on time, especially the third prayer of the day' – and a lovely decorated *mihrab* in the prayer room on the right. *Mashrabeya* panels line the courtyard in between the pillars. *Zelije* tiles line the walls and are topped by friezes of calligraphy in black cut-out tiles; above these are stucco motifs. Upstairs, some 100 students used to occupy the 48 rooms, with small wooden windows opening out on to the *sahn*. Climb to the roof for a view of the Medina and its minarets.

Palais des Idrissides
11 rue Kermouni, Medina (035 556285/ palais_Idrissides@hotmail.fr). Open 9am-7pm daily. Admission free.
Palais de Idrissides, built by the family of Moulay Ismail, is actually a shop but entrance is free and it's worth nipping in to admire the stunning interior and Carrara marble floor. The walls are decorated with an unusual frieze of red ribbon imagery above the stucco line and there's a beautiful wooden ceiling in the side room. The fountain has *zelije* tiling and a gun collection hangs on the wall.

FURTHER AFIELD

MOULAY IDRISS
The holy city of Moulay Idriss stands on a hill, cradled by mountains, just two miles (four kilometres) east of Volubilis. From a distance it appears as a white, higgledy piggledy pile of buildings, surrounded by slopes of cacti.

The town – with steep slopes, marvellous views and a refreshing lack of hassle – is built around the tomb and *zaouia* (religious school) of Sultan Moulay Idriss I (reigned 788-792), a direct descendant of the Prophet Mohamed. Fleeing war in what is now Saudia Arabia, he managed to unite and convert local tribes, and build a powerful kingdom. He is thus seen as the father of not just the nation but of Moroccan Islam. The town is a peaceful corner for most of the year, but that all changes in September, when thousands of pilgrims come to the moussem in his honour. Non-Muslims can't enter the mausoleum and zaouia complex, but they are welcome to enjoy the town at any time of year.

Shop

The souks in the Meknès Medina and the covered market, south of place El-Hedim, are the best places to shop. Rue Sebat, which runs in front of the Medersa Bou Inania, is crammed with

Clockwise from top left:
Mausoleum of Moulay
Ismaīl; the souks;
Mausoleum of Moulay
Ismaīl; Riad Meknès;
place El-Hedim.

La vie en rosé – and red, and white

In a country where religion forbids the consumption of alcohol, the wine business is, perhaps surprisingly, booming. In the region around Meknès, altitude, hours of sunshine and temperatures combine to make ideal vineyard conditions. **Les Celliers de Meknès**, with estates covering over 2,000 hectares, is the largest of five wine companies in Morocco, making 27 million of the 55 million bottles produced in the country each year. Of these only two million bottles are exported, leaving 25 million bottles to be consumed on home ground. So is it the tourists who quaff the lot? Not according to Les Celliers' export manager, Jean-Pierre Dehut; he reckons that only around two per cent of his company's wine is drunk by visitors.

Despite the fact that sales prove that many Moroccans aren't averse to a glass of wine now and again, the industry had a hard time in the immediate post-independence period and at one time its chances of survival looked bleak. 'At the end of the French protectorate, the president of this company, Brahim Zniber, was the only one who didn't uproot his vineyards', said Jean-Pierre Dehut. 'Moroccan viticulture only exists because of him. He is 86 years old now, and still working.'

These days Celliers is confident in its future. It is about to invest €11 million in infrastructure, as well as building a 12-room riad focusing on vinotherapy, and a *route du vin*. But even without exploiting the potential for oenotourism, the company is making vast strides. According to Dehut, the home market remains the most important. 'We have just produced a sparkling wine – a new local product. We produced 25,000 bottles and we sold 20,000 bottles at the end of the first year,' he said.

Despite the success of the home market, Celliers is keen for its wines to be recognised on the world stage. It is the only company in Morocco to be awarded an Appellation d'Origine Contrôlée (AOC): Le Coteaux de l'Atlas. From the AOC area come the company's flagship Château Roslane red and white wines. Three other areas have earned Appellation d'Origine Garantie (AOG) designation.

Château Roslane, the company's wine-making centre, is surrounded by 700 hectares of estate and set in a beautiful landscape of bright green hills dotted with cypress trees, olive groves and vineyards. Some 1,000 people are employed to harvest grapes by hand from the end of July to October each year, and this is where those grapes end up, to undergo a process that involves both modern technology and traditional skills. It is now possible to visit the château and watch the Moroccan wine-making process at first hand.

Les Celliers de Meknès

11 Ibn Khaldoun Street (035 504 693/visites@lescelliers demeknes.net/www.lescelliers demeknes.net). Tours by appointment, reservations required 14 days in advance.

stalls most likely to interest the visitor. Freshly decapitated sheep, olives and mounds of pastry can be found in the covered market. Meknès is noted for its damascene ware, found in the Kissaria Lahrir in the Medina, where visitors can view the manufacturing process.

Palais Damasquini
Kobt souk no.10, Kissariat Lahrir, Medina (061 50 30 43/essaidi762000@yahoo.es). Open 9am-6pm daily.
Essaidi Hicham has been making damascene ware ever since his father taught him the skills as a youngster. At his workshop in the Medina you can see him inlaying the silver thread into vases and jewellery while colleagues fire moulds of birds and owls. The silver is mined in Morocco, then exported and made into thread in France before being imported to Meknès. Essaidi will explain that it takes approximately 12 days to finish a pot – from design stage to completion.

L'Art des Villes Imperiales
2 Der Hamman My Ismail, opposite Koubbet Soufara (035 55 37 40). Open 8.30am-6pm daily.
Mohamed Chalia will take the time to explain the symbols on Berber kilim in the carpet shop. About the traditional marriage kilim, he explains: 'Women don't make rugs for future husbands anymore; they send them text messages.' Next door is a treasure trove of goods stacked floor to ceiling, with embroidery made by the orphans at the San Franciscan convent in town, Berber daggers and saddles, kilim belts and old silver Berber jewellery such as bangles, rings, earrings and pendants.

Eat

Because Meknès doesn't have many overnight visitors, the restaurant scene has remained small. Most offer set menus of Moroccan food. Place El-Hedim has stalls with tables and chairs, which sell brochettes, fruit and drinks. Eating here will give you a good view of the evening entertainment in the square. At night you will need to eat early, as places may close if there are no customers.

Multicoloured sweet pastries and biscuits are a Meknès speciality; you can buy them at the covered market on the south side of place El-Hedim.

Le Collier de la Colombe
Place Lalla Aouda *67 rue Driba (035 55 50 41). Open 11.30am-3.30pm, 6.30-11pm daily. £££. International.*
A hit for its views and its fish dishes. The roof terrace has an all encompassing view of the Ville Nouvelle and the fountain marking the entrance to the New Town. And if the weather's bad, you can catch the same view from the huge upper windows of the three-storey building. The dining area is huge and the decor is smart Moroccan, with maroon-

covered wooden chairs, white tablecloths, stucco work ceiling and mosaic-tiled columns. The restaurant is known for its Atlas trout: the Collier de la Colombe is a two-trout affair with rice and mushrooms, and it's highly recommended, as is the leg of lamb. There's a decent wine list, including champagnes, and a selection of beers too.

Dar Sultana
Medina *4 der Sekkaya-Tiberbarine (035 53 57 20/ www.dar-sultana.com). Open 8am-11pm daily. £. Moroccan.*
A little restaurant, hidden in a small Medina house down an alley close to Ryad Bahia. Diners eat at courtyard tables or in the more slouchy, fuschia-pink area to the side. Here there's a beautiful mosaic-topped carved coffee table, dishes of orange blossom, a sheesha and candlesticks. A traditional Moroccan menu includes densely flavoured salads of beans, lentils, aubergine in tomato and sweetened carrots, served in little white dishes with great hunks of bread, as well as tagines and a reasonably priced pastilla. There's also a set menu of the day.

> ## "If the weather permits, the patio garden is a mellow place to dine in this riad, with its off-the-wall collections of clocks and face masks."

Palais Didi
Dar El-Kebira *7 dar El Kebira (035 55 85 90/ www.palaisdidi.com). Open 11am-3pm, 6-10pm. ££. Moroccan.*
Diners can eat upstairs on the terrace in susmmer, or inside in the cosy bare-brick interior, beside a roaring fire, when it's cold. The traditional Moroccan menu lists several soups, couscouses and tagines. A hearty soup of vegetables and chick-peas comes with fluffy bread and a plate of pale green olives. Tagines include beef with prunes (ours was a tad dry); and a more luscious Meknassi tagine of chicken with olives and pickled lemon. Chicken and beef pastillas are also available. The waiting staff are friendly and delightful, and the fresh flowers on the tables are an appreciated touch. Diners can bring their own alcoholic drinks.

Restaurant Le Dauphin
Ville Nouvelle *5 avenue Mohamed V (035 52 34 23). Open 12.30-3pm, 7.30-11pm daily. ££££. French/ Moroccan.*
Popular with well-heeled Moroccans and anyone else who enjoys fine French cooking, Le Dauphin is a special occasion kind of restaurant, with bow-tied staff and a long menu. Good French bread and multicoloured olives are served on arrival. Fish is a speciality: mains include fried

calamari, fillet of trout, paella, sole, dorado, and trout in Meknès wine, as well as succulent steaks and brochettes. Puddings are trad treats such as bananas flambé, crêpe suzette, crème caramel, fruit tart, and peach melba. The good-value three-course *menu du jour* might include a house salad, beautifully presented calamares in sauce, served in a tagine dish with rice, and crème caramel. Wine and beer are served.

Restaurant Riad

Dar El-Kebira *Riad Meknès, 79 Ksar Chaacha (035 53 05 42/www.riadmeknes.com). Open 11am-3pm, 6-10pm daily. ££. Moroccan.*
If the weather permits, the patio garden is a mellow place to dine in this riad, with its off-the-wall collections of clocks and face masks. Someone here can rustle up a wonderful chicken tagine: tender chicken delicately matched with green olives, peas and carrots, soaking in a big-flavoured juice. Mint tea is accompanied by mini meringues or little blobs of nougat. Food is available in the usual set menu format (salads or soup; tagines, couscous or pastilla, then fruit or pastries), and there's a carte too. No alcohol is served, but you can bring your own.

"Magical views across the Medina are best enjoyed with a sunset drink in one hand."

Ryad Bahia

Medina *Tiberbarine (035 55 45 41/www.ryad-bahia.com). Open noon-3.30pm, 7-10.30pm daily. £££. Moroccan.*
The dining area at the Ryad Bahia is set off the main courtyard, in a wing with a long banquette and round tables. A herby *salade aromatisée* (tomatoes, cheese, oregano), Moroccan salad or a vegetable or onion soup can be followed by a choice of nine tagines: the tagine Arabe – lamb with dates and almonds – is deeply, sweetly flavoursome. Couscous, pastilla and brochettes are also available. Unusually, there is also a long list of desserts, including a tangy Dessert Berbère (oranges with sugar and cinnamon) and a tart of the day. Alochol isn't served, but you can bring your own.

Nightlife

Hotel Transatlantique

Le O'Night Club, Hotel Transatlantique, Zankat El-Mariniyine, Ville Nouvelle (035 52 50 50). Open 10pm-6am Tue-Sat. Admission 100dh.
If you must go clubbing in Meknès, this is the place to come. It will cost you, though. In a new building on the premises of the Hotel Transatlantique, the club attracts only a

wealthy clientele. Not only must you stump up 100dh to gain entry but the drinks are an astonishing 100dh each. Music is a crowd-pleasing mix of house, electro, trance, Latin and R&B.

Stay

Meknès does not have a great many places to stay, as visitors tend to come here for the day from Fès. There are some riads in the Medina, and more standard hotel accommodation in the Ville Nouvelle.

Hotel Majestic

Ville Nouvelle *19 avenue Mohamed V (035 52 20 35). £.*
The Hotel Majestic belongs to another era. It dates from the 1930s and has kept some original features, such as the handsome brass banister on the marble staircase and the old-fashioned telephones set into the headboards under art deco lamps in the bedrooms. There are 47 spacious, spick and span but spartan rooms; bathrooms feature showers only, but these days there's hot water round the clock. The friendly manager will climb down from his cubby hole of a reception – replete with dozens of hanging keys – to show you around and escort you to the under-utilised roof terrace. There are Moroccan and European dining rooms on site.

Hotel Transatlantique

Ville Nouvelle *Rue Myrenne (035 52 50 50/ ansar4242@hotmail.fr). £££.*
The Transatlantique is a sprawling complex set in five hectares of grounds in an inconvenient location in the Ville Nouvelle. The compensation is magical views across the Medina, best enjoyed with a sunset drink in one hand. The hotel is split into two buildings; the old building dates from 1926, the new building from 1968. Prices are the same, but rooms in the new building are smarter, with lovely crafted bronze lamps and balconies with great Medina views. Older rooms are fairly plain but spacious. All 120 rooms front patios overlooking gardens and beyond to the Medina. A second, larger pool and expensive nightclub are opposite the newer wing.

Palais Didi

Dar El-Kebira *7 dar El-Kebira (035 55 85 90/ www.palaisdidi.com). ££.*
This beautifully restored 17th-century palace is a place for quiet repose. Five suites are arranged around the tranquil courtyard, while the six rooms are on the first floor overlooking the fountain and courtyard. All are individually designed: the red suite boasts a luxurious, curtained four-poster; the desert room is dominated by a four-poster made from Zaharawi carved desert tent supports. A camel frieze runs around the walls. Palais Didi belonged to the grandfather of Raouf Ismaïli and he runs it, in very welcoming fashion, with his wife, Houda. The couple also own Riad Meknès (*see p123*).

Clockwise from top left:
Dar Sultana; Riad
Meknès; Palais Didi;
Riad Meknès (2).

Volubilis

The Roman ruins of Volubilis, and their wonderful mosaics, sit in a spectacular natural environment on an enormous plateau, surrounded by swathes of cereal fields and olive groves. It's a beautiful setting; orange calendula and white asphodel flowers flourish across the site, which is at its most atmospheric in the late afternoon and at dusk, especially in summer.

A World Heritage Site, Volubilis is about 18 kilometres north of Meknès. There were neolithic and Carthaginian settlements here long before the Romans arrived in the first century BC and built what was to be the southernmost city of its empire. As a Roman provincial capital, Volubilis was a centre for the trading and exporting of grain in this fertile region. The Romans headed off home in the third century AD but the city was inhabited until the 11th century. In the 18th century, it suffered at the hands of Sultan Moulay Ismail, when he began demolition to provide materials for his palaces in Meknès. Nature got in on the act and the site was further damaged by the 1755 Lisbon earthquake.

The town plan is clear, and the remains of a Capitol, with corinthian columns, Basilica (a hall for legal and business transactions) and Forum mark what was once the administrative centre. Little remains of the public baths, but the triumphal arch built in AD 217 to honour Emperor Caracalla and his mother Julia Domna has survived. The town's Decumanus Maximus runs from the triumphal arch to the Tanger Gate; it's possible to walk the road, which would once have been lined with shops. Behind these were a series of grand villas.

The highlights of the site today, though, are the stunning mosaic floors – many still intact and remarkably unfaded – which remain in their original locations. Amethyst, quartz, marble and granite were the materials used to create memorable images of Roman life. The best are at the House of the Ephebe next to the triumphal arch, the House of Orpheus near the olive oil presses, the House of the Labours of Hercules on the Decumanus Maximus and those at the House of Venus in the northeast of the site.

Most of the site's portable artefacts have been removed and put in the Musée Archéologique in Rabat (*see p129*). A museum is under construction next to the site and it is hoped to transfer the mosaics here by 2012.

There are a handful of guides on the site who charge 120dh for a 45 minute tour, but if you want a serious tour, it's best to bring an official national guide with you.

Volubilis
Open 7am-sunset daily. Admission 10dh. Parking 5dh.

Top: Dar Sultana.
Bottom: place El-Hedim.

Riad Meknès

Dar El-Kebira *79 Ksar Chaacha (035 53 05 42/ www.riadmeknes.com). £.*
Part riad and part small museum, this is another of Moulay Ismail's palaces in Dar El-Kebira, set around a cool courtyard and patio garden. The ten rooms are scattered around the large building, and include one dominated by a four-poster antique bronze bed surrounded by dark drapes, with an attractive painted wooden ceiling. Ask Raouf to show you his old radio collection – apparently they all work – and the ancient piece of ceiling in an upstairs room. There's also a clock collection on the walls and face masks – some a little sinister looking – from the south of the country. A filling breakfast is served in the restaurant or on tables around the lovely patio garden.

Riad Safir

Medina *Bab Aïssi, 1 Derb Lalla Alamia (035 53 47 85/ www.riadsafir.com). £.*
Philippe and Chantal, originally from Lyon, fell in love with Meknès and have opened up this small, cosy guesthouse in the Medina. There are just three rooms, off a central sitting room area. They are alcoved and decorated in earthy hues: paprika, saffron and camel. The saffron room has a sweet mezzanine. Restored in 2007, attention has been paid to detail in the interior, with plenty of attractive local artefacts decorating the place. A slice of Place El-Hedim can be seen and heard from the terrace, which also has good views of the mountains. Guests can dine with the owners by reserving dinner. Ask for the honey and sesame pastry, *chebekia*, and for the secret sweet of the house. Massage and 4x4 excursions can be arranged.

Ryad Bahia

Medina *Tiberbarine (035 55 45 41/www.ryad-bahia.com). ££.*
This spacious riad, just inside the Medina and very close to place El-Hedim, belonged to owner Bouchra's grandmother. The building actually dates from the 16th century. It's quite a gathering place for people to meet for mint tea in the communal area or for dinner in the inviting downstairs courtyard amid the brightly coloured cushions and small tables. There's a roof terrace and rooms on several levels. These vary in size; some are tiny and rustic and perched on the roof terrace; others are larger and brightly decorated. Bouchra and her husband, Abdel, are helpful and can arrange excursions. The star of the show is Samar, the riad cat.

Volubilis Inn

Volubilis *BP144, Dourar Fartassa, Oualili, Moulay Idriss, Zerhoun (035 54 44 05/www.ilove-morocco.com/ hotelvolubilisinn). ££.*
Overlooking the Roman site of Volubilis, this modern hotel has 54 fully equipped rooms, all with balconies. From these, the views of the site are incomparable – best at sunset in summer, amazing at any time. There's a mosaic-tiled pool, dedicated children's pool, tennis court, facilities for *boules* and volleyball, and a café and snack bar amid the orange trees and enormous flowering cactus in the gardens. Inside is the Massinissa restaurant, with an inviting open fire in winter, and an à la carte international menu that includes the likes of Caesar salad, swordfish, pasta dishes and a selection of pizzas. There's also a smart Moroccan-style bar. Don't leave without making the kilometre-long trip down to the archaeological site on the kitsch blue Roman chariot.

Factfile

When to go

The weather is most pleasant in spring and autumn, while June, July and August can be very hot. The city gets crowded in late August and September as people descend on the area for the *moussem* of Moulay Idriss.

Getting there & around

Meknès has two railway stations: the main station and the more central El-Amir Abdelkader station. There are trains from Fès to El-Amir every two hours from 6.50am until 6.50pm, with an additional two services at 1.10pm and 5.15pm. The journey takes 37 minutes. On Sundays, the two additional services do not run.

From Rabat Ville there are ten trains a day from 7.17am until 11.17pm; the journey takes two hours and ten minutes.

Hiring a car with a driver from Meknès to Volubilis will cost 300dh for half a day and 500dh for a full day. The cost of hiring a car with a driver from Fès to Meknès and

Volubilis for the day will depend on your negotiating skills, but 800dh is the official price and a good one to aim for.

Grands and *petits taxis* can be found down the hill beyond and east of Bab Mansour and Place El-Hedim.

Tourist information

Meknès Regional Tourist Office, place Administrative (035 51 60 22/dtmeknes @menara.ma), open 8.30am-4.30pm Mon-Fri, is of limited use. It's always worth asking for advice at your hotel, or you could try the CRT cabin in Place El-Hedim, open 9am-noon, 2.30-6pm Mon-Sat; here you can at least get a decent map of the area.

A recommended registered local guide who speaks very good English is Noureddine Mrani, (07 47 41 552/nmrani_67@yahoo.com).

Internet

Cyber Café Bab Mansour, Dar Smen, rue Rouamzine, Medina. Many riads have Wi-Fi.

Clockwise from top left:
Café Maure; herb seller;
Avenue Mohamed V;
Villa Mandarine (2); Riad
Oudaya; Chellah walls;
Andalucian Garden;
Riad Oudaya.

Rabat & Salé

When it comes to the successful rebranding of a city, look no further than Morocco's capital Rabat, and Salé, its sister city across the river. Once a breakaway republic, nest of piracy and hub of the trade in captured white slaves, today the twin cities are models of law and order.

Now a modern administrative capital – host to foreign embassies, the Moroccan monarchy and the machinery of government – Rabat was once a medieval imperial city, and vestiges of this illustrious past remain in the form of city walls and imposing gates built by Sultan Yacoub El-Mansour in the late 12th century. In another era it became a city revived by refugees. After years of decline, an ailing Rabat was handed over to Moors expelled by Phillip II of Spain in 1610. It didn't take long for the returnees to breathe new life into the place, and then – along with Salé – to declare independence as the pirate republic of Bou Regreg.

Today, while Rabat is the seat of government, in national life it takes a back seat to the economic powerhouse of Casablanca down the road. The city's focus on government and away from tourism means visitors can enjoy the sights in a pleasantly low-key fashion: the picturesque kasbah overlooking the Atlantic; the core of the medieval city, and the peaceful beauty of the walled Chellah.

But Rabat has certainly not been overlooked, and a huge amount of investment is pouring in. Above the northern curve of the Bou Regreg river, vast works are under way; a new construction project will incorporate a marina, new homes and businesses at a cost of $11 billion. By 2009 the city will have the country's first tram system, and Rabat and Salé will be linked by a tramline that incorporates a new, dedicated bridge.

Explore

Fronting the Atlantic ocean, the city's blue and white Kasbah stands sentinel. Further south are the neat Medina, the broad avenues of the Ville Nouvelle, monumental Hassan Tower and the scattered ruins of the Chellah.

KASBAH DES OUDAYAS

Kasbah des Oudayas is a compact and picturesque enclave of cobbled streets, blue-and-white houses and a handful of dead ends. Its entrance gate is the honey-hued, carved Bab Oudaya; note the shells on the stone work above the arch.

The Arabs built a *ribat* – a monastery and garrison combination – on the site of the current kasbah in the 10th century; it was replaced with a kasbah by the Almohads in the 12th century.

Its name derives from the Oudaya tribe of the Sahara, some of whom served as soldiers here. The Bab Oudaya, one of the masterpieces of Almohad architecture, was added to the existing walls in 1195 by Sultan Yacoub El-Mansour.

Rue Jemaa runs straight through the quarter. Halfway along is the Kasbah mosque, the Jemaa El Atiq, founded in 1150 and the city's oldest. Rue Jemaa continues to Le Platforme, a broad promontory with views over the ocean and Salé across the river.

The city had suffered years of decline when, in 1610, Phillip III of Spain expelled thousands of Moors, many of whom fled to Rabat. In 1627, a reinvigorated Rabat, along with sister city Salé, established themselves as the independent republic of Bou Regreg. Its chief business was organised piracy, and it was from Le Platforme that the Sallee Rovers (as they were known to the

Rabat & Salé

Historic sites	Eating & drinking
● ● ● ● ◦	● ● ● ◦ ◦
Art & architecture	**Nightlife**
● ● ● ◦ ◦	● ◦ ◦ ◦ ◦
Hotels	**Shopping**
● ● ● ◦ ◦	● ● ● ● ◦

SPAIN

Rabat & Salé

ATLANTIC

OCEAN

MOROCCO

ALGERIA

0   100km

WESTERN SAHARA

English) could shell merchant ships lured on to the submerged sandbank spanning the estuary mouth.

Nowadays, you can watch wetsuit-clad surfers ride the waves and climb down to the city beach, a popular spot for sunset smooching, with a smattering of cafés. Return along rue Jemaa and turn left down rue Bazzo for the open-air Café Maure (*see p128*), with its 180-degree view of the River Bou Regreg and Salé.

Beside the café is the entrance to the peaceful Andalucían Garden. The garden, which was actually laid out in the French colonial period, between 1915-18, is stuffed with orange trees, hibiscus and poinsettia. Fronting the garden is the Museé National des Bijoux.

The square by Bab Oudaya dates from the 16th century and was where captive Christians were auctioned off as slaves.

Le Museé National des Bijoux

Kasbah des Oudayas (037-731537). Open 10am-4.30pm Mon, Wed-Sun. Admission 10dh.

The National Jewellery Museum is housed in a palace built between 1672 and 1992, during the reign of Moulay Ismail. Exhibits include shiny pieces of Almoravid, Almohad and Alaouite coins, Roman rings from Volubilis and a beady collar from Tamude. There are pistols adorned with precious stones and mother-of-pearl, and a magnificent dagger of gold and leather, inlaid with gems and enamel, dating from the early 20th century. Labels are in Arabic, French and Spanish.

MEDINA

Saadian Sultan Zaidan gave the city to Muslim refugees from Andalucia in the early 17th century, and it was they who built the Medina. Today, it is an unflustered affair with spacious streets and a conspicuous lack of hassle. The main drag is rue Souika, which cuts north-east from the Medina continuation of avenue Mohammed V, just past the Marché Central. Rue Souika runs past both the mosque of Sultan Moulay Sliman, on the corner of rue Sidi Fatah, and the Grand Mosque, which was founded by the Merenids, and rebuilt in the 19th century. Rue Souika continues as the covered rue Souk Sebbat, and then meets rue des Consuls. There's a flea market between here and Bab El-Bahr, and the Mellah, the old Jewish quarter.

Rue des Consuls was the diplomatic quarter before the French built the Ville Nouvelle. Today, it is the Medina's most upmarket shopping street. As one of Morocco's least aggressive bazaars, it's a great place to buy local crafts, particularly the rugs and carpets for which Rabat is renowned.

The Almohad wall runs for two kilometres from the northern edge of the Medina south to Bab Er-Rouah (Wind Gate). The 1,400m-long Andalucian wall, built during the 17th century, marks the division between the Medina and the Ville Nouvelle along boulevard Hassan II. It is punctuated by four gates – Bab El-Jedid, Bab El-Bouiba, Bab Chellah and Bab El-Mellah.

SOUTH OF THE MEDINA

Most of the city's principal sites lie south of the Medina. Walking from one to the other is a pleasant experience as it will take you in and around the city walls.

Chellah

Open 8.30am-5.30pm daily. Admission 10dh.

The walled Chellah (Merenid complex, necropolis and Roman ruins) is one of the city's most beautiful sights, pervaded by a peaceful poignancy. From the unusual entrance gate, a stepped path descends through overgrown gardens of palm and bamboo, banana and fig. There are freshwater springs in the hillside here and this patch was probably inhabited even before the Phoenicians set up shop, followed by the Romans – there was a city here for 1,000 years before it fell into ruin. Centuries later, Merenid Sultan Abou Youssef Yacoub chose the derelict site to build a tomb for himself and his wife, taking his place here in 1286. His grave is adorned with blue and white tiles on the right after the necropolis entrance. The second mausoleum contains his son, Abou El-Hassan, the black king, who was responsible for building the enclosing walls and entrance gate. Various other tombs are here too. The complex contained a mosque and *zaouia* (religious school) as well as the necropolis. Much is now in ruins except for the lovely minaret, home to nesting storks. Below the *zaouia* is a formal garden, defined by a double line of orange trees. Hibiscus, bamboo, bananas and yucca flourish here, as do the noisy storks.

In a corner of the enclosure, enfolded by a group of seven domed *koubbas* (tombs) containing the remains of seven saints, is a walled rectangular pool populated by dark eels. Someone will be sitting at its edge, selling candles and hard-boiled eggs. Women seeking a cure for infertility will buy an egg, symbol of fertility, and peel it. Throw the white into the pool and watch as phallic eels writhe from the dark recesses to swallow it.Some women also light a candle.

Adjacent to the Merenid complex, the Roman ruins of Sala Colonia are down to the left, occupying the northern half of the enclosure. The line of the main street is clear, flanked by the remnants of a triumphal arch, a bathhouse, a forum and temple to Jupiter.

La Tour Hassan & Mausoleum de Mohammed V

Open 8am-sunset daily. Admission free.

On a rise at the eastern edge of the Ville Nouvelle, overlooking the bridge to Salé, La Tour Hassan has been Rabat's main landmark for over 800 years. Originally the minaret of Sultan Yacoub El-Mansour's grand mosque, it was intended to be as tall as the Koutoubia in Marrakech, but was only three-quarters finished when the sultan died in 1199. It's an impressive structure with four different façades, and solid enough to have mainly survived the 1755 earthquake that destroyed what was left of the mosque. The paved expanse dotted with a grid of 355 re-erected pillars gives some idea of its former dimensions.

On the site are the Mosque and Mausoleum of Mohammed V, the father of independence who died in 1961 (buried in the centre), Hassan II (south-east corner), who died in 1999, and Hassan's brother Prince Moulay Abdellah

Clockwise from top left:
Le Platforme; Salé; La
Tour Hassan; Bab El-Had;
Royal Guard; Medersa
Abou El-Hassan.

(south-west corner), who died in 1983. The 40 flags between the three tombs represent the 40 provinces of the country. The entire complex is guarded at the two entrance gates by impressive mounted guards.

Musée Archéologique

Rue Brihi 23 (037 70 19 19) Open 9am-4.30pm Mon, Wed-Sun. Admission 10dh.

The draw of the archaeology museum is its abundance of fine Roman pieces. Highlights include the Carrara marble statue of Ptolemy of Mauretania (1 BC-40 AD), the son of Berber Juba II of Mauretania and Cleopatra Selene II, who was assassinated by the order of Emperor Caligula. Note the Berber nose and his beautiful behind. There's also a head of Juba II from Sala Colonia and an enormous, striking 2000-year-old head of Juno discovered at Banasa, near Volubilis. Other highlights include a small bronze dog, in attack mode; a youth with a crown of fruit, found at Volubilis; a reclining, portly Bacchus, also from Volubilis; and a first-century bronze Neptune surrounded by sea animals, from Lixus. Look out for the first-century one-legged fisherman statue with a round mark branded on to his chest, the symbol of a slave. Signs are in French and Arabic only.

PALAIS ROYAL

The 44 hectares of palace enclosure contain the monarch's residence, a cream-and-green modern-looking structure that actually dates from 1757, and an assortment of working buildings including the Cabinet office, the Prime Minister's office, the Supreme Court, the Royal Library and various ministries. You can't enter any of these, but walking down the main avenue of the palace enclosure is no problem. On the eastern side you'll pass El-Fas Mosque, used for official royal Friday prayers. The highlight, though, is the throne room, entered through Bab Essaada – a stunningly beautiful bronze door. The guards, in crimson ceremonial outfits, change every 90 minutes at the principal gate. Inside the compound, the king's personal servants wear cream jellabas, babouches, and fezes.

SALÉ

Salé, on the opposite side of the Bou Regreg river from Rabat, was founded around the time that Sala Colonia was abandoned. While the Merenids buried their dead in the Chellah, over the river in Salé they were building the celebrated Medersa Abu El-Hassan. During the Middle Ages, while Rabat was little more than a village, Salé was a prosperous port. In 1627 Rabat and Salé established themselves as the pirate Republic of Bou Regreg and seceded from Morocco. The Sallee Rovers ruled the high seas, not only taking out Christian ships that passed their way, but also raiding as far afield as Iceland and the southern coast of England, where they made slave raids.

But Salé's supremacy began to erode when the Alaouites took power in the late 17th century and began building and living in Rabat, although piracy – no longer state-sponsored – continued until 1829, when the Habsburg navy took revenge for the loss of a ship by shelling all of Morocco's coastal cities. Once the French decided to make Rabat their capital and Casablanca the Protectorate's principal port, Salé was condemned to relative obscurity.

Today, Salé is, effectively, a suburb of Rabat – its centre consisting of quaint old houses, alleys and artisans still clustered together and contained within four kilometres of walls. It has a different personality from its neighbour: traditional where Rabat is modern; devout where the capital is secular.

Most of what's worth seeing is in the Medina. From the tree-shaded Souk El-Kebir radiate streets of blacksmiths, carpenters, leather workers and stonemasons. The main landmark is the Grand Mosque, which stands in an area full of merchants' mansions. You can't enter the 12th-century mosque, but it's worth looking around the fine 14th-century Medersa Abou El-Hassan (open 9am-3pm daily; admission 10dh). This small *medersa* is covered with ivory-coloured arabesque stucco work and has a lovely decorated *mihrab*.

Eat

Many of the city's smarter restaurants are in the Ville Nouvelle. As a coastal city, the fish is excellent here.

Café Maure

Kasbah des Oudayas *Open 9.30am-7.30pm daily. Café. £. Café.*

A rambling café that is perfect at sunset but a dreamy spot at any time of day. To find it, take any alley right of rue Jemaa. These will connect with rue Bazzo, and as you descend you will hit the café. Pull up a blue stool next to a blue wooden table or perch yourself on the *zelije* seating and sit back and enjoy the panoramic view of Salé and the sea. The novelty here is the café extension jutting out on a peninsula – it's reached down a winding side alley. Waiters carry plates of local pastries and biscuits around; pick one to enjoy with your mint tea. Very popular with young folk and sunglass-clad lovers.

El-Bahia

Medina *4 avenue Hassan II (037 73 45 04). Open 7am-11pm. £-££. Moroccan.*

Set in the southern wall of the Medina, El-Bahia is a cool and leafy refuge from the hectic artery that announces the beginning of the Ville Nouvelle, with courtyard seating set under umbrellas scattered around a central fountain. Tart green olives soaked in lemon and garlic precede the likes of tagines, squid, sole, shrimp pil pil, *briouates de fromage*, omelettes, kofta (minced lamb), and brochettes of turkey, lamb and beef. The myriad varieties of juice include unusual flavours such as avocado and strawberry.

Le Grand Comptoir

Ville Nouvelle *279 avenue Mohamed V (037 20 15 14/ www.legrandcomptoir.ma). Open 9am-1am daily. £££. French.*

Occupying a prime position on the Ville Nouvelle's main boulevard, this 'brasserie parisienne' and lounge bar, with an appealing art deco interior, serves traditional French food: *boeuf à la provençale*, fricassée of rabbit, steak tartare, and so on. There is also a children's menu. Alternatively, stop for a coffee and a snack in the more laid-back café area with windows looking out on to the bustle of Avenue Mohamed V. A long drinks list even includes non-alcoholic beer.

Le Petit Beur

Ville Nouvelle *8 rue Damas (037 73 13 22). Open 10am-2pm, 6pm-1am Mon-Sat. £££. Moroccan.*

Locals and expats in the know pack into this small, congenial Moroccan restaurant for some of the best tagines, brochettes and *briouates* in town. Seven kinds of tagines include an unusual aubergine variety, and there is a fish version of the traditional *pastilla*. The atmosphere is convivial, with candlelit tables and live music in the evenings. Alcohol is served.

Riad Oudaya

Medina *46 rue Sidi Fateh (037 70 23 92/www.riad oudaya.com). Meals by appointment. ££. Moroccan.*

Riad Oudaya's five-course set meal – served in one of the central salons or at candlelit tables next to the open fire in winter – is a showcase for some of the best of Moroccan cooking. It begins with a tangy selection of Moroccan salads – tomatoes with herbs, spicy puréed carrots and so on, followed by pigeon *pastilla*, or chicken tagine, stuffed squid or fillet of bream *à la tapenade*. A second main course of vegetable couscous, shoulder of lamb or bream tagine with caramelised onions follows. If you have any room left there are two rounds of desserts including a delicious apple and cinnamon tart, crêpes or fruit. Alcohol is served.

Villa Mandarine

Ville Nouvelle *19 rue Ouled Bousbaa, Souissi (037 75 20 77/www.villamandarine.com). Open 7-11pm daily. ££££. French/Moroccan.*

Upmarket food in the intimate surroundings of the Villa Mandarine (*see p133*). Chef Christophe Vauthier applies a light touch to create sophisticated French dishes, with dishes on the daily-changing menu incuding the likes of *tronçon de sole* on a salad of potatoes and avocado, for example. There's the odd Moroccan touch with the use of local ingredients like argan oil. Desserts are a highlight: orange soufflé perhaps, or something extremely indulgent made with chocolate. A Moroccan menu is also available. Alcohol is served.

Shop

Comptoir de L'Artisanat

Medina *214-216 rue des Consuls (037 72 63 03). Open Winter 9am-8pm daily. Summer 9am-10pm daily.*

As the staff and the guest book will testify, this shop is a favourite with expats and diplomatic staff looking to buy antique or modern carpets and rugs. Try to meet Larbi, who speaks English and French and has worked in the shop since 1967. There's a huge range of cushions too.

Maison d'Argent

Medina *244 rue Consuls (037 72 38 28). Open 10am-8pm Mon-Thur, Sat, Sun.*

Silver is sold by the gram and comes in everything from necklaces to earrings to multiple versions of Hand of Fatima pendants. The Silver House also sells a wonderful range of giant collars and tribal jewellery, bangles and swords, old silver stirrups, and beautiful antique babouches. Vases, candlesticks, teapots, figurines, silver pots and rings round out the collection. Ask to see the second room out at the back. With antique belt clasps, old kaftans, bowls of coral and lapis lazuli and elephant tusks, it's like a museum.

Nightlife

Hotel Balima Terrace

Ville Nouvelle *Avenue Mohammed V (037 70 77 55/ www.hotel-balima.com). Open 7am-11pm daily.*

The lively terrace bar of the Hotel Balima (*see p133*) is a hugely popular place to pass the time or take a pre-prandial drink. The terrace faces Avenue Mohammed V and the parliament building and attracts locals, tourists and female groups of friends. There's also a small bar in the lobby of the hotel in case of rain or chilly weather. Drinks are reasonably priced and beer drinkers can sup on foreign imports such as Heineken and San Miguel.

Stay

Rabat doesn't have as many appealing guesthouses as Morocco's other, more tourist-oriented, imperial cities. That said, there are some gems that are worth seeking out.

Dar Al Batoul

Medina *7 derb Jirari (037 72 72 50/www.riad batoul.com). ££.*

The nine guestrooms in this lovely house – which dates from 1785 – feature metre-high four-posters with colourful bedcovers, desks with lamps, and finely embroidered chairs. Around the plant-filled central courtyard are a library and sitting area. Climb to the top terrace for a view of the cemetery and sea. Leisurely breakfasts are served in the courtyard and guests are attended to by the two sisters who own the *dar*, Lamia and Nabila Khribeche. The location, in the north of the Medina very close to road access, is another advantage.

Dar Baraka

Kasbah des Oudayas *26 rue de la Mosquée (037 73 03 62/www.darbaraka-rabat.com). ££.*

Dar Baraka means 'House of Blessing', and this house certainly feels blessed: its multilevel spaces are covered in flourishing fig, lilies and heliconia, and an enormous citron

Clockwise from top: Café Maure (2); Riad Oudaya (2); Villa Mandarine.

Top: Villa Mandarine.
Bottom: Riad Oudaya.

tree dominates the patio; a horseshoe-shaped terrace covered with crisp white cushions faces the river and the Hassan Tower. Hidden away at the end of the Kasbah, the house dates from the 1920s. Proprietor Pauline de Mazières was once a gallery owner and the walls are adorned with paintings. There are just two rooms: the very large, bright white double, with 1950s original features in the bathroom, and the smaller twin with a sweet balcony, blue-shuttered window and privacy afforded by the giant citron tree. Moroccan or European meals are served on request – and standards are high.

Hotel Balima
Ville Nouvelle *Avenue Mohammed V (037 70 77 55/ www.hotel-balima.com). £.*
The terrace bar at the Balima, facing the parliament building on Avenue Mohammed V, is one of Rabat's social hotspots. It would be a stretch to make the same claim for the hotel. Some rooms are smallish, old-fashioned and sparsely decorated. Renovated double rooms, however, are more appealing, spacious and come with bathtub. All rooms have satellite TV and heating. Service – from red-uniformed staff, whose outfits include a fez – is wonderfully old-school.

Hotel Le Pietri
Ville Nouvelle *4 rue Tobrouk (037 70 78 20/www.le pietri.com). ££.*
This small, stylish, modern hotel in a quiet street in the Ville Nouvelle is very good value for money. Its 35 rooms are minimalist in style, with wooden floors, TVs, air-conditioning, built-in desk spaces and sleek granite bathrooms – the antithesis of riad style. The next door restaurant, Le Bistrot, is stylish and modern, with live music concerts on Tuesdays, Fridays and Saturdays. It also offers free WiFi.

Riad Kasbah
Kasbah des Oudayas *49 rue Zirara (037 70 52 47/ www.riadoudaya.com). ££.*

Tucked into the kasbah, is this tiny riad with three petite rooms set around a courtyard. This is stuffed with palm and bougainvillea that unfortunately rather thwart the light, but otherwise the rooms are appealing, with old furniture and individual colour schemes. The Kenza has an old wooden chest and unusual carved metal bed. Naïma is twin-bedded; an old wooden wardrobe decorated with scissors stands in the corner. Zahra is a riot of jewel colours: lemon yellow and green. There are also three rooms upstairs.

Riad Oudaya
Medina *46 rue Sidi Fateh (037 70 23 92/www.riad oudaya.com). ££.*
Four beautifully furnished rooms and suites are set around the first floor and terrace of this riad buried in the Medina, sister property to the Riad Kasbah (*see above*). In one, guests gaze up at the carved wooden ceiling from their carved wooden bed, and an attached room with a fireplace and living area leads to a tiled bathroom with arches and stone shower surround. The sun-trap terrace is fairly enclosed, allowing for privacy. The riad's restaurant (*see p130*) serves a great five-course set meal.

Villa Mandarine
Ville Nouvelle *19 rue Ouled Bousbaa, Souissi (037 75 20 77/www.villamandarine.com). ££.*
The allure of this large villa complex in the diplomatic quarter is the abundant orangerie and lush gardens, a veritable Garden of Eden, overflowing with trees, shrubs, flowers and the scent of hibiscus. If this wasn't incentive enough there's also an inviting pool set amid the luscious greenery. The huge, modern rooms, with very comfortable large beds, televisions, desks, ample wardrobes and spacious bathrooms are set around the central villa courtyard. Guests can enjoy the subterranean spa, savour a cocktail or two in the African bar and dine at the renowned French restaurant (*see p130*).

Factfile

When to go
Rabat is pleasant to visit all year round, even in the summer months when cities in the Moroccan interior suffer from excess heat.

Getting there & around
Aéroport de Rabat Salé (037 80 80 90/ www.onda.ma) is 10 kilometres from the city, with international flights from Royal Air Maroc. There are no *petit taxis*, only *grand taxis* waiting at the airport; the taxi fare is 150dh-200dh to city the centre.

There are trains from Casablanca Port station to Rabat Ville every 30 minutes, 6.30am-9.30pm, daily (journey time one hour); nine daily from Fès, 6.50am-6.50pm (journey time 2hrs 50mins); and nine trains daily (4hrs 15 mins) from Marrakech.

A taxi from Casablanca to Rabat officially costs 600dh. From Fès to Rabat, 800dh. It's wise to negotiate a price before setting off.

Most of Rabat and Salé is walkable, and taxis are readily available and reasonably priced.

Tourist information
Regional Tourism Council of Rabat (CRT) is at 23 avenue de la Victoire (037 77 99 69/ www.visitrabat.com).

MFeddel ben Hammou (067 37 00 16) is a registered English-speaking guide who lives in the Kasbah des Oudayas.

Internet
Teleboutique 113 avenue Hassan II, next to Café Chahrazad. Open 7am-11pm daily; 8dh per hour.

Clockwise from top left:
Kasbah (2); La Marshan
(2); beach; Medina;
Cap Spartel.

Tangier

Like a crumpled wad of sweat-stained banknotes, Tangier has changed hands, been fought over, argued about and pocketed more times than it cares to remember. Its past inhabits its present, in the jumble of its architecture, and in the currents of languages and cultures that move beneath the surface of its cafés and bazaars. Tangerines have a front-row seat at the gateway to Africa, a chance to watch human tectonics at work. This is where people come to leave, to jump continents, either legally or by stealth in the dead of night. And, coming the other way, Tangier has had more than its fair share of European chancers and adventurers looking to make their mark. They have come seeking ownership, advantage, fortunes of one kind or another, only to be finally beaten back by the sheer unmanageability of it all. In the end, all that remains of them is a residue of language, a ghost of their customs, another layer to Tangier's unmistakeable tumbling skyline.

Here you will see the old haunts of the Interzone years, when the city was the playground of Western artists and tycoons, you will see the anatomy of the medina's ancient streets and alleyways, and the sturdy walls of the kasbah. The louche cafés of the Petit Socco, the sharpers and hustlers on the Corniche, even the way the sunsets shimmer in from the Strait to gild the city's rooftops: everything here lives up to the hype.

Tangier is not a city to be taken lightly, not somewhere to be toyed with. And yet at the same time, it is one of the most beautiful places in Morocco. Not just in the ragged glory of its streets and buildings, but in its spirit. Creative geniuses, spies, exiled dissidents, tearaways hoping for a last chance and families in search of a new beginning have all, at one time or another, made this their home. It's easy to see why.

Explore

MEDINA & GRAND SOCCO

The two main squares of the city's Medina are the Grand Socco (also known as place du 9 Avril) and the Petit Socco (also known as Zoco Chico). While the Grand Socco is not, strictly speaking, in the Medina (in fact, it represents the main gateway to the ancient walled city, standing right next to the walls at the Bab Fahs entrance), it is notionally the starting point for any exploration of the city's oldest quarter. Formerly a market square, the **Grand Socco** is now a busy thoroughfare of hurried locals, map-flapping tourists, traffic, donkeys, handcarts, small boys on jerry-built scooters and old men with home-made walking sticks. Dominated by the impressively revamped façade of the **Cinema**

Rif (*see p144*), with a fountain at its centre and the leafy boughs of the Jardins de la Mendoubia peering over its perimeter, the Grand Socco is a mellow place to sit down on a bench and get your bearings.

From here, you can either proceed south along rue de la Liberté in the direction of place de France and the New Town, or head on into the Medina itself, via the arched gateway at the northern edge of the square. This will take you along the (relatively) broad and (always) busy rue des Siaghines, which continues in a straight shot more or less due east to the Medina's second square, the **Petit Socco**. Here, several cafés and the minaret of the nearby Grande Mosquée remain pretty as they were from the early part of the last century, when this was ground zero for the intrepid artists and socialites who had made Tangier their home.

Tangier

Historic sites
● ● ● ◌ ◌

Art & architecture
● ● ● ● ◌

Hotels
● ● ● ● ◌

Eating & drinking
● ● ● ● ◌

Nightlife
● ● ◌ ◌ ◌

Shopping
● ● ◌ ◌ ◌

SPAIN

Tangier

ATLANTIC

OCEAN

MOROCCO

ALGERIA

0   100km

WESTERN SAHARA

Top left: view from the Kasbah. Other shots: beach and port.

Any of several dozen tortuous streets will lead you north from here to the **Kasbah** (*see below*), which stands at the highest (northernmost) point of the Medina, surveying the port and the distant prospect of the beach to the south. En route to the Kasbah, you will pass all manner of stalls, shops, tiny eateries and, of course, various locals trying to interest you in any of the above or, more commonly, in a tour of the Medina. Of course, the choice is yours whether you decide to accede to a person's offer of help or guidance. There are only two things to remember: despite any claims to the contrary, a payment of some kind will almost always be expected; and if your answer is no, say it politely, firmly and with no indication that further discussion is required.

American Legation

8 Zankat America (039 93 53 17/www.legation.org). Open 10am-1pm, 3-5pm Mon-Fri. Admission free.

Although its remit (to commemorate the American presence in Morocco, the first country to recognise the States as a foreign power) may perhaps be of limited interest, this museum is second to none in its power to evoke the atmosphere of a now-vanished period of Tangier's past. It may be located within the Medina's walls (follow signs from the American Steps) but, once you have crossed the threshold of its unassuming alleyway entrance, the patchwork of lovingly preserved salons, drawing rooms and elegant courtyards bears no resemblance to anything else you will see in the city. Exhibitions include an intriguing array of maps and charts to the coast and mountains around Tangier, a somewhat random collection of memorabilia and photographs dedicated to Paul Bowles and his Tangerine dream, and some fascinating correspondence (including a comical letter from Thomas Carr, the ambassador landed with the tricky task of dealing with a sultan pressing upon him the gift of a pride of fierce and unruly lions). It's all great stuff, but the real value of the place lies in simply drifting between its rooms and balconies and stopping to look at whatever catches your eye. Also, opposite the museum's entrance, is a small library richly stocked with a diverse selection of English-language fiction, as well as more arcane material on the Maghreb and its history. You'll need an appointment to visit but, if you have a morning to spare, it is certainly worth it, if only to sit in one of the worn armchairs and flick quietly through a volume to the sound of birdsong in the courtyard and the occasional gutteral burst of Arabic from the alleyway outside.

Fondation Lorin

44 rue Touahin (039 93 03 06). Open 10am-4pm Mon-Sat. Admission free.

It may not look much like a museum from the outside (follow the grimy signs to an equally down-at-heel flight of stairs in a back alley near the Medina gates), but this small collection of photographs from Tangier's International Zone heyday is neatly displayed in a bright, modern and spotlessly white exhibition space. Set out over two floors and partly illuminated by the elegant atrium roof, the pictures themselves are fascinating (if, in parts, rather

sketchily catalogued – don't expect to always know who everyone is or when each picture was taken). Street scenes of the city's seething Medina hang alongside snaps of formally attired Europeans doing their best to put a brave face on the heat and noise. Musty travel literature (including a great Spanish brochure for the El-Minzah hotel) and some vintage posters are also scattered around – as are one or two musical instruments (the reason for which is the Fondation's occasional use as a live music venue).

Kasbah & Musée d'Al-Kasbah

Sahat Al-Kasba (039 91 20 92). Open 9.30am-12.30pm, 2-5pm Mon, Wed-Sat. Admission (Museum) 10dh.

With a little imagination, it is easy to reconstruct something of the former glory of this grand, 17th-century Kasbah from the bare, echoing courtyards that greet you on arrival. Walled off from and perched strategically on the highest seaward shoulder of the Medina, the Kasbah has a considerable air of romance (even if the relentless chatter of its self-appointed 'guides' intrudes a little too frequently on the daydream). Intricately decorated arches and colonnades, narrow streets, secret gateways and lush gardens carry a whiff of a now-vanished splendour, while various traditional living quarters are fascinating in their way (as are those of the Interzone heyday, including the nearby former home of intrepid American heiress Barbara Hutton). But the real historical interest lies in the Kasbah's museum, housed in the Dar El-Makhzen building (formerly the sultan's palace). Architecturally, it is an appealing setting for a museum, as is evident from the very first exhibition space, which features a wonderful dodecagonal cupola. But, aside from the building itself – and its elaborate plaster mouldings and cedarwood carvings – the museum shows off various artefacts and treasures, ranging from vases and statuettes to coinage and weaponry.

VILLE NOUVELLE

Encompassing the port area, the nerve centre of place de France and the seafront, the Ville Nouvelle is Tangier's modern, bright and often hectic centre of operations.

Up top, looking down over the harbour is the famous **place de France**, a hornet's nest of whining mopeds and blaring car horns, tamed by smartly attired traffic cops and surveyed by hundreds of onlookers at the square's peripheries, where half a dozen cafés sport European-style terraces with ringside seats. The most famous of these is the worldly **Gran Café de Paris**, whose terrace has seen the best of them come, go and linger for hours on end. Simply put, if you haven't sat down for an espresso here, in the company of academic old-timers, rowdy young lads and cosmopolitan girls, not to mention the advance patrols of shoe-shiners and cigarette salesmen on their way to the Medina, then you haven't properly visited Tangier.

Just along the way is the **Terrasse des Paresseux**, named after the myriad slackers and idlers who spend their days sitting on its low wall or draped across its seaward-facing cannons,

Clockwise from top left:
La Marshan; Grand
Socco; Medina; city
view; Kasbah.

taking in the view, smoking and chatting. Head down from here to reach the seafront, with its many cheap hotels, rather bleak city beach and lively corniche. Bars and cafés abound, as do hustlers and touts – so be prepared to adopt your 'get out of my face' face from time to time. The city's **port** (scheduled for significant investment at the time of writing and, ultimately, for transformation into a 'super marina' for leisure shipping) is where the frequent ferries from Europe dock.

On the other side of the Medina from the port, bab El-Kasbah leads out into the exclusive residential area of **Marshan**, and other beaches.

Musée d'Art Contemporain
52 avenue d'Angleterre (039 94 99 72).Open 10.30am-12.30pm, 2.30-5pm Mon, Wed-Sat. Admission 10dh.
Housed in a villa that was built in 1890 to accommodate the British Consulate (and was converted exactly one century later into an exhibition space devoted to modern Moroccan art), this museum is certainly worth a look. Each of its rooms has a different theme (the abstract movement of the 1950s, say), although the conspicuous absence of any figurative art tends to have a homogenising effect. Only the biggest names in the Moroccan art world, such as Abdallah Hariri, make it on to the walls here, while lectures and other cultural events are frequently staged on the premises (keep an eye out for posters or announcements in the local press).

St Andrew's Church
Rue d'Angleterre (no phone). Open 9am-5.30pm daily. Admission free (small donation appreciated).
It is worth setting aside a little time to wander around this colonial Anglican church and its equally fascinating churchyard where, in typically eclectic Tangerine style, a hotch-potch of headstones commemorates Victorian philanthropists alongside fallen RAF servicemen, or, say, a long-serving correspondent for the *Times*. It's beguiling stuff, even more so if you're lucky enough to catch *guardien* Mustapha at a time when he's not too busy to give you a personal tour of the place. Otherwise, just read it from the sheet: built on land given to Queen Victoria in 1883 by Sultan Moulay Hassan I, the church is built in exquisite Moorish style thanks to the labour of artisans, woodcarvers and masons shipped in specially from Fès. The result is gorgeous, notably the intricate cedarwood ceiling of the chancel. Intrepid members of the church's former congregation and administration peer out from the black-and-white and sepia photos on the walls, while a faded Union Jack (inside) and a jaunty flag of St George (atop the spire) remain as reminders of where these long-since departed ghosts appeared from.

Eat

In the Medina are many hole-in-the-wall eateries, offering no frills and very little in the way of service, beyond the preparation of the food. There's not much to choose between them

but a consistently reliable option is Restaurant Andalus, a short walk from the Petit Socco. Also a common sight are Tangier's famous Juice Bars (such as the excellent Caraibe Jus, *see p142*), as well as a smattering of drinking dens left over from the Interzone years, some of which have aged well (like Atlas Bar, *see below*), some of which haven't (witness the once legendary, now seedy, Dean's Bar on Rue d'Amérique du Sud).

Agadir
Ville Nouvelle *21 rue Prince Héritier (068 82 76 96). Open noon-2pm, 6-10pm daily. ££.*
Mercifully, this intimate, self-deprecating little gem of a bistro bears no resemblance to the brash tourist joints of Agadir. Instead, you can expect red wine, big portions of tasty grub and, inevitably, conversations with your neighbours (there can't be more than half a dozen tables jammed into the tiny dining room and the place is never less than full). The menu is a roll call of unambitious but well-prepared international classics (steak, roast chicken, paella, grilled fish) and the staff are efficient, friendly and, on the right night, great fun. Just one word of warning: since this is very much the restaurant of choice among Tangier's discerning ex-pats and clued-up visitors, you may not manage to bag a table first try. But be sure to give it another go – it's definitely worth it.

Anna e Paolo
Ville Nouvelle *72 avenue Prince Héritier (039 94 46 17). Open 12.30-2.30pm, 7.30-10.30pm Mon-Sat. £££.*
Let's face it, there's going to come a point in every Moroccan holiday when what's needed is a break from the daily tagine. And where better to take a little culinary time out than at this lovely little trattoria whose rows of wine bottles, blackboard menu and cosy tables make you feel as if you could be in some Neapolitan hideaway. The menu has a good choice of pizzas (Siciliana, say, or maybe *frutti di mare*), pasta (classics of the penne all'arrabiata school) and meat dishes such as *saltimbocca* or *scaloppine alla Romana*. It's all good fun and very convivial, but if you'd rather just chow down in your hotel room, all the pizzas and various other bits and pieces are also available to take away.

Atlas Bar
Ville Nouvelle *Rue Prince Héritier (no phone). Open 6pm-midnight daily. £.*
Appropriately named for such a worldly bar, the Atlas has seen its fair share of drinking and devilment in the last 80 years. But don't be put off by its gruff façade (little more than a weathered neon sign and a wordless doorman with hands the size of frying pans) because deep down there beats a heart of gold. It's a small basement, skirted by a sturdy wooden bar and lit by low-wattage lamps, where those who have popped in for a post-work snifter mix happily with others who seem as much of a fixture as the antique ceiling fan or the worn and polished barstools on which they are perched. Mahou on draft, bottled San Miguel and tapas-style snacks, together with clouds of cigarette smoke, create a Spanish vibe, but the hum of Arabic conversation, the exclusively male clientele and the backstreet, almost speakeasy atmosphere is pure Morocco.

Café Hafa

Ville Nouvelle *Opposite stadium, avenue Mohamed Tazi (no phone). Open noon-sunset daily. £.*

Little seems to have changed at this elusive hideaway since Paul Bowles used to come to seek shade beneath its corrugated iron awnings and gaze out at the spectacular seascape that unfurls from its terraces. And when presented with its patchwork of handkerchief-sized patios, hewn from the cliff face to provide grandstand views of passing ships and yachts, it seems a minor miracle that this site has remained untouched by the tourist development that has swept through the nearby Medina. The downside of this authenticity comes in the form of rudimentary facilities, battered furniture and a primitive catering set-up (mint tea, very strong coffee, soup from the cauldron, maybe an omelette). That said, it's still well worth a visit – but you'll need to take a *petit taxi* here: it is a complicated route through unnamed side streets, with nothing but a few sea shells pressed into the cement by the doorway to alert you to the fact that you've arrived.

Café Roxy

Ville Nouvelle *Corner rue Bouthouri & rue Al Mansour Dahabi (no phone). Open 10am-6pm daily. £.*

Affiliated to the cinema of the same name, the Roxy is a meeting point for many of the neighbourhood's students, who can usually be found tapping away at laptops or wrapped in earnest conversation at its terrace tables. A prominent corner site and the copperplate lettering on its storefront windows lend a vaguely Parisian look, but the fare is stalwartly local – mint tea, strong (Mécafé) coffee and a few snacks – and the inevitable cabal of talkative old geezers squirrelled away in the back places it firmly in the Moroccan mainstream. An excellent pit stop, then, before heading back up to the main drag, but nothing more.

> # "What they can conjure from the simplest ingredients is nothing short of amazing."

Caid's Bar

Ville Nouvelle *El Minzah, 85 rue de la Liberté (039 33 34 44/www.elminzah.com). Open noon-midnight daily. ££.*

First and foremost, Caid's is a great place to simply hunker down in a comfy chair, listen to the pianist tickle out some smooth melodies and remind yourself what Bombay Sapphire poured over ice cubes and freshly sliced lemon tastes like. It's also pretty good for pretending you're the protagonist in some slightly racy novel, for impressing a not easily-impressed date or simply soaking up the old-world atmosphere of a clubby bar that has enough decent cigars and good-quality booze to keep a load of raffish spies swapping intel for years on end. Which indeed it did, during its heyday before and during World War II.

Evocative photos of bygone eras adorn the walls, waiters appear with Jeevesian silkiness… in short, the reason you threw a smart shirt into your suitcase.

Caraibe Jus

Ville Nouvelle *36 rue de la Liberté (no phone). Open 9am-6pm daily. £.*

If you want to get your five a day in one lip-smackingly delicious shot, look no further than this zesty little juice bar. The blokes here will whizz up pretty much any combination you fancy of what they have to hand (which usually comprises about ten types of seasonal fruit). Freshly squeezed orange juice forms the basis for any shake, with everything from avocado and banana to mango, pineapple, kiwi and strawberry getting lobbed into the blender for good measure – and all for under a quid (13dh was what we paid for a recent springtime mash-up). And if this leaves you feeling a little too healthy, retox your system with one of the gorgeous Moroccan or European pastries. For breakfast in a rush, you won't find anywhere better.

DARNA (Maison Communautaire des Femmes)

Ville Nouvelle *Rue Jules Cot, place du 9 Avril (039 94 70 65). Open 9.30am-5.30pm daily. £.*

If you only have time for a couple of meals in Tangier, you simply must make this one of them. Run by a collective of industrious ladies, this bright but simple refectory serves up some of the best Moroccan grub you're liable to come across, and all at absurdly low prices. There's no actual menu as such, so you'll have be prepared to roll with the results of that morning's trip to the market, but what they can conjure from the simplest ingredients is nothing short of amazing. Our last trip turned up a deliciously pungent soup crammed with juicy prawns and fresh coriander, a generously filled and sweetly spicy pastilla, and (the highlight of the meal) a richly reduced and subtly seasoned fish tagine with fat fillets of anchovy and chunks of bread for sauce mopping (of which there was a great deal). Service is smilingly efficient.

La Giralda

Ville Nouvelle *Opposite Terrasee des Parasseux, boulevard Pasteur (no phone). Open 6.30am-10pm daily. ££.*

On the first floor of an unprepossessing building, this popular café does a roaring trade, partly because of its unrivalled views of the Terrasse des Paresseux and also because of the selection of good-quality snacks and drinks that are laid out in Technicolor splendour on its gaudily designed menu. You're better off sticking to things like the shakes (which come in juice, milk or yoghurt varieties), ice-cream sundaes or the fine selection of crêpes – the 'nuts and honey' filling is especially good. What are not so impressive are the paninis, which could probably more truthfully described as rather mediocre toasted sandwiches. Still, the coffee's good, the mint tea (for once) arrives without migraine-inducing levels of sugar and the elaborate ceiling design and ornate furniture are a pleasant change from the prosaic norm.

View from the Kasbah.

Clockwise from top left: around the port; Riad Tanja; beach cafés; Petit Socco.

Gran Café Central

Medina *Petit Socco (no phone). Open 6am-midnight daily. £.*
Readers of Bowles, Burroughs and the boys will already be familiar with this well-established café whose terrace fans out around the ever-lively Petit Socco. After this many years, the place has seen its fair share of brigands and chancers come and go, which means the management is not overly tolerant of lascivious behaviour (in other words, take heed of the sign on the wall forbidding the smoking of hash). But provided you stay out of trouble, this is a more than pleasant place to take a load off and fuel up on a decent breakfast, a tostada or two and a heart-starting caffeine kick in the form of the famous 'café royale'. You may possibly encounter a little attention from the Medina's hustlers, but it's nothing that a few minutes of silently staring at your plate can't make disappear.

Gran Cafe de Paris

Ville Nouvelle *Place de France (no phone). Open 6am-midnight daily. £.*
If this genteel café seems at all familiar it might be because it recently featured in the Hollywood blockbuster *The Bourne Ultimatum*, but it could also be because it resembles in many ways the classic prototype of the European *grand café*. Smart, worldly waiters, who waste no time on small talk (but who've probably never got a drinks order wrong either) float among the languishing punters as the tumult of place de France whirls around them like a river in full spate. It is probably one of the best people-watching spots in all of Morocco, and this tradition, inaugurated back in the era of covert agent shop-talk during World War II, continues unabated. So get hold of a newspaper, order a coffee and take your seat on the terrace, and let Tangier put its succubus spell on you.

El Korsan

Ville Nouvelle *El Minzah, 85 rue de la Liberté (039 33 34 44/www.elminzah.com). Open noon-3pm, 7-10.30pm daily. ££££.*
One of, if not *the* best fine-dining restaurant in Tangier, El Korsan needs to be booked (and saved for) well in advance. Although some have defected to the Relais de Paris (*see below*), El Korsan remains the restaurant of choice for the city's high-fliers. The dining room's ornate ceilings and vaulted arches don't let you forget altogether that this is Morocco, but the menu, the service and the wine list are tailored to more international standards. Expect dishes like *magret de canard au miel du gharb*, grilled sea bass with fennel or sauteed lamb cutlets with sauce provençale, and expect to pay London prices for them. Service is always there but never intrusive, and the restaurant's occasional live music takes the form of a discreet and welcome accompaniment (as opposed to the brand of aural ambush that can rear its wailing head in some of Tangier's more low-brow diners).

Pâtisserie Le Petit Prince

Ville Nouvelle *Boulevard Pasteur (no phone). Open 8am-8pm daily. £.*
You'll find both Moroccan and European-style pastries at this excellent pâtisserie, and for once, both varieties are equally well turned out. The house version of the *pain aux raisins*, for example, includes a recklessly immoderate amount of candied fruit on the inside and a sprinkling of chopped pistachios on top. Extremely tasty, especially if you're under the age of five. More grown-up choices include croissants that taste like a little piece of France, and some sinfully creamy cakes. To get the most mileage out of your purchase, take it across the street to the Café Metropole and enjoy it with a cup of their delicious Renka coffee.

Le Relais de Paris

Ville Nouvelle *Complexe Dawliz, 42 rue Hollande (039 33 18 19). £££.*
One of the hippest spots in town, this popular, upmarket restaurant is decked out in the kind of style that does not make its designer-suited clientele feel out of place. Over-sized blood-red lampshades hang down from the ceiling, vintage posters adorn the walls and, in the evening, when the stunning views over the city and the Strait are not stealing the show, candlelight flickers discreetly at each of the linen-clothed tables. The menu is pretty much as you would expect – packed with Parisian brasserie favourites with a particularly strong showing of seafood – and the wine list is one of the best in the city. Its location in the mall-like Dawliz complex does not bode well, but once inside, this is soon forgotten. Especially if you kick off the meal with a nicely mixed cocktail in the restaurant's sleek lounge bar next door. It goes without saying that you will need to book ahead.

Restaurant Tanja

Medina *Rue de Portugal, Escalier Americain (039 33 35 38/www.riadtanja.com). Open noon-2.30pm, 7-10pm daily. £££.*
Located inside the charming riad of the same name (*see p151*), this excellent restaurant brings a sense of inventiveness and culinary know-how to the usual line-up of Moroccan staples. Pastilla, for example, is extended beyond its classic pigeon filling (although they do that too) to encompass delicately spiced monkfish or a robust vegetarian version with an aromatic coulis. But it is the sea bass tagine that really steals the show – subtle spicing, a richly reduced sauce and perfectly cooked fish make this a dish you won't forget in a hurry. The surroundings are stylish too, with big picture windows overlooking the chaotic sprawl of the Medina providing a nice counterpoint to the refined order of the dining room, with its antique etchings, oil paintings and beautifully crafted lamps.

RJ's Irish Bar

Ville Nouvelle *63 rue Amr Ibn Ass (039 37 28 01). Open noon-midnight daily. ££.*
There are a few reasons why this new pub-style joint in the Ville Nouvelle backstreets has already garnered a loyal following of ex-pat locals. First, it is a great place to watch the rugby or football with a pint in your hand and a selection of tasty tapas on the bar in front of you. Failing that, it's also a good spot to tuck into some hearty pub grub (champ and bacon, cottage pie, Irish stew), also with a pint in your hand. And lastly, despite its poky proportions, it has the feel of one of those vaguely smart, dangerously cheerful little boozers in which one suddenly realises that a whole

afternoon has slipped past and very little has been achieved. Unless, of course, drinking beer and having a laugh with the bar staff can be counted as an achievement.

Rubis Grill
Ville Nouvelle *3 rue Ibn Rochd (039 93 14 43). Open 12.30-2.30pm, 6.30-11pm Mon-Sat. £££.*
No matter where you are in the world, when you see a wagon-wheel chandelier suspended from the ceiling of a restaurant, you know you're in for a serving of no-nonsense, blokey cooking with side orders of beer, more beer and cheesy live music. And the Rubis is no exception to this rule – as conclusively proved by its drawing-pinned gallery of photos in which smilingly drunken tourists and musicians in Mexican hats feature prominently. The pidgin-English menu boasts a variety of fish dishes as well as various carnivorous options (not least, the intriguing 'lamb shops'), plus a few tagines and whatnot. Basically, you'll either be counting the seconds until you can politely leave or still be there at the end of the night giggling until red wine comes out of your nose. It's just one of those places.

Shop

Galerie de la Kasbah
Medina *67 rue Riad Sultan (039 94 82 45). Open 10am-5pm daily.*
There are usually some interesting paintings by local artists on display at this pleasant and laidback gallery in the lee of the kasbah walls. Beneath your feet, too, you'll notice an impressive piece of work in the form of the gallery's floor, which has been inlaid with all manner of unlikely objects from knives and forks to pairs of old pliers. The staff are happy for you to simply browse and leave or, should you express an interest in a piece, they will talk to you about it at length without giving you the hard sell. This may be because they have bigger fish to fry (the gallery also functions as a successful estate agent) or it may just be because they are a particularly chilled-out crowd. Either way, it's good for a gander.

Mgharbi Bazaar
Ville Nouvelle *31 boulevard Pasteur (039 93 79 90). Open 9am-7pm daily.*
The fascinating collection of 18th- and 19th-century coins in this small, hassle-free shop is particularly worth a look, as are the well-made leather goods, lamps and ornaments. The owner probably won't deign to enter into a haggling match, so if you had your heart set on a classic Moroccan shop show, then you might be better off taking your dirhams elsewhere. But if you see something you like and you reckon the price is fair, then you can at least be sure of the quality.

Salima Abdel-Waheb
Ville Nouvelle *Rue du Cinéma Goya (018 29 90 18/ www.salimaabdel-wahab.com). Open 10am-6pm Mon-Sat.*
A native of Tangier, Salima Abdel-Wahab is a talented and accomplished designer, with a line of hip, contemporary women's clothing. The inspiration for many of the designs comes from the cosmopolitan nature of Tangier, resulting in simple flowing fabrics that combine the discreet elegance of traditional Moroccan cuts with sexier, more modern styles. There is a second boutique in Asilah.

Arts

Cinemathèque de Tanger
Medina *Grand Socco (039 93 46 83/ www.cinemathequedetanger.com). Opening times vary according to programme.*
You'll notice the elegant white façade of this newly restored 1940s cinema as soon as you walk on to the Grand Socco, and even if you're not planning to catch a movie, it's worth wandering inside just to check out the beautifully decorated lobby. But if you are thinking of spending an hour or two ensconced in the splendour of its *grande salle* (an old-style movie theatre with vintage posters, grand seating, ornate lighting and all the fixings) then you may just be in for a cinematic treat. French-language film seasons are common (when we last visited, *The Umbrellas of Cherbourg* was showing) and cutting-edge Moroccan offerings are always subtitled in French. Or, if your parlez-vous is a bit rusty, you might prefer just to get a coffee and a pastry in its impossibly cool café. Kids' screenings are on the third Sunday of every month (for programme details, check out www.lanterne-magique.org).

Nightlife

Tanger Inn
Medina *Hotel El Muniria, rue Magellan (039 93 53 37). Open 7pm-midnight daily. £.*
Much discussed and once the hallowed haunt of Burroughs, Ginsberg and the gang, the Tanger Inn is now little more than a louche night haunt, with thumping house music where once there was the hum of hip beatniks making cool conversation. Oh well, at least there's a nice portrait of the Queen hanging on the blood-red bar room wall, and there is, of course, still the possibility of a nice cold beer. The adjoining El Muniria hotel (where William S knocked out *The Naked Lunch*) is like a Moroccan version of Barton Fink's hotel and only worth checking into if you are seriously strapped or hoping that the ghost of writers past will come and pay you a visit.

Le Tricam's
Ville Nouvelle *Avenue Mohamed VI, opposite Hôtel Solazur (039 32 33 80). Open noon-2pm, 7pm-midnight Mon-Sat. £££.*
The cool and the curious are drawn in great numbers to this slick new restaurant and piano bar, where ambitious modern cooking and interesting programming provide a welcome break from the somewhat cheesy norm of Morocco's 'dinner with music' scene. The understated monochromatic decor is pepped up by bold splashes of red, warm lighting and the weekend sounds of performers getting to grips with the piano in a variety of styles, ranging from jazz to traditionally inspired compositions.

Clockwise from top left: view from Hôtel Nord Pinus; Kasbah; Church of St Andrew; Dar El-Makhzen, Kasbah (2).

The menu (featuring dishes like spinach fondant with smoked salmon or freshly made pasta) is fortified by a decent wine list and a well-stocked bar.

Stay

Dar Nour

Medina *20 rue Gourna (062 11 27 24/ www.darnour.com). ££.*

This slick and stylish little riad is by no means easy to find, so resign yourself to the fact that you'll probably need to ask (and, more than likely, pay) someone to show you the way, but it's certainly worth it once you get there. The usual arrangement of Moorish salons and terraces is given the personal touch here through the careful distribution of meaningful artefacts – from designer lamps and *objets* down to the merest detail, like a vintage *Tintin* annual left lying on a coffee table. The furnishings (sourced as much from Europe as the Maghreb) are lovely, bedding is smart and bathrooms are of the kind you positively enjoy spending time in. Ornate shutters keep the daylight out when you don't want it, pretty terraces are on hand for when you do. A lovely spot.

Le Dawliz

Ville Nouvelle *42 rue de Hollande (039 33 33 77/ www.ledawliz.com). ££.*

For its views of Tangier's skyline, the Strait and the shimmering prospect of Spain in the distance, the Dawliz cannot be bested. But its location (in the eponymous 'Dawliz complex', whose McDonalds and loud, brash pool hall attract gaggles of excitable teenagers) will not be the envy of other hotels. Still, the comforts within are all commensurate with the Dawliz's four-star status (spacious rooms with good-sized balconies, a small pool, in-room TVs and fridge), albeit in an essentially characterless way. There's also secure parking, for those with their own wheels, as well as banks of *grands taxis* right outside the door, for those who don't. Recommended, then, as a base from which to explore the city that is neither crammed into the seething heart of the Medina nor removed to an impersonal distance.

El Minzah

Ville Nouvelle *85 rue de la Liberté (039 33 34 44/ www.elminzah.com). £££.*

Despite being owned by the upmarket Le Royal chain, this grand institution of Tangier has retained much of its original character. The lobby, with its grandfather clock and fabulous reception area (complete with the original 'cash' window and various smartly framed photographs of tuxedoed revellers), is a fitting introduction to what is still the town's most stylish hotel. The bedrooms have also been sensitively updated, so that the sturdy 1930s wardrobes and doors sit comfortably alongside flat-screen TVs and other artfully distributed mod cons. The drinking and dining options are some of the best around (notably at El-Korsan, see *p145*, and Caid's Bar, see *p142*), and there's a separate spa and fitness centre offering everything from seaweed wraps to step classes. But perhaps most decadent of all is to sit by the picturesque pool and enjoy the taste of a well-mixed cocktail as the pulse of Tangier's irrepressible street life beats faintly in the background.

Hôtel Continental

Medina *36 rue Dar El-Baroud (039 93 10 24). £.*

A cut above the town's budget beds, the Continental may not be as cheap as some of its lower-end counterparts but it's a lot more cheerful. The magnificent terrace (overlooking the port), where breakfast is served, is a great place to start the day, while its public areas feature some exquisite tiling and stained glass. Its past of housing notable guests (among them, Winston Churchill) has trailed off into a more modest present, but the guest rooms retain a certain something of the *Baedeker*-clutching era of intrepid foreign travel that has vanished from much of the rest of Tangier. Great fun, then, and, if you're wanting to stay in the Medina, undoubtedly the best budget option. All of which means advance booking is essential.

Hôtel de Paris

Ville Nouvelle *42 boulevard de Pasteur (039 93 18 77). £.*

A good place to bunk down on a budget, the Hôtel de Paris may not be swanky but it has plenty of charm. The ancient switchboard on the reception connects to equally antiquated phones in the bedrooms, where tiled floors, big sunny windows and quirky little shutters put a cheerful spin on what are essentially bog-standard furnishings. Standards are high (meaning impeccably clean bathrooms, tirelessly cheerful staff and hearty breakfasts) and the location is great for cafés, shopping and wandering down to the beach.

> "You might look up to see a ceiling adorned with a surreal constellation of 19th-century coloured glass baubles."

Hôtel Nord Pinus

Medina *11 rue Riad Sultan 061 22 81 40/ www.hotelnord-pinus-tanger.com). ££.*

There are riads and then there's this place. Simply put, Hôtel Nord Pinus is the best of the city's boutique accommodation, not only because of its peerless bedrooms and triptych of gorgeous terraces, but also because of the sheer volume of stunning features that are so casually distributed around the place. You might look up to see a ceiling adorned with a surreal constellation of 19th-century coloured glass baubles or a David Hick chandelier, or a wall enlivened by a smattering of Peter Lindbergh's photographs. And in the rooms themselves you'll find stunning bathrooms (complete with Occitane toiletries), expensive bedding, original artwork and individual furnishings – maybe a grand ducal bed, a lacquered oriental wardrobe or antique French chairs upholstered in vibrant Indian fabrics. Views of the city on one side and

To the lighthouse

At the northernmost tip of Africa, the Mediterranean and the Atlantic wash into one another like the confluence of two mighty cultures: a wild, empty ocean and an enclosed, sunlit sea. And on this peninsula, balanced on the very tip of a massive continent, stands Cap Spartel lighthouse, a beacon to shipping and an emblem to one and all, heralding the nearest shore of a vast and mysterious world.

That was, at least, how it must have appeared to European mariners passing through the Strait in 1864 when this lighthouse was built, just 14 kilometres (nine miles) from Tangier. Situated to the west of the city, Cap Spartel lighthouse can be visited in a leisurely half day and is far more interesting and entertaining than a trip to the nearby and often more enthusiastically touted Grottes d'Hercule. Better, then, to use your spare time wisely and head to the lighthouse.

Built by Sultan Mohammed III, it sits among lush vegetation on a precipitous perch, its stout square tower protruding just high enough over the treetops to send its nightly signal to shipping. Next to the lighthouse is a small car park (with a smart, good-quality restaurant offering a pretty panoramic terrace and fresh, tasty seafood that has been caught just 200 metres from your table) and from here the views are good. Many visitors leave it at that and, having snapped the pics, return to car or coach for the onward journey. But that would be to miss the point.

For a small fee (20dh on our last visit), the *guardien* (lighthouse keeper) will take you inside the pretty walled courtyard of the lighthouse and up its marvellous spiral staircase to the viewing platform on top. From here the views are amazing and, on the way up, you will also have been treated to the equally arresting sights of the elaborate pulley system that operates the light and to the light itself. The current light is a beautiful object (designed and installed in 1930 by Barbier, Bénard & Turenne of Paris), surrounded by a balustraded walkway.

To get to Cap Spartel, pick up a *grand taxi* from outside the Dawliz Complex, or if driving yourself, head west on rue Belgique, continue straight over the big roundabout at place Koweit and continue west until you have passed through the chic suburbs of La Montagne and California. From there, follow signs for Cap Spartel.

From top left: El Minzah (3); Hôtel Nord Pinus.

the port on the other can be admired from the lovely network of roof terraces, from various balconies and salons or from the grand picture windows of the dining room.

Hotel Rembrandt

Ville Nouvelle *Boulevard Mohamed V (039 93 78 70/ www.hotel-rembrandt.com). £.*

From the gorgeous leather armchairs in the lobby to the antique piano in the bar and the garden's palm-shaded pool, the Rembrandt is a very decent little hotel. Rooms aren't going to win any design awards but they are comfortably appointed and some have decent views. The restaurant does a good line in modern Moroccan grub, and more often than not, there's a pianist in the bar to keep you company while you sip your J&B nightcap. And in the morning, you can be sure that a nicely spoken member of staff will come and find you on your sun lounger and ask if you'd like a cup of coffee.

Le Mirage

15km W of Tangier *Les Grottes d'Hercule (039 33 33 32/www.lemirage-tanger.com). £££.*

Worth every one of its five stars, Le Mirage is an exquisite hotel with the kind of oceanfront location that is worth crossing continents for. A few miles out of town, the hotel occupies a rocky promontory that commands spectacular views of surf-fringed Robinson Plage, the city's Atlantic beach. There are steps leading down to a private stretch of sand, or else you can take a dip in the beautiful pool up top (set amid lawns and fragrant rose bushes). Accommodation takes the form of plush, modern bungalows, all with spacious sitting room, tastefully furnished bedroom and a large and luxuriously appointed bathroom. Various terraces are on hand to admire the Atlantic sunsets, including that of the hotel's popular restaurant. And should you feel any sense of guilt about lounging around the pool all day, there's a small but well-equipped fitness centre (whose large windows also make the most of the stunning views).

Riad Tanja

Medina *Rue de Portugal, Escalier Americain (039 33 35 38/www.riadtanja.com). ££.*

Follow the signs to the Tanja's unassuming doorway from the American Steps and let yourself be ushered into a discreetly exotic interior that winds up through various staircases towards the open air of a roof terrace. From here the rooftops of the Medina and the blue horizon of the bay are at your feet. There are five suites and one ordinary double, all decorated to a very high standard and liberally furnished with hefty Moorish antiques. Attractive wooden shutters keep the evening sun at bay while you drift into the immaculate, prettily tiled bathroom to wash away the dust and heat of the city. For the lowdown on the excellent restaurant, *see p145.*

La Tangerina

Medina *19 Rue Riad Sultan (039 94 77 31/ www.latangerina.com). ££.*

Virtually next door to the Nord Pinus (*see p148*), this gorgeous little riad is another example of the high-end boutique accommodation that is starting to spring up in the city's Medina. Clean white walls enlivened by carefully selected vintage poster art give the place a hip feel, while pretty Moroccan lamps and lovingly preserved architectural features keep the mood in the Maghreb. The occasional addition of an antique mirror or faded croquet set are pleasing reminders of Tangier's Interzone heritage, without being overpowering or stuffy. A sweet little hammam has been painstakingly restored (over a period of two years) to a sleekly contemporary facility, and the bedrooms are bright and quietly luxurious (gorgeous sheets, nice bathroom products – all the little touches are here). The riad's husband and wife team are pleasant, switched-on people with modest directions to give both to sightseers and to those who simply want to find a comfortable sunlit spot to watch the sightseers trudge past.

Factfile

When to go

Winter can be chilly in Tangier. In summer, temperatures are Mediterranean.

Tangier is home to a wide range of annual festivals, notably the Tanjazz music festival (www.tanjazz.com), which operates from May to June each year, and the national film festival, which takes place in October. For full listings on both, contact the city's Tourist Office (*see below*).

Getting there & around

Petits taxis are the most reliable form of transport within the city itself (local bus routes tend to serve the suburbs as well as off-the-track residential neighbourhoods).

Journeys to and from Tangier can involve any combination of bus, rail, plane and ferry. The latter leave from and dock at the city's port,

where tickets are available for immediate or advanced sailings inside the terminal building itself. CTM buses (039 93 11 72) meanwhile, also come and go from the port and will take you pretty much anywhere in the country. For trains, head to the spanking-new Tanger Ville station (a few kilometres out of town; 039 95 25 55/ www.oncf.ma). Flights go into Ibn Batouta Airport in Boukhalef (around 15 kilometres out of town; 039 39 37 20/www.onda.org.ma).

Tourist information

Tourist Office 29 Boulevard Pateur (039 94 80 50). Open 9am-noon, 2-5pm Mon-Fri.

Internet

Cyber Café Pasteur 31 Boulevard Pasteur, Ville Nouvelle (039 37 07 27). Open 8am-2am daily.

Coast

Clockwise from top left:
Riu Tikida; Les Trois
Chameaux; Suerte Loca;
Yacout; Sidi Ifni;
Les Trois Chameaux.

TERRASSE
PANORAMIQU

Agadir to Sidi Ifni

Morocco's Atlantic coast is strangely, wonderfully dislocated from the rest of the country. It is a land of broad and luminous brushstrokes, on whose canvas the marks of man have made little impression. A region of uninterrupted shoreline, vast canopies of blue sky and blood-red sunsets, and towering cliffs. People come here to explore, to walk, to parascend, to surf and swim; they come to get a lungful of fresh air, to feel the sting of saltwater on their skin. They come here because this is nature, in its pure, unpackaged form. Welcome to Morocco's wild side.

That said, landing at Almassira airport and getting a taxi into downtown Agadir feels about as close to nature as eating a Big Mac at a Brixton bus stop, but don't be discouraged by first impressions. Agadir is a springboard from which to launch yourself into the brackish greenery of the Souss Massa National park, the down-tempo delights of sleepy Mirleft and the art deco sea treasure that is the faded colonial outpost of Sidi Ifni.

If time, budget and itinerary allow, the best way to discover this vastly varied area is by car. The journeys that take you along the coast roads running parallel to the main spine of the N1 are an experience in themselves, as you find yourself sandwiched between the thumping tempo of the Atlantic breakers on one side and the silent mass of hills on the other. You'll see Berber goatherds meandering along the roadside, hawks sailing and circling high overhead and gulls following the fishermen out to sea.

Explore

Functional Agadir is the gateway to the lush wilderness of the Souss Massa region, where deserted beaches, unspoiled wetlands and wide-angle horizons of sea and sky provide the perfect antidote to summer in the city.

Sidi Ifni, at the south of our area, is Agadir's antithesis: a romantic art deco ruin, now being gently prodded into revival by a burgeoning tourist industry.

AGADIR

In touristic terms, Agadir is a buckct and spade destination. It is Morocco's package-tour centre, with a resort-style hotel industry, a swathe of bars and nightclubs and any number of formulaic restaurants ready to greet the latest plane arrivals with open arms. But it is also (and always has been) one of the most strategically located towns in southern Morocco for those wishing to explore the many delights of the varied and fascinating Souss-Massa-Drâa region (of which Agadir is the capital). With a busy international airport, and the mysteries of the Maghreb laid out at its feet, Agadir is an essential stop on any itinerary – whether you're sporting a lilo and a beach resort wristband or not.

Once a beautiful and highly prosperous port, Agadir was devastated by an earthquake in 1960, which razed many of its historic and residential buildings and caused widespread loss of life. The prolonged reconstruction project that followed had neither the means nor the aim to recreate the city's former aesthetic credentials but worked simply towards the resumption of normal life; thousands of people had been buried alive, causing a degree of trauma whose aftershock can still be felt today. In these terms, then, the city has recovered well, exceptionally well, in fact – a testament to the flinty steadfastness of its 700,000 inhabitants.

The centre of Agadir (those streets that cross and run parallel to the twin arteries of Avenue Hassan II and Avenue Prince Moulay Abdellah) is a drab but relatively smart cityscape of modernist architecture, with a northern (more rundown) appendage known as Talborjt. The majority of the city's budget accommodation is here, along with the lion's share of its takeaway and cheap eateries. But both of these areas play second fiddle to Agadir's principal attraction: its beach.

Agadir to Sidi Ifni

Historic sites
● ● ● ● ●

Art & architecture
● ● ● ● ●

Hotels
● ● ● ● ●

Eating & drinking
● ● ● ● ●

Scenery
● ● ● ● ●

Outdoor activities
● ● ● ● ●

Cap Rhir

0   10km

ATLANTIC

OCEAN

Agadir

Parc National de Sous-Massa

Aglou Plage

Tiznit

Mirleft

Sidi Ifni

Sidi Ifni.

Plage Sauvage.

The city beach is an inviting curve of golden sand whose easternmost reaches (under extensive remodelling at the time of writing) are the preserve of the upmarket resort hotels, while the western end is where the public are free to do their sunning, swimming, footballing and strolling. There is always a bit of a wave stirring the shoreline (although nothing like the pounding surf of the beaches a little way around the coast at Taghazoute, see p161), hence the stilted lifeguard towers that are dotted across the sand. The 'town end' of the beach is also where you'll find the majority of the seaside restaurants and cafés (especially along rue de la Plage, aka La Corniche), not to mention the chi-chi shops and civilised waterside enclave of the town's marina (which bursts into life when the carnival of the Transat Classique sailing race makes its one stop here in November).

Beyond the marina is the no-frills fishing port, where ocean-going trawlers return to empty their catch, pursued by squadrons of raucous wheeling gulls. It is in this somewhat unlikely location that you might get a taste of the real life that goes on in this hard-working town if you happen to come across one of the open-air fish grills that are often to be found sizzling away on the quay.

SOUSS MASSA NATIONAL PARK

South of Agadir, the dramatic coastal steppe of the Souss Massa National Park is well worth devoting a day to. For this, you'll need your own wheels or those of a *grand taxi* (just be sure that the driver takes you to the proper entrance, which is a further ten-minute drive along a pot-holed track that branches off the main road to Sidi Rabat). A small car park opposite a mud-red fortress of a building (destined to be the region's ecological museum) marks the head of the trail. Informative signs punctuate the footpath as it leads on from here, detailing the migratory and feeding habits of the many rare birds that take sanctuary in these parts. Eventually, the path leads out, along with the estuary it borders, to the open sand and the sea. Depending on the wind and tide (both of which determine just how much plastic flotsam and other rubbish gets washed on to the shore here), this can either be a magnificently exhilarating or a really rather disheartening sight. Still, the birds don't seem to mind, and nor does the quiet army of bearded twitchers, who assemble from far and wide to peer through binoculars, wrestle with sound booms and eat sandwiches in the ardent hope that a black-crowned tchagra or a tawny pipit might one day pass their way.

MIRLEFT

Do not expect it to be love at first sight: Mirleft is no great beauty. It has no UNESCO-protected medina to boast of, no ancient kasbah or mighty city walls, no Saharan dunes whispering in the distance. Instead, what you will find is a small seaside town of low-rise buildings threaded together by unmetalled roads, sandwiched between the low barren hills of the landward side and the heavy swells and strong currents of the Atlantic to the west. And yet. And yet this town remains one of the best-loved destinations along the whole of the Atlantic coast. Why? You can only find that out by booking a room for a few nights, getting into step with the sleepy pace of life and walking from beach to secluded beach.

Mirleft lies in the lee of a small hill on whose summit stand the remains of a 1930s colonial fort (which serves more as a focal point for a morning's walk rather than a destination in itself). The street plan is not a complex one, featuring just one or two dusty roads that branch off the main rue du Souk (a kind of Wild West strip of dirt and donkeys), whose arched eaves provide the shade and space for various shopkeepers to tout their wares (everything from halal meat to litre bottles of argan oil, artisanal soaps and odds and ends of craft and jewellery). It is also along this road (and the road that leads into town, the route de Sidi Ifni) that the majority of Mirleft's hotels, restaurants and cafés are to be found. The latter being the key centres for local lounging and chatting, of which there is a great deal.

"Head a little further in search of peace and sand to the remoter, stunningly feral reaches of Plage Sauvage and Plage Sidi Ouafi."

But it is the proximity of a handful of genuinely pretty beaches that elevates Mirleft from the status of just another low-key Moroccan town to a point on the map that is actually worth drawing a ring around. The first, and most popular of these, is Imln Tourga (aka 'Grande Plage'), which has a tendency to become crowded and litter-strewn in the summer months. Best, then, to head just that little bit further in search of peace and sand space to the surf-fringed Aftas Plage, Plage Sidi Mohamed Ben Abdullah (sometimes referred to as Marabout Plage, in reference to the stunning tomb that juts out into its bay) and the remoter, stunningly feral reaches of Plage Sauvage and Plage Sidi Ouafi.

As evening falls, the sleepy pace of rue du Souk picks up a little, as shoppers hurry home and mosque-goers are drawn by the call to prayer.

The restaurants begin to fill up with tourists whose appetites have been sharpened by the sun and sea air, and volume levels briefly swell as a few cold Storks are downed. And then the tiredness kicks in, everyone melts away to bed and the sound of a faraway car and a dog barking in the distance is all that's left.

SIDI IFNI

Finally abandoned by the Spanish in 1969, the crumbling art deco buildings of Sidi Ifni stand perched on their clifftop like some monument to colonialism, to the sheer magnificent folly of Europe in Africa. There are shades of small-town Cuba in the carious, caved-in state of its once-grand administrative buildings, but there's something else too, a sense of romance that is unique to this extraordinary place. The atmosphere is that of a film set that has been left standing or even, when the Atlantic mists settle over its streets and squares, of a sequence in a dream. And yet, despite its strangely mesmeric quality, Ifni (as it is known to the locals) is an increasingly vibrant and modern town, with a healthy (booming, even) tourist industry, which sees everyone from septuagenarian camper-vanners to gap-year surf bums pouring into the town's hotels, apartments and campsites.

With a Spanish presence that can be traced as far back as 1476, Sidi Ifni is a mixed bag when it comes to its architecture and, to an extent, its culture. The hub of the town is the leafy Place Hassan II (also known as the Plaza de España), and this is where most of the interesting architecture is concentrated. Standout examples are the former Spanish Consulate (the splendidly dilapidated building on the north-west corner of the square, whose curved portico still bears a weathered coat of arms) and the squat lighthouse hidden down a side street off the square's south-west corner. Continuing north from the square, along avenue Moulay Youssef (rather grandly named for such a diminutive street), you will come to the wide balustraded steps that lead down to the beach, and the interesting spectacle of an art deco building constructed in the form of a barge, whose prow points due west, towards the setting sun.

South of the square is the former airstrip, a vast tract of disused land stretching off towards the distant mountains, which has the distinctly eerie feel of a no-man's-land, a buffer zone between man and nature. It is here, just set back from the busy avenue Hassan II, that the town's main market is to be found. This open-air arcade is worth investigating, even if only to marvel at the sheer variety of produce crammed into such a small area, from kiosks piled high with leather slippers to stalls groaning with chillis and spices, and the fishmonger's slab out back, a glistening tangle of burnished sea life.

Sidi Ifni's beach is a long, cliff-backed expanse of sand primarily favoured by surfers, due to its reliably powerful swells (*see p161*). But it's also a great place for a long, meandering walk (just beware of the tide, which comes up higher and faster than you might expect). Quite a few kilometres to the south is the town's fishing port. As a guide for distance, it is more or less in line with the peculiar concrete structure jutting out of the sea to the south of town (it was once a docking station for commercial shipping).

Eat

Fish and seafood are, unsurprisingly, the specialities of this region of surf, sun and sand. Whether grilled over a flash of coals or simmered at length in a tagine, the catch is always fresh, even in the most modest restaurants. As ever, carnivores have plenty of choice here too (the countryside is never far away in Morocco), while plentiful salads, fresh fruit shakes and cocktails, and the ubiquitous omelette, mean that vegetarians won't be left out either.

Avenida Pâtisserie

Sidi Ifni *Avenue Hassan II (no phone).*
Open 8am-10pm daily. £. Café/pâtisserie.
Really no more than a small room with a chiller cabinet and a few cheap tables and chairs, Avenida is not the kind of place you visit to soak up the surroundings. It is, however, somewhere to come for excellent pastries (the fruit millefeuilles are especially mouthwatering) and fresh fruit juices. And if you require something a little more fortifying than sugar, staff will happily fetch you a cup of coffee from the café next door. It's cheap (juices weigh in at around 8dh; pastries even less), it's spotlessly clean and it does the job with a little more class than its neighbours.

Les Blancs

Agadir *Marina d'Agadir (028 82 83 93/68).*
Open 9am-1am daily. £££. Seafood/Spanish.
Enviably located right next to the marina at the head of Agadir's sweeping bay, Les Blancs is the most sophisticated restaurant in town. A gleaming white bunker of a building, it exploits its position (right on the water's edge) with an elegant terrace, an outdoor bar and two walls of floor-to-ceiling windows in the restaurant itself. Flagstone floors, understated furnishings and sleek table settings combine to create an atmosphere that is more connected to the well-kept, yachty vibe of the marina than to the package tour crew further up the beach. Food ranges from the likes of a delicious *grillade de poissons et fruits de mer* (260dh for two) to a wide selection of decent tapas and light bites. Good wines, too.

Le Jour et Nuit

Agadir *Rue Tawada (no phone).*
Open 24hrs daily. £. Café.

Wave goodbye to stress

Heading north out of Agadir along the easygoing N1 (any *grand taxi* will take you, or take the No.12 or No.60 bus from Place Salam), it's a short (half-hour) drive to the beaches around the villages of **Tamraght** and **Taghazoute**. En route, it soon becomes obvious what the chief attraction of the area is, as the views from the car window reveal glimpses of headlands and beaches wreathed by perfect, glassy swells. And by the time you roll into happy-go-lucky Taghazoute, with its giant Billabong flag fluttering in the breeze and its myriad surf shops, there can be no doubt about it: everyone here has only one thing on their mind, namely to spend as much time as possible in the water and on a surfboard. Which means, of course (this being Morocco), that you should expect some persistent offers of equipment, lessons and lodgings.

Rather handily, all three of these assets can be procured in advance from the region's most competent operators, Surf Maroc (00 44 1794 322709/www.surfmaroc.co.uk), whose Taghazoute-based surf camp is a comfortable, reliable base from which to explore the area's beaches and breaks. Its English owners, Ben and Ollie, have made an art form out of the relaxed welcome, sending their guests on fully supervised surf outings (for all ages and abilities), and supplying them with the wetsuits, boards and, most importantly, the confidence they need to get the hang of what are some of the most consistent and accessible waves in Morocco. And come sundown, the scene is set for whatever you want to do, be that kick back and indulge in lazy post-mortems of the day's surfing or simply find a quiet corner on the camp's oceanfront terrace to read a book and have a doze.

The more energetic and body-conscious may want to surrender themselves to the team's yoga practitioners, who will bend them into submission at sunset sessions on the wild shores of the Atlantic, or indeed take them on for a whole week of intensive yoga training. But whatever you've been doing during the day, dinnertime is the one communal moment, when all the guests come together at the long open-air dining table for warm nights of cold beer and the famous house tagine.

Similar operations exist further down the coast too, near to the thumping beach breaks of Mirleft and Sidi Ifni. The best of the bunch is Aftas Trip (066 02 65 37/www.aftastrip.com).

Les Blancs.

Wealthy Moroccan families, young professionals with business to discuss and beachbound tourists are drawn to the breezy, upmarket terrace of this insomniac bar and café. The best time to visit is at breakfast, to eat Moroccan pancakes with plenty of jam and honey and drink strong coffee; what is less likely to attract the discerning punter is the selection of bog-standard main courses on offer, or indeed the increasingly desperado nature of the crowd as *jour* turns into *nuit*. But in daylight and at sunset, the views of Agadir's broad scimitar of golden sand are unsurpassed, and the sounds of big-screen sport and pumping Euro dance music are mercifully absent.

Mar Pequeña

Sidi Ifni *Rue de la Mer, off Avenue Moulay Abdellah (no phone). Open noon-10pm daily. £. Seafood/Moroccan.*

Its name may be a reference to an early Spanish settlement in this area (Santa Cruz de la Mar Pequeña) but there is nothing old-fashioned about this promising new restaurant. An interesting reprise of traditional camel meat couscous and oven-roasted fish of the day *à la provençale* are a couple of the contemporary spins to a menu that also lists more everyday Moroccan dishes such as pastillas, tagines and the like. There's not a great deal of elbow room inside or on the tiny terrace, but with the great westerly stage of Atlantic breakers and sunsets right on its doorstep, Mar Pequeña manages not to feel claustrophobic.

Le Marin

Agadir *Rue Tawada (no phone). Open 6am-midnight daily. £. Café.*

Elegant wave patterns in the building's design, along with huge windows and high ceilings give this beachfront café an impressively spacious feel, despite its compact terrace and an interior that's actually rather small. The furnishings are smart (as are the waistcoated waiters), making this the kind of place where flip-flopped tourists think twice before plonking themselves down for a drink and a snack. Instead, seaside strollers and weekend families choose this spot to gorge on wonderful ice-creams and a rainbow of freshly squeezed juices, alongside smartly attired gents who know that this is somewhere they can drink a coffee and leaf through the morning's issue of *L'Opinion* in relative peace.

Nomad

Sidi Ifni *Avenue Moulay Youssef (062 17 33 08). Open noon-10pm daily. £. Seafood/Moroccan.*

Still the best restaurant in town, Nomad has been going strong for several years now and, once seated in the bright, convivial dining room, it's easy to see why. For one thing, the food is uniformly excellent, whether it's a plate of simply grilled fish, heavenly calamari or a chicken tagine with a twist. But it's also got a lot to do with the atmosphere of the place, which seems just that bit sunnier than its competitors (thanks, in no small measure, to the good humour of the proprietor, Abdullah). When people talk about Sidi Ifni, this is the restaurant they always mention; when visitors return to Sidi Ifni, Nomad is part of the reason why. It's not fancy, it's not even especially pretty, it's just somewhere that has kept its personality when all around it are losing theirs.

Ocean Miramar

Sidi Ifni *Avenue Moulay Youssef (no phone/ www.miramar-ifni.com). Open 9am-8pm daily. £. Café/restaurant.*

For grandstand views of the town beach, with its thumping waves and perennial population of local and visiting surfers, the Ocean's terraces (the largest one is up on the roof) are second to none. This makes it a lively spot, popular with everyone from tourists whose camper vans are parked up in the bays down below to groups of surf-crazy kids surveying the conditions. And as a result, the menu has a stab at catering to all tastes, with a reasonable selection of seafood, a smattering of salads, soups, omelettes, pizzas and ice-creams. The latter (piled high in sundae dishes) is what most people end up ordering – that, and the good-quality coffee.

La Pizzeria Siciliana

Agadir *Boulevard Hassan II (028 820973). Open noon-11pm daily. £. Pizzeria.*

Had one tagine too many? Then this busy, unpretentious little pizzeria has everything you need to give your taste buds a restorative mini break. Around 30 different pizzas are on offer (all of them generously topped and with convincingly crispy bases) and, provided you're not expecting culinary miracles, the quality is gratifyingly high. A dozen or so pasta dishes shore up the second half of the menu with a hit parade of comfort food featuring passable cover versions of lasagne, spag bol, carbonara and the rest. Decor follows the school of thought that a few strings of coloured lights go a long way, and service is tailored to a brisk business from local families, teenage kids, tourists, and those in a hurry for a post-work takeaway. No alcohol licence.

> "The beguiling candlelit interior of this restaurant provides an almost decadent counterpoint to the dusty frontier-town vibe of the rue du Souk."

Restaurant Abertih

Mirleft *Hôtel Abertih, Rue du Souk (028 71 93 04/ www.abertih.com). ££. Moroccan/French.*

Come nightfall, the beguiling candlelit interior of this hotel restaurant provides an almost decadent counterpoint to the dusty frontier-town vibe of the rue du Souk. The blood-red walls of the dining room are hung with arty monochrome prints, a constellation of ornate lamps are suspended from the high ceiling, the cosy bar is propped up by colourful locals and the restaurant's banquettes are strewn with plump, caravan-style cushions. The cuisine is mainly Moroccan (although the hotel's French ownership means a few bistro classics steal onto the menu), with elaborate salads and delicate preparations of local seafood two of the kitchen's strong suits. A handful of wines and bottled beers are what you can expect in the way of drinks; friendly efficiency characterises the service.

La Scala

Agadir *Rue de L'Oued Souss, Complex Tamlalt (028 84 67 73). ££££. Seafood.*

The neon lobster sign that hangs outside this smart red-brick restaurant is no empty boast. You'll find the best shellfish and fish in town here, along with a decent wine list and competent, discreet waiting staff. The dining room is smart but not stuffy, and there's a pleasant terrace surrounded by greenery (although the restaurant's location in a complex of large hotels means that the views are nothing to look twice at). Dishes like the bountiful *salade de mer* or exquisitely tender bream roasted in a salt crust are worth every dirham, while a smattering of meat dishes (duck breast cooked with ginger, honey and orange being a fine example) prevent carnivores from getting restless.

Yacout

Agadir *Avenue 29 Février (048 84 65 88). Open 6am-10pm daily. £. Café/Pâtisserie.*

One of those places that does a bit of everything and does it all well, this friendly neighbourhood joint majors in delicious breads and pastries (of the European, Moroccan and Lebanese varieties), along with good-quality coffee and mint tea. But it also offers a cheap (65dh) three-course menu of simple, well-rendered tagine, couscous and pastilla staples, with pâtisserie for pudding. Or failing that, you could wait for them to fire up the outdoor pizza oven and see what you fancy there. All in all, it's a mellow place to hang out (fragrant flora and twittering birdsong on the terrace, sleepy local caff within), which makes it a favourite among budget travellers lodged just up the street in Nouveau Talborjt.

Stay

Agadir is Morocco's most conventionally touristy destination, favoured by package tours and independent sunseekers in search of a beach and a break. And it is to this market that the city's hotels are skewed, so if you're looking for lodgings with a little more Moroccan flavour, you'll need to head out of town and continue south, towards the low-key resorts of Mirleft and Sidi Ifni.

Abertih

Mirleft *Rue du Souk (028 71 93 04/www. abertih.com). £.*

Bright, friendly and run to a scrupulously high standard, this hotel has plenty to recommend it. True, the guest rooms are pretty basic (some have shared, albeit spotless and nicely appointed, facilities) but they have big personalities,

and the lovely restaurant (*see p163*) is a truly pleasant place to pad down to in the morning for pancakes and coffee. There's a roof terrace too, whose immediate view (of the workaday rue du Souk) is not overly charming but whose distant prospect (of the glinting ocean) should be enough to lure you down to the beach each day. Staff are a good laugh and always ready to help out by answering questions, organising excursions or simply pointing you in the right direction for a stroll about town.

Ait Bâamrane

Sidi Ifni *Avenue de la Plage (028 780217). £.*

The only real reason to check into this weather-worn hotel would be if everywhere else in town were full. In such an eventuality, the (immaculately clean) rooms here will do as a convenient holding cell until something better crops up, or simply as a base to lay your head at night. On a positive note, its location (at the foot of the steps that lead down to the beach) means that you'll be sleeping about as close to the sea as it's possible to get without actually being in it. But the flip side is that surfers on a budget are also drawn here for the same reason, and tend to be the ones who make extensive use of the hotel's basic but (again) cheap waterside bar. In other words, there may be a bit of noise.

"Everyone is able to share in the sunset-watching that is a popular pastime on the spacious roof terrace."

Atlas

Mirleft *Centre de Mirleft (028 71 93 09/ www.atlas-mirleft.com). £.*

On first impressions, this wonderful budget hotel can seem a little poky. The lobby, which is a welcome escape from the heat in summer months, is a little starved of natural light, but once up the narrow flight of stairs that leads to the guest rooms, all of that changes. Vibrant primary colours, glimpses of blue sky from the open corridors and cheerful, immaculately maintained shared bathrooms give an upbeat spin to the place (there are also some rooms with their own bathroom). Rooms are clean and comfortable, but about as small as it is possible for a room to be (you can sit on the edge of your bed and still be able to wash your hands in the sink, open the window and answer the door). Still, the large roof terrace, delicious breakfast, convivial (licensed) bar and switched-on, friendly staff more than make up for these spatial challenges.

Bellevue

Sidi Ifni *Place Hassan II (028 875072). £.*

With the atmospheric Place Hassan II on one side and the luminous expanse of the Atlantic on the other, the Bellevue is in a pretty peachy spot. It makes the most of its sea views with the clean, functional rooms that are located in the main building (these are the ones to go for; the cabana-style alternatives out back are cramped and impervious to the noise generated by the hotel's alfresco bar). Everyone, though, is able to share in the sunset-watching that is a popular pastime on the spacious roof terrace, whose steps feature a small landing with a well-used open-air bar. It's worth hanging around for dinner, too, especially if you're a seafood fan – ask what's fresh that day, as it may not always be marked on the menu.

Hôtel Aglou Beach

Aglou Plage 048 86 61 96/57/www.agloubeach.com). £.
In the the remote outpost of Aglou Plage, a one-horse holiday town on the whisker-thin road that skirts the coast between Mirleft and Agadir, Hôtel Aglou Beach is a restful place to lose yourself for a day or two. The town itself, with its brace of café-restaurants and diminutive, charmingly faded boardwalk, will take all of ten minutes to see, which leaves plenty of time for a less focused brand of holidaymaking. Mile after mile of open beach gives all the room you need for walking, talking and getting some salt air in your lungs; otherwise, take on the Atlantic breakers for a brief, invigorating dip in the ocean. The hotel's guest rooms are light, spacious and equipped with satellite television, while its splendid terrace is a symphony of sea and sky with views that take in the entire sweep of the coast. Decent restaurant too.

Hôtel Kamal

Agadir Boulevard Hassan II (028 84 28 17). £.
A welcome plot of middle ground between the fancy resort hotels on the beach and the budget bunks in Nouveau Talborjt, the Kamal is a smart and comfortable base from which to explore the town. Rooms may not be chic or especially cosy, but the mattresses are firm, the facilities are spotless and the windows are double-glazed. A modest pool along with a bar boasting cold beer and big-screen sport give the package crowd what they came for, while everyone else can get on with exploring the town in the knowledge that a hot shower and a decent night's kip awaits them on their return.

Résidence de Sidi Ifni

Sidi Ifni 4 Avenue Moulay Abdellah (028 87 67 76/ www.residencesidi-ifni.com). £.
Since opening its doors in July 2007, the ever-popular Résidence is regarded by many locals as admissible evidence that Sidi Ifni really is experiencing a tourist boom. And it is with just such a tidal drift of European travellers in mind that this block of rental apartments has been fitted out. The town's trademark turquoise, splashes of summertime yellow and a pleasingly open-plan design wrest a breezy and attractive interior from what is a rather ordinary building, while the ballustraded roof terrace has all the space and comfy furniture required to make the most of the spectacular sea views. The German proprietor, Artus Matthiessen, is an easygoing and helpful host, who has some good contacts for those interested in trying their hand at parascending.

Riu Tikida

Agadir Chemin des Dunes (028 84 54 00/ www.riu.com). £££.
Let's face it, if you're booking a hotel room in Agadir for a few days you're hoping for one of two things. Either you're looking for somewhere that will serve as a base for exploring the region, in which case a comfy bed, a decent shower and pleasant surroundings are the sole requirements. Or you're hoping for sunny days on the beach followed by evenings of resort-style dining and nightlife. Welcome, then, to the Riu Tikida, which delivers the best of what Agadir has to offer, on both these counts. It's comfortable (apartment-style accommodation, thalasso-therapy spa), it's convenient (and positively bristling with tour and excursion options), and there are one or two smart restaurants, not to mention the city's most popular nightclub (Papagayo), just a short, Tommy Hilfiger-scented stroll away. Also, for flying visits, the Riu Tikida makes a soothing and luxurious place to dust off for a night before embarking on the flight home.

> "Back in the first half of the last century, this charming art deco hotel was the first to open its doors in what was then a remote outpost of the Spanish Sahara."

Sofitel Agadir

Agadir Baie des Palmiers, Commune de Bensergao (028 82 00 88/www.sofitel.com). £££.
It may be part of a chain but the Sofitel Agadir is still a stunning and luxurious hotel. Built in a low-rise kasbah style (a series of bright white buildings tumbling through lush gardens down to the shoreline) and with plenty of pristine white fabric billowing in the breeze beside the glassy surface of its infinity pool, the hotel has more than just a touch of Maghreb opulence. The rooms are furnished with taste and restraint (and are hooked up with all the usual five-star amenities, including wifi), a gorgeous spa is on hand to smooth out the kinks of office life with massages, wraps and the rest, and there are a few drinking and dining options on site. The cafés and restaurants of Agadir are only a leisurely wander away.

Suerte Loca

Sidi Ifni Avenue Moulay Youssef (028 87 53 50). £.
Back in the first half of the last century, this charming art deco hotel (whose name literally translates as 'crazy luck') was the first to open its doors in what was then a remote outpost of the Spanish Sahara. These days, the amiable owner Ayad Essaidi continues his grandfather's work, and

Top: Suerte Loca.
Middle & bottom:
Les Trois Chameaux.

Suerte Loca remains if not the only, then certainly the most characterful hotel in town. The tiled reception area is a friendly, laidback space, just right for tucking into one of the hotel kitchen's famous pancakes or chalking up your cue for a lazy afternoon of pool. If you can, bag one of the rooms facing the beach because, come nightfall, you can open up your windows, lie back on the bed and let the thunder and hiss of the surf send you off to sleep. As well as those first-class waves right on the doorstep, there's also a roof terrace for lounging, a library of left books, and fresh, hearty breakfasts.

Tikiout
Mirleft *Route de Sidi Ifni (028 719463). £.*
Run by the vivacious Lamiae, who moved from her native Agadir to open this bright new hotel in winter 2007, the Tikiout is a very welcome addition to the town's accommodation scene. The half dozen or so guest rooms are brightly painted and playfully furnished (think large, vibrant photo portraits of Berber villagers), although the rooms themselves are a bit on the small side. The shared showers are all in decent nick, and the hotel's restaurant is a thriving operation in its own right, serving café fare (*quiche au chèvre*, lasagne) and full-blown meals (catch of the day *en papillote*, fruit crumble) to locals, guests and those on their way to or from the nearby beaches. You can also get a very decent cup of coffee here – in fact, it's the very best coffee in town.

Les Trois Chameaux
Mirleft *Rue des Trois Chameaux (028 71 91 87/ www.3chameaux.com). ££.*
If you hadn't already guessed from its strategic location on the map (dominating a hilltop that surveys Mirleft and its surrounding coastline), your first glimpse of this beautiful hotel will leave you in no doubt that this was once a military fort. It has an undeniably *Beau Geste* aspect, with sturdy arches and castellations, and a sweltering parade ground (albeit one that is now given over to parking spaces, pretty plants and hand-made furniture). The romance continues inside, where ascetic barracks have been transformed into luxurious rooms and suites with high-quality fabrics, stunning tiling and panoramic terraces. The attractive *tadelakt* pool has the same wrap-around views, as well as white sails of cotton shading its perimeter and old-fashioned wooden sunloungers with gorgeous, fluffy towels to drip dry on. The restaurant and hammam both put a contemporary spin on their respective Moroccan traditions, and the results are excellent.

Factfile

When to go
In terms of climate, spring, autumn and early summer are lovely times to visit this region of Morocco, when it's warm enough for shorts and shirtsleeves but not so hot that a portion of the day needs to be spent in the shade. Several regional festivals are also worth noting, such as the Honey Festival held in April and May, Agadir's Timitar world music festival in July and the Transat Classique sailing race, which makes for a colourful stopover at Agadir Marina in November.

Getting there
Agadir's Almassira Airport (28 839 102/ www.onda.ma) is the main hub for international arrivals. For flights from the UK, see British Airways (www.britishairways.com), Thomsonfly (www.thomsonfly.com) and Royal Air Maroc (www.royalairmaroc.com). There is no bus service into town but *grands taxis* are in plentiful supply and operate a fixed fare of 180dh to downtown Agadir.

Getting around
Most of Agadir is walkable, but there is no shortage of the city's ubiquitous *petits taxis* (nippy little orange hatchbacks) – just be sure to remind them to turn on the meter. Otherwise, for longer distances, either visit Supratours in Agadir (Rue Les Orangers, 48 841 207/www. supratours.ma), which runs a regular coach service to Mirleft and Sidi Ifni, or take one of the *grands taxis* that depart from rue de Fes, opposite the Royal Palace. For independent travel, a number of car hire services are represented at Almassira Airport (try Avis, 028 839 244, www.avis.co.uk) and in the city centre (such as Europcar, Boulevard Mohamed V, 028 840 203, http://car-rental.europcar.com).

Drivers can either hurry down the N1 south from Agadir, turning off at Tiznit for Mirleft and Guelmim for Sidi Ifni, or else head to the tiny village of Aglou-Plage (again, taking the sign-posted road west from Tiznit) and take what must surely be one of Morocco's prettiest coast roads to Mirleft and then on to Sidi Ifni.

On a smaller scale, Mirleft's Speed Motos (Route de Sidi Ifni, 028 719 364) hires motorbikes, scooters, quads and mountain bikes at very reasonable rates.

Tourist office
Office du Tourisme (ONMT), Place Prince Héritier, Agadir (028 846 377/www.visitmorocco.com). Open 9am-12.30pm, 2-6pm Mon-Fri.

Internet
Globenet (33 Boulevard Hassan II, Agadir, no phone) Open 9am-midnight daily.

Clockwise from top left:
Asilah Medina (7);
Asilah harbour.

Asilah & Around

Walking along Asilah's 15th-century ramparts, with the sound of the ocean crashing on the rocks below and the pristine white buildings of the Medina tucked snugly into their dense map of ancient alleyways, gates and passages, it is hard not to feel a connection to the past. This is where Barbary pirates made their landfalls, where Riffian rebels holed up in the walled palace, and where European travellers came to marvel at the architecture and the feral beauty of the coast, long before it was safe to do so. Romantic (or at least romanticised) tales of kidnappings and daring escapes, fights and feuds crowd Asilah's history, and yet today it has become one of the cosiest, most abundantly charming coastal resorts in Morocco.

Asilah's Medina is cleaner, prettier and more compact than most, and its picturesque setting (perched on the water's edge) and the superior quality of the ocean light have made it an increasingly popular destination for European artists, many of whom have made the town their home. As a result, the annual art festival is now big business and not only attracts a great number of visitors, but also a huge influx of visiting artists, film-makers and writers, who come to exhibit their work and hold discussions and debates late into the summer evenings.

To the north, a huge unspoilt beach stretches into the distance as far as the eye can see; to the south lies the modern port of Larache with its laid-back seaside vibe and legacy of Roman ruins, and beyond it, the tiny fishing village of Moulay Bousselham, whose lagoon teems with birdlife and whose long, sandy beaches are fringed with oceanside villas and dotted with picnicking tourists.

Explore

ASILAH

Asilah is the sum of the usual two parts that make up a classic Moroccan town: the Medina and the *Ville Nouvelle*. What does, however, confound expectations is the pristine condition of its walled Medina. Enclosed by 15th-century ramparts, and surrounded by tall, spindly palms, the Medina is a largely residential area and has a sleepy and – out of season – even slightly deserted air. The principal entrance is Bab Kasbah, which leads on to the smartly paved rue El-Kasbah, with the magnificent *grande mosquée* overshadowing the pavement to the left and the vast whitewashed wall of the Centre Hassan II (*see p173*) to the right. A few paces along this road is the Medina's main square, place Sidi Abdellah Guennoun, dominated by the El-Kamra tower, a picturesque vestige of the city's Portuguese heritage. This is a popular meeting point for locals and a rallying point for tourists about to embark on a sweep of the Medina's main shopping street, rue Tijara, where artisans, craftsmen and less high-brow souvenir salesmen compete to peddle their wares.

But to get a real flavour of the Medina's swashbuckling past, enter via the Bab Bhar gate (just to the north of Bab Kasbah, next to the large car park) and hug the path that runs next to the ramparts (rue Ibn Khaldoun). This takes you past the castellated sea defences, and buildings whose facades are adorned with pretty frescoes and ornate tiling, and from whose rooftops hang decorative street lamps. An observation point, behind Palais Raissouli (*see p173*), allows you to take stock of the sweep of the beach in both directions and the inland view of the Medina's jumbled geometry of angular walls, Moorish window arches and blue-painted roof terraces. It's quite a sight.

The hub of the new town, meanwhile, is the smart and busy place Zallaka, where half of the town's decent restaurants are to be found. The spokes leading off this square are: the seafront strip of avenue Moulay Hassan ben Mehdi, home to the other (fishy) half of Asilah's restaurants; avenue Abdel Moumen Ali Bnou, flanked by the town's somewhat overgrown and unkempt cemetery; and avenue Hassan II, cheap eats central and the starting point of the local souk, whose fruit, veg and household goods stalls curl around the southern and western walls of the Medina. Otherwise, the eastern portion of town is its administrative heart (look in this quarter for the post office, the police station, the library) and is worth a visit if only to see the beautiful Catholic Iglesia de San Bartolomé. You'll spy its twin towers from some way off (on the corner of avenues Mohamed V and Prince Héritier) and it's always worth ringing the buzzer beside the church door. If the sisters aren't busy running courses

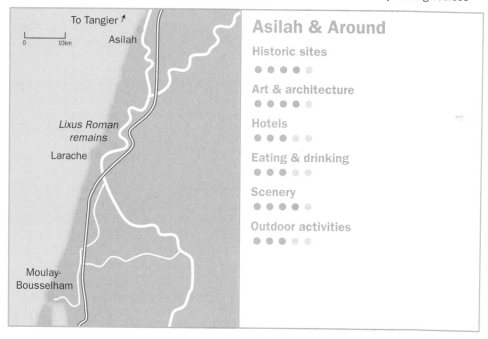

To Tangier ↗

Asilah

0   10km

Lixus Roman remains

Larache

Moulay-Bousselham

Asilah & Around

Historic sites
● ● ● ● ○

Art & architecture
● ● ● ● ○

Hotels
● ● ● ○ ○

Eating & drinking
● ● ● ○ ○

Scenery
● ● ● ● ○

Outdoor activities
● ● ● ○ ○

Asilah.

Clockwise from top left: postcards; countryside outside Asilah; Asilah Medina (3); Iglesia de San Bartolomé.

for the local womenfolk, they'll happily show you around the church's fascinating hotchpotch of architectural styles.

Centre Hassan II des Rencontres Internationales

Asilah *Rue Al-Kasbah (039 21 70 65). Open 9am-noon, 2-7.30pm Mon-Wed, Sat, Sun. Admission free.*
During the month of August, when Asilah's annual culture festival is in full swing (for which, *see p178*), this spacious, well-equipped cultural centre becomes a bustling hub of activity. During the rest of the year, though, it is little more than a peaceful retreat from the heat, with a series of interconnected atrium spaces displaying a changing selection of locally produced, mainly abstract artworks. A custodian is on duty during the day and is happy to let visitors wander around and admire the exhibition, just don't expect the café (of which there is evidence in the neatly ordered rows of tables and chairs dotted around the place) or the lecture theatre to be operational.

Palais Raissouli

Asilah *Place Raissouli, Medina (no phone). Open by appointment only. Admission free.*
The seat of the notorious Sharif of the Riffian Berbers Moulay Ahmed ben Mohammed er-Raissouli (depending on your view, a Barbary pirate, a despot, a brigand or a freedom fighter), this wonderfully evocative building was where the great man (known simply as Raissouli) held court at the beginning of the last century. The building is only open to the public during the annual culture festival in August (*see p178*) or by special appointment (although you would need a specific reason to be allowed entry and would have to make arrangements via the Centre Hassan II des Rencontres Internationales; *see above*). But go along anyway to have a look, as you might find it open. And if you do strike it lucky, while there are no real exhibits as such, you'll be treated to some fascinating glimpses of what life was like on the wild side back in the 1900s – such as the terrace from which the big man meted out his own brand of capital punishment by hurling wrong-doers over the edge and on to the rocks below. Nice guy? Not so much, but a key historical personage of the decades leading up to the Rif War, and someone whose life and actions still provoke animated discussion today.

LARACHE

The nucleus of Larache's new town is the large, busy place de la Libération. Surrounded by cafés and (informal, cheap) restaurants, this square has an appealing air of faded grandeur, not unlike the rest of Larache. From the square, a short sloping street leads on to the corniche (rue de Casablanca), where the smarter cafés are to be found, along with many of the townsfolk when, come sunset, they turn out in force to take the sea air. Dominating the northern tip of the boulevard are the crumbling ruins of the town's 16th-century kasbah (built by the Portuguese and left thereafter to slowly decay in the warm salt air).

Behind the kasbah and to the north of place de la Libération is the Medina, a lively, working market and residential area whose chaotic and often rather scrubby streets will appeal to some more than others. On the port side of the Medina are a number of open-air fish stalls, which are reliable, fresh and great fun for a snack on the go. To the south of the main square lies the bulk of the new town, where most of the hotels but little of any real architectural or cultural interest are to be found, and further still (a short *petit taxi* drive out of town) is the Spanish Cemetery where French writer Jean Genet is buried. And, perhaps most famously of all, a short hop to the north of town, are the Roman ruins of Lixus (*see p175*).

MOULAY BOUSSELHAM

A few clicks down the coast from Larache, the tiny, adorable Moulay Bousselham is the epitome of a one-horse town. It will take all of five minutes to explore the place (a collection of fish grills and a smattering of hotels) but you could spend weeks losing yourself in the coastal wonderland that surrounds it. To the south, the vast lagoon and wetlands that comprise the Merdja Zerga national park are significant not only in their capacity as protected and well-conserved bird sanctuaries but also as a glorious setting for morning strolls and afternoon siestas. To the north: a huge, empty, surf-fringed beach that seems to go on forever.

Eat

Al Madina

Asilah *Place Sidi Abdellah Guennoun (no phone). Open 9am-8pm daily. £. Moroccan.*
Perfectly located on the quaint place Sidi Abdellah Guennoun just inside the Bab Bhar, this unassuming little café-restaurant sits right opposite El-Kamra tower. Its terrace, a small cluster of tables set against a background of whitewashed, blue-shuttered houses, is a very pretty spot from which to observe shoppers spilling out on to the square from busy rue Tijara next door. Given the proximity of Asilah's enclave of decent restaurants, you're probably better off just grabbing a Coke or a cup of coffee at Al Madina, but if you find that you're really quite comfortable where you are, then there are a few standard local dishes on offer (tagines, couscous et al), as well as occasional Moroccan pastries.

Balcon Atlantique

Larache *Rue de Casablanca (039 91 01 10). Open 7am-10.30pm daily. £. Café/Pizza.*
Sporting what is undoubtedly the nicest terrace in town, this upmarket café is popular among well-heeled Moroccans and visiting Europeans. While not exactly smart, the Balcon Atlantique is as close as Larache gets to chic, hence the

decorously attired waiters and the upmarket furniture, but you'll fare best if you stick to what the place does best: decent coffee, tasty crêpes and kid-friendly ice-cream sundaes. The selection of pizzas and panini do the job if you have a gap to fill or are blessed with the rare combination of a child who is hungry and not fussy. Otherwise you're probably better off fuelling up on the real thing at Restaurant Commercial (*see below*). Behind the café's tinted windows lies an interior of faintly gaudy wood and pastel furnishings, which is recommended only if the terrace is full or the weather bad.

Casa Garcia

Asilah *51 avenue Moulay Hassan ben Mehdi (039 41 74 65). Open noon-3pm, 7.30 10.30pm daily. ££. Fish.*

A small, genuinely beguiling restaurant, there's something of a taverna feel to its seaside shtick of fishing nets suspending plastic lobsters from the ceiling, wooden model galleons and photographs of trawlers laden down with giant tuna. A much more appealing picture is that of the wet counter at the front of the restaurant, whose glistening still-life of fish and shellfish has clearly arrived fresh from the day's catch. Choose from the extensive menu if you wish, but more fun is to select a specimen from the counter and wait for it to be delivered to you boned, butterflied and perfectly pan-fried. Classic accompaniments are a plate of golden chips, a wedge of lemon and a bowl of pickled garlic, but there's a wide range of salads to choose from too. Friendly bow-tied waiters and quaffable wines make the experience even more enjoyable.

Casa Pepe

Asilah *22 place Zallaka (039 41 73 95). Open 12.15-2.30pm, 7-11pm daily. £££. Fish.*

It may have a few swish touches – not least, the waiters' use of electronic touch pads to take down orders or the chef's habit of producing daintily presented *amuse-gueules* – but this cosy restaurant is still very much a holiday joint. The spectacle of rustic beams, brickwork, still-life artwork and red tablecloths mixes easily with the rowdy chatter of coach tourists and the happy sound of bottles of Moroccan plonk being divested of their corks. The menu is long and varied, with a few interesting choices, such as cuttlefish, among the seafood options and various Spanish specialities (the paella, in particular, is good here). Unusually for small-town Morocco, the wine list also has a few French labels, which are a touch more drinkable than their home-grown cellar-mates. Staff are friendly and know what they're talking about, especially when it comes to the local fish and how to eat it.

Restaurant Commercial

Larache *Place de la Liberation (no phone). Open 7am-10pm daily. £. Moroccan.*

It may be virtually indistinguishable in style from the many other cafés and restaurants that encircle Larache's busy main square, but the Commercial is actually something quite special. Not that you'd know it, of course, to look at its frankly unattractive brown tiling and plastic tablecloths, but then it makes no claims to beauty or sophistication.

What it does say it can do, however, is cook up a decent plate of seafood or a more than passable paella, and with that there can be no dispute. Catering without discrimination to hungry hordes of locals and tourists, the kitchen here cranks out cheap, tasty plates of sole, squid, prawns, paella and brochettes with little ceremony and lots of flavour. Bring along a 50dh note and you'll leave here full, happy and with plans to return.

Restaurant El Espigon

Asilah *Avenue Moulay Hassan ben Mehdi (039 41 71 57/41 88 39). Open 12.30-2.30pm, 7-10pm daily. ££. Fish.*

An evening stroll along the beachfront of avenue Moulay Hassan ben Mehdi will lead you to this busy restaurant with views that stretch beyond the harbour towards the surf-fringed beaches north of town. The *fruits de mer* mentioned on the bright blue awning that shades the restaurant's terrace is of a high standard (on a good day, this is the best place in town to be tucking into lobster or crab), and the small wine cellar visible through the archway at the end of the dining room has a few half-decent bottles tucked away in its stacks. You may have to endure a bit of 'where you come from?' banter from the well-meaning waiters, but it's worth it for the quality of food that they're bringing.

Restaurant de la Place

Asilah *Avenue Moulay Hassan ben Mehdi (no phone). Open noon-2pm, 7-10pm daily. ££. Fish.*

Generally (and perhaps unfairly) regarded as a reliable 'plan B' when its more popular contenders, Casas Garcia and Pepe, are fully booked, this pleasant little restaurant is actually worth a visit in its own right. While the kitchen here is able to turn its hand to the same kind of fish and seafood specials you'll see on every menu along this strip, it also knocks out a very decent omelette, a tasty steak and a not-too-shabby 'brochette oriental'. There's a pleasing simplicity to the clean, compact dining room, and the terrace is a lively kind of place, with the amenable English-speaking boss joking and chatting with punters in a way that feels welcome and refreshing, as opposed to intrusive or annoying.

Restaurant Le Pont

Asilah *Avenue Moulay Hassan ben Mehdi (no phone). Open 12.30-2.30pm, 7.30-9.30pm Mon-Sat. £. Fish*

You can expect a comparatively limited choice of fish and seafood at this diminutive, family-run restaurant, but what they do, they do well. Like most of Asilah's restaurants, Le Pont has its share of Iberian-influenced dishes (paella, Spanish omelette and the like) but it is at straightforward seafood grills that they really excel. Sardine, swordfish, sole and many other locally caught specimens are simply served, with no heavy-handed seasoning or over-complicated adornments to spoil what is essentially the unimprovable flavour of very fresh fish gutted, grilled and plated. The tiny dining room has a similarly unfussy feel: a handful of cheaply framed photos hang on the walls, tables have thick plastic cloths, and the menus are laminated in the style of an East End pie house. No wine, no ceremony, just honest-to-goodness tasty grub.

Ancient mariners

At the mouth of the Loukkos river, where its long journey ends at the sparse marshes and flood plains of the Atlantic coast, the Phoenicians established a trading post in the seventh century BC. This modest settlement soon fell under Carthaginian control and, ultimately, into the hands of the victorious Romans, who established it as Lixus, an imperial colony that thrived with the growing fishing industry, reaching the height of its prosperity under the reign of Claudius I. And yet, for the amateur visitor who pitches up at what is now an only partially excavated, overgrown (albeit very atmospheric) hilly outcrop of ruins located in the northern outskirts of Larache, there is little to indicate that this is one of the most important archaeological sites along this stretch of the Mediterranean. But persevere because there is much to see here.

If you are arriving by car, park at the side of the site (where you see the overturned rowing boat and anchor on a traffic island) and not at the layby near the entrance to the site (where you see some broken and rusted green gates), as this is where scurrulous *faux guides* and other miscreants tend to try their luck. There are three official guides to the site (know them by their municipal ID tags) but you are not obliged to enlist their services. It is perfectly acceptable to visit the site independently.

To this end, start at the main gates and follow the path that leads up towards the summit of the hill. On your left, you will pass the remains of what were (quite literally) the guts of the settlement: the *garum* (fish sauce) processing plant. Further up (directly to the right of the path) are the more easily discernible remains of the amphitheatre, complete with a mosaic depicting the god Oceanus (sadly, the mosaic depicting Neptune that was to be found in the public baths, just along the hillside from the amphitheatre, was destroyed by local children in 1998). From here, it is a short walk to the summit, where the views of the river and the coast (some three or four kilometres distant) and of the remaining ruins below (on the western hillside) are spectacular. Indeed, it is here that on a good (meaning, not too crowded) day that the magic of the place comes alive. It is easy to associate this breezy, sunlit hilltop with its tumultuous historical past and its equally exciting legendary status – this is believed to be the location of the mythical Garden of the Hesperides, scene of Hercules' penultimate labour, that of the 'golden apples'. *Lixus, N1 north of Larache. Open 10am-5pm daily. Admission free.*

Hôtel Patio de la Luna.

Restaurant Sevilla

Asilah *Rue Imam El-Assili (no phone). Open noon-2pm, 7-10pm daily. ££. Moroccan/fish.*

In some senses the dowdy cousin of the more conspicuous, tourist-oriented establishments down the road, Restaurant Sevilla is no less appealing for its altogether unpretentious atmosphere and seemingly impromptu decor of assorted prints and random objects (ships' wheels feature prominently). But, while the front of house may have a thrown-together vibe, the kitchen is clearly very well ordered and is able to turn out more than respectable renditions of all the usual fish dishes, plus a few more adventurous choices besides, such as the spindly, delicious *angulas* (elvers or baby eels). Where Sevilla does not, however, live up to the pedigree of its near neighbours is in its scope. Beyond the seafood section, the menu rather loses its way and gets bogged down in a catch-all no man's land of spaghetti bolognaise, questionable paellas and the dreaded macaroni. There's no wine list on offer here, so you'll have to choose between mineral water, orange juice or lemonade.

La Symphonie des Douceurs

Asilah *26 place Zallaka (no phone). Open 7am-10.30pm daily. £. Café.*

It may not be big but it is clever, as witnessed by the fact that, even when other bars and cafes are standing empty, the Symphonie is perennially busy. And it's easy to see why. For one thing, staff here make some of the best fruit juices you'll ever taste (the panache of seasonal fruit is like a spa treatment in a glass), they rustle up a mean breakfast ('menu B' of eggs, juice and strong coffee is especially good) and they seem genuinely pleased to be serving you (which is something of a novelty in increasingly touristy Asilah). The tiny terrace is the place to be in early morning or as the sun is heading for the horizon, while the tunnel-like interior offers a welcome retreat from the high-noon heat blast – albeit one in which Arab pop videos are playing rather too loudly on the wall-mounted televisions. But then nothing's perfect.

Stay

Berbari

7km S of Asilah *Dchar Ghanem, Cercle de Tnin Sidi Yamani (062 58 80 13/www.berbari.com). £.*

Like Thoreau's *Walden* updated to a post-digital age, Berbari is the ideal base from which to experiment with the idea of changing down several gears and falling into step with the rhythms of nature. A few kilometres out of town, its tasteful but simple rooms are constructed around a delightful courtyard, with the design-literate lounge and dining area a focus: surrounded by floor-to-ceiling glass, it features a battered piano, a stove that was once an oil drum and a lampshade that was at one time a dress. The bedrooms are similarly playful and are steeped in the same brand of shabby chic, while the terrace looks out over miles of uninterrupted countryside. There are no televisions, few electric lights and no telephones to compete with the

lullaby of the birds and the profound stillness of the starry nights. Storks nesting up on the rooftops survey the scene with mild curiosity.

Dar Aziz

Asilah *Above Aplanos Art Gallery, 89 rue Tijara (039 41 74 86/061 99 80 30). £.*

What is immediately appealing about these spacious, dead-central apartments is the arty European style that has been subtly folded into their typical Moorish mixture of open-plan living areas, sunlit windows and tasteful tiling. An antique armoire here, a corner bookcase there – the vibe is very much that of a northern European atelier transposed to northern Africa. No surprise, then, to discover that the owner, Anne-Judith Van Loock is a Belgian-born painter who also runs a wonderful art gallery, situated on the ground floor of the building. The two main apartments can comfortably accommodate three guests (or, say, parents with a couple of kids in tow), while a smaller third apartment consists simply of a bedroom and bathroom (the others have spacious, well-equipped kitchens). Private terraces and a charming roof space allow plenty of opportunities to admire the Medina's multi-hued rooftops from on high.

Dar Walili

7km S of Asilah *Outskirts of Asilah (00 336 07 32 26 82). ££.*

It comes as quite a surprise to discover what looks like an art-house film set at the end of the long dirt track that branches east off the N1 road a few kilometres south of Asilah. And yet, there it is, the creation of French ex-pat Andrée Douchet, who has clearly invested a great deal of her time (and money) into transforming a simple country farmhouse into a chic bolthole complete with verdant courtyard, *Arabian Nights* roof terrace and all the trimmings. On offer to groups or families who want to take the place over for a week or more, Dar Walili has everything the design-conscious traveller could hope for. Antique mirrors and beautiful fixtures adorn the vast bathrooms, old-world charm drips from every corner of the bedrooms and the kitchen shelves are stocked with the trappings of a *cuisine provençale*. The roof terrace has to be seen to be believed, with its views of fields rolling down towards the Atlantic set against a foreground of cushions, carpets and billowing sunlit fabrics.

Hôtel Espana

Larache *6 avenue Hassan II (039 91 31 95/www.hotel-espana.fr.gd). £.*

Walking into the lobby of the Hôtel España, it is immediately clear that someone, at some point (probably around the mid 1970s), said to themselves, 'Let's jazz this place up a bit.' Which is a shame, since this was obviously at one time quite a classy joint. Still, if you can squint hard enough to see past the faded, slightly bizarre decor, or concentrate hard enough to convince yourself that it is, in fact, retro cool, then you should be perfectly happy here. The rooms are nicely proportioned and the polyglot staff can tell you in as many as six different languages that General Franco once spent a restful night here.

Hôtel Mansour
Asilah *Avenue Mohammed V (039 41 73 90/ www.hotelmansour.fr.fm). £.*

This has long been the most popular choice at the economy end of Asilah's accommodation and, once inside the place, it's easy to see why. Cheerful tiling, dark wooden furniture and large windows are common themes throughout the hotel, both in the bedrooms and in the open-plan dining room. Of course, it's also easy to see why prices are so low (the tiny bathrooms, for example, are more like wardrobes fitted with tiles and plumbing) and rooms overlooking the road can be a little on the noisy side. But it's a friendly base for exploring the town, and if you're thinking of an excursion or need to rent a car or bike, there's also a travel agency on the ground floor of the hotel that has a reliable track record for finding good deals with reputable operators.

Hôtel Patio de la Luna
Asilah *12 plaza Zelaka (039 41 60 74). £.*

This Tardis-like hotel opens out into a world of understated style that you would never guess at from its modest little entrance opposite the Medina gates. The rooms are sequestered in a peaceful area at the back, where a leafy courtyard provides shade and birdsong, and artful touches bring the place to life in the evening. The rooms are simply furnished but much thought has clearly gone into their overall effect, with lambent blue walls and painted furniture perfectly offsetting earth-toned tiling. The only downside is that no meals are provided, which means that even breakfast must be found elsewhere. But the hotel's location means you'll not have far to go.

Hôtel Riad
Larache *88 avenue Med Ibn Abdellah (039 91 26 26/ www.hotelriad.com). £.*

If you're looking for a turndown service and a marble bathroom, this is certainly not the place for you. It may have been, a century or two ago, when the mansion that houses the hotel and its landscaped grounds were newly completed, but these days it has become one of those grand old establishments of undeniable charm but questionable levels of refurbishment. That's not to say it isn't clean (it is – spotless, in fact), it's just that the rooms, the restaurant and the splendidly proportioned lobby have all seen better days. But then, who hasn't? And the point about Hotel Riad is that even the remnants of its former glory (beautiful stained glass, a wonderful antique switchboard on the reception, ornate tiling and wrought iron at every turn) have more charm than a dozen chain hotels stitched together. Although perhaps not as much hot water (which is more of a morning and night affair at the Riad).

Villanora
Moulay Bousselham *Front de Mer, Moulay Bousselham (037 43 20 71/www.villanora.ifrance. com). £.*

A little piece of beachfront paradise, this former family villa is now a *maison d'hôte* of rare charm and sophistication. It has the same natural advantages as many similarly located properties along this stretch of coastline (think panoramic ocean views, the nightly lullaby of Atlantic rollers) but it is what the owners have chosen to do with it that elevates Villanora above the norm. The six guest rooms and the beautiful sitting rooms are decorated with original artworks (many of them from the family easels), the sweet private terraces and communal lawn are secluded and fragrant with the scent of flowers and salt air, and just-caught fish is roasted over open coals (either in the garden or at the enormous fireplace). Foodies return for Selma and Karima's wonderful cooking, twitchers for Hassan's inside knowledge of the lagoon-dwelling birdlife, and the rest just come back for their annual shot of vitamin sea. Be sure to book well ahead. At the time of writing, work was well under way on Villanora's new bird-watching outpost, Farm Nora, located a short drive out of the town on the shores of Lake Barghat.

Factfile

When to go
The most exciting (and therefore busiest) time to visit Asilah is during its annual culture festival (www.perle-de-culture.com). Otherwise, spring and autumn walks along the beaches in and around Moulay Bousselham are certainly something to plan a trip around.

Getting there
In Asilah, buses arrive at and leave from the *gare routière* on avenue de la Liberté. Try CTM for timetables and destinations (039 41 80 91). Otherwise, there's a train station a couple of kilometres north of town (039 41 73 27).

Buses to Larache arrive at the small station just next to the roundabout behind avenue Hassan II, while Moulay Bousselham is most easily accessed via *grand taxi* (you'll see them lined up at the roadside just along from the Hôtel Le Lagon), although buses do go there from Larache and Asilah.

Getting around
Asilah, Larache and Moulay Bousselham are all easily navigable on foot, although *petits taxis* are cheap and plentiful in both Asilah and Larache.

Tourist information
Tourist Office 29 boulevard Pasteur (039 948050). Open 9am-noon, 2-5pm Mon-Fri.

Internet
Cyber Plaza Zelaka, next to Patio de la Luna (no phone). Open 9am-10pm daily.

Clockwise from top right:
Restaurant de la Place;
Casa Garcia (3).

Clockwise from top left:
ramparts; port; souks;
Villa Maroc; ramparts;
place Moulay Hassan;
Villa Maroc.

Essaouira

Essaouira is one of those places that looks too good to be true. For many years this picturesque, pocket-sized port luxuriated in a laid-back timelessness all of its own, out on a limb from the rail network, no longer important as a commercial port. The Moroccan tourist boom has begun to have an impact recently, but this is still a place geared to quiet days, big sunsets and brisk Atlantic breezes.

Sandy-coloured ramparts shelter the clean and bright Medina built around French piazzas, carved archways and whitewashed lanes and alleys. The fishing port provides a constant fresh catch for local restaurants, while the wide, sandy beaches to the south, combined with high winds, have put Essaouira on the international windsurfing map.

The Medina, laid out in the late 18th century by a French architect along the lines of a European fortified seaport town, is now a UNESCO World Heritage site. In the 18th and 19th centuries Mogador, as Essaouira was known for much of its history, was a busy port and centre for foreign trade, linking Morocco and its Saharan hinterland with Europe. A now-disintegrating Jewish quarter and the former European consulates that dot the Kasbah testify to these old commercial connections. When the French took over, the town became something of a backwater, before being 'discovered' by the hippies in the late 1960s. Today the Europeans have returned in force, with more than ten per cent of Medina houses now owned by foreigners.

Essaouira also has another, very different, strand to its identity – as a centre of culture for the gnawa, descendents of sub-Saharan African slaves now constituted as an itinerant brotherhood of mystic musicians, with its own school of naive painters and an annual June music festival that attracts tens of thousands of visitors.

Explore

Essaouira has next to nothing in the way of formal sights, such as monuments and museums. The interesting part of town is contained within the walled **Medina**, and this is one big sight, with highlights including the ramparts (**Skala de la Ville**), **souks** and the **Mellah**. You can march from one to the other in ten minutes; a more leisurely exploration, however, can take days. The **port** is a separate entity, worthy of at least a stroll. Connecting the two is place Moulay Hassan.

Coming into town through Bab Sba (one of five gates and the most likely route if you're travelling from Marrakech or Agadir), the narrow, shady avenue du Caire intersects the broad, open avenue Oqba Ibn Nafia, spine of the Medina. Left, this leads to the port. Right, it dips under

an arch, changes its name to avenue de l'Istiqulal and becomes Essaouira's main commercial thoroughfare, leading to the souks. The Mellah district is beyond.

Opposite avenue du Caire, the arch in the wall leads into the Kasbah district, and, bearing left, to the place Moulay Hassan. As well as connecting the Medina to the port, place Moulay Hassan is Essaouira's social centre. Early in the morning, fishermen pass by on their way to work and the first wave of itinerant musicians and shoe-shine boys appears. By mid morning the café tables have begun their secondary function – as al fresco offices from which most Souiris conduct business at some time or another. Purveyors of sunglasses, watches and carpets sweep from table to table, only occasionally selling something. It's a popular spot for tourists, who can be found sitting at any of the cafés watching the theatre of

Essaouira

Historic sites	Eating & drinking
● ● ● ○ ○	● ● ● ○ ○
Art & architecture	**Scenery**
● ● ● ● ●	● ● ● ● ○
Hotels	**Outdoor activities**
● ● ● ● ●	● ● ● ● ●

SPAIN

ATLANTIC

OCEAN

MOROCCO

Essaouira

ALGERIA

0   100km

WESTERN SAHARA

Clockwise from top left:
souks (2); beach;
place Moulay Hassan.

Beach and port.

the town unfold or buying the previous day's international newspapers from Jack's Kiosk.

Musée Sidi Mohammed Ben Abdellah

7 Derb Laâlouj (024 47 23 00). Open 8.30am-6pm Mon, Wed-Sun. Admission 10dh.

This renovated 19th-century mansion was used as the town hall during the Protectorate and today hosts a fairly boring collection of weapons, woodwork and carpetry. There are also gnawa costumes and musical instruments and a few pictures of old Essaouira.

Phytolacca Dioca tree

Just inside Bab Marrakech, turn right into the Centre Artisanale opposite the L'Heure Bleue hotel. At the far end, beyond various small workshops, a small passage on the right leads to a courtyard containing nothing but the oddest remnant of Essaouira's cosmopolitan past: an enormous Phytolacca Dioca tree, a species native to parts of Argentina and Brazil, planted here centuries ago by Portuguese traders and still clearly thriving, so very far from home.

SOUKS

The souks can be found at the centre of the Medina, in cloistered arcades around the intersection of avenue Mohammed Zerktouni and avenue Mohammed El-Qouri. On the eastern side, just south of the arch from avenue Zerktouni is the grain market. Slaves were auctioned here until the early 20th century. The neighbouring cloistered square, the Joutiya, comes to life between 4pm and 5pm for a daily auction. The auctioneers walk in a circle holding up old alarm clocks, fishing reels, slippers, transistor radios – like a demented Moroccan version of *The Generation Game*.

On the west side of the avenue, the fish and spice souk is lively and interesting, but beware of unscrupulous stallholders, expert at the hard sell. It is here that Souiri women come to buy chameleons, hedgehogs and various weird and wonderful plants for use in sorcery and magic.

The jewellery souk curls around the outside of the mosque to the south-east of the junction. It's a surprisingly quiet corner where it's possible to browse in peace and pick up pieces of traditional silver jewellery.

MELLAH

Essaouira's old Jewish quarter, the Mellah, can be found just inside the ramparts beyond the Skala de la Ville – or by walking along avenue Sidi Mohammed ben Abdellah. When the shops and businesses start to peter out, the Mellah begins.

During the 19th century, British merchants outnumbered other nationalities to the extent that 80 per cent of the town's trade was with Britain and sterling was the favoured currency. Muslims were not permitted to conduct financial transactions with the British, so the sultan

brought in Jews from all over the kingdom; by 1900 they outnumbered the locals. All but the wealthiest lived in the Mellah district within the Medina, between the North Bastion and Bab Doukkala.

The area has been so neglected since mass emigration to Israel in the 1950s and 1960s that many buildings have fallen down or been demolished due to disrepair; alleys are grubby and dilapidated. At one time, though, Essaouira was known as the Sanhedrin (Jewish cultural centre) of North Africa. As recently as the 1950s the city still claimed 32 official **synagogues**. One of those that still functions remains at 2 derb Ziry ben Atiyah, which is the last lane on the west off derb Laâlouj before it intersects with avenue Sidi Mohammed Ben Abdellah. The synagogue was founded by British merchants from Manchester; at the height of Essaouira's importance this section of the Medina was the location of various consulates and administrative buildings. Another functioning synagogue is at 3 rue de Mellah (call 076 04 83 52 if you want to arrange a visit).

These days there are perhaps two dozen Jews left in Essaouira, some still distilling fiery *eau de vie de figues*, but they don't necessarily live here.

> "Locals gather here to watch the sunset, and lovers cuddle in the crenellations, where ancient cannons offer places to perch."

SKALA DE LA VILLE

The Skala de la Ville is the only place where you can walk on top of the town's ramparts. There is one ramp up to the top near the junction with rue Ibn Rochd at the southern end, and another can be found near the junction with rue Derb Laâlouj at the northern end. Locals gather here to watch the sunset, and lovers cuddle in the crenellations, where ancient cannons offer places to perch. At the far end is the tower of the North Bastion, the top of which offers good views across the Mellah and Kasbah.

Painters lay out their work for sale on and around the ramparts. Artisans sculpting *thuja* – a local coniferous hardwood with a smell like peppery cedar – have their workshops in the arches below and here you can find all manner of carvings and marquetry.

PORT & BEACHES

Essaouira's **beach** is wonderful, but the north-westerly winds, known as the Alizés, make it cold and choppy for bathing. It's ideal for windsurfing, though, and the beach stretches for miles to the south, backed by dunes once the town peters out. Closer to the Medina it serves as a venue for local youths to play football. There's always a game going on and at weekends there are several played simultaneously, their kick-offs timed by the tides. You'll also find guys with camels, or they will find you, insistently offering rides. It can be fun to trek around the bay to the ruined old fort of Borj El-Berod, but wait until you find a camel guy you feel comfortable with, and agree a firm price before setting off.

The **port**, although pleasant at any time of day, is most interesting in the late afternoon when the fishing fleet rolls back into the harbour. Essaouira is Morocco's third-largest fishing port after Agadir and Safi. The catch is auctioned between 3pm and 5pm at the market hall just outside the port gates, and fresh fish are grilled and served up at stalls on the port side of place Moulay Hassan.

Eat

Les Alizés Mogador

26 rue Skala (024 47 68 19). Open noon-3pm, dinner 1st service 7pm, 2nd service 9pm, daily. £. Moroccan.
Opposite the wood workshops under the ramparts, and thus sheltered from the winds that lend the restaurant its name, this is one popular restaurant. It is known for its stone-arched interior, friendly, candlelit atmosphere, and above all for hearty portions of good and reasonably priced Moroccan home-cooking from a set menu. You can't make reservations, so expect to wait for a table sometimes – especially when it's feeding time for backpackers from the Hotel Smara upstairs.

Bar

1 boulevard Mohamed V (no phone). Open 9am-8pm daily. ££. Bar.
Attached to the beachfront restaurant Chalet de la Plage (*see below*) on the side furthest from the port, and accessed by a discreet entrance signed only with the single word 'Bar', this is a simple drinking den where Moroccans gather over cold bottles of Flag Spéciale either on a small terrace overlooking the sands or indoors in the cosy saloon. It's a friendly place, but it's their place.

La Cantina

66 rue Boutouil (024 47 45 15). Open 11am-8pm daily. £. Mexican.
Whatever possessed the congenial Steve Murphy and Sharon Hallom from South Yorkshire to open a 'vaguely Mexican' café on this square near the Mellah, the result

is good news for those looking for a change from couscous and tagines – especially vegetarians, who are catered for with understanding and flexibility. Jacket potatoes, burgers, chilli, stews, stir-fries and wonderful home-made cakes and desserts form the spine of a menu that is constrained by the availability of local ingredients. Guacamole is served only in late autumn when avocados are in season.

Chalet de la Plage

1 boulevard Mohamed V (024 47 59 72/www.le chaletdelaplage). Open 6.30-10pm Mon; noon-2.30pm, 6.30-10pm Tue-Sat; noon-2.30pm Sun. £. Fish/international.
Built in 1893 entirely o ut of wood, this Essaouira beachside institution – just outside the Medina, opposite place Orson Welles – has been a restaurant forever. Good fish dishes are the highlight of a solid, unfussy menu, there's beer and a small wine list, and the overall vibe is friendly and efficient. It's at its best for lunch, when the terrace affords a tremendous panorama of the bay. The owners have also opened a terrace café on the harbour side of the building, where coffee, tea and soft drinks can be enjoyed with an ocean view.

Chez Driss

10 rue El-Hajali (024 47 57 93). Open 7am-10pm daily. ££. Café.
This pâtisserie at the end of place Moulay Hassan, founded back in 1925, serves a mouth-watering selection of croissants, tarts and cakes at prices everyone can afford. You can eat them with coffee here in the small, sheltered courtyard, or take them to one of the cafés with tables on the square where no one will mind you bringing your own breakfast pastries.

Chez Sam

Port de Pêche (024 47 62 38). Open noon-3.30pm, 7-11pm daily. £££. Fish.
Right by the harbour, the building occupied by Chez Sam is a waterside wooden shack, designed like a ship, cramped and full of clutter. Continuing in the nautical vein, you can even peer out of the portholes to see fishing boats bringing in the catch. It's a no-nonsense kind of fish restaurant where you'll always find some local seafood, even if you rarely get anything exceptional, but the staff seem to know what they're doing. The new balcony out the back, overlooking the entrance to the harbour, is a nice spot for lunch.

Côté Plage

Boulevard Mohammed V (024 47 90 00). Open noon-3pm, 7-10.30pm daily. ££. French.
On the promenade opposite the Sofitel, by which it is owned and operated, this is a good spot for mildly upmarket beachside lunches and interminable menu descriptions, both epitomised by the likes of 'duo de melon du pays au jambon cru de parme et pain tomate' or 'escabèche d'ombrine et saumon frais aux epices de la médina et herbes fraîches de l'Atlas, toast chaud'. It's about a ten-minute stroll from the Medina. Barbecue on Sundays.

Clockwise from top: Café Taros (2); fish market; Villa Maroc.

Something fishy

Essaouira is no gourmet paradise, but in one department it bows to no man: fresh fish. At the fish market on the harbour side of place Moulay Hassan, there's a fresh catch on offer twice a day. The first lot arrives around 10am, just in time to be bought and prepared for lunch. The second catch appears around 4pm, ready for the evening meal.

There are various specialist fish and seafood restaurants, such as Chez Sam (*see p186*) and Le Patio (*see p189*), and most other places will have fish on the menu. But nowhere is the produce fresher or cheaper than at the fish stalls, clustered in an L-shape on the Medina side of the fish market.

OK, there are few trimmings. But with open-air tables overlooking the square, and prices ranging from 10dh for a plate of sardines to 400dh for a kilo of 'spiny lobster', there's also not much to bemoan. It's the best budget lunch option in town.

The catch varies by season. January to March is the time for sea urchins and shrimp. The sardines are at their best in July and August. Shark, sole and turbot are good all year round, and there's also a lot of red snapper. You can sample a selection for 60dh.

Choose what you want from the produce on display, and it will be sprinkled with salt, grilled over charcoal, and served on a plastic plate with a slice of lemon, salad, soft drink and a chunk of baguette. These are included in the fixed prices, displayed on a notice board as you approach the stalls. Chips are extra, and you'll have to wait while they run off to get them from one of the cafés on the square.

Stall-owners can get a little hassly when trying to usher you into their joint, but this shouldn't deter you from comparing what's on offer before choosing where to sit. We favour Ali's stall at No.33, Les Bretons du Sud (067 19 42 34), but they're all pretty much the same, and open from around 11am to 4pm daily.

Elizir

1 rue de Agadir (024 47 21 03). Open noon-3pm, 7.30pm-1am daily. £££. Moroccan-Mediterranean.

Elizir opened back in 2006 with a Moroccan-Mediterranean menu and an atmosphere of idiosyncratic cool; it quickly became one of the best restaurants in town. Young owner Rharbaoui Abdellatif, who lived in Italy for a few years, still tinkers keenly with the restaurant's stylish interior, where a few traditional elements set off an impressive retro-futurist collection of 1960s plastic furniture and fittings in orange and white – all of them sourced in Moroccan flea markets. Meanwhile, he's serving a menu that veers from a camel tagine to home-made pasta via organic chicken and the catch of the day. In winter, ask for a table in the room with the open fire; in warmer months, go for the sheltered roof terrace. The louche, jazzy playlist sounds good wherever you're sitting.

"The venue is an old house with a roofed-over courtyard, dark red palette, and fabrics hanging to create a tented effect."

Fanatic

Boulevard Mohamed V (024 47 50 08). Open 8am-11pm daily. £££. Seafood.

This seafront seafood restaurant opened by what was otherwise a surfer operation is a surprisingly formal place offering a cheaper beachside lunch than the nearby Côté Plage (*see above*). The kitchen is competent if unimaginative, but you can enjoy a drink with your *loup de mer* on the terrace and there are plenty of inside tables if it's too windy for al fresco dining.

Ferdaouss

27 rue Abdessalam Lebadi (024 47 36 55). Open 12.30-2.30pm, 6.30 10.30pm Tue Sun. ££. Moroccan.

Ferdaouss is a cute and cosy place where traditional Moroccan food is served with an imaginative twist at prices so reasonable that you usually need to book a couple of days in advance. It's quite a way down an alley off rue Sidi Mohamed ben Abdellah in the central Medina, from which it is signposted.

Gelateria Dolce Freddo

25 place Moulay Hassan (063 57 19 28). Open 7.30am-10pm daily. ££. Café.

A prime location facing across the open part of the town's main square is one reason why this is the most fashionable of the central cafés; good Italian coffee is another. A selection of garish ice-cream adds colour to the proceedings and helps keep outdoor tables full.

Le Patio

28 bis rue Moulay Rachid (024 47 41 66). Open tapas 5.30 11pm, dinner 6.30 11pm Tue Sun. £££. French-Moroccan.

Fish dishes are the highlight of a French-Moroccan menu, presented on a blackboard that can be hard to read in the dingy, candlelit interior. The venue is an old house with a roofed-over courtyard, dark red palette, and fabrics hanging to create a tented effect. Tables are cramped, though the room is spacious; music so insipid you almost don't notice it adds little to a rather bland atmosphere. That said, it's a good place to sample a selection from the day's catch, and there's a beautiful bar where you can order from a small but respectable tapas selection (around 35dh per item).

Silvestro

70 rue Derb Laâlouj (024 47 35 55). Open 11.30am-3pm, 6.30-11pm daily. ££. Italian.

Silvestro is a cool and unpretentious first-floor Italian restaurant. Run by Italians, the place feels authentic, with an open kitchen, an espresso machine and a basic but sensible menu of antipasta, pasta and pizza. The food's very well prepared and served with a smile. Accompany it with something from the short but reassuring list of Italian wines.

Taros

Place Moulay Hassan (024 47 64 07/www.taroscafe. com). Open 11am-4pm, 6pm-midnight Mon-Sat. £££. Bar/international.

Perched above the town's main square on a corner overlooking the sea, Taros is a multi-purpose venue with a prime location. It has a first-floor salon and library, where you can drink tea and read quietly during the afternoons or have a beer and listen to live music in the evenings (from Thursday to Saturday nights). Then there's a cocktail bar on the fine roof terrace (serving Mojitos, Margaritas, Caipirinhas and the like) with tables and bar stools. Food is served in either area, and the menu includes a modest vegetarian selection, complemented by the best steaks in town. An art gallery and small shop round off this much-loved institution.

Le Trou

Rue Mohammed El Ayachi (no phone). Open 11am-11.30pm daily. £. Bar.

At the cul-de-sac opposite and beyond the restaurant El-Yacoute, the entrance to 'the hole' is obvious at night, with a small barrow selling cigarettes and snacks outside, and a beery glow emanating from within. It's a disreputable sort of place, full of fishermen in *djellabas* drinking bottles of Stork beer, with a drunken hubbub and the occasional row. Tourists are tolerated rather than welcomed.

Shop

Essaouira has a lively artesanal and trading culture radiating out from the souks at the centre of the Medina to the shops selling knick-knacks and craft items on and around the avenue de l'Istiqlal and place Moulay Hassan. It's renowned for the quality of its cabinet-making, marquetry and woodworking – particularly in thuya wood – and various workshops can be visited under the ramparts. The jewellers' souk behind the Grand Mosque is also worth a look.

Afalkay Art
9 place Moulay Hassan (024 47 60 89). Open 9am-8pm daily.
This is the one-stop shop for all your Essaouiran woodwork needs. Searching the wood workshops under the ramparts might turn up the odd different item, but pretty much anything they can make out of fragrant thuja wood – from tiny inlaid boxes to great big treasure chests, toy camels to bathroom cabinets – can be found somewhere in this big barn of a place opposite the cafés of place Moulay Hassan. Staff speak English and are used to shipping larger items.

Azurrette
12 rue Malek ben Morhal (066 45 44 12). Open 9.30am-8pm daily.
At some remove from the hassle and hustle of the spice souk, this traditional Moroccan pharmacy has the largest herb and spice selection in the Medina and also offers perfumes, pigments, remedies, incense and essential oils. The big, cool space is lined with shelves of common condiments, exotic ingredients, mysterious herbs and colourful powders, all in glass jars or baskets. English is spoken by amiable young owner Ahmed, who's happy to explain what's what.

> # "It offers silver jewellery, select ceramics, ancient wooden doors, vintage kaftans, treasure chests and old portraits of King Mohamed V."

Bazaar Mehdi
5 rue de la Skala (024 47 59 81). Open 9am-8pm daily.
As good a place as any to buy a Moroccan carpet. It's no match for the big dealers of Marrakech, but there are literally heaps of rugs, with floorspace to lay them out and nimble helpers to unfurl them. The owner, Mustapha, is a good sort, speaks excellent English, and will provide detailed biographies of each carpet. Don't expect any bargains, though. If nothing here takes your fancy, there are other carpet shops further up rue de la Skala.

Chez Aicha
116 place aux Grains (024 47 43 35). Open 9am-8pm daily.
Moroccan ceramics can be much of a muchness – and much Essaouiran pottery is poorly glazed and chips easily. Aicha

Hemmou's stock is a cut above. It's mostly Berber pottery, made near Marrakech. Some of the designs are a bit fussy, but others are clean-lined in warm, solid colours. There's also a bit of glassware and argan oil in gift bottles.

Chez Boujmaa
1 avenue Allal Ben Abdellah (024 47 56 58). Open 8am-midnight daily.
Expats call this small, central grocery 'Fortnum & Mason's'. That's a bit of a stretch, but Chez Boujmaa is the place to find English teas and biscuits, plus a range of Italian pasta and parma ham, French cheeses and tinned haricots. At the basic deli counter they'll make up a sandwich to your specifications.

Galerie Aida
2 rue de la Skala (024 47 62 90). Open 10am-1pm, 3-8pm daily.
A big place filled to bursting with an intriguing selection of old jewellery, paintings, glassware, crockery and other Moroccan antiques, plus a small but good (and pricey) selection of secondhand books.

Galerie Damgaard
Avenue Oqba Ibn Nafiaa (024 78 44 46). Open 9am-1pm, 3-7pm daily.
Danish expat Frédéric Damgaard opened Essaouira's only serious commercial gallery in 1988 and has helped to nurture and develop the work of around 20 local artists, now collectively known as the 'Essaouira school'. The work is bright and colourful, almost hallucinogenic, heavy with folk symbolism and pointillist techniques. Gnawa artist Mohammed Tabal is the star: his 'paintings of ideas' are inspired by the gnawa trance universe of colour-coded spirits. We also like the paint-splattered wooden furniture sculptures of Saïd Ouarzaz and the dreamlike canvases of Abdelkader Bentajar. Damgaard himself has now retired, and the gallery retains his name under new ownership.

Galerie Jama
22 rue Ibn Rochd (024 78 58 97/galeriejama@ hotmail.fr). Open 9am-8pm daily. Open 9am-noon, 1-9pm daily.
The brother of Mustapha from Bazaar Mehdi offers an interesting and nicely displayed selection of antiques and old pieces – silver jewellery, select ceramics, ancient wooden doors, vintage kaftans, treasure chests and old portraits of King Mohamed V.

Hassan Fakir
181 Souk Laghzel (070 23 00 17). Open 9am-8pm daily.
Second on the right among the row of babouche stalls as you turn into the fish and spice souk from rue El-Fachtaly, Hassan sells the usual Moroccan slippers and sandals and speaks decent English.

Jack's Kiosk
1 place Moulay Hassan (024 47 55 38). Open 9.30am-10.30pm daily.

Souks.

Villa Maroc.

In a key location on the square, Jack's is the place to find the previous day's international newspapers and other foreign periodicals, plus a small selection of new and second-hand English, French, German and Spanish books – mostly guides and bestsellers. Jack also rents sea-view apartments by the ramparts.

Kifkif

204 place du Marché aux Grains (061 08 20 41/ www.kifkifbystef.com). Open 10am-noon, 4-8pm Mon-Sat.
This sister shop to the Kifkif in Marrakech sells the same eclectic assortment of colourful bags and purses, along with nice notebooks, electric lamps, jewellery and lots of things for children.

Mogador Music

52 avenue de l'Istiqlal (070 72 57 79). Open 10am-noon, 4-8pm Mon-Sat.
Gnawa, arabo-andalucian, grika, bellydance, rai, desert bles – Mogador Music is well stocked with all varieties of North African and West Saharan music on CD and cassette. If you can't find it here you probably won't find it anywhere: owners Youssef and Azza know their stuff and distribute to all the other music shops.

Ouchen Mohammed

4 rue El Attarine (024 47 68 61). Open 9am-9pm daily. No credit cards.
On a corner by the Riad Al Madina, Ouchen Mohamed is our favourite of the various leatherwork shops. It's good for pouffes, bags and belts, but there's also a big slipper selection and a few non-leather items, such as boxes, mirrors and old musical instruments.

Trésor

57 avenue de l'Istiqlal (no phone). Open 9am-8.30pm daily.
On the Medina's main avenue, jeweller Khalid Hasnaoui speaks good English and offers a more discerning selection than that found in the nearby jewellers' souk. His stock is a mixture of Berber, Arab, Tuareg and other pieces – some of it old, some new, and some new but using old designs. Look out for work in the local filigree style, made by Essaouiran Jews.

Stay

Beau Rivage

14 place Moulay Hassan (024 47 59 25/ www.essaouiranet.com/beaurivage). £
The pick of the inexpensive options, Beau Rivage has been operating above the Café Opera on the Medina's main square since 1939 – and was renovated in 2002. There are 15 bedrooms and six suites. All are clean, colourful and bright and have toilets and showers en suite. Rooms on the second floor also have balconies overlooking the square. The location can be noisy but is as central as it gets; though still offering big views from the roof terrace, it is cosier and more sheltered than those places overlooking the ramparts. Breakfast is

extra, but it's just as easy to nip downstairs for croissants from Chez Driss and a coffee at one of the tables on the square.

Casa Lila

94 rue Med El-Qorry (024 47 55 45/www.casalila-riad.com). ££.
Half-way between the souks and Bab Marrakech, this tasteful, unfussy *maison d'hote* has eight rooms and suites plus one two-bedroom apartment ranged around the usual central courtyard. Most of the rooms come equipped with baths (three just have showers) and all except the apartment boast open fires. Common areas include a salon off the courtyard and a rambling roof terrace. It's all nicely decorated in bold pinks and purples with lots of grey tadelakt in the bathrooms, complemented by a few well-chosen knick-knacks.

Dar Adul

Rue Touahen 63 (024 47 3910/mobile 071 52 02 21/ www.dar-adul.com). ££.
Houses on the ocean side of the Medina need a lot of maintenance if they're not to fall into decline and the five bedrooms of this unpretentious French-owned former notary's house have been renovated to good effect. The owners have also added – the first in Essaouira – a skylight to close off the atrium in inclement conditions. The shared sitting room with open fire is comfortable and there are excellent views from the roof terrace, where breakfast is served when it's not too windy.

Dar Al Bahar

1 rue Touahen (024 47 68 31/ www.daralbahar.com). ££.
The 'House by the Sea' is right on the northern ramparts, with waves crashing on the rocks below – there's no place in town quite as close to the ocean. The French-Dutch couple who own the place have decorated their nine rooms in clean, bold colours, bright fabrics and local naïve art. Not all of them have sea views and they're not the biggest lodgings in town, but even the non-view ones are nice enough and more economically priced. The big roof terrace affords breakfast with a tang of sea spray.

Dar Beida/Dar Emma

067 96 53 86 in Morocco/07768 352190 in UK/ www.castlesinthesand.com.
For something a bit special, consider the 'White House'. Deep in a corner of the Medina, a twist or two off the tourist trail, this is a wonderful 200-year-old house owned by English partners Emma Wilson and Graham Carter. They've renovated and furnished with playful good taste, mixing Moroccan materials and flea-market finds with imported antiques and a retro vibe. The result manages to be both idiosyncratically stylish and unpretentiously comfortable. It can sleep up to four couples, has two bathrooms, two roof terraces, a lounge, a small library, open fires and a well-equipped kitchen and comes with two amiable cats. In addition, Emma Wilson also runs the less luxurious and slightly smaller Dar Emma. This compact 19th-century house in an alley off rue Derb Laâlouj has a kitchen, two double bedrooms and a roof terrace.

Dar Loulema

2 rue Souss (024 47 53 46/mobile 061 24 76 61/ www.darloulema.com). ££.

A well-run place at the Kasbah end of the Medina, just behind the Taros café (*see p189*), which the terrace overlooks. It's a nice old house, more generously proportioned than many of its competitors. There are eight rooms, mostly named, and vaguely themed, after Moroccan cities, so 'Essaouira' is blue and white and 'Marrakech' is pink. Breakfast can be served in your room, on the terrace, in the patio, by the central fountain, in one of the living rooms with open fires – just about anywhere, really.

Dar L'Oussia

4 rue Mohammed ben Messaoud, Bab Sbaa (024 78 37 56/www.dar-loussia.net). ££.

More of a hotel than a *maison d'hote*, this place near the Bab Sbaâ still consists of a house with rooms ranged around a central courtyard. It's just a very big house with a very grand courtyard, and 24 rooms in its upper reaches. Well fitted and colourfully decorated, these come in three categories. Standard rooms are a decent 25 square metres with king-size beds and big bathrooms. 'Deluxe' rooms are 35 square metres with bigger beds and bigger bathrooms. And 'junior suites' are a whopping 50 square metres with enormous beds and big bathrooms. To top it all there's a vast roof terrace, but the architectural highlight is the spectacular carved archway in the courtyard by the entrance. Beyond it there's a vaulted dining-room where the menu is prepared by a former chef from Taros.

Dar Mimosas

Route d'Agadir km1 (024 47 59 34/www.dar-mimosas.com). ££££.

On the right-hand side of the Agadir road about a kilometre after it forks away from the route back to Marrakech, this is a walled compound of peace and luxury around the bay from Essaouira proper. Four suites and four villas are scattered in beautiful Italianate gardens. Two of the suites have their own gardens; the other two have terraces with views of the sea – 15 minutes' walk away across scrubby dunes. The villas have one or two bedrooms, sitting-rooms, well-equipped kitchens, two bathrooms each and walled gardens with fountains. All of the lodgings have log fires. You need never see another guest if you don't feel sociable, but it would be a shame to miss out on the gorgeous swimming pool, tiled in blue and white. The main house, coloured a brilliant terracotta, has dining rooms, TV room, a terrace, a well-stocked bar and the apartment of Morocco-born French owner Philippe Cachet. Service is nicely pitched between attentive and discreet and the food is excellent – staff bake their own bread for breakfast and serve honey from their own hives. Ridley Scott, Orlando Bloom, the Pet Shop Boys and King Mohamed VI have been among the guests.

L'Heure Bleue

2 rue Ibn Batouta, Bab Marrakech (024 78 34 34/ www.heure-bleue.com). ££££.

This upmarket renovation of what was once a private mansion has 16 rooms and 19 suites around a spacious, leafy courtyard. It also has the Medina's only lift ascending to the Medina's only rooftop pool. The standard rooms (on the first floor) are spacious and African-themed – black marble, dark wood, zebra-patterned upholstery. Suites on the second floor, which get more light and seem better value, also come in Portuguese (blue and white), British colonial (19th-century engravings) and 'Eastern' (gold and burgundy) flavours. The British colonial theme – the 'clubroom' bar has big armchairs and mounted animal heads – seems a touch daft. There's also a DVD screening room, a beautiful hammam in black *tadelakt*, and a decent restaurant.

Hotel Smara

26 bis, rue de la Skala (024 47 56 55). £.

Upstairs from Les Alizés Mogador are simple rooms with bed, sink and table; the better ones overlook the ramparts and ocean. Bathrooms and toilets are shared. Breakfast is extra. It's all basic and the staff are a bit brusque, but you can't argue with some of the lowest room rates in town. The owner also has apartments in the Medina.

Hotel Souiri

37 rue Lattarine (024 47 53 39/www.hotel souiri.com). £.

The budget option when the Beau Rivage or Hotel Smara are full has a central location but no sea views. There are 39 cool and colourful rooms, of which 24 have bathrooms en suite. Nice stained glass throughout.

La Maison des Artistes

19 rue Derb Laâlouj (024 47 57 99/mobile 062 60 54 38/www.lamaisondesartistes.com). ££.

A characterful French-run guesthouse that makes the most of its oceanfront location and the slightly eccentric taste of its original owners. It has six comfortable rooms, three of them overlooking the sea, three facing on to the patio, all furnished differently and some boasting intriguingly odd pieces. The suite is splendid, with the ocean on three sides and, lording over all, the roof terrace is like the bridge of a ship. It's pretty exposed, however, and can get a bit rattly in high winds. La Maison seems to be a home from home for an assortment of young and vaguely arty French folks, and whether you'll like it here depends greatly on whether you get on with the crowd. Manager Cyril is also proud of his 'Judeo-Berber' kitchen and lunch or dinner can be served on the terrace with the ocean view.

Madada

5 rue Youssef El Fassi (024 47 55 12/ www.madada.com). ££.

At the south-west corner of the Medina, this is a smart and stylish six-room affair with accents that are more Parisian than Souiri. The four rooms on the first floor have their own crenellated terraces overlooking the town and the port, though these are separated from each other only by wrought iron fences so there's not a lot of privacy. Two of the rooms are on the roof, where breakfast is also served, and there's a panoramic view of the whole bay from a small upper level.

Castles made of sand

'Welcome to the village of Jimi Hendrix!' So runs the patter of shoeshine boys and dope dealers. 'Hendrix stayed here!' is the proud claim of at least two hotels. In nearby Diabat, where Jimi supposedly spent time with the hippy community, there is a Café Hendrix and a Hotel Hendrix, both overlooking the decidedly unrocking new golf resort.

Orson Welles may have a square named after him, but Hendrix is Essaouira's claim to street cred. The stories pour forth. Jimi jammed with the gnawa! He tried to buy one of the islands! He met with Timothy Leary! The most enduring tale is that he was inspired to write 'Castles Made of Sand' (which melt into the sea, eventually) by the ruins of the Borj El-Berod.

It seems almost plausible. The Borj El-Berod is a small, ruined fort at the ocean's edge, quite clearly melting into the sea. But the story has one small snag. 'Castles Made of Sand' appeared on the *Axis: Bold as Love* album, released on 1 December 1967. And Jimi didn't visit Morocco until July 1969.

Just ten days long, it was the only vacation Hendrix ever took. Stressed out after the break-up of the Jimi Hendrix Experience, moving from London to New York, getting busted by the Mounties in Toronto, and

rehearsing a new band, Jimi accepted his friend Deering Howe's suggestion that they go to Morocco, and ran off in defiance of his management. The pair flew to Casablanca in late July, where they met up with two Moroccans they knew from New York, Stella Douglas and Colette Mimram.

They stayed at the Casablanca Meridien, the Mamounia in Marrakech and the Hotel des Iles in Essaouira, travelling by limo and doing tourist things – eating out, smoking kif, shopping for clothes. Far from jamming with local musicians, Hendrix enjoyed his anonymity and kept a low profile. He had a spooky fortune-teller experience, conducted a romance with Colette Mimram, and spent an evening in Essaouira with a couple of actors from the Living Theater. But he didn't meet Timothy Leary, bought no islands, probably didn't visit Diabat, certainly didn't stay at the Riad Al Madina, and likely never even saw the Borj El-Berod.

It's a lot of myth from a short visit, but that's what you get from a good rock legend. By 6 August Hendrix was on his way back to New York, stopping off in Paris to get up closed and personal with Brigitte Bardot. Twelve days later he was playing Woodstock.

Top: Dar Beida.
Bottom: Elizir.

Ocean Vagabond Guest House
4 boulevard Lalla Aicha (024 47 92 22/
www.oceanvagabond.com). ££.
In a modern villa on the seafront, just a short walk outside the old city walls, Ocean Vagabond boasts a few features alien to converted Medina houses, such as a garden and a pool. Opened by the crew from the Ocean Vagabond café and surf station, it's a breath of fresh air in all senses. Common areas are cool, bright, stylish and simple. The 14 rooms are themed ('Bali' is vaguely Indonesian, 'Geisha' vaguely Japanese, and so on). Try to get one of the four ('Dogon', 'Felluca', 'Pondichéry' and 'Inca') that have balconies with an ocean view (two others have balconies with a view of the Medina – and the post office). A garden bungalow is the place for pampering: it houses a hammam and rooms for massage, beauty treatments and a hairdresser.

Riad Al Madina
9 rue Attarine (024 47 59 07/www.riadalmadina.com). ££.
Once the location of the Hippy Café, this is now a rather lackadaisical mid price hotel that trades on the myth that Jimi Hendrix once stayed here. The beautiful courtyard is one of the nicest breakfast spots in town, but the rooms that overlook it, though colourfully decorated, tend to be poky, dark. The owners have also bought the house next door and added a hammam and 30 new rooms to make a total of 54.

Ryad Watier
16 rue Ceuta (024 47 62 04/www.ryad-watier-
maroc.com). ££.

The building was formerly a school, which means a more rambling, less predictable arrangement than in the usual converted Medina house. There are seven double rooms and three suites with two bedrooms, all with small writing desks (a rarity in Essaouira) and all en suite, but none with baths, only showers. There's also a big dining-room, a terrace on what used to be the playground, a hammam and a massage room, a pair of roof terraces, and a pretty decent library by Moroccan riad standards. Rooms and common areas are decorated with paintings and old film posters from the idiosyncratic collection of French owner Jean Gabriel, for whom the whole thing is obviously a labour of love. Every picture tells a story which he'll cheerfully relate.

Villa Maroc
10 rue Abdellah ben Yassine (024 47 61 47/www.villa-
maroc.com). ££.
The first boutique hotel in Morocco when it opened in 1990, Villa Maroc is now a mature establishment. It's nicely located just inside the walls of the Kasbah quarter, its roof terraces overlooking the square and the fishing port. Twenty rooms and suites are nicely furnished and arranged around a warren of open terraces, narrow staircases and small, secluded spaces – the result of knocking together four old merchants' houses. No two rooms are alike; some are a bit cramped and gloomy, and the suites are built around a central patio, so you can hear what's happening on the next floor. The 'oriental spa' has a beautiful small hammam for individuals or pairs, and offers a variety of massage and beauty treatments – also open to non-residents.

Factfile

When to go
High winds from May to August are the trade-off for a break from the searing temperatures of the Moroccan interior, but a boon for windsurfers. When they subside in September, the weather is just about perfect.

Getting there
Royal Air Maroc (www.royalairmaroc.com) runs five flights a week from Paris and a further five from Casablanca into the tiny Aéroport de Mogador (024 47 67 09), 15 kilometres south of town on the route d'Agadir.

Essaouira is three hours by bus from Marrakech. Timed to connect with the Casablanca train, buses depart from the Supratours terminal (024 43 55 25) near Marrakech train station four times a day and arrive at the south side of the big square outside Essaouira's Bab Marrakech, where tickets are sold at a kiosk (024 47 53 17) next to the Telecom building. Buses from other destinations arrive at the *gare routière* (024 78 47 64) about 400 metres north of the Medina.

Shared *grands taxis* from Marrakech (80dh per person) leave from Bab Doukkala. In the other direction, they leave from outside Essaouira's gare routière. You can also hire your own taxi for around 700dh.

Getting around
The only way to get around the Medina is on foot. *Petits taxis* can whisk you round the walls from one gate to another, or to destinations south along the ocean front.

Tourist information
There's a tourist information office near Bab Sbaâ (10 rue du Caire, 024 78 35 32, www.tourisme.gov.ma, open 9am-noon, 2-4.30pm Mon-Fri) but it's not a great deal of use. Your hotel will likely be of more help.

Internet
Many hotels now have Wi-Fi. If yours doesn't, Espace Internet Café (5 avenue de l'Istiqlal, 024 47 50 65) is open 24 hours daily.

Clockwise from top:
El-Jadida beach (2);
Hôtel de Provence;
Cité Portugaise, El-Jadida;
Restaurant Tchikito (2).

El-Jadida, Oualidia & Azemmour

The stretch of azure Atlantic, butterscotch beaches and rugged caramel cliffs between Casablanca and Safi is a landscape of bright colours, big spaces and a distinctive light. The coast road passes mile after mile of deserted beaches, the occasional tiny village the only sign of human habitation. It's a haven for wildlife, birdlife, surfers and windsurfers.

Punctuating the wilderness are some unique gems of towns. Western Morocco throws the added ingredient of Portuguese occupation into the heady mixture that is its past – and present. The 16th-century Portuguese Medina of El-Jadida is now a UNESCO World Heritage Site; outside the Medina, El-Jadida is a popular modern resort town. In Oualidia a ruined Saadian kasbah stands sentinel over the ethereal beauty of a crescent-shaped lagoon, cut off from the Atlantic waves by a breakwater; but this little town is probably most famous for its oysters, which you can sample straight from the water, with a slice of sun-kissed lemon and a glass of cold white wine. The whitewashed artists' enclave of Azemmour, meanwhile, is now a backwater on the edge of the Oum Errebia river, but at one time it was a busy and strategic Portuguese port. In its Medina you can go from 16th-century Portuguese architecture to a Mondrian-inspired mural to a Moorish minaret in the space of a few turns.

Explore

AZEMMOUR

The highlight of Azzemour, a tidy town just 30 minutes from El-Jadida on the Oum Errebia river, is the historic Medina, built by the Portuguese, who conquered the area in 1513. From the place du Souk, a 16th-century gate opens on to the largely ruined Kasbah and the town's ramparts. The local *gardien* will lead you around; if he isn't there, just ask one of the locals to call him.

From the Medina entrance near the Hotel Riad Azama you can take a stroll around little hills and slopes with whitewashed Portuguese-style houses, where each door is a different and striking colour and shape. It's a charming, lived-in Medina, and – for now – visited by few tourists. Look one way and you'll see women baking bread in traditional kilns. Look the other and you'll find a man working a loom to make Azzemour's renowned embroidery. Children play ball in shadowy alcoves. Old ladies sit in circles on stone floors.

Past the Jewish Mellah, at the northern end of the Medina, some steps lead down to a modern promenade along the river. Quite a few of the 18th-century buildings nearby have been purchased by foreigners for renovation. The arrival of these Europeans, added to the guests from the two existing boutique hotels, will no doubt change the vibe of this little gem of a town for good.

PLAGE HAOUZIA

This dazzling 15-kilometre beach stretches from Azzemour to El-Jadida. From September to June it is virtually empty and a paradise for surfers, windsurfers and horse-riders. Two dramatic shipwrecked oil rigs punctuate the shoreline. A Sofitel resort complex and the El-Jadida Royal Golf course are the two most ambitious signs of development so far, but plans are supposedly underway to begin building a large resort in 2010.

EL-JADIDA

Half a mile back from the ocean, Hollywood-style holiday homes line palm-flanked residential streets, but the real action in El-Jadida happens down by the sea, which borders the old Medina and its ramparts – the beach fronting Parc Mohammed V is awash with ice-cream parlours and pizza joints galore.

El-Jadida, previously known as Mazagan, was seized in 1502 and occupied by the Portuguese until 1769. After being settled by Sultan Abdel-Rahman in the 19th century the town was renamed 'El-Jadida' ('The New'). In 2004 the old Medina (Cité Portugaise) was made a UNESCO World Heritage Site due to its status as an 'outstanding example of the interchange of

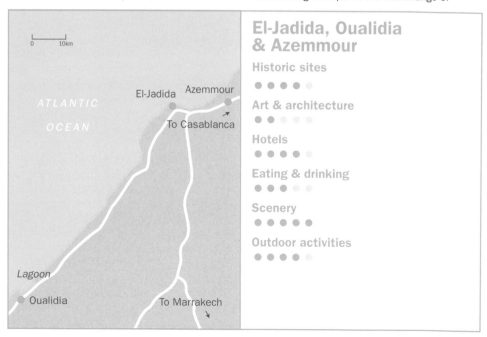

El-Jadida, Oualidia & Azemmour

Historic sites
● ● ● ● ●

Art & architecture
● ● ● ● ● ●

Hotels
● ● ● ● ●

Eating & drinking
● ● ● ● ●

Scenery
● ● ● ● ●

Outdoor activities
● ● ● ● ●

influences between European and Moroccan cultures'. Outside the fortress walls, the pleasant streets are set up for the local tourist influx from July to September. Beach balls, DVDs, plastic spades and swimwear dangle from open shop fronts. However, inside the Cité Portugaise, life steps back in time.

From the entrance to the Church of the Assumption, now used as a cultural centre, a path leads down to a small strip of tourist shops across from the **Portuguese Cistern** (rue Carreira, open 9am-1pm, 3-6.30pm daily). Built in 1541 to hold water for the town, the cistern was discovered by a Jewish merchant in 1917 when he knocked down a wall to make his house bigger. The eerie subterranean chamber contains 23 gothic columns and a thin layer of water that reflects a circular shaft of light from the ceiling. The cistern was used to dramatic effect in Orson Welles' film of *Othello* in 1954.

As you walk through the residential streets, with wrought iron details and Dickensian street lamps used as nesting places by housemartins, the perfect curves of the ramparts become visible. The ramparts themselves are accessible from the **Bab El-Bahr** (Sea Gate), the original port gate where ships unloaded their cargo, at the end of rue Carreira. It is possible to walk all the way around them (and also to go on to the bastions). From here, the beach can be glimpsed beyond the port.

SIDI BOUZID

Just 30 minutes south of El-Jadida, with a much cleaner and less crowded stretch of ocean, Sidi Bouzid is known by locals as the 'Ibiza of El-Jadida', though it lacks the clubs. Life in this tiny town is centred along the crescent-shaped coastline with its vast promenade and residential stretch of suburban American-style 1950s Futurist houses; cookie-cutter homes in Easter egg colours of pistachio, pale pink and baby blue border the windy Atlantic. In the mid-summer months people come to watch the sunset and surfers take advantage of consistent windswells and groundswells, before darkness falls and everyone retires to their bungalows for seafood and some sleep.

A few kilometres further on, the tiny village of **Moulay Abdallah** is surrounded by the ruined walls of a 12th-century fort. Also within the walls is a *zaouia* (religious school) complex. There's not a lot to see here most of the year, but an important *moussem* is held in August, attracting thousands of pilgrims and known for its parades and demonstrations of horsemanship.

OUALIDIA

Oualidia is an attractive little port, and its beauty is enhanced by the 11-kilometre inland lagoon that forms a focal point for villagers, German camper vans, French surfers and a bohemian tourist industry distinctly more tranquil and nature oriented than El Jadida.

Oualidia was the childhood holiday destination of King Mohammed V (1909-61) and a redundant **Royal Palace** now sits empty. This doesn't mean that Oualidia's popularity has diminished, though, and the resort remains dear to the hearts of many Moroccans. Its other striking construction is the crumbling and atmospheric **kasbah**, built in the 17th century by the Saadian Sultan El-Oualid, after whom the town is named, overlooking the lagoon.

A lot of the accommodation options sit up on a hillside, with grand views of the pristine lagoon. Popular holiday pastimes include barbecuing seafood on the beach, tipping a fisherman to take you out on his boat or hiring a quad bike from one of the many stands and zipping across the sand dunes.

The coastal wetlands, cliffs and saltpans of Oualidia and the surrounding coast (particularly **Cap Beddouza**, 32 kilometres south of Oualidia) make it a birdwatcher's paradise, with species including avocets, pink flamingoes, storks, house martins, spits, swallows and egrets. But despite the ethereal beauty of its lagoon, Oualidia's main pull is arguably its oyster farms. The first farm opened in 1957, and harvests 200 tonnes a year for sale throughout Morocco and export to Japan. Stop by Ostrea restaurant (*see p202*) at the entrance to town from El-Jadida for premium oysters and chilled wine.

South of Oualidia, on the way to Safi, the landscape becomes more dramatic, with high cliffs separating road from shore, and a series of completely deserted beaches, of which Cap Beddouza is one of the finest.

Eat

Ali Baba
El-Jadida *Route de Casablanca (023 34 16 22). Open noon-2.30pm, 7.30-11pm daily. £££. French.*
When you feel like a special evening out in El-Jadida, Ali Baba is the upmarket pick, with crisp white tablecloths, candles and scattered rose petals, dramatic ocean views and high-quality, traditional French fare on offer. Another definite bonus is the well-stocked cellar with French and Moroccan wines.

La Broche
El-Jadida *Place El Hansali 46 (no phone). Open noon-11pm daily. £. Café-restaurant.*
This modest café-restaurant has a wide selection of dishes – bountiful salads, fish and meat tagines, pasta, calamare, couscous and more – and portions are large. A blackboard listing daily specials hangs above the few small tables set out on the wide pavement.

El-Khaima

El-Jadida *Avenue des Nations Unies (023 37 21 74).*
Open 11.30am-3pm, 7pm-midnight daily. ££. Bar-restaurant.
A five-minute drive from the main beach, El-Khaima is perhaps the only female-friendly bar in El-Jadida. Patronised mostly by expats and foreign tourists, the restaurant area upstairs serves the usual array of burgers, pizzas and seafood dishes, while a casual downstairs bar gets going around 10pm with hip hop, Arabic tunes and laser lights.

Ostrea

Oualidia *Parc à Huitres no.007 (023 36 64 51).*
Open noon-10pm daily. £££. Seafood.
You don't need to work for MI6 to find the 007 Oyster Park and adjoining restaurant, Ostrea. Here you can sit on the terrace, right on the lagoon, and enjoy a glass of chilled rosé and a plate of oysters on ice – oyster farmers work a few metres away carrying crates straight from the lagoon. As well as oysters, the restaurant serves up salads, grilled and fried seafood dishes and pasta, and has a good selection of French and Moroccan wines to choose from. The views over the water are magnificent.

Le Requin Bleu

Sidi Bouzid *Centre balnéaire (023 348 067/*
www.requinbleu.com). Open noon-11.45pm daily.
££. French.
This two-storey restaurant has an outdoor terrace with ocean views and an inside area with a bar. A TV shows football or music videos while a bow-tied waiter serves delicate salads, poached sardines, garlic prawns and perfectly cooked steaks. Le Requin Bleu is regarded by many as the best restaurant in Sidi Bouzid, and the French-inspired food is good value.

Restaurant Tchikito

El-Jadida *Rue Mohammed Smiha (no phone).*
Open noon-10pm daily. £. Seafood.
If you like fish and you like it fried you're in business. Tucked away down a small lane beside the market, this eaterie has a buzz not found in any other seafood restaurant in El-Jadida. Religious texts in Arabic calligraphy, some in the shape of a fish, and a photo of the former king fishing, have pride of place above the cooking area. This is a no-fuss lunch spot where plates of delicate, mixed fried seafood, a bowl of harira-based dipping sauce and a hunk of bread are served without much ado on linoleum tables. Choices are extremely limited so if you don't like fish and you don't like it fried, head elsewhere.

Snack Costeau

El-Jadida *Avenue Suisse, près de la Cité Portugaise 6*
(067 01 13 20). Open 11am-10pm daily. £. Seafood.
Conveniently located across from the Medina and with outdoor seating, this sparkling canteen makes things easy with photographs of its dishes on the outside – mainly fried seafood with salad options and some skewered meat selections. Meals are well-prepared, fresh and the portions are large. Honour a bad pun and dive in.

Stay

Hotel Beach View

Oualidia *Avenue Hassan II 301 (023 36 60 10/*
www.beachviewoualidia.com). ££.
This large hotel is a good bet for mid-range accommodation in a town with few options between camping out and camping it up at the luxurious La Sultana. Situated on top of a hill and decorated with white tiled floors and blue and yellow chaises longues, Hotel Beach View has duplex suites for families with direct access to the pool, single room suites and single rooms with terraces overlooking the lagoon. The spa comprises a hammam and sauna, plus massage and beauty treatments. Unlike the hotel, the downstairs Jet Set nightclub doesn't quite live up to its name.

Hôtel Florence

Sidi Bouzid *Centre Sidi Bouzid, Lotissement Sammra*
BP57 (023 34 85 55). ££.
Five kilometres from El-Jadida and a short walk to the sea, this well-managed, family-friendly hotel has 11 rooms, a large parking area and a good restaurant that serves steak, pizza, paella and more. There are quite a few hotels in the backstreets of Sidi Bouzid, but Hotel Florence is probably the best option for families.

Hôtel de Provence

El-Jadida *Avenue Mohammed Errafi 42 (023 34 23 47/*
www.gazal7.com). ££.
Built in 1922, with the framed sepia photographs to prove it, this barmy, charming inn, owned by an Englishman since 1986, is two parts English working men's club and one part 1920s Parisian *hôtel*. Bedrooms that sleep one, two or three people are basic and clean, if slightly worn out, while the public areas are decked out in rich colours. Breakfast is served outside, but the main highlight is a restaurant and nicely stocked bar that seems to be modelled on a London East End pub. Just don't expect a bar brawl. The hotel's security guard is one of Morocco's champion bodybuilders – or so he boasts – and will gladly flex his muscles on request.

Hôtel Royal

El-Jadida *Avenue Mohammed V 108 (023 34*
28 39). ££.
'Viva El-Jadida!' seems to be the vibe at this esteemed but slightly bizarre hotel with Moroccan mosaics, Las Vegas-inspired neon signs and outlandish stained glass windows. Rooms are oversized and very basic, connected by intricately decorated hallways. A large international restaurant and bar area in the back of the hotel becomes a local drinking den in the afternoon, beloved of middle-aged men who stack up the empty Casablanca beer bottles and dance for one another in the courtyard. Service is good and the hotel is conveniently located within walking distance of the Medina.

Ibis Moussafir

El-Jadida *Place Nour El-Kamar, Route de Casablanca*
(023 37 95 00/www.ibishotel.com). £££.

Clockwise from top left: Cité Portugaise, El-Jadida (2); Medina, Azemmour; Portuguese Cistern, El-Jadida; Medina, Azemmour; Cité Portugaise, El-Jadida.

Clockwise from top right:
Riad Azama (2);
La Sultana (2).

The only hotel right on the beach in El-Jadida, the Ibis makes up for lack of individuality with the perks of a chain hotel, including room service, an international restaurant, satellite TV, swimming pool and a disabled-adapted room. The hotel can arrange surfing trips, watersports in Oualidia and golf at the 18-hole El-Jadida Royal Golf course. El Morabitine Hotel, 200m back from the beach on Avenue Mohammed VI, has many of the same amenities without the beach views.

L'oum Errebia

Azemmour *Impasse Chtouka 25, Ancienne Medina (023 34 70 71/www.azemmour-hotel.com). £££.*
The recently built L'oum Errebia is more of a spacious home-cum-art gallery than a hotel. Rooms are hip, minimalist and plastered in beige *tadelakt*, a good foil to display the contemporary North African paintings and installations that cover much of the available space, many of which are for sale. The hotel sits right above the river and some of the rooms overlook it. If you can't nab one of these, make sure to spend sunset on the splendid roof terrace where you can also enjoy a set dinner. There are three family suites with direct access to the terrace.

Riad Azama

Azemmour *Impasse ben Tahar 17, Ancienne Medina (023 34 7516/www.riadazama.com). £££.*
Riad Azama is a guesthouse with the allure of an award-winning boutique hotel minus the cost. You would never guess from the simple exterior what lies inside this converted 18th-century building. Six uniquely designed suites fitted with Moorish arches, intricately carved walls and dark wood furniture look on to a central courtyard in shades of sage and terracotta with a hanging banana flower and free-flying parakeets. Run by Daniel, a former chef from Brittany, meals don't disappoint. The set menu features sumptuously presented tagines and other Moroccan dishes. Mornings can be spent reading on the rooftop daybeds that overlook the Medina and river. Staff can organise golf, surfing, horse riding and fishing day trips.

La Sultana

Oualidia *Parc à Huitres no.3 (023 36 65 95/ www.lasultanaoualidia.com). ££££.*
La Sultana Oualidia is in a different league to any other hotels in the area. It is a member of Small Luxury Hotels of the World, and this 21st-century honey-coloured stone fortress on the lagoon is designed for sybaritic living. Set down an unassuming dirt road, it features its own pier and private beach overlooking the lagoon and is bordered by green pastures and salt-water marshes, best viewed from the infinity pool. Rooms are castle-like in proportion and design with enormous four-poster beds, fireplaces, marble fittings and paintings by Régis Delene Bartholdi, the great grandson of the creator of the Statue of Liberty. Each room has a private deck and outdoor saltwater Jacuzzi. A vault houses a heated, ionised soft water pool flanked by Moorish spa treatment rooms and saunas, and there is also a bar and restaurant on site. Non-guests are welcome to come for drinks, dinner and spa treatments.

Factfile

When to go

While visitor numbers to Azzemour are fairly consistent all year round, El-Jadida and Sidi Bouzid see a sharp rise during August when Moroccans come on holiday. Hotel rates vary dramatically according to season; if you're coming in midsummer it's a good idea to book accommodation well in advance.

Late April to mid June is an enjoyable, crowd-free time to visit, with consistently warm, sunny weather and breezy evenings.

Getting there and around

There are direct flights from most major European cities to Casablanca's Mohammed V Airport. From there taxis are available to El-Jadida for around 700dh, though the cost should be agreed with the driver beforehand.

Trains leave every two hours from Casa Port station in Casablanca to El-Jadida, journey time 1hr 30mins. Timetables and prices are available in French and English on the national rail service's website, www.oncf.ma. There are also six daily trains from Marrakech to El-Jadida and trains from Fès, Agadir and Rabat.

One of the best ways to explore the coast is to hire a car. A good rental agency in El-Jadida is Sami Car (Samicar.com, 023 35 08 20). A *petit taxi* from El-Jadida to Sidi Bouzid and back, including a 4hr wait, will cost around 200dh. Trains from El-Jadida to Azzemour and back run every 2hrs and journeys take just 15mins. *Petit taxis* are also available to Azzemour and back from El-Jadida.

Tourist information

There is a tourist information centre on the main strip in El-Jadida (023 34 47 88), although it seems to be perpetually closed. Most hotel reception desks can probably offer all the information you need.

Travel agency Agence de Voyage Jacaranda (012 02 08 98), at the corner of avenue Ibin Toumert and boulevard Brahim Roudani, has tourist information and can organise day trips.

Internet

Mellah Net (rue Carreira 40, open 9am-midnight daily). There are also a couple of internet cafés on place El-Hansali near the Medina.

Small Gems

Chefchaouen.

Chefchaouen

There is a bewitching, storybook atmosphere to this remote mountain hideaway, whose history reads like a *Boy's Own* tale of high adventure and derring-do. The stronghold of the town walls and the squat, sturdy kasbah were originally intended to harbour the rebels who launched audacious attacks on the Portuguese in Ceuta. Then came the Jewish and Muslim refugees who had fled across the water from religious persecution in Spain. Over the years Chefchaouen evolved into a mysterious, cloistered outpost, a territory to which Christians were forbidden entry on pain of death. And yet the natural strategic advantage of its location, folded into the inaccessible crags of the Rif Mountains, continued to attract countless attempts at conquest and capture: over the centuries, Chefchaouen has been wrested from the control of chieftains and warlords, and even from the mighty Spanish, who occupied the town in 1920.

In the 19th century, one or two steely European adventurers had gained access to its forbidden Medina cloaked in cunning disguises. But it wasn't until the 20th century that the first travellers came wandering in from Tangier and Tetouan to discover a community in glorious isolation, its ancient crafts and diverse cultural heritages as perfectly preserved as insects in amber. The brilliant blue and dazzling whitewash of its houses, the Andalucian roof tiles, the eaves and terraces – here was a unique townscape made all the more distinctive by being stuck in the midst of hostile mountain terrain. The same sight greets visitors today. They come in their droves to Chefchaouen (known to locals simply as Chaouen) to soak up the history and gun smoke in which the very walls seem steeped, to glory in the stunning setting and the famously freewheeling atmosphere.

Explore

MEDINA

The hub of Chefchaouen's small but perfectly formed Medina is the busy plaza Uta El-Hammam. This is a lovely pedestrianised square with a massive pine tree at its centre and terraced cafés and restaurants scattered liberally around its perimeter. It's a relatively large open space – around 3,000 square metres – and is the focus for much of the Medina's activity (musicians, craft shops, locals and tourists taking their evening strolls) and a great deal of its inactivity (the café terraces are where countless old men eke out coffees and mint teas over lengthy discussions; the galleries above the terraces are generally the haunt of the town's not inconsiderable contingent of hash, or *kif*, smokers, whose economy of movement and glazed spectatorship of the world around them is something to behold).

Overlooking the plaza is the impressive Kasbah (*see p211*) and the *grande mosquée* (which is strictly off-limits to non-Muslims). Directly to the east of plaza Uta El-Hammam is place El-Makhzen, a quaint-looking, much smaller square, home to a couple of decent hotels, a dinky but highly convenient car park and several rather tacky souvenir and craft stalls. This is one of the main access points to the Medina proper, whose narrow, steep streets can only be explored on foot and reward more of an unfocused, meandering approach since there are no real 'sights' as such, just the breathtaking beauty of the town's unique *andalous-maghrébin* architectural style. The most famous attribute

Chefchaouen

Historic sites
● ● ● ● ●

Art & architecture
● ● ● ● ●

Hotels
● ● ● ● ●

Eating & drinking
● ● ● ● ●

Scenery
● ● ● ● ●

Shopping
● ● ● ● ●

SPAIN

Chefchaouen
●

ATLANTIC

OCEAN

MOROCCO

ALGERIA

0   100km

WESTERN SAHARA

of this style is that many of Chefchaouen's buildings are painted in the town's trademark two-tone of brilliant blue and bright, crisp whitewash. Many reasons for this will be offered to you by the locals you might happen to meet (to ward off mosquitoes, to symbolise the clouds and the sky – the list goes on); the truth is that the blue was introduced by Jewish refugees who favoured it over the more traditionally Arabic green that was there to begin with. Still, despite the prosaic explanation, the effect of the glowing streets and the Spanish tiles and overarching eaves above is one that never fails to enchant even the most trail-hardened visitors.

"It is an attractive set-up, with the rushing water weaving among the steps that connect a series of mini squares, walkways and platforms."

The Medina is, in many ways, an area of stark contrasts. Its closed-in streets set you up for an even greater level of oohing and aahing when the mountains suddenly come into view in the gaps between buildings or at the top of a whitewashed stairway. And even in the atmospheres of the intertwining streets and alleyways, there is a distinct element of contrast. You can walk up a tiny backstreet full of small carpentry *ateliers* crowded with the fragrance of cedarwood, with flurries of chisel-curled shavings swept out on to the cobbles. You can stand and watch the craftsmen as they pare out intricate patterns with no worry of a hard sell, or indeed of even the slightest acknowledgement of your presence, so profound is their concentration. Then, at the next turn, you can find yourself in a narrow thoroughfare of tacky souvenir shops and Pepsi signs, as if you had suddenly been catapulted forward through the centuries to land in the Mont Saint-Michel of Morocco. Which, in some ways, you have.

At the eastern edge of the Medina is an area known as Quartier Sebbanin or Barrio Lavaderos. The name refers to a small waterfall whose flow is directed through a series of sluices to stations where local women are able to do their washing at communal troughs. It is an attractive set-up, with the rushing water weaving among the steps that connect a series of mini squares, walkways and platforms, and many people come to the area to enjoy the sunshine, stretch their legs or sip a tea at one of the nearby cafés.

Kasbah

Plaza Uta El-Hammam (039 98 67 61). Open 9am-1pm, 3-6.30pm Mon, Wed, Thur, Sat; 9-11.30am 3-6.30pm Fri. Admission 10dh, 3dh under 12s.

Built by the 'father of Chefchaouen' Moulay Ali ben Rachid in 1471, this picturesque Kasbah is in better nick than most. Its sturdy crenellated walls enclose a beautiful courtyard, where well-tended formal walkways, fragrant with the scent of lilies and roses and dusted with orange blossom in spring, seem a lifetime away from the comings and goings of the square on the other side of the gates. Looking up from the garden, extraordinary views of the ridges and peaks of the surrounding mountains and of the lonely white sentinel of the Spanish Mosque (*see p212*) appear framed in the gaps between the battlements. And once up on the walls themselves, and thence to the summit of the beautiful tower, it becomes clear why this mountain stronghold was built in this exact spot: the views extend for miles in all directions, leaving no possibility of an unnoticed approach.

There are a few things to see around the Kasbah's grounds, notably the Musée de la Kasbah, housed in the largest of the outbuildings, just to the left of the main entrance. Consisting of a few rooms spread over two floors, the museum houses an interesting, albeit amateurishly displayed, collection of traditional artefacts and regalia. The Berber muskets with long, ornately decorated barrels and the collection of traditional musical instruments stand out among the displays, which also include bits and bobs of weaving equipment, Berber costumes and some blurry old photographs. Otherwise, on the opposite side of the courtyard, there is a small gallery hosting temporary exhibitions by local artists, and you can also visit the remains of a poky, somewhat sinister prison, complete with manacles and an oppressively dungeon-like atmosphere.

VILLE NOUVELLE

Easy as it might be to forget once you're ensconced in the ancient bastion of Chefchaouen's Medina, there is nonetheless a Ville Nouvelle here, a modern, rapidly expanding town that extends far beyond the medieval walls. Most visitors tend to see little of the Ville Nouvelle other than for transport purposes (buses and taxis arrive and leave from here; drivers will pass through the new town on the way to the car park at place El-Mekzhen in the Medina). Or else for other logistical reasons (cashpoint, post office – that kind of thing). But, as well as being home to most of the town's services and the bulk of its newer residential areas, the Ville Nouvelle is an interesting place to walk around, if only as a break from the sometimes overwhelming prettiness of the Medina.

Aesthetics is not among the Ville Nouvelle's strong suits (it is essentially a characterless conurbation of modern buildings and soulless avenues and squares) but the municipal market, which takes place just to the west of the Medina, behind Avenue Hassan II, can be a fun place to wander. That said, you will have to expect a certain degree of hassle that is not present

– or is at least uncommon – in the Medina, particularly from lads trying to sell you *kif* (the principal source of annoyance in and around Chefchaouen). To borrow a well-tested cliché, just say no, and do it politely.

What the Ville Nouvelle does have is a number of no-frills budget hotels, which differ from the cheaper options intramuros only in the sense that they lack the potential saving grace of any real character or charm (with some notable exceptions, of course, such as the lovely Hotel Rif; *see p219*). Somewhat predictably, these pockets of flophouse accommodation tend to attract a certain type of tourist – in this case, gap-year stoners with beads and beards, and refugees of '70s counter-culturalism with little more in the way of revolutionary spoils than some ratty tie-dye T-shirts and a thousand-yard stare.

To get the best of what's outside the Medina walls, you'll need to stray a little further afield than the streets of the Ville Nouvelle and get hooked in to the network of footpaths and mountain trails that surround the town. The most acccessible of these is the pretty path that leads from the north-eastern edge of town up to the ruined Spanish Mosque (*see p212*). From here, the views are simply incredible, the air is fresh and clean and, as ever in this incredible place, the sense of history and romance is palpable.

Spanish Mosque
Chefchaouen (no phone). Open dawn to dusk daily. Admission free.
A leisurely walk to the east of town (quit the town's walls via the Bab El-Ansar gate, in the Barrio Lavaderos), this Spanish-built mosque was an attempt on behalf of the colonisers to curry favour among the locals, but it was poorly received and, ultimately, completely abandoned in the years following the Rif War. Still, even in its ruined state, it presents a rare opportunity for the secular visitor to have a poke around inside a Moroccan mosque and get a feel for the layout, and the walk up the hillside path leading to the mosque is scenic. On a bad day, though, your enjoyment can be completely spoiled by the dozens of local boys who seem to operate a kind of relay system along this track, hassling and pestering tourists with endless offers of *kif*. The best policy is to simply ignore them (even if you did want to sample some of the local produce, this is definitely not the place to do it), and they will eventually go away.

Eat

There are many eateries clustered around the central, pedestrianised plaza Uta El-Hammam and, with the exception of Café Snack Mounir (*see below*), there's not a great deal between

them. Of course, the waiters who dart like Moray eels from their terraces to solicit your custom will be bound to tell you otherwise. But stick to your guns. In a touristy town like Chefchaouen, a bad meal is never far away.

Café Snack Mounir
Medina *Plaza Uta El-Hammam (039 98 75 84). Open 8am-10pm daily. £. Snack/Moroccan.*
The only one of the cafés that encircle plaza Uta El-Hammam to really stand out, this simple set-up of sheltered terrace tables and kiosk kitchen is the ideal place to come and have a rest and refreshment while you get your bearings. The very tasty juices will slake your thirst, while fresh fast food (of the omelette and salad varieties) and a handful of tagines and couscous dishes fill the lunchtime gap with a certain degree of style. Its position at the far end of the town's liveliest square also makes it an excellent vantage point from which to observe many people doing many different things – as well as many people doing very little at all (the café opposite is especially favoured by *kif*-smoking locals).

"A small huddle of tables is arranged around a tiny terrace that looks beyond plaza Uta El-Hammam towards the distant mountains."

Casa Aladin/La Lampe Magique
Medina *17 rue Targui (039 98 90 17/065 40 64 64). Open noon-2.30pm, 7-11pm daily. ££. Moroccan.*
It doesn't get much more romantic than this. Casa Aladin's dining area spills over a few floors, all of them candlelit and well supplied with secret corners and private, cushion-strewn snugs, and all aromatised by the delicious cooking smells that emanate from the open kitchen up on the roof. And it is here, at the top of the restaurant, that things go from good to stellar: a small huddle of tables is arranged around a tiny terrace that looks beyond the commotion of plaza Uta El-Hammam towards the distant mountains and (at dinner) the first stars peeping out of the darkening sky. The menu does justice to this setting with a simple but well-executed roll-call of tagines, couscous and brochettes –the chicken and preserved lemon tagine we tried was memorably rich and sticky. Understandably, this is the most popular restaurant in town, so you'll definitely need to book ahead.

Jardin Ziryab
Medina *Avenue Ras El-Maa, Barrio Lavaderos (039 98 77 70). Open 8pm-1am daily. ££. Spanish.*
Describing itself as a *cafeteria y teteria musical*, Jardin Ziryab is as close as sleepy Chefchaouen ever gets to a proper night spot. The eponymous Ziryab, a 16th-century

Top left: Quartier Sebanin.
Others: Chefchaouen.

oud player, is the inspiration for many of the nightly performances of live music that take place here, although world and country music also feature in what is an eclectic and interesting mash-up of styles. The place itself is a characterful little joint dominated by a bar-room style piano and drum kit, with a liberal scattering of tables, chairs and comfy sofas within easy listening range. Two menus cover a range of tasty Spanish bases, from snacky fare (*bocadillos*, *tostadas* and the like) to more substantial dishes, as well as several excellent salads. There's no booze licence but the party keeps going until past midnight most nights, which is due in no small part to the talented line-up of local (and the occasional visiting) musicians. There's also a garden at the back, which acts as a peaceful retreat for those who want to take a break from the music inside.

"The *harira*, which is properly served with a thick wedge of juicy lime, is some of the best we've tasted."

Restaurant Al Kasbah
Medina *Corner rue Targui and Place Uta El-Hammam, (no phone). Open noon-3pm, 6-10pm Mon-Sat. £. International.*
The first of the little gaggle of excellent restaurants just behind the main square – Tissemlal (*see below*) and La Lampe Magique (*see p212*) are just a couple of doors down – this cosy restaurant does a roaring trade pretty much all year round. There are a few tables on the tiny terrace, with the rest of the seating stretching back into the atmospheric, albeit slightly cavernous interior. The menu tries to bring together various loose strands of international cuisine, resulting in a slightly jumbled mix of omelettes, Greek salad, pasta dishes and all the usual Moroccan staples. Stick to the latter (tagines, pastilla, couscous) if you want to be guaranteed a good feed, try a step in a more adventurous direction (towards 'olive oil spaghetti', say) and the outcome is less than certain. Still, everyone seems to like it here, from local business bods at lunchtime to a steady and varied stream of tourists.

Restaurant Tissemlal
Medina *22 rue Targui (039 98 61 53/ www.casa hassan.com). Open noon-2.30pm, 7-11pm daily. £. Moroccan.*
Under the same ownership as Casa Hassan (*see p216*), this perennially packed restaurant is a fabulous place for an evening meal. There are perhaps better spots for lunch but, come nightfall, it's hard to beat. Warmed by firelight in winter and by the evening sunshine that streams down through the atrium in summer, Tissemlal's courtyard dining room makes for an enchanting setting. The menu is

unambitious but everything is done well, so much so, in fact, that the harira, which is properly served with a thick wedge of juicy lime, is some of the best we've tasted. The clientele is a roughly equal mix of Moroccans and visitors – another good sign – and the waiters work hard to establish a rapport with them, although this can get a bit wearisome if you're not in the mood.

Shop

Bazar Kenidi
Medina *Plaza Uta El-Hammam (no phone). Open 9am-7pm daily.*
With no name to announce it, this shop can be identified simply as the delightful collection of lamps, lanterns and mirrors that opens out on to the west of plaza Uta El-Hammam. Tourists and locals drift in from the square to wander among the beautifully crafted bronze and iron candle lanterns that hang from the ceiling and the ornate mirrors that lie propped against or hung from the walls. The personable young owner, Hamid, can be readily engaged in conversation but if you're not in a talkative mood he will happily leave you to look around in peace. Which is a strategy that seems to work well for him, as it is rare to walk past here on a busy afternoon and not see someone buying something.

Librairie Al Nahj
Ville Nouvelle *15 avenue Hassan II (061 30 26 02). Open 7am-7pm daily.*
A hole-in-the-wall bookshop a few doors down from the post office, Al Nahj mostly stocks French and Arabic paperbacks but it also does a handy line in local maps. If you're thinking of heading for the hills, even on a day trip, it is worth dropping by to see what's here (often a far cheaper and more hassle-free way of seeing the countryside than enlisting the services of one of the town's many self-proclaimed 'guides'). Also good to know is that it also stocks a regular selection of English-language magazines, such as *The Economist*, *Time* and *Newsweek*. And, on a more esoteric note, there are a few editions of plays by local writers such as Zoubeir Ben Bouchta that have been translated into English.

Textile Souk
Medina *Rue Abi Hassan Chadli (no phone). Open 9am-9pm daily.*
For any kind of clothing or fabric, come to the dozen or so shops that constitute the textile souk on rue Abi Hassan Chadli, the steep street that winds down from the side of the mosque on plaza Uta El-Hammam. There is very little variation in the kind of material that they stock – mostly hemp and cotton clothing, from jellabas to shirts and trousers, with a sideline in throws, cloths and shawls – so it's just a case of milling about and seeing what tickles your fancy. The merchants here are far less hectoring than their counterparts around place El-Makhzen, which makes the whole experience enjoyable and even quite relaxing. The first of the shops, Bazar Berber, also sells a few antiquey bits and bobs, and has a reputation for good-quality workmanship.

Arts

Théâtre de la Kasbah
Medina *Plaza Uta El-Hammam (039 986761). Open June-Sept; times vary with programme. Admission varies with programme.*
There's always plenty going on in summertime at this smart, modern open-air theatre adjacent to the Kasbah. It's a wonderful setting, with the thick walls of the Kasbah and the leafy boughs of the surrounding trees lining the edges of the seating area, and the unreal backdrop of the mountains looming behind the stage. Performances range from the accessible (*musique andalouse*, children's puppet shows) to the erudite (poetry recitals in classical Arabic, scholarly interpretations of medieval musical scores), and are concentrated around the many summer festivals that take place in Chefchaouen. For precise information, see Fatima Bushmel at the Kasbah administration office, or keep an eye out around town for posters and flyers announcing forthcoming events.

Stay

Casa Hassan
Medina *22 rue Targui (039 98 61 53/ www.casahassan.com). ££.*
Almost a mini Medina in itself, this bewitching riad is an elaborate maze of staircases, terraces and sleepy corners. Squishy chairs and the spit and crackle of an open fire make winter evenings here something special, while the cool shade of its arched walkways and the leafy roof terrace were designed with long, hot summers in mind. The rooms are nicely proportioned and very comfortable, and the bathrooms are well supplied with fluffy white towels and piping hot water. Myriad design details (from the delicate patterns on the ceiling to the tiles underfoot) conspire to create a sense of opulence that leaves you feeling like one of the sultan's houseguests. Great fun, and well worth the price.

Dar Mounir
Medina *Zankat Kadi Alami Hay Souika (039 98 82 53/ www.hotel-darmounir.com). £.*
Run by the same family that owns the thriving café of the same name on plaza Uta El-Hammam (*see p212*), this excellent hotel is one of, if not *the* best place to stay in Chefchaouen. For a start, it is gorgeous to look at, from the beautiful ensuite *tadelakt* bathrooms with their beaten bronze sinks and monsoon showerheads to the guest rooms themselves, whose fragrant, beautifully crafted cedarwood ceilings, fine fabrics and discreetly modern central heating put them in a category of their own in Chefchaouen. Communal areas are lovely too, from top (a roof terrace with decadent, Bedouin-style seating) to bottom (a craftily designed ground-floor restaurant with a partially open ceiling that funnels fresh air and daylight into what is effectively an enclosed courtyard setting). The cooking (courtesy of a team led by the owner's mother) is of a particularly high standard, and the same can be said of the staff in general, who are a helpful, friendly and intelligent lot. Highly recommended.

Dar Terrae
Medina *M'daka, quartier Andalous (039 98 75 98). £.*
One of the first riads in Chefchaouen, this small, Italian-run place is still going strong, and deservedly so. Its cosy blue-painted rooms all face one another around an intimate arrangement of stairs and balconies, and when the house is full and the boss's CD player is circulating the sounds of some nice jazz, it all begins to feel very convivial. On cold nights, most of the rooms have roaring fires to curl up in front of, or when the weather is warm the staff will happily cook you a plate of delicious pasta and bring it to the table on the walkway outside your room, above the inner courtyard, for a spot of al fresco room service. It's all very laidback and good-humoured – on which note, a brief aside: if you are at all prudish about dope smoking, you may feel a bit uncomfortable here.

Hostal Gernika
Medina *49 Onssar (039 98 74 34). £.*
On a steep, narrow cobbled street with just a simple carved wooden sign to announce it, the Gernika is the epitome of the kind of modest hostel that has earned Chefchaouen the reputation of a charming, laidback mountain town. Inside, a smart but simple reception area has attractive floor tiles, bare white walls and a lovingly restored stone hearth; shafts of coloured sunlight stream merrily through the stained glass panels of the doorway. It's all very cheerful, and the guest rooms are reassuringly uncluttered – no dusty wall hangings or damp corners, just simple beds and furniture, and clean, crisp linen. The roof terrace might be tiny (just big enough to accommodate a decent-sized table and chairs and a few little pot plants) but it has choice views of the mountains. Staff are friendly and relaxed (and we mean in a nice way, rather than a just plain stoned way).

Hôtel Hicham
Medina *Place El-Makhzen (066 26 79 00/ 039 98 81 09). £.*
Completed in summer 2008, the Hicham is Chefchaouen's newest hotel. Situated right on the edge of quaint place El-Mahkzen (bang opposite the Parador; *see p219*), this smartly appointed hybrid of *maison d'hôte* and formal hotel hits all the right buttons: guest rooms are decorated in a style more in keeping with a traditional riad (think plenty of stained glass, beautiful tiles and Moorish arches) but have been finished to a level more usually seen in a four-star hotel (a high quality of workmanship in the fittings and fixtures, discreet lighting, beds with top-quality mattresses and decent linen). The accommodation options are also particularly well suited to families (of the nine rooms, six are large enough to accommodate four people, all with lovely little lounge areas), and a small internet station and a tasty café operation add to the overall convenience factor. The roof terrace is exemplary too, with dual views of the square on one side and Théâtre de la Kasbah (*see above*) on the other.

Clockwise from top:
Restaurant Al Kasbah; La
Lampe Magique;
Casa Hassan.

Top: Casa Hassan.
Bottom: Dar Terrae.

Hôtel Madrid
Ville Nouvelle *Rue Hassan II (039 98 74 96/97). £.*
A popular extramural option, this Ville Nouvelle hotel sports some impressive decorative touches in its public areas (notably the ceiling in the lounge on the ground floor) and its staff are a friendly bunch. The guest rooms, meanwhile, are perhaps a little more eccentric than usual (the wrought iron beds, for instance, sport bizarrely incongruous tasselled curtains). The fact that they are also equipped with various modern touches (such as the digital safes, which are mounted on the walls more like ersatz paintings than security devices) makes the place popular with package tours. Some rooms benefit from the out-of-Medina location with great views of the mountains, which seem closer than ever down here. Sadly, though, the roof terrace is a domain that has been given over entirely to washing lines and satellite dishes and is therefore not somewhere you'd want to slink off to with a paperback and a pair of shades.

Hôtel Molino
Medina *Plaza Sebbanin (039 98 74 23). £.*
The set-up at the Molino is ideal for independent travellers on a budget but, that said, this is far from being a backpacker flophouse. The guest rooms are cosy and prettily decked out in classic Chefchaouen blue with colourful textiles and attractive striped blankets on the beds, and some of the top rooms, nestled up in the eaves, have lovely sloping ceilings. There's always a fire going downstairs when the weather's not hot (where genial German owner Rene is often to be found warming his feet with a good book) and the communal kitchen is immaculately clean and well appointed. The small back garden has plenty of sunshine and, when it comes round to laundry day, lots of washing lines too.

Hôtel Parador
Medina *Place El-Makhzen (039 98 61 36/www.hotel-parador.com). ££.*
Traditionally, this centrally located touristy hotel has been viewed as Chefchaouen's top accommodation option, even if some of the town's prettier riads had started to seduce those tourists who preferred traditional charm to the Parador's dated version of luxury. But now, after a comprehensive facelift in mid 2008, the Parador is looking a lot more spiffy, especially in the remodelled third-floor suites, complete with fresh paint jobs, recessed spot lighting and spanking new bathrooms. On the whole, though, this remains a comfortable if undeniably kitsch address, where the terrace boasts great views and a nice enough swimming pool, and the licensed bar sports the kind of bar stools Austin Powers would feel right at home on.

Hôtel Rif
Ville Nouvelle *Rue Hassan II (039 98 69 82). £.*
A stalwart ally of the budget traveller, the Rif has been around forever and it continues to earn its reputation as an easygoing, convenient, cheap and (genuinely) cheerful bed for the night. The bright and homely reception is festooned with gaudy pictures and sprawling houseplants, while the adjoining café area (where breakfast is served) is similarly fun and lively, and filled with the sounds of the various songbirds that occupy ornate little cages around the room. A traditionally tiled staircase leads to the various guest rooms (most of which have great mountain views, all of which have plain furniture and tiny, curtained-off bathrooms) and, ultimately, to the comfortable but unglamorous roof terrace. Here, café-style tables and chairs are at the disposal of those who want to eat picnics in the sun or under the stars, and a few washing lines have been rigged up for guest use.

Factfile

When to go
The annual Festival Alegria, a celebration of traditional music and arts, takes place in July (for precise dates, phone 039 98 61 47). The most romantic times to visit this mountainous region are snow-capped winter and flower-carpeted spring.

Getting there & around
Chefchaouen's gare routière (bus station) is a 20-minute walk south-west of town on avenue Mohamed V (the road that leads south from plaza Mohamed V, just to the west of the cemetery). Alternatively, *grands taxis* leave in all directions (usually in the morning) from plaza Mohamed V and from the main market area just behind the post office on avenue Hassan II.

Drivers coming from the north are best off on the N2/N13 from Tangier via Tetouan, a long, scenic road that takes in some spectacular scenery with minimal disruptions from poor surfaces or heavy truck traffic. Those driving up from the south will wish to avoid the N2 on both sides of Ketama, which is in the dead centre of one of the largest hash-producing areas in the world, and as such, is no stranger to crime.

Getting around Chefchaouen is best done on foot (the Medina is the preserve of pedestrian traffic) and even the short excursions out of town (to the Spanish Mosque, say) are most enjoyable in the form of a short, untaxing walk. That said, *petits taxis* are, as ever, ubiquitous.

Tourist information
The nearest tourist office is in Tangier (*see p151*).

Internet
Cyber Outahammam Plaza Uta El-Hammam (039 989822/www.outahammam.com). Open 8am-midnight daily.

Clockwise from top left:
Hôtel Palais Salam;
Dar Zitoune; Hôtel Palais
Salam; Riad Maryam (2);
Dar Zitoun; town
ramparts; Dar Zitoun.

Taroudant

Taroudant is a town that seems completely connected to the landscape around it, not only in the deep ochre earth colouring of its pisé ramparts, whose hue seems to shift with every movement of the sun, but also in its population, many of whom are agricultural traders.

In the 16th century, Taroudant was the stronghold of the Saadian dynasty, and its magnificent ramparts were literally raised from the ground to fortify this key position. And those thousands of tons of rammed earth, packed and pounded into position by thousands of men, are still the first thing you glimpse as you drive towards the city, with its sentinel guard of snow-capped Atlas peaks crowding the horizon behind it. Now, though, its strategic significance has long since vanished, and Taroudant is simply a busy market town where the produce of the Souss Valley is traded and crafts continue to be worked in time-honoured fashion by the town's artisans.

To walk through Taroudant's souks and the lively quarters around its central squares is to find yourself in a living museum. You may have to concentrate a bit to fade out the occasional blast of Arabic pop music, the ubiquitous ring tones of mobile phones and all the other aural trappings of modern life, but not too much. Because, mixed in with all the 21st-century noise, is the tireless ring of hammer on anvil, the cries of traders hawking their wares, and the sound of the hooves of mules being lead to market.

Explore

At heart, Taroudant is a parochial place and, despite its handful of fancy hotels life here still revolves around the central souks and the bustle of trade and commerce.

Your first landmark, then, should be place Assarag and its neighbouring square, place Talmoklate. Also known as place El-Alaouyine and place An-Nasr, respectively, these two squares are the heart of the city. You'll not find much that is beautiful there, save for the odd sightline of a souk alleyway or a faded hotel façade, but this is ground zero for seeing the sights.

These extend principally to the two main souks (Arabe and Berbère; see p226) and to the magnificent *pisé* walls that surround the city. It is possible to get up on to the ramparts in a few places (notably at the main gate of Bab El-Kasbah). But as the walkways up top don't go all the way around the most coherent and relaxed way to see the walls is simply to make the six kilometre circumference on foot or in one of the horse-drawn carriages (*calèches*) that are stationed at various points along the way.

Really, though, Taroudant is somewhere to follow your nose and not be burdened by the imperative of 'seeing the sights', as, strictly speaking, there are none. And that's the beauty of the place.

Eat

There is a relatively high traffic of tourists in Taroudant and, as a result, there are a good many restaurants to feed them. To be avoided are most

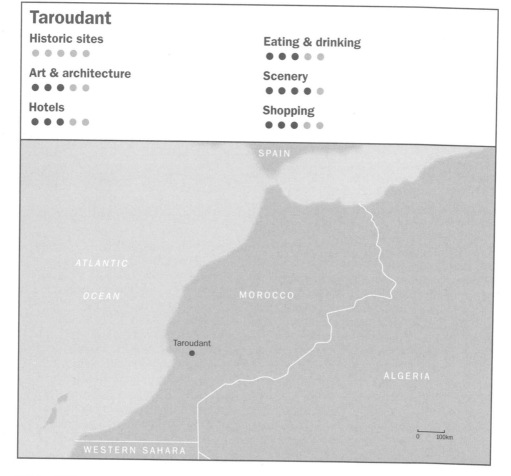

Taroudant

Historic sites
● ● ● ● ●

Art & architecture
● ● ● ● ●

Hotels
● ● ● ● ●

Eating & drinking
● ● ● ● ●

Scenery
● ● ● ● ●

Shopping
● ● ● ● ●

SPAIN

ATLANTIC

OCEAN

MOROCCO

Taroudant
●

ALGERIA

WESTERN SAHARA

0   100km

Top: souks. Bottom: town ramparts.

The clean team

'This is Mohamed. He will wash you.' These are perhaps not the words most men long to hear, especially when the object of said declaration is a vast man in swimming trunks whose only hairless body-space is the small clearing of skin between beard and brow. And yet it is quite surprising how easily these initial inhibitions may be overcome and how quickly one adjusts to the etiquette of steam-shrouded banter that is the Moroccan hammam.

For men and women, the function of the hammam is essentially the same (although, obviously, never at the same time: most hammams have separate days for men and women, some larger ones have separate baths and entrances). It is a coded and highly traditional environment in which to relax, somewhere to let your guard down and get some things off your chest. The hammam is as sacred to the Moroccan way of life as the village pub is to the British or the café terrace to the French. It just involves a little more bare flesh, and a lot more back slapping.

This is how it works. Leave your clothes in the changing room and follow (wearing a swimming costume and flip flops) your designated washer and scrubber into the warm room. This tiled chamber is where you become accustomed to the gentle warmth that emanates from the ancient concealed furnaces that are stoked by the bundles of rough-cut wood you might see stacked in giant piles at the back of some of the older hammams. After a period of adjustment,

and a good deal of sprinkling (and/or tipping) of water from buckets distributed around the place, you proceed to the hot room. Here you can expect to be washed with liquid soap (usually with an olive or argan oil base – don't get any in your eyes, it stings), scrubbed, shown the worms of skin that have appeared on the scrubbing mit, scrubbed some more, shown more skin. All punctuated by good-natured laughter from your neighbours. Then comes the crunch.

Those with delicate bones may want to liberally employ the word *doucement*, meaning 'gently', during the various back and limb manipulations that ensue. Be prepared for a certain amount of cracking and crunching, muscle stretching and tendon twanging. But be prepared, too, to feel as supple as a newborn baby by the end of it. At which point (when you may or may not get a bucket of cold water tipped on your head), you can withdraw to the warm room to decompress, before finally heading back to the changing room. There, you are free to take your time, read the paper and enjoy the strong coffee liberally seasoned with twigs of wild thyme that will be handed to you.

To arrange an authentic hammam in Taroudant, contact the Maison Anglaise (*see p226*). Staff there will be only too pleased to arrange a trip for you to a local place far from the coach tours and mini shampoo bottles of the tourist trail. You'll need a towel, cozzy and flip flops, plus some dirhams for the washer and nominal entrance charge.

of the hotel restaurants and snack stops surrounding Place Assarag (where many of the coach tours stop). Be prepared, instead, to take a punt on some of the local places, especially those little grill joints that orbit the souks, whose fish and lamb brochettes might turn out to be some of the tastiest grub you'll eat anywhere in town.

Chez Nada
Avenue Moulay Rachid (028 85 17 26). Open noon-11pm Mon-Sat. ££. Moroccan.
There are two sides to Chez Nada, one is the café on the ground floor, whose seating area (which extends out the back to a small slice of terrace down the side of the building) and menu (complete with lurid food photos) are perhaps a little more low-brow than those of its main restaurant. Which means it's probably best to confine your visit to the first and second floor and to the roof terrace, where you can choose from the restaurant's classic Moroccan menu (salad or harira, followed by cous cous or tagine) and relax in a world of potted plants and genial service. And if, by the end of it, you fancy a dessert, they'll happily sprinkle some cinnamon over a few orange slices for you. Worth knowing about, then, but not somewhere to bust a gut to get to.

Cocktail Oasis
3 Immi Tiouti, avenue Moulay Rachid (061 941293). Open 9am-10pm daily. £. Juice bar/crêperie.
Spanish football is one of the obsessions at this characterful little juice bar (as is often apparent not only from the massive Barça and Real Madrid flags on its walls, but also from the live matches playing on the big plasma-screened TV in the corner). But another, even greater obsession is the pulverisation of vast quantities of apples, oranges, bananas, avocados, melons, apricots, papayas and the rest to create the zingiest smoothies in town. They simply have to be tried to be believed. And, somewhat unusually for a Morrocan juice bar, the solid food is better than average too, taking the form of substantial Moroccan pancakes both savoury (stuffed with tomatoes, olives and onions) and sweet (slathered with honey).

Ezziani
Between Place An-Nasr and Grande Mosquée (no phone). Open 11am-10pm daily. £. Fish/seafood.
Run by a couple of energetic young lads, this lively little restaurant is the place in Taroudant for simply cooked, beautifully fresh fish. Find a seat at one of the handful of tables that are wedged into the small caff-style space behind the hiss and spit of the grills and take your pick from the wet counter. A typical selection would include the likes of sole, hake, bream, bass and a good selection of shellfish (such as the giant langoustines that were the highlight of our last visit). Snap open a can of Coke to wash it down and mop up the juices with fresh bread. Just one word of advice: try to avoid Sundays, when there's no morning delivery; on any other day, you'll be getting fish that has come in from Agadir harbour that same morning.

Pâtisserie Ettais Fatiha
Rue Atlas Ferk (028 551094). Open 10am-6pm Mon-Sat. £. Café/pâtisserie.

Keep your eyes peeled because this one is easy to miss – except for the discreet swirl of Arabic script on its window, there is no sign to announce it, and the few tables and chairs that are set out on either side of its doorway don't look much like a terrace. But despite these modest first impressions, Ettais Fatiha's cakes and pastries really are something worth seeking out. Prettily arranged in spotless glass cabinets are two varieties of pâtisserie: European and Moroccan. The former consists of a more limited range of croissants, millefeuilles, *pains aux chocolat* and the like, but the latter is a wonderland of sinful treats, ranging from classics like *cornes de gazelle* and all manner of jam-filled biscuits to heavenly *sablés aux noix de coco* (balls of coconutty goodness), *caissettes* and nameless gooey pistachio cookies. Should you want to make a meal of it, there are usually about half a dozen savoury *pastillas*, not to mention excellent espresso-based coffees and milkshakes, to help you on your way. And if you need to sit down, there are a few plastic-covered tables inside too.

Restaurant Maryam
Avenue Mohamed V, derb Maalem Mohamed, 140 Bab Targhounte (066 12 72 85). Open noon-3pm, 7pm-midnight daily. £££. Moroccan.
Serving what is, without question, the best Moroccan cuisine in Taroudant, the restaurant operation of the diminutive Résidence Riad Maryam (*see p229*) is effectively an open-air dining room, with tables arranged around the greenery of an open courtyard and the secluded niches of its eaves. The chef's specialities (and these are where the real culinary fireworks are) need to be ordered some time in advance (drop by in the morning to request an evening meal), and include a traditional sweet and meltingly succulent pigeon *pastilla*, lamb shoulder cooked *choua* (steamed) or *mechoui* (barbecued) and the house 'roudani' veal tagine. Other standouts from the menu are the various succulent brochettes, garden-fresh salads and hearty tagines glistening with slices of preserved lemon and fat locally grown olives. To finish, delicate orange flower salad, honey-soaked pastries scattered with chopped pistachios – the list goes on. Wine, beer and excellent coffee are all on offer too.

Shop

One of the main pleasures of Taroudant is shopping, and much of the real pleasure of shopping here is in the browsing. And not just among the craft and carpet shops of the Souk Arabe or the colourful, fragrant produce of its sister market, but in the many unmarked streets that surround them. Stroll, for example, to the east of Place Assarag and breathe in the combined aromas of myriad coffee merchants, each with their own little hill of beans. Or stop in at a bakery or a juice bar, or drink hot, sweet tea at one of the district's innumerable cafés: follow your senses and you are sure to be well-rewarded.

Ali Baba

95 Joutia, Souk Arabe (048 852435). Open 8am-8pm daily.
No hard sell, no trickery, no 40 thieves: Ali Baba is a straight-up, unintimidating carpet shop, and for that fact alone it deserves a mention. Its massive stock of high-quality Berber textiles (as well as various leather goods – pouffe covers and the like) is probably enough to satisfy most people's tastes. The roll-call of famous former customers (Mick Jagger, Charlie Watts, yada yada) is well documented in a visitor's book that you will inevitably be made to look at but probably not asked to sign.

Art de Souss

113 Avenue Biranzaran (061 530143).
Open 8am-8pm daily.
Mohamed El-Meski, the owner of this newly opened, high-quality craft shop is something of an expert on local artisanal tradition, and it shows in the pieces that he has on display. Ironwork is what's on offer here, in its myriad forms, with many items (including some exquisite lamps, mirror frames and tables) coming from Meski's own forge. Beautiful inlays and coloured glass panels decorate some of the more intricate pieces.

Souk Arabe

Place Assarag. Open dawn-dusk daily.
Also known as Souk Assarag, the Souk Arabe is where the real action is. It is impossible to classify what is really sold here (it would be quicker, so the joke goes, to enumerate what is not) but suffice to say that this is where the citizens of Taroudant come to do their shopping, their socialising and – for those who run stalls here – a good deal of their talking, arguing, haggling and downright shouting. Broadly speaking, the areas of the souk break down as follows: secondhand stalls, leather goods and sandal-and slipper-makers in the western quarter (nearest to Place Assarag; fresh fruit and vegetables in the northern section; clothes shops, tailors and general stores (from decorative woodwork and pottery to halal butchers and traditional apothecaries) to the east; jewellery in the southern section. A couple of highlights among these many areas include: the Antiquaire Haut Atlas (a serious antique, furniture and objets vendor in the Kabir section, just south of the BMCE bank on Place Assarag); and Mouyel Hamad's spice and tea shop (also in the Kabir section).

Souk Berbère

Place Talmoklate. Open dawn-dusk daily.
Even the humblest stall offering nothing but bucketfuls of fresh mint looks and smells good at this colourful, busy and friendly fruit and veg market. It's a great place to breeze through in a state of mild sensory overload, as the clamour of Berber and Arabic fills your ears, the scents of spices, herbs and juicy thick-skinned oranges get your mouth watering, and colourful jellabas swish past in every direction. You'll probably also find a smattering of stallholders flogging household goods (from tea towels through to some quite splendid ceramics), as well as a number of interesting herbalists and tea-sellers. (Not to mention the occasional tea leaf, so keep your wallet tucked away somewhere safe.)

Stay

CECU (La Maison Anglaise)

Derb Afferdou (048 55 16 28/
www.naturallymorocco.com). ££.
The Taroudant headquarters of the English-operated Naturally Morocco travel group, this excellent guest house is a genuinely inviting place to stay. Rooms are clean, bright and homely, and the communal dining room (where first-rate meals are served) is decorated with dozens of maps of the region (into which a number of excursions, treks and wildlife-themed forays are offered by the staff here). Said, a local ornithologist, is an indispensable companion on any outing to the Souss coastal steppe, while his wife Latifa is on hand at the guest house to offer advice and pointers on everything from where to find the town's best tagine to how much to expect to pay for a ride in a *calèche*. Hassle-free, clued-up and committed to sustainable tourism, these guys know what they're doing and they do it well.

Dar Zitoune

Boutarialt El-Barrania (028 55 11 41/42/
www.darzitoune.com). ££.
A little way out of the town centre, this immaculate new hotel is where the pampering gets done in Taroudant. Luxury cabins are distributed among the rambling, lovingly tended gardens, and the overall aesthetic is one of organic refinement: traditional building materials, fabrics and artworks conspire to create interiors that evoke the spirit of the Maghreb without conceding any points on contemporary luxury or technology. The result is a pleasing blend of past and present: enjoy the glow of a real log fire while watching a film on your plasma-screen television – that kind of thing. There's also a gorgeous pool, a nice little hammam and treatment centre, and a decent restaurant to complete the picture. The staff are the kind of friendly, highly efficient bunch you'd expect to find in a place like this.

Hôtel Gazelle d'Or

Rue d'Ameskroud, outskirts of Taroudant (028 85 20 48/www.gazelledor.com). £££.
With enough old-world charm to furnish a Merchant Ivory film set, the Gazelle d'Or is a bewitching relic of a long-past colonial age. Its croquet lawn, its leafy garden and perfect pool, its spacious, stylishly appointed guest pavilions, its sleekly designed hammam and treatment centre – everything here draws on the legend of Moorish opulence and hospitality, which seems ingrained in the building and gardens themselves. This is somewhere to saunter along secluded pathways and corridors of fragrant roses, to read a novel in the shade of a giant tree, to open your eyes and hear birdsong in the morning. Or, for the more adventurous, it is somewhere to trot out of the picturesque gates on horseback for a day's trekking in the nearby foothills, or perhaps to stay put and play a few sets on the leafy clay tennis courts. The half board rates include fine Moroccan dinners and elegant al fresco breakfasts.

Clockwise from top left:
Pâtisserie Ettais Fatiha;
Cocktail Oasis; Chez Nada
(2); Hôtel Taroudant.

Clockwise from top: Riad Maryam; Dar Zitoune (2); Riad Maryam; Hôtel Palais Salam.

Hôtel Palais Salam
Kasbah (028 85 25 01). ££.
Despite the presence of one or two more overtly luxurious hotels, Palais Salam remains the first choice of many Taroudant aficionados. And it's easy to see why. The building that houses the hotel was once a pasha's palace and, in the old wing at least, a residue of that former glory remains: lush greenery enlivens the courtyards, the rooms have a certain old-world charm, and the main series of secluded terraces that encircle the pretty pool and nestle against the palace walls provide the kind of setting in which a safari-suited Charles Dance wouldn't look out of place. Breakfasts take the form of mighty buffets piled high with fruit, pastries, all manner of hot foods, and plenty of good, strong coffee. And finally, the location couldn't be more central.

Hôtel Saadiens
Bourj Oumansour (028 85 25 89). £.
Constructed around a large inner courtyard, this spacious budget hotel has decent-sized rooms, plenty of sunlight and a relatively peaceful location working in its favour. Its down sides, which are pretty much typical of any hotel in this price range (the odd squishy mattress, a pool that doesn't always look that inviting) are by no means deal-breakers. The point is, it's a cheap and (for the most part) cheerful joint with a breezy roof terrace overlooking the Medina, and for the price it costs to spend the night here, you really can't ask for a great deal more than that.

Hôtel Taroudant
Place Assarag (028 85 24 16). £.
It has a great location (right on the south-west corner of Place Assarag) but there is also something to be said for the low-rent vibe of the Taroudant's old-school reception area, the plastic chairs and beer bottles of its courtyard bar and the no-fuss, no-frills aesthetic of its guest rooms. It's not for everyone, of course, but for those whose intention is to get right into the heart of things and spend a few nights feeling like a Moroccan version of Philip Marlowe, it's pretty much perfect. Also worth knowing about, whether you're planning to stay here or not, are the excellent treks and excursions that can be organised through the hotel's outward bound partner, the oddly named Djebel Emotions (028 72 24 65 79).

Résidence Riad Maryam
Avenue Mohamed V, derb Maalem Mohamed, 140 Bab Targhounte (066 12 72 85/www.riad maryam.com). ££.
The inimitable, irrepressible Habib is master of this brilliant little riad that lies somewhere in a spaghetti tangle of lanes behind Avenue Mohamed V (go looking on foot if you must, but a few dirhams in a *petit taxi* will save you a lot of trudging, false turns and small-time extortion at the hands of wily young boys who have a sixth sense for when a person is lost to the point of paying for directions). But once there, you'll be pleased you bothered. An elaborately tiled, verdant courtyard is surrounded by four beautifully appointed, air-conditioned rooms. Three of the rooms (two triples, one quadruple) are large enough to accommodate a family, and have a suitably cosy feel to them, with coloured glass lanterns, spotless bathrooms and old-fashioned, wrought-iron bed frames. Traditional artwork, wall-mounted Berber muskets, colourful throws and intricately carved furniture spice up the alcoves in the courtyard, where breakfast and dinner (*see p229*) are served.

Factfile

When to go
Spring and autumn are wonderful times to visit this city, when the colours of the surrounding countryside are either exploding into life or deepening to a palette of luscious earth tones Although, on a more practical note, drivers wishing to journey here via the spectacular Tiz'n'Test pass are better off coming in snow- and fog-free months of summer.

Getting there
The gare routière (just outside Bab Zorgane on Avenue Mohamed V) is the main arrival and departure point for Taroudant, which is served by various bus companies, notably CTM (Place Assarag, information 022 75 36 58). *Grands taxis* also depart from and arrive at the *gare routière*. Those driving on their own will find the N10 from Agadir to be the most efficient route and the tortuous Tiz'n'Test pass to the north-east of town to be the most spectacular one.

Getting around
Most of the city is easily accessed on foot (indeed, the streets around the major souks are probably easier to navigate for pedestrians) Otherwise, *petits taxis* swarm around the city centre. You can hail them from anywhere around the town (the large roundabout near to Palais Salam Hotel, at the intersection of avenues Moulay Rachid and Hassan II, is normally a good bet).

Tourist office
Office du Tourisme (ONMT), Place Prince Héritier, Agadir (028 846 377/www.visitmorocco.com). Open 9am-12.30pm, 2-6pm Mon-Fri.

Internet
There are several internet cafés in town, including Club Roudana Jeux & Internet, avenue Bir Anzarane Imm Hadj Menani, 028 55 16 51. Open 10am-midnight daily.

Clockwise from top left:
Mdiq; Martil; Mdiq (2);
Tetouan Medina (2).

Tetouan
& Around

In a fertile valley dusted with almond blossom, ripe with orange and pomegranate groves, Tetouan sits at the foot of the Rif mountains, whose towering, silent mass dominates the city's skyline. But it is something entirely man-made for which Tetouan is most famous, namely its ancient Medina, now a UNESCO World Heritage site, and still home to the crafts and traditions on whose prosperity it was founded more than five centuries ago. A rich mix of architectural styles reflects the multicultural heritage of the city, within whose walls Jewish, Muslim and Spanish settlers have built their homes during a long and fascinating history.

The sea is not far distant, with the tiny coastal town of Mdiq, the rugged headland of Cabo Negro and the larger, busier port of Martil just a stone's throw from the city centre. Massive investment has, in recent years, transformed these long, sandy beaches into world-class resort territory, with everything from private beach clubs to watersports centres providing some sun-kissed respite from the cultural attractions of Tetouan.

Explore

TETOUAN

Tetouan's Medina sprawls up the hillside in gleaming white splendour. To its west, the new town is an orderly network of broad avenues and tidy streets centred around the busy place Moulay El-Mehdi, a broad square dominated by the sepia façade of the city's Spanish church. South of here is avenue Moulay El-Abbas, a raised promenade from which the views of the surrounding Rif mountains are quite spectacular.

The main access point to the Medina is from the smart and grandly proportioned place Hassan II, which is overlooked by the Royal Palace and is now a far cry from the bustling, workaday market it once was. The spine of the Medina is the (relatively) broad rue Terrafin, which runs due east from the square and disappears into a spaghetti of streets, alleyways, myriad souks, bazaars and stalls, and time-worn residences. You will need a reliable inner compass and a certain degree of confidence to navigate the Medina in any meaningful way, without assistance. Otherwise, enlist the services of a guide in advance of your trip (ask at the tourist office; *see p234*) but avoid hooking up with one of the many *faux guides* who still work the Medina entrance (despite the best efforts of a small police force tasked with the job of stopping this kind of thing).

Highlights include the carpentry souk and the tannery – both at the northern tip of the Medina near the Bab Sebta exit, which leads out to an interesting hillside cemetery just beyond the Medina walls.

Archaeological Museum

2 rue ben H'sain (039 96 73 03). Open 8.30am-4.30pm Mon-Fri. Admission 15dh.

It may not be the most effectively signposted tourist attraction in the world but, if in doubt, keep an eye out for the several large artefacts (urns, architectural fragments) that adorn the small garden in front of this compact but highly informative museum. If you have the chance to combine a visit here with a trip to the ancient site of Lixus (*see p177*), you will undoubtedly get more out of both experiences, since it is at this museum that almost all of the treasures excavated at Lixus are stored. That said, though, the museum is still well worth devoting time to in its own right.

The rooms are small and, on the whole, the presentation is far from inspiring, but there is a chronological coherence to the layout that is instantly absorbing. Follow the progress of pre-Roman Moroccans through the remains of tools, pottery and jewellery found at the nearby cave of Kaf Taht El Ghar and the more distant coastal cave of Ghar Cahal. The Roman period is comprehensively dealt with (due, of course, to the wealth of artefacts unearthed at digs around Lixus and Tamuda) and displays the expected range of ceramics, sculptures, weaponry, masks and jewellery. Most striking by far, though, are the large-scale mosaics in Room Two, depicting Venus and Adonis, and Mars and Rhea

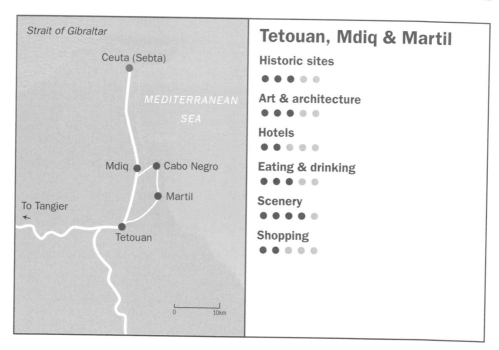

Strait of Gibraltar

Ceuta (Sebta)

MEDITERRANEAN SEA

Mdiq · · Cabo Negro

To Tangier

· Martil

Tetouan

0   10km

Tetouan, Mdiq & Martil

Historic sites

● ● ● ● ○

Art & architecture

● ● ● ● ○

Hotels

● ● ● ● ○

Eating & drinking

● ● ● ● ○

Scenery

● ● ● ● ○

Shopping

● ● ● ● ○

Silvia (Ilia). Also of note are some gorgeous vases and striking 15th- and 16th-century *zellig portugais* tiles in the comparatively limited display covering the Islamic period.

MDIQ

Lots of cash has been injected into this lovely seaside town, and it shows. The corniche is smart and a genuinely pleasant spot for an evening stroll (especially when heading towards the eastern end, where an old colonial church stands as a reminder of the Spanish colonial presence here). To the south of the boardwalk is the main town itself, which comprises little more than a few streets, with pleasant cafés, ice-cream stalls and the occasional souvenir shop. Following the sweep of the beach (north) out of town soon brings you to the resorts, mini marinas and high-end holiday complexes of Restinga-Smir.

MARTIL

Essentially a busy, working port, Martil has its harbour and its fishing industry to keep it going, but what markets and shops there are hold little attraction for the visitor. What do, sustain its tourist industry, however, are the beautiful beaches that skirt the town (alongside them, a wide, slightly sparse but gloriously spacious corniche) and some opportunities for a bit of laidback sightseeing. Particularly appealing is the plaza de la Gaviota, where an extraordinary colonial church has been transformed into the Centro Cultural Lerchundi (039 97 95 53/www.lerchundimartil.blogspot.com), a community centre for local women and students run by a group of French, Spanish and Congolese nuns; the classes have had a hugely positive impact on the local community. During the week, it may be possible to look around the classrooms and speak to one or two of the nuns, or it may not – ring the bell and see if anyone's around. Summer programmes with opportunities for volunteer work run on a regular basis.

Eat

Café Hela-Go
Tetouan *9 avenue 10 Mai (039 71 20 38). Open 9am-8pm Mon-Sat. £. Café/pâtisserie.*
A bright, funky café in the thick of the new town, Hela-Go's slightly eccentric decor (lurid tissue-paper models of ice-cream sundaes dangle from its purple ceiling) might not be too easy on the eye, but its line of Moroccan pastries, Illy coffee and, above all, speciality ice-creams (10dh a scoop but worth every *santimat*) are heaven on the palate. First and foremost, this is a traditional ice-cream parlour or *heladeria* (hence the name) and is a meeting point for local students and couples wanting to steal some precious moments alone. For those with a savoury tooth, a few simple (but very nicely presented) sandwiches are on offer at lunchtime.

Café Jenin
Tetouan *Rue Al-Wahda (039 96 22 46). Open 9am-7pm daily. £. Café.*
A classier version of its near neighbour, Hela-Go (*see p233*), this excellent café is decorated in impressively grand style for its workaday town-centre location (exposed brick walls give a modern feel, while a magnificent antique chandelier floats overhead). This is where the town's suits and smart set get their juices (to which end, a bank of blenders stand lined up and ready for action on the far counter), along with coffees and lunchtime snacks. Hot food (pizza slices, panini and the like), pastries and ice-creams are what's on the menu. There's also a *traiteur* arm to the business, meaning bespoke orders of exquisite European-style pâtisserie can be ordered in advance and collected later in the day.

La Casa de Tu Gusta
Martil *Avenue Mohamed VI, next to Cinéma Rif (061 34 26 26). Open 12.30-3pm, 7-9.30pm Mon-Sat. £££. International/fish.*
A welcome addition to Martil's limited dining scene, this smart, ambitious new restaurant offers a little of everything, but what it does best is fish. A wet counter of locally caught sole, bream, squid and mullet, to name but a few, is set out in front of the gleaming stainless steel counters and vast extractor hood of the open kitchen, allowing you to spectate every stage from the quick, professional gleaning and prep work to the flash and fizz of the cooking. It's good fun to watch, and the cute little dining room, with its stained glass windows and smart new tiling, is a comfortable setting to relax with a (soft) drink and a fresh, simple salad while you wait for the main course. A groovy little tropical aquarium (made with stones found on the beach) is home to a few exotic fish, pretty (and small) enough to be spared the grill.

Restaurante Restinga
Tetouan *21 avenue Mohamed V (061 24 33 74/068 08 74 90). Open noon-2.30pm, 6.30-10.30pm daily. £££. International/fish.*
Set back from the busy main drag of Avenue Mohamed V, the Restinga is a leafy courtyard restaurant illuminated, come evening, with strings of fairy lights and chock-full, at all times, with tourists and wealthy locals. The menu has plenty of fodder for the unadventurous eater – burgers, paella, brochettes and so on – but it also has an outstanding selection of simple, ultra-fresh fish (whiting, mullet, swordfish steaks). Also of note is the booze licence (not so common in Tetouan), enabling them to sell 'wine pink' and 'wine red' as well as a couple of beers (the ubiquitous Flag and Heineken combo).

La Vitamina del Mar
Martil *Avenue Miramar (no phone). Open noon-3pm, 7-10pm daily. ££££. Fish.*
Exceptional seafood, first-class service and unbeatable value is what you can expect at this wonderful little restaurant. The bright dining room has a cheerful but smart seaside decor of wicker lampshades and blue-painted chairs, and the spiffy, polyglot waiters are attentive, without being overly so, and are knowledgeable counsellors to seafood novices or those unable to decipher the (Spanish) names of the various fish on the menu. Last time we visited, sea bass was fish of the day

and it arrived grilled to perfection, accompanied by an artfully presented selection of baby veg and preceded by a starter of fresh anchovy fillets drizzled with deeply green, pungently fruity olive oil. Around us, platters of langoustines were being merrily devoured, dishes of garlic-infused calamari wafted past bound for other tables, and a nearby starter of lightly grilled bream had us vowing to return.

Stay

El Reducto
Tetouan *38 Zanqat Zawya (039 96 81 20/ www.riadtetouan.com). ££.*
This smart riad is without doubt the finest accommodation that Tetouan has to offer. Down an inauspicious alley just behind place Hassan II, it comes as a pleasant surprise, with splendid high ceilings, masterfully inlaid wood panelling and ornate tiles and wrought iron work. A glass-covered ceiling floods the atrium lobby with daylight and long silk pennants drape down from the mezzanine adding a note of courtly elegance. The guest rooms have the same high ceilings and craftsmanship as the lobby, on a cosier, more intimate scale, and en suite bathrooms are clean and bright. The restaurant, which specialises in seafood, is worth staying in for.

La Ferma
Martil *BP16, Outskirts Martil (039 97 80 75/ www.laferma.com). £.*
Just on the outskirts of town, this hacienda-style hotel is a real gem: peaceful, stylish and housing a fully equipped equestrian centre, it's the epitome of the idyllic rural getaway, but still only a few minutes' drive from the beach. Rooms are decorated with a kind of *caballero* flair (whitewashed walls, prettily restored rural paraphenalia scattered about, Mexican-style rugs) and the bathrooms are spotless and well-appointed. There's a great restaurant on the ground floor, decked out in the same *Border Trilogy* aesthetic. Tons of fresh fish, Moroccan, Spanish and a smattering of international dishes are on offer, as is a fully stocked bar and pool table. Oh, and it's got amazing views from nearly every window, taking in the plains, the sea and the mountains beyond.

Golden Beach
Mdiq *Route de Sebta (039 97 50 77/www.golden-beachhotel.com). £.*
A classic tourist-dollar hotel with decent room facilities, switched-on reception staff, a pool and views over the beach (and, of course, a nightclub next door), the Golden Beach is what it is. But there's no denying it's comfortable, affordable and perfectly located right on Mdiq's lovely corniche, a few steps away from the Spanish church. And the sea-facing rooms have splendid views of the bay (sitting on the balcony as the sun slips down, watching the fishing fleet chugging out to sea is a very agreeable experience).

Riad Dalia
Tetouan *25 Rue Ouessaa, Souika (039 96 43 18/ www.riad-dalia.com). £.*
The only classy place to stay in Tetouan's labyrinthine Medina, Riad Dalia makes the most of the miserly light down in the medieval alleyways with a large, beautifully tiled interior courtyard, which clears a space for the sunshine to come flooding in. There are a number of small lounge areas (including one lovely space upstairs with giant windows and billowing diaphanous curtains), and there's also a great roof terrace with unrivalled views of the Medina. But watch your step up there: the tiles, even when dry, are as slippery as ice. Guest rooms, while very nice, are not the highlight of the hotel (they lack the sense of light and space that gives the rest of the riad its charm). Finding the place is not easy, so you may have to end up paying someone to lead you here. But hey, it's not as if you'll be short of offers.

Factfile

When to go
June and July brings the Nuits de la Mediterrán ée world music festival (www.maghrebarts.ma) to Tetouan. Tetouan gets cold during the winter. Spring or summer are better times to visit.

Getting there
The bus station (039 711654) is located between boulevard Mouquauama and avenue Hassan II; there's a large *grand taxi* rank to the south of the new town, just below avenue Hassan II.

Drivers coming from the north are best off on the N2/N13 from Tangier via Tetouan, a long, scenic road that takes in some spectacular scenery with minimal disruptions from poor surfaces or heavy truck traffic. Those driving up from the south will wish to avoid the N2 on both sides of Ketama, which is in the dead centre of one of the largest hash-producing areas in the world, and as such, is no stranger to crime.

Getting around
Tetouan, Martil and Mdiq are all easily navigable on foot. *Petits taxis* are also plentiful (especially in Tetouan, around place moulay El-Mehdi).

Tourist information
Délégation du Tourisme 30 avenue Mohamed V (039 96 1915/16). Open 9am-noon, 2-4.30pm Mon-Fri.

Internet
Cyber Primo place Moulay El-Mehdi (no phone). Open 10am-10pm daily.

El Reducto (top);
Restaurante Restinga
(bottom).

Mountains

Clockwise from top left:
La Roseraie; Kasbah du
Toubkal; Tin Mal; Kasbah
du Toubkal; La Roseraie;
La Bergerie; Ouirgane.

Toubkal Atlas

With its lush valleys, stony Berber villages, terraced hillsides and stark volcanic peaks, the Toubkal region seems dramatically rugged and remote; once amid its vertiginous scenery it's easy to forget how close you are to Marrakech. Roughly bounded by two passes, the Tizi-n-Tichka to the east and the Tizi-n-Test to the west, the Toubkal Atlas is also the location of North Africa's highest peak, Jebel Toubkal, at 4,167 metres.

The Tizi-n-Test road, which ends up at Taroudant, leads into the bucolic forested area around Ouirgane, home to the area's best hotels. The Tizi-n-Tichka leads eventually to Ouarzazate and the Sahara, but there isn't much up this way besides spine-tingling hairpin bends. The Ourika Valley, on the other hand, is an easily accessible and popular day trip from Marrakech. Here, as elsewhere in the region, life is lived at altitude. Berber villages cling to the steep valley sides, camouflaged against a red-earth backdrop that forms a brilliant contrast with the deep, luminous greens of the valley floor. The boulder-filled Ourika river runs in a deep gorge alongside the road; isolated houses on the far side are accessed by precarious bridges of bundled branches.

To travel the few miles from Marrakech into the Atlas is to encounter both a different landscape and a different, distinctly Berber, culture; these fiercely independent people were the last to be pacified by the French. With the Marrakech region continuing to grow, things are changing in these parts. But the Berbers cling proudly to their own traditions much as their villages hug the hillsides. These mountains have a life of their own, and so do its people.

Explore
OURIKA VALLEY

Ourika is a spectacular cut, slashed deep into the High Atlas. It's not a pass – the road stops at the village of Setti Fatma – and there's not much in the way of quality accommodation. So unless you're interested in skiing or trekking, it's best thought of as a day trip from Marrakech or an excursion from elsewhere in the Toubkal region.

Oukaimeden, home to Morocco's best skiing, is also best reached from Ourika. Work is soon supposed to begin on a billion-euro 'golf and skiing' development near the existing resort, the scale of which is likely to affect the whole area. Expect new roads, improvements to existing ones, and a lot more traffic. There is also talk, as yet vague, of a tunnel under the Atlas with its mouth at Setti Fatma.

Just before the valley scythes into the mountains, the village of Tnine de l'Ourika has a Monday souk and is home to **Nectarome** (024 48 24 47, www.nectarome.com, open 9am-6.30pm daily, admission 15dh). This is a one-hectare organic garden full of aromatic and medicinal plants, plus a small shop selling natural wellness products made with their essential oils. First you are invited to a tour of the fragrant gardens, where the properties of plants are explained. Then you can browse the soaps, shampoos and oils, or take mint tea and a snack. Call ahead to try the foot bath or foot massage. Nectarome is on the eastern side of the village, and is signposted from the centre.

Once you enter Ourika proper, the landscape becomes a dramatic combination of steep slopes, red earth and green vegetation in the valleys. Terracotta pottery, made from this local earth, is on sale at stalls all along the road.

The turn-off for Oukaimeden is at **Arhbalou**. There are also a couple of decent lunch spots here, notably Ramuntcho (*see p244*).

SETTI FATMA

After a final gorge-like stretch, the Ourika road peters out at Setti Fatma. The actual village is nothing special – cafés and souvenir shops, breeze-block houses and some rudimentary accommodation – but the setting is wonderful, ringed by mountains with lots of streams and grassy terraces. If you arrive in mid August there's a big four-day *moussem* that's both religious occasion and sociable fair. The village also has a *bureau de guides* where you can arrange treks and hikes; Noureddine (070 78 10 96) is the English-speaking one.

The shortest and simplest hike is the Walk of the Seven Waterfalls. It begins on the other side of the river from the main body of the village. Clutching the steep bank on the far side –

reached by footbridges made of bundled branches – are a number of small tagine-and-brochette joints. Concealed behind these is a steep sided valley, and a climb up this will bring you to the first of the seven cascades. It's quite a strenuous scramble, over big river boulders and up a cliff or two. Anyone will point (or lead) the way, and there's a basic café at the foot of the first waterfall, where you can rest with a cool drink. The other six are a more serious climb.

OUKAIMEDEN

The road up here hairpins all the way from the valley, rising eventually to 2,650 metres, and the ski resort of Oukaimeden. The season runs from December to May but snow is most likely between February and April. These are no slopes for beginners but anyone can go up the ski lift, once the highest in the world and still, at 3,273 metres, the highest in Africa. It's not always in operation, though.

The area's other attraction is the prehistoric rock carvings – of animals, weapons, battle scenes, and symbols with forgotten meanings – that can be found nearby with the help of a guide.

In summer, the area below Oukaimeden becomes what is known as an alpine prairie. The pastures are opened on 10 August and become crowded with Berber tents and livestock, each tribe sticking to its own, traditional area.

TOWARDS THE TIZI-N-TEST

TAHNAOUTE, MOULAY BRAHIM & ASNI

The last town on the plain before the road heads up towards the Tizi-n-Test is a boring administrative sort of place called **Tahnaoute**. Recently designated an official satellite town of Marrakech, it's certain to grow in the near future. For now, only two things might detain you. **Al Maqam** is a residence for artists equipped with a restaurant and surprisingly good gallery and bookshop.

Terres d'Amanar (024 45 81 05, www.terres damanar.com), is a big adventure park spreading over a nearby hillside, with attractions such as mountain biking tracks, perilous rope bridges, and aerial runways. There's also a restaurant and some bivouac accommodation. The track up there is signposted from the main road just south of Tahnaoute.

After Tahnaoute, the road winds uphill through a slightly perilous stretch known as the Gorges of Moulay Brahim. **Moulay Brahim** also has a village named after him, the road to which is off up to the right just before Asni, and in the middle of the village he has a green-roofed shrine (entry is forbidden to non-Muslims.) Nearby stalls sell charms, incense, nougat, chameleons and other esoteric supplies. Beautifully situated above the gorges, it's a popular summer day-trip destination for Marrakchi families and can get quite busy.

Asni is a few kilometres beyond the gorges. The lively Saturday souk draws people from all over the area and is worth a look. The village is bigger than it first appears, with clumps of houses dotted about the valley, but there's nothing else to see. Beyond Asni the road continues towards Ouirgane and Tin Mal. The road for Imlil forks off to the left.

IMLIL

The road to Imlil hugs the side of the broad Mizane Valley, its bottom a wide bed of shale. Not far out of Asni, surrounded by high walls and cypresses, is the restored Kasbah Tamadot (*see p247*), a hotel owned by Richard Branson.

The surfaced road runs out at Imlil, beyond which the valley forks. This small village at the foot of Jebel Toubkal, North Africa's highest peak, serves as the centre for trekking in the region. Guides can be hired at the *bureau des guides* in the centre of the village. There are also several small café/restaurants, a sprinkling of souvenir shops, and a few small guesthouses. Overlooking the village, and involved in a host of local initiatives, is the area's premier hotel, Kasbah du Toubkal (*see p247*).

OUIRGANE

Ouirgane ('weer-gan') at first seems like the tiniest place, consisting of little more than the cluster of buildings around the two

well-known hotels – La Roseraie and the Au Sanglier Qui Fume – facing off at the centre across the Oued Nifis. But after a while you realise that the houses are hidden in forest and scattered up the valley sides. It's a pretty location, in a basin surrounded by wooded slopes and, since spring 2008, partially filled by a new reservoir. This has submerged part of the village (including Chez Momo, a well-liked hotel; Momo will soon bounce back at a higher altitude) and added watersports to the area's small portfolio of activities.

This is the most comfortable base from which to visit Tin Mal, though if you don't have your own transport this will involve commandeering a taxi. But Ouirgane is a place for chilling rather than sightseeing, with a little light trekking or riding on the side.

TIN MAL

Tin Mal, the 12th-century mosque that is the area's most significant historical site, is a further 40 kilometres uphill from Ouirgane, and around three kilometres beyond the village of Ijoujak.

The landscape up here is overlooked by various kasbahs that crown strategic heights. These were fortresses of the Goundafi tribe, who ran the Tizi-n-Test until 'pacified' by the French. Though they look ancient, the kasbahs mostly date from the late 19th and early 20th centuries. Feudalism is still a living memory around here.

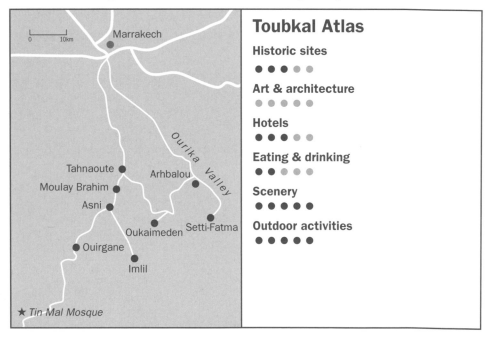

Toubkal Atlas

Historic sites
● ● ● ● ○

Art & architecture
○ ● ● ● ○

Hotels
● ● ● ● ○

Eating & drinking
● ● ○ ● ○

Scenery
● ● ● ● ●

Outdoor activities
● ● ● ● ●

★ Tin Mal Mosque

Ouirgane.

The turning to Tin Mal is on the right, where a recently surfaced road leads down and across the river. The ancient mosque, built in 1153, stands above the undistinguished modern village. Soon after you arrive, someone will appear with a key.

Back in the 12th century this remote settlement was the spiritual heart of the Almohad empire. Tin Mal had become the headquarters and garrison of one Ibn Toumart, a vociferous opponent of the Almoravid regime. He retreated here in 1125, creating a sort of Moroccan Lhasa – a fortified religious community run with a pitiless, puritanical discipline. He and his supporters called themselves El-Muwahhidoun ('unitarians') – and hence their European name, the Almohads. Ibn Toumart died in 1130 but his right-hand man, Abdel-Moumen, kept up his work. Tin Mal proved a good base, as the Almoravids' strength was in cavalry, and horses couldn't get up here. In 1144 Abdel-Moumen laid siege to Marrakech and went on to conquer most of North Africa and much of Iberia. Back here, in 1153, they used some of the resulting loot to build the mosque that stands today. It was modelled after that of Tata, near Fès.

Following centuries of decay, restoration took place in the 1990s. There is no roof but the framework of sandy-coloured transverse arches is complete, offering receding perspectives of light and shade. For the non-Muslim visitor it's a rare chance to see inside a Moroccan mosque, but note that the minaret is almost never above the *mirhab*, as it is here. Normally it's over on the north wall, rather than the one facing east towards Mecca; no one knows why it's different at Tin Mal.

The precise future of the site is uncertain. Maybe it will become a museum, maybe a mosque, or maybe it will stay exactly as it is. Little has changed here in the last few years. The roofless structure is currently used for prayers on Friday, which is the one day you can't visit. There isn't so much as a postcard on sale, and absolutely no information about anything. The attendant with the key will appreciate a tip.

Eat

Al Maqam
Tahnaoute *Douar Lamgassem (024 48 40 02). £££.*
This peaceful complex (west off the Marrakech road just north of the roundabout with the turn-off into Tahnaoute's small town centre) has the area's only noteworthy restaurant that doesn't come attached to some hotel or hotel. Instead, it's attached to a residence for artists, with rooms and a shared studio surrounding a murky pool. There's a small but worthwhile shop with art books, guides and pottery; a gallery featuring a small selection of work by some of the better Moroccan painters, including Binebine, Belkahia and Al Maqam owner Mohammed Morabiti, and a café/restaurant serving assorted tagines in a shady courtyard space.

Ramuntcho
Arhbalou *(024 48 45 21/www.ramuntcho.ma). ££.*
The best lunch stop in the Ourika Valley, where meals are served on one of two sunny terraces, or indoors in an air-conditioned saloon. It's a pleasant spot, in one of Ourika's deep and narrow stretches, with the valley walls towering high above. Despite the name's Basque reference (Ramuntcho was the smuggler hero of an 1897 novel by Pierre Loti) the menu is standard French-Moroccan, though a cut above the other cafés and tagine joints around here, and accompanied, if you wish, by wine or beer. It's also a hotel, with 14 rooms.

Stay

Most of these places charge for half board, which is fair enough as there's nowhere else to eat.

Au Sanglier Qui Fume
Ouirgane *(044 48 57 07/www.ausanglierquifume.com). ££.*
The inn of the smoking wild boar (there's a mounted boar's head with a pipe behind the bar) is the oldest hotel around here, founded in 1945 and still owned by the same French family. Two dozen chalet-style rooms and suites, all with log fires, are ranged around a good-sized pool. The restaurant serves French country food, and there's a big lounge with a pool table and huge fireplace for after-dinner activities. It's all very affordable, but the place could use a little TLC.

Bab Ourika
35km S of Marrakech *Tnine Ourika 061 25 23 28/061 44 77 89/www.babourika.com. ££££.*
On a hilltop overlooking the mouth of Ourika Valley, this newly opened (October 2008) hotel makes the most of a splendid location. It was formerly the site of a caidal kasbah, nothing of which remains. The new building, in vernacular style, has a restaurant and 15 rooms with views; more rooms will be added in the next couple of years, as well as a hammam/spa and some further pavilions in the airy gardens. There's already a pool. Work was still going on when we looked around, so we can't speak for the finished product, but English owner Stephen Skinner and partner Beatriz Maximo know what it's all about, having already made a success of the Riyad Edward in Marrakech.

La Bergerie
3km S of Ouirgane *Marigha (024 48 57 16/ www.labergerie-maroc.com). ££.*
Downstream from Ouirgane, 'the sheep pen' comprises 18 rooms, bungalows and four-bed 'family suites' (all with open fires and private terraces) scattered across six hectares of gently sloping hillside. A central building has a library/ games room and a bar and restaurant with a rustic, country pub atmosphere and Flag beer on tap. Elsewhere there's a ping-pong table and a small pool with loungers. It's a no-nonsense kind of place and is great accommodation for the price, particularly for families and groups. It's been expanding slowly since it opened under French ownership in October 1999, and further rooms are still being added.

Kasbah du Toubkal.

La Roseraie.

Douar Smara

Imlil *Tamatert (024 37 86 05/ www.douar-samra.com). £.*
Up the valley from Imlil, accessible by mule or 4x4, the Douar Smara offers modest accommodation in the tiny hamlet of Tamatert. There are two bungalows as well as seven small, colourful rooms, a tiny hammam and dining room in the main house, which has been restored in traditional style using local labour. Owner Jacqueline Brandt describes it as a 'hobbit house', built around living rock and with lots of slightly rickety wooden stairs – perilous when her family of shitsu dogs get underfoot. It's arguably the best budget accommodation in the High Atlas.

Ksar Shama

Ouirgane *(024 48 50 32/www.ksarshama.com). ££.*
The newest hotel in the Ouirgane area (it opened in spring 2008) is Moroccan-owned and follows the familiar pattern of rooms and bungalows scattered around peaceful and extensive grounds – 14 hectares in this case, plenty of space for the ten new rooms they are soon to add. They're all tastefully done out and made cosy with fireplaces, but only the bungalows have baths; rooms are limited to showers. At the heart of the place is a restaurant (French-Moroccan kitchen, dinner is extra) and a big, eccentrically shaped pool.

Kasbah Tamadot

Asni *(024 36 82 00/www.virgin.com/kasbah). ££££.*
Sir Richard Branson's Kasbah Tamadot feels like it's been dropped into the Atlas from another planet. Just up the road from Asni, built in the 1920s as the residence of the caid of the Mizane Valley, it's kitted out with every luxury amid four hectares of landscaped gardens. Yes, there are pools and tennis courts and experienced staff, and, as has happily become the fashion in this area, it contributes funding for community projects. But it's otherwise detached from local life, a citadel of sumptuousness where the surroundings serve only as backdrop and the chef is from South Africa.

Kasbah du Toubkal

Imlil *(024 48 56 11/www.kasbahdutoubkal.com). £££.*
A wonderful restoration of an abandoned kasbah perched on an outcrop above Imlil, Kasbah du Toubkal is both one of the most atmospheric places to stay in southern Morocco, and an admirable exercise in the delicate balancing act of 'sustainable tourism'. Conceived as a partnership with the local community, it's staffed by locals rather than outside professionals. Other community employment comes via a commitment to local sourcing and work for the muleteers who transport guests (and everything else) up from the village. Guests enter the compound by a tower constructed for Martin Scorcese's *Kundun*. Accommodation ranges from simple dorm rooms to a huge, split-level apartment suite with two terraces, and there are breathtaking views in every direction. Food is hearty rather than haute cuisine, and though the Kasbah has no alcohol licence, guests may bring their own. Staff can arrange every kind of trek from short rambles to ascents of Jebel Toubkal and recently opened a comfortable trekking lodge with three en-suite bedrooms in a nearby valley, about four hours walk away.

La Roseraie

Ouirgane *(024 48 56 94/bookings 024 43 91 28/ www.laroseraiehotel.com) £££.*
The classiest accommodation in Ouirgane, this is a tranquil place where 44 rooms and suites are strewn around 22 hectares of beautifully maintained gardens with lawns and citrus orchards, three swimming pools and thousands of rose bushes. The decor is beginning to look a little dated, but when we last stayed, the hammam and spa were among facilities being renovated for 2009, the hotel's 40th anniversary. A 'multimedia room', doubling as disco, was the latest addition. An equestrian centre makes this a great place for horse-riding, bird-watchers will find plenty of twitter in the treetops, and anyone will appreciate the fact that you can always find a quiet corner. The breakfast terrace is beautiful, though dinner (not included) can be a rather routine set of Moroccan standards. But the unique gardens remain attraction aplenty.

Factfile

When to go

In spring the valleys are full of wild flowers. Visibility is great and there is usually still some snow on the higher peaks. In summer, it's a pleasant notch or two cooler than down on the plain. Early winter can be cold and wet but late winter snow adds skiing to the area's list of attractions. Trekking is possible all year round.

Getting there & around

The area is naturally approached from Marrakech. Buses heading for the Ourika Valley and Setti Fatma, or Taroudant via Asni, Ouirgane and the Tizi-n-Test, leave from the bus station outside Bab Er Rob, not from the main bus station at Bab Doukkala. *Grands taxis* leave from the same place.

Asni is about an hour's drive from Marrakech, Tin Mal or Setti Fatma about two hours.
    The simplest way to get here is to ask your hotel to arrange a car from the airport or your hotel in Marrakech. The swankier places have their own cars for the purpose; any place will be able to arrange a taxi. Hiring a car and driver is also by far the easiest way to explore the area.

Tourist information

The nearest tourist office is in Marrakech (*p109*).

Internet

Most hotels will have some kind of internet access and this is your best bet. The nearest internet cafés are in Marrakech.

Clockwise from top left:
Dar Ahlam; Kasbah Ait
Ben Moro; Auberge Chez
Famille Ben Moro; Skoura;
Dar Ahlam; Toundoute.

The Dadès Valley & the Gorges

Stretching east from Ouarzazate, the Dadès Valley runs between the High Atlas to the north and the jagged formations of the Jebel Sarho to the south. It's sometimes referred to as the Valley of the Kasbahs, which is appropriate – there are dozens of old kasbahs along the route, a haunting reminder of the civilisation that flourished here in past centuries.

The Dadès is the most barren of the southern valleys – a thin strip loomed over on either side by bare reddish mountains – but the juxtaposition with such rugged surrounds just makes the palm-strewn oases seem more beautiful. Skoura at sunset, for example, has an ethereal quality that can make it seem unreal.

However, it's the dramatic slashes into the Atlas made by the Dadès and Todra gorges that take the prize for nature as spectacle. North off the main valley road, the road into the Dadès Gorge swoops and twists, climbing through curvaceous formations of red rock and passing old kasbahs on rugged outcrops before reaching a narrow and deep reddish canyon. The Todra Gorge, accessed along the edge of Tinerhir's lush palmeraie, is even more spectacular, its cliffs rising to around 300 metres.

Explore

Skoura, at the westernmost end of the Dadès Valley, can be done in a day trip from Ouarzazate. The Dadès Gorge too. But trying to pack in the Todra Gorge as well is pushing it. There's decent accommodation along the route, and all this can be done with overnight stops on the way to the Tafilelt.

The town of Ouarzazate is covered in the chapter Ouarzazate & Drâa Valley, *see pp270-281*.

SKOURA

About 40 kilometres east of Ouarzazate, Skoura is a big oasis but a small settlement. The main road bypasses what there is of the town centre – just one street with a few basic shops, a couple of down-at-heel cafés and signs still pointing to a long-closed women's goat's cheese cooperative. Most of the population is scattered about the extensive palmeraie, which is beautiful, and sprinkled with kasbahs. If you want to explore some of these, it's worth considering a guide for the day, most easily arranged through your hotel.

One of the kasbahs, on the far side of the *oued* (*wadi*, or dry river bed) from the road, to the west of the centre behind Kasbah Ait Ben Moro (*see p257*), is the famous **Amridil** (open dawn-sunset daily, admission 10dh), which features on both the 50-dirham note and on the packaging of Marrakesh Orange Juice (an example sits proudly on display).

Built by a Middle Atlas tribe in the 17th century, it's now being restored. Resident guide Aziz Sadikln brings everything to life with humour as he shows you around. Aziz can also do a tour of the oasis; call him on 064 91 45 53. Another dramatic old kasbah, **Dar Aït Sidi El-Mati**, is ten minutes' walk to the south-west of Amridil. And if you're still not kasbahed out after that there are plenty of others, including ones you can stay in.

The road that heads north out of Skoura up to the village of **Toundoute** is a beautiful drive through what's known as the **Vallée des Amandes**.

EL-KELAA M'GOUNA

Fifty barren kilometres east of Skoura, the oasis resumes at El-Kelaa, which ribbons along the road. It's famous for its rose products. All over the country, women rub rosewater into their face and hands, and most of it comes from here. It seems

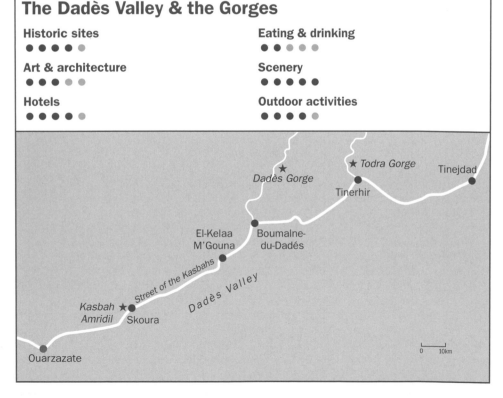

The Dadès Valley & the Gorges

Historic sites
● ● ● ● ●

Eating & drinking
● ● ● ● ●

Art & architecture
● ● ● ● ●

Scenery
● ● ● ● ●

Hotels
● ● ● ● ●

Outdoor activities
● ● ● ● ●

Toundoute.

Top: road near Toundoute.
Bottom: Amridil.

the most Moroccan of things, yet it was French perfumiers who, in the early 20th century, realised that this area offered ideal growing conditions for the leafy rosa centifolia. You'd barely notice them among the palms when they're not blooming, but there are hundreds of thousands of rose bushes around here. The harvest is in May, celebrated by a rose festival with dances, processions and lots of petal-throwing.

Essences are distilled at two factories and every other shop sells rose soap, rose skin cream, rose shampoo, rose shower gel and, of course, rosewater. It's not otherwise a very interesting place.

With a 4x4 you can drive north towards Tourbist through what's known, naturally, as the **Vallée des Roses**. From here you can follow the piste around to the top of the Dadès Gorge.

DADÈS GORGE

Leaving El-Kelaa and continuing east, ribbon development continues for another 20 kilometres or so, with kasbahs left to crumble among new buildings made from concrete rather than pisé. There's not much of interest at the next major settlement, **Boumalne Dadès**, but it does mark the mouth of the Dadès Gorge. The road up to the gorge climbs the side of the valley, twisting its way past rock formations and a series of old kasbahs. The valley is at its most dramatic and gorge-like after the village of Aït Oudinar, about 27 kilometres along, where it turns into a deep, reddish canyon – though only for a couple of hundred metres.

It's a good road up to this point, but from here it gets more difficult. You'll need a 4x4 to proceed beyond **Msemrir**, but could then take the spectacular piste that runs east over the mountains to Aït Hani, whence you can come back down through Todra. This is also excellent hiking territory, and any hotel can arrange guides and excursions.

Back on the main Dadès Valley road, just east of Boumalne Dadès, is the turning for the **Vallée des Oiseaux**, signposted to Ikniouin. Here amateur ornithologists can spot Houbara bustards, Egyptian vultures, eagle owls and bar-tailed desert larks.

TINERHIR

There's another desolate stretch beyond Boumalne, but after about 50 kilometres the road arrives in Tinerhir, the most interesting town on this road. The new part of it ribbons east and west along the road; the old part stretches out in huge kasbah-dotted palmeraies to the north and south. There's a pocket-sized Medina where you can find rug-weavers from the Aït Atta tribe at work on their looms. The carpets these women make are brilliantly coloured and of high quality, but you'll need an interpreter to negotiate as few speak anything but Berber. The main street is called the rue des Femmes because it mostly

sells kaftans and suchlike. There are also lots of spice merchants. The small Mellah (Jewish quarter) on the far side of the Medina, closed off behind a big wooden door, is these days occupied by about 20 Berber families.

The modern part of town has all mod cons – post office, banks, cybercafés, and a small supermarket that's the last stop for alcohol. It's on the south side of the main road, between Kasbah Lamrani and the old centre. Opposite Kasbah Lamrani is where you'll find Tinerhir's Monday souk.

TODRA GORGE

The road up to Todra winds north around the edge of Tinerhir's lush palmeraie. There are a couple of spots here with good views back over the town.

Once in the valley, the road runs along the bottom, never climbing the sides as the road does in Dadès. After about ten kilometres of palmeraie and campsites, the road fords the river and beyond this someone will usually be waiting to charge you 10dh to proceed. It's worth getting out and walking to enjoy the last, canyon-like stretch – it's not as narrow as at Dadès but it's much grander and more spectacular. Here the cliffs rise to about 300 metres, and provide a habitat for assorted birdlife, including a pair of Bonelli's eagles. There are two hotels here on the other side of a cold, clear stream, which is crossed by stepping stones, carefully placed just far enough apart that you might want to pay the boys who hang around to offer a helping hand in return for dirhams.

With a 4x4 it's possible to head on up beyond the gorge and follow the mountainous piste from **Aït Hani** to **Msemrir**, and then enter the Dadès Gorge from the north.

Going back down the road towards Tinerhir, notice the **Source des Poissons Sacrés**, a spring-fed pool full of 'sacred' fish, these days on the grounds of a rather tawdry campsite. We wouldn't recommend staying here, but you can go and have a look at the fish. According to local folklore, bathing here on three successive Friday afternoons will help women conceive.

TINEJDAD

Beyond Tinerhir the road continues in the direction of Er Rachidia. After about 50 kilometres, just short of Tinejdad, there's an eccentric roadside attraction on the left-hand side. The **Sources de Lalla Mimouna** (8am-sunset daily, admission 50dh) is a walled garden housing an assortment of small 'museums' (of agriculture, manuscripts, horses), each built around a gurgling spring.

It's the pet project of multilingual Zaïd Abboa, who also owns the Galerie d'Art (really more of a museum and antique shop) in downtown Tinejdad. It's on the main road, which is otherwise full of shops selling chickens. There are also some antiques and paintings on sale at the Sources. The springs themselves are disappointingly devoid of special significance.

On the outskirts of Tinejdad, a left turn at the sign for the **Musée des Oasis** leads, after a few twists and turns, to the beautiful 18th-century **Ksar El-Khorbat**. Part of this fortified village has been transformed into a fascinating museum of oasis life (admission 20dh). It's the best exhibit this side of the Atlas: well organised, with informative captions in five languages, supplied by Spanish writer Roger Mimó.

Just after Tinejdad there's a turn-off to Erfoud and the Tafilelt that takes you through towns inhabited by members of the once widely feared Aït Atta tribe.

Stay & eat

There are places to stay, which usually double as the only places to eat, all along the Dadès Valley, but the highest concentration of hotels is to be found in Skoura. Not that you'd notice that when driving through; from the road the oasis seems a huge sprawl of palm trees dotted with an incredibly confusing tangle of dirt tracks and dotted with innumerable mud-brick kasbahs. Travelling east along the road there are further hotels, scattered in the imposing landscapes, but stand-alone restaurants are all but unknown.

Auberge Chez Famille Ben Moro

Skoura *(024 85 22 12/drissbenmoro@caramail.com). £*. An appealing budget guesthouse next door to the Kasbah Ait Ben Moro, and with similarly superb views over the Skoura palmeraie and Kasbah Amerhidl. The auberge occupies a recently renovated traditional building arranged around a pleasant central courtyard, with comfortable rooms (all en suite) enlivened with Berber rugs and assorted Moroccan trinkets. There's also a cute little dining room and a breezy rooftop terrace, and the welcoming family atmosphere is another major draw.

Berbère de la Montagne

Dadès Gorge *(024 83 02 28/www.berbere-montagne.ift.fr). £*. Near La Kasbah de la Vallée, Berbère de la Montagne offers somewhat simpler accommodation and, for the hardy or the impecunious, camping. Six of the rooms have their own showers, four don't (but are cheaper), and the whole place is well, if simply, furnished. It's no palace, but it's more than adequate.

Dar Ahlam

Skoura *(reservations via Paris office +33 (0)1 53 63 42 30/www.maisonsdesreves.com). £££££*. One of the most beautiful – and most expensive – hotels in Morocco, Dar Ahlam offers a surreal haven of designer luxury buried deep in the dusty depths of the Skoura palmeraie. Hidden away behind high walls, the hotel boasts an aura of fiercely guarded exclusivity guaranteed to appeal to film stars on vacation and other cash-rich, publicity-shy visitors. Inside you'll find one of the country's ultimate kasbah designer makeovers, its traditional 19th-century building superbly refurbished in chic modern style, with nine mouthwatering suites scattered among a labyrinth of artfully embellished lounges, terraces and corridors. The gag is that you find your way from one of nine austere but tasteful suites or three sumptuous garden villas to the enormous lounge, then they escort you to where you'll eat dinner – somewhere different from the evening before, with different place settings and different food. You'd have to stay here for about ten days before you dined in the same place twice. The kitchen is excellent. Outside there are exquisitely manicured gardens and three villas with private pool, plus a large communal pool. Also thrown in is a gorgeous hammam, professional masseur, swimming pool set in lush gardens, three small libraries, and the use of a 4x4 and experienced guide, while staff can also set up a wide range of excursions into the local countryside. The hotel makes its own luxurious soaps and shampoos and you can enjoy them in big bathtubs, or buy some to take home at the small but interesting shop.

Hotel Yasmina

Todra Gorge *(024 89 51 18/www.todragorge.com). £*. This enclosed section of the gorge is an atmospheric place to stay the night, and feels remote despite being just 15 kilometres north of busy Tinerhir. At the bottom of the cliffs by the river is the Hotel Yasmina. Run by a Moroccan/American husband and wife team who also arrange tours throughout the country, the Yasmina has a fine restaurant and striking views over the palmeraie. While the building itself is not particularly remarkable, the setting is, and it has a tented 'Berber' dining area by the river.

Les Jardins de Skoura

Skoura *(024 85 23 24/www.lesjardinsdeskoura.com). ££*. Set deep inside the Skoura palmeraie (follow the red triangles painted on the telegraph and electricity poles), this tranquil French-owned hideaway offers supremely comfortable and peaceful lodgings in a meticulously restored old pisé building surrounded by extensive gardens stuffed full of fruit trees, flowering shrubs and medicinal herbs. Inside, each of the light and spacious rooms sports a different style of Moroccan decor; each is beautifully put together using local arts and crafts: traditional rugs, bedspreads, wall-hangings, wooden furniture and assorted artefacts. There's also a larger-than-average pool and inventive Moroccan cuisine.

Kasbah Aït Arbi

Boumalne *Aït Arbi (024 83 17 23/www.kasbah aitarbi.com). £*. Back down towards Boumalne, the Kasbah Aït Arbi, in the hamlet of the same name, is the region's star budget option. Cheaper rooms are on the roof but the romantic might well choose them for their wonderful views of the surprisingly lush immediate area, set against the bare, rose-tinted rocks of the surrounding hills. The more practical will note that the showers are two floors below. The more expensive (relatively speaking) rooms have their own bathrooms.

Auberge Chez Famille
Ben Moro.

Dar Ahlam.

Kasbah Ait Ben Moro
Skoura *(024 05 21 16, hotelbenmoro@yahoo.fr). ££*
One of Skoura's largest and most eye-catching buildings, topped by a soaring quartet of finely carved towers, the 18th-century Kasbah Ait Ben Moro sits on the main Ouarzazate road, with spectacular views down across the long green sprawl of the palmeraie and the dramatic Kasbah Amridil, best enjoyed from the beautiful rear-facing garden terrace. Converted into a hotel in 2000, the kasbah retains much of its original character, with chunky old wooden doors and crepuscular corridors and stairwells arranged around the traditional central airwell. The whole place is stronger on atmosphere than contemporary creature comforts, and rooms are small, rustic, and dark (those in the rooftop towers get a bit more daylight – albeit the windows are still tiny), but for an authentic taste of kasbah living, it's difficult to beat.

La Kasbah de la Vallée
Dadès Gorge *(024 83 17 17/www.kasbah-vallee-dades.com). £.*
Clambering up the steep valley side shortly before the canyon, La Kasbah de la Vallée is big and friendly, with traditionally decorated rooms, some of which look out over the Dadès river. Since the river runs year round, fed by rain falling on the Atlas Mountains, it brings a welcome coolness, particularly on summer nights. Not all the rooms have air-conditioning, so be careful to specify when booking. The owners, Hammou and Mohammed Sahbi, have an alcohol licence as well as a fine kitchen serving Moroccan cuisine. The athletic can hire a mountain bike and test themselves against the gorge, arranging for hotel staff to pick them up later in the day rather than having to slog all the way back again.

Kasbah Lamrani
Tinerhir *(024 83 50 17/www.kasbahlamrani.com). £.*
Given the scale of the place – there are three restaurants – Kasbah Lamrani can seem a bit Disneyfied, but that's not unusual in mid-range hotels in this part of the world. The rooms are a good size and more colourful than most in an area not averse to bright colours (on the inside at least). But if you're looking for 21st-century comforts at a reasonable price, you'll find them here: the 21 rooms have air-conditioning, heating, telephones, fridges, TVs and nice bathrooms. Other facilities include a swimming pool. What sets the Lamrani apart is that it's exceptionally well run.

El Khorbat
Tinejdad *(035 88 03 55/www.elkhorbat.com). ££.*
When Roger Mimó and his Moroccan partners set about creating the museum of desert life and culture at Ksar El-Khorbat, they also opened a restaurant and converted some village houses into a six-room hotel. The rooms, all with en suite bathrooms but few other luxuries, are big and dark and cool – great when it's hot, but not so welcoming in winter. The restaurant serves both Spanish and Moroccan dishes. Icy gazpacho is a welcome treat during a hot Sahara lunchtime, and if you're ever going to try camel tagine, this is probably the place to do it. Note that the hotel does not accept credit cards.

Sawadi
Skoura *(024 85 23 41/www.sawadi.ma). ££.*
Out on the far edge of the oasis, Sawadi is very attractive and a great option for travellers with children. As well as houses and bungalows scattered in extensive grounds and equipped to accommodate groups of all sizes, there's a pool and a small farm with a flock of sheep and donkeys to ride. It also supplies meat and vegetables for the kitchen. Philippe Ferrer Mora took over running the hotel in 2007 and has set about widening its already considerable appeal with sports (badminton, table tennis, boules, among others) and conference facilities, while paying careful attention to issues such as water use (and its disposal after use) and local employment. All in all, an excellent place to stay.

Factfile

When to go
High daytime temperatures mean that midsummer (July and August) is too hot to be able to explore the desert routes in comfort. March to May, or October and November, are ideal times to visit.

Getting there & around
There are daily flights from Casablanca to Taourirt Airport, two kilometres north of Ouarzazate. Otherwise the nearest airport is at Marrakech, four to five hours away.

Infrequent buses run along the main road from Ouarzazate, and *grands taxis* shuttle between the bigger towns. If you don't have your own transport and want to visit the gorges, you can commandeer taxis at Boumalne or Tinerhir, and hotels can also arrange transport. This is an area where it really does make sense to have a 4x4 to explore a little of the Atlas beyond the various valleys or gorges, or to detour into the strange, sculpted landscapes of the Jebel Sarho.

Tourist information
In Ouarzazate, the Délégation Régionale du Tourism is at avenue Mohammed V, opposite the post office (024 88 24 85, open 8.30am-4.30pm Mon-Fri). You will probably find, though, that staff in your hotel are more able to help you.

Internet
Many of the hotels and maisons d'hôte featured in the listings above offer internet access to guests. If not, your choices are limited to a small number of rather hit-and-miss internet bureaux in Ouarzazate (mostly towards the west end of rue du Marché) and towns along the Dadès Valley, particularly Tinerhir. Rates at these places are usually around 10dh an hour.

Clockwise from top left: Shepherds, Cirque du Jaâfar (2); Aïn Leuh market (2); Timnay Inter-Cultures Centre; Barbary macaque; Timnay Inter-Cultures Centre.

Middle Atlas

AZROU, MIDELT & AROUND

What could be more different from the Morocco of popular imagination than ancient cedar forests where Barbary macaque roam wild, trout-filled lakes, and steep-roofed, chalet-style gîtes? But the area around Azrou and Ifrane has all of these. Further south, the mountainous and snowy barrier of the Jebel Ayachi greets the visitor to Midelt. Here the land is radically different, with rusty red soil and gorges that strike deep wounds through the earth.

Heading from Fès south to Midelt across the Middle Atlas reveals a whole gamut of landscapes: first a plateau of green oak and tumbledown Berber nomad shacks; then the land opens out to a plain spattered with millions of shards of rubbly rock and Dali-esque gnarled limestone sculptures. Ifrane, at 1,600 metres, is something of a surprise. A rural retreat for the well-off from the summer heat of Fès and Meknes, it sports new roads, lemon-curd hued mountain chalets and European-style cafés. Beyond Ifrane, the cedar forest comes into view, before a descent into an area of volcanic lumps and bumps decorated – in season – with the pink of apple blossom. South of Azrou and the cedar forests, off the main road, the human landscape of this rugged region is in evidence with the busy weekly market of Aïn Leuh. Midelt, over 100 kilometres across the mountains, sits on a wide plain, home to eerie abandoned mines and deep rocky gorges; the line of the Jebel Ayachi peaks looms beyond.

Explore

AZROU & THE CEDAR FORESTS

Azrou is spreadeagled on the floor of the Tigrigra Valley, surrounded by cedarwood factories and apple, cherry and peach trees, and towered over by forested mountains, whose peaks reach heights of 2,400 metres.

The Atlas cedar forests of Ifrane National Park extend for some 125,000 hectares, and some of the trees are 500 or 600 years old. In addition to the dominating cedars, there are juniper trees. The forests provide a habitat for Barbary macaque, wild boar, falcons and other birds, and wildlife preservation is an important function of the park. Macaque numbers have fallen dramatically since the 1970s. Then there were 50 to 70 monkeys per kilometre; now there are only five to seven.

The 30-kilometre Circuit Touristique drive begins on road No.7217, a couple of kilometres from Azrou. At its end, at the junction of Route 13, there's a parking lot where macaques gather at La Maison de Cèdre. Here you can buy nuts to feed a collection of tame monkeys.

It's more fun to walk in the forest than to drive, though (you'll need a guide as there are no marked trails). You'll probably spot the monkeys – watch out for them pissing from the trees. It's a peaceful place, with sunlight filtering through the branches; the forest floor is laden with cedar cones, and there's a faint whiff of thyme in the air. Every now and then there are clearings, littered with basalt stones, with sweeping views of the hills beyond. In April, May and June, the glades are carpeted in daffodils. In summer, there's white hawthorn blossom.

From the summit of Rss Kharzouza, at 1,850 metres, a dramatic landscape unfolds. Below are red-roofed Ifrane, at 1,700 metres, and chalky-toned Azrou, at 1,400 metres. Beneath the peak of Rss Kharzouza is a sheer rock face. It's a dramatic landscape, isolated and a touch eerie, with falcons gliding by silently and the only sound that of the flapping wings of ravens above.

AÏN LEUH & SOUTH TO OUM ER-RBIA

Aïn Leuh, 34 kilometres from Azrou, at an altitude of 1,500 metres, is home to the Beni M'Guild Berber tribe. Shepherds and dusty brown sheep mill about the big volcanic stones that are strewn across the area around the town. Here the hills are harsh, steep slopes, either bare or with green oak trees, changing to cedars as the altitude increases.

The weekly Wednesday market is just north of the town (follow the trucks carrying sheep and look for the sea of white-grey tents). The souk itself is a place to meet and trade for people for miles around – a raggedy mix of tents and stalls, with chickens, giant sacks of flour, mini jewellery stalls and mounds of fruit.

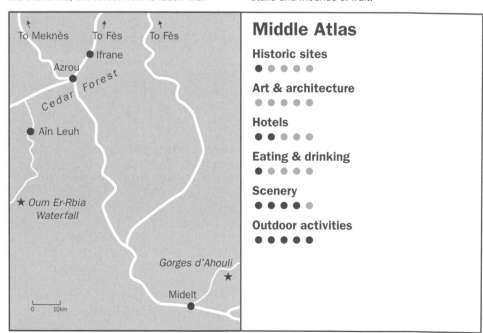

Middle Atlas

Historic sites
● ● ● ● ●

Art & architecture
● ● ● ● ●

Hotels
● ● ● ● ●

Eating & drinking
● ● ● ● ●

Scenery
● ● ● ● ●

Outdoor activities
● ● ● ● ●

Jaâfar Gorge.

Clockwise from top: Jaâfar Gorge; cedar forest; Jebel Ayachi; Ifrane.

South of Aïn Leuh is the source of the Oum Er-Rbia river. The road down to it winds around rocky slopes and nomadic campsites before the treeline begins. It then goes around Lake Ouiouane, which is surrounded by poplars. Red patches start to taint the green- and brown-toned earth; here the soil is saline and iron-rich. Sat is collected in piles under plastic mounds at the side of the road. Beyond the road you can see the caves where the salt has been extracted. Around here, agave cactus plants start to appear, along with fig and oleander trees.

The Oum Er-Rbia flows to the Atlantic at El-Jadida. Its waterfall source is surrounded by a landscape streaked white from salt evaporation. Climb up through the car park, where you can pick up a *melwi* (pancake) for sustenance. Walk past a line of cafés either side of the small river to see the waterfall cascading off the earthy brown rock.

MIDELT & AROUND

Route 13 travels south out of Azrou to Midelt, which sits at an altitude of 1,500 metres. A short detour, two kilometres off the road, leads to Aguelmane Sidi Ali, an enormous blue lake. Passing through the Col du Zad, the road emerges to face the snowy Middle Atlas mountains of the Jebel Ayachi *massif*, towering at 3,747 metres. This wide band of mountains stretches east to west across the horizon, with dark lower reaches and sharp fingers of snow. The road, meanwhile, pushes through a reddish-brown landscape towards Midelt.

Midelt itself is a workaday small town at the foot of the Jebel Ayachi range. Its Sunday market (6am-2pm) is one and a half kilometres from the centre of town, rolled out on a vast, exposed concrete and gravel plain, with a dramatic backdrop of snowy mountains. The sheep market is crushed with herders and animals. In a nearby tent, a 'dentist' works extracting teeth. Women hawk furry rabbits and piles of maize, star anise and onions are for sale.

The **Gorges d'Ahouli** is 25 kilometres north-east of Midelt. The desolate road narrows and then twists through the stunning steep-sided gorge – it's especially beautiful in the late afternoon sun, when the rich red of the rock is illuminated. Ahouli is a linear settlement of derelict mines, truncated railway tracks and abandoned buildings. Some of the fortress-like housing is pressed into the rock face. Steps and doorways have been blocked, giving the whole site a mournful air. A few Berber shepherds wander amid the silent ruins, and a smell of lead pervades. The French mined lead here until the end of the 1970s.

The road to Ahouli passes Me-bladen, where men will try and sell minerals and advertise mine viewing; it's best to push on. The entrance to the mines can be seen in the rock faces but they are all blocked off for safety reasons.

The **Cirque du Jaâfar** route that begins half a kilometre south of Timnay requires a guide, as the cross-country roads are unsigned. The dirt tracks (a 4x4 is best) cut through a valley of apple trees (they blossom in March) and pass adobe homes and walls of Berber villages.

The road meanders towards the snow-draped mountains, their dark lower slopes spotted with green oak and juniper, before you descend in to the limestone gorge of the Cirque du Jaâfar. In the higher levels of the gorge are caves that were used by shepherds to store materials. The flat riverbed can be walked, although the rubble surface requires proper walking boots; take advice about flash floods.

The red, craggy walls of the gorge sprout hardy vegetation; rock fragments litter the sides. After an hour's walk, the gorge emerges beneath the snowy mountains at Old Jaâfar's Hut, on a right-hand ledge. The gorge is named after Jaâfar, a Berber, who would welcome passersby in for tea; he is buried in an unmarked spot behind the hut.

Atelier des Soeurs Franciscaines, Broderie and Tissage Berbères

Kasbah Myriem, Midelt (035 36 12 55/ debono_menara@yahoo.fr23). Open 8am-noon, 2-5.30pm Mon-Thur, Sat.

Franciscan sisters have been living and working in the Monastère Notre-Dame de L'Atlas since 1926. There are six sisters at present, with five nationalities between them. Around 60 women work in the workshop, which the nuns run as a charitable institution to help the women earn and develop their skills. They produce some stunning carpets and embroidery work; make sure you see the display room at the back.

FURTHER AFIELD

The village of **Imilchil**, south-west of Midelt, holds a huge market in September – a chance for local Berbers to meet and replenish their stocks before the first winter snows cut them off. But it's not this that draws tourists by the busloads: it's the fact that this is also a 'marriage market', where young men and women can enjoy entertainments from dancers and musicians, all the while checking each other out with a view to engagement and marriage. Contact a local tourist board for the exact date each year.

Eat

Hotel Kasbah Asmaa

3km E of Midelt *Route Errachidia (035 58 04 08/ asmksb@menara.ma). Open Winter 11am-3pm, 6.30-10pm daily. Summer 11am-3pm, 7-11pm daily. £. Moroccan.*

This hotel is a regular stop for tour groups and so its restaurant is always busy. Large groups eat in the spacious Moroccan salons, leaving individuals to dine in the more appealing interior courtyard or next to the roaring fire in winter. The menu does not vary from the usual protein-heavy options of Atlas trout, beef brochettes, beef tagine, chicken and lemon tagine, couscous and roast chicken. In the evenings, a white-robed musician plucks melancholy tunes on a *gimbri*. Alcohol is served.

Hotel Panorama Restaurant
Azrou (*035 56 20 10/www.hotelpanorama.ma).*
Open noon-3pm, 7.30-10pm daily. £. French.
The Panorama has gone for the 'proper restaurant' look, with starched napkins and tablecloths, and wine glasses on the tables. The menu follows suit. The three-course *menu du jour* consists of soft French bread accompanied by curly butter, vegetable soup or hors d'oeuvre, followed by Atlas trout, roast lamb, rabbit or lamp chops, then crème caramel. Add a glass of chilled white wine, and you have a respectable European-style restaurant meal, probably the best in Azrou; gatherings of local bigwigs attest this. Service is prompt and efficient. Alcohol is served.

Hôtel Restaurant des Cèdres
Azrou *Place Mohammed V (035 58 23 26).*
Open Winter 11am-3pm, 6.30-9pm daily. Summer 11am-3pm, 6.30-11pm daily. £. Moroccan.
It's underused, it's down-at-heel – in fact, the less said about the decor the better, especially the blackamoor drum holder – but friendly staff at this hotel restaurant serve winning roast potatoes, tender green beans and chunky, tasty beef brochettes. The *menus du jour* list fish, beef, and rabbit and prune tagines, alongside trout meunière and spaghetti Milanese.

Restaurant de Fès
Midelt *Boulevard Mohammed V (062 05 77 54).*
Open 11am-9pm daily. £. Moroccan.
The Restaurant de Fès is proud of its marathon vegetable dish – a platter of 11 vegetables (and fruits), including quince and sweet potatoes. There are more multiple combinations when it comes to meat dishes: a tagine of lamb and beef with nine vegetables. It's not just a numbers game, though. The cooking is good here and the welcome, from owner Driss, is warm.

Timnay Inter-Cultures Tourist Midelt Centre
Midelt *Route principale No.13 (035 58 34 34/www.timnay-tourisme.com). Open 7.30am-10pm daily. £. Moroccan.*
This vast restaurant, surrounded by black and white photographs of Moroccan scenes, provides dining at long tables or salon-style, with banquette seating and low tables. Choose from several tagines, two couscous dishes, grilled trout with potato and sautéed vegetables, grilled sardines, steak brochettes and grilled chicken. There's also a fine selection of salads, among them a spicy Moroccan salad of onion, cucumber, tomatoes and black olives, an orange and carrot salad, and a good, fresh green salad. Alcohol is served.

Stay

Making a booking can sometimes be less than straightforward in this part of Morocco, as international tourism is in its infancy. The Association des Maisons Touristiques des Montagnes, Moyen Atlas has recently created the http://ifranetourisme.com site, which includes a useful list of accommodation.

Auberge La Forestiere
Timahadit, 33km S of Azrou *Route d'Errachidia-Timahdite Centre (035 56 04 03/www.laforestiere.moonfruit.com). £.*
Right by the roadside on the way from Azrou to Midelt, the Auberge has a café, warmed by a wood stove, which is a good place to stop for a cup of tea on the drive south. Hungry visitors and guests can be catered for in the Moroccan restaurant (noon-3pm, 7-10pm), where Atlas trout is a speciality. Upstairs there are just three wood-panelled rooms, with twin beds and a basin and lavatory inside mini wooden cabins within the rooms. Goat skins hang on the walls, each room has a TV and there are modern heaters for winter nights. Unfortunately, the one shower is shared, which means the place isn't such great value for money.

Camping Caravan Amazigh
5km NE of Azrou *Ougmès, route d'Ifrane (065 36 16 40/www.campingamazigh.com). £.*
A handy pit stop right on the road just north of Azrou. Amazigh has five guestrooms as well as quality camping facilities, with clean, warm showers and toilets, and space to accommodate 40 campervans (and an area for tents too), set amid cherry trees. Simply furnished guestrooms have a good dose of rustic charm. They're spacious, with rough-hewn walls, double beds and wood stoves for the winter. Small terraces capture the sun; one has a good view of the resident stork and her nest. Showers are separate. Trout, tagines and couscous can be cooked up on request.

Gîte de Charme
8km NE of Azrou *Ras El-Ma, RN8 (035 56 00 08/http://giterasalma.ifrance.com). £.*
This lodge, tucked below a rolling spread of Atlas cedar, is the stuff of rural homestead fantasy, all roaring fires, country simplicity and good home-cooked food. It was the family home of former civil servants Mehdi and Aziza Naceur, who decided to open the house to guests after the children flew the nest. Kick back on the sofas by the fire and tuck into Mme Aziza's superb food: a wonderful harira soup, and a very tasty tagine with smulchy prunes, perhaps, plus green salad. Breakfast is also a treat, with mounds of fig jam. Rooms are rustic and basically furnished, but they're comfortable, and the isolated setting means that they're completely quiet. The Auberge is eight kilometres from Azrou, 11km from Ifrane, and one kilometre off the Number 8 main road. Take the turn-off marked 'Ras El-Ma 5km', and then take the first right after half a mile; there's a very small sign there for the Gîte.

Kasbah Asmaa.

Clockwise from top: Gîte de Charme; Gîte Dayet Aoua (3); Gîte de Charme.

BIENVENUE

WELCOM

BIENVENIDO

Le Gîte Dayet Aoua

7km NE of Azrou *d'Immouzer à Ifrane, RN8 (055 60 48 52/www.gite-dayetaoua.com). £.*
This attractive whitewashed gîte is a little off the beaten track, close to the Dayet Aoua lake (this had been dry for a while at the time of writing). Berber carpets, bags and saddles decorate the white interior and the four suites and one room are all attractively done out. In addition to the restaurant (open 6-9pm daily) there's a small library, board games, patio seating with umbrellas and the chance to sleep in a Berber tent in the garden from May to July. The owner, Abdelhamid Ghandi, can arrange a variety of activities for you, including donkey riding, horse riding, canoeing and walking trips.

Hotel Atlas

Midelt *3 rue Mohamed Amraoui (035 58 29 38). £.*
This tiny hotel in the centre of Midelt is run by a Berber family, who speak Spanish and French as well as a little English. Most of the nine spotlessly clean rooms share a bathroom, but there are a couple with ensuite bathroom. On the roof terrace is a cute, tiny double with its own toilet but no bathroom. Next door, on the ground floor, there's a small restaurant serving tagines, couscous, brochettes and tea.

Hotel Kasbah Asmaa

3km E of Midelt *Route Errachidia (035 58 04 08/ www.kasbah-asmaa-midelt.com/asmksb@menara.ma. £.*
This is the top hotel in the area and it's an imposing sight – its terracotta towers look suitably fortress-like against the blue sky and the bright white snow of the distant mountains. The 35 ensuite rooms, a mix of double, single, triple and twin, are comfortable and have amazing views towards the mountains over the swimming pool. The newer, more expensive 10 rooms, while extremely spacious, each with a balcony and nicely furnished, do not have such astounding views. There's also a peculiar bathroom design fault. The

bathtubs have been attractively encased in long alcoves – the trouble is that it's impossible to operate the taps without climbing into the bath first. Half-board deals are available.

Hotel Panorama

Azrou *(035 56 20 10/www.hotelpanorama.ma). £.*
An attractive alpinesque hotel with a great restaurant. The pleasant rooms, with balconies, are equipped with TVs, desks, bed lamps and radiators; the downside is the tiny bathrooms with showers – and some rooms are smarter than others. Note also that the doubles are larger than the twins. There is one spacious suite with a bathtub in the bathroom and a separate loo. There's outdoor seating and a bar area that sits incongruously with the rest of the hotel.

Timnay Inter-Cultures Tourist Centre

18km NW of Midelt *Route principale N13 (035 58 34 34/www.timnay-tourisme.com). £.*
Timnay, whose frontage looks like a mini kasbah, faces a spectacular view of snowy mountains. This walled compound is one of the friendliest places to stay in the area, and there's a good chance you'll meet other visitors in the dining room. The Centre is 18km north of Midelt. From here you can hire a 4x4 and driver for expeditions to the Cirque du Jaâfar, ancient mines d'Ahouli, and villages of the Taâraârt upper valley and the Zaouit confraternity. Timnay can also arrange visits to Imilchil, the Berber village that has become famed (and overrun with visitors) because of its 'marriage market' (*see p263*); it also hosts an annual music festival. Owner Youssef Aït Lemkadem has rooms set right back off the road and close to the restaurant and pool. Each room has air-conditioning and a TV. A riad with eight rooms (Riad Mouna) was due to open on the premises at the time of writing. There's also parking space for campervans and an area for pitching tents.

Factfile

When to go

Winters in the Middle Atlas are cold, and snow can lie on the peaks until June. Spring is beautiful as the landscape is covered with flowers; days can be hot but the nights are still cold. Summer days are also hot, of course, and it's a good time to visit, but bear in mind that people from Fès and Meknes come here to get away from the heat, so you will need to book well in advance.

Getting there & around

You will need to hire a car to drive yourself, or a car with a driver. If you are staying in Fès your hotel can probably help with this, or see p63 for Youssef Maamri's details. The Fès tourist board lists prices at 800dh per day to the Middle Atlas but 300dh one way to Ifrane.
    Perfect Car, www.perfectcarfes.com is a recommended car hire agency in Fès.

Tourist information

Ifrane Provincial Tourist Office, Boulevard Mohammed V (035 56 68 21/dtifrane@ menara.ma) Open Sept-May 8.30am-6.30pm Mon-Fri. June, July, Aug 8.30am-6.30pm daily. **Guides** Abdellah Lahrizi (062 19 08 89/ lahrizi37@yahoo.co.uk) is president of the Association Provinciale des Guides et Accompagnateures de Montagne d'Ifrane (www.tourisme-vert-ifrane.com). He also runs two websites: www.moyen-atlas-trekking.com and www.lemarocautrement. com. Guides can be arranged by contacting guides.moyenatlas.ifrane@gmail.com or phoning 035 56 68 21.

Internet

Cyber Canadien, 2nd floor, Kissariat Al-Azhar, Azrou (035 56 19 01). Open 9am-10pm daily.

Into the Desert

Clockwise from top left:
Kasbar des Juifs (2);
road to Zagora;
Kasbar des Juifs;
Auberge Jardin Chez Ali;
sand dunes at Tinfou.

Ouarzazate & the Drâa Valley

South of Marrakech, the N9 national highway climbs slowly up into the Atlas Mountains, twisting around endless hairpins and past Berber villages clinging to vertiginous gradients before finally breasting the crest of the range at the breezy 2,260-metre Tizi-n-Tichka pass.

Beyond here, the change of scenery is abrupt and dramatic, as the highway plunges down towards Ouarzazate, then into the Drâa Valley and the barren fringes of the Sahara desert. This is Morocco in the raw: a memorably biblical landscape of stony plains and rocky mountains, flecked with surreal mineral shades of red, yellow and green. The overwhelming sense of natural desolation is relieved only by the scattered oases that cling to the valley floors, their lovingly tended thickets of palm trees sucking whatever moisture can be found out of the arid soil and providing a precarious living for the local population, whose traditional mud-brick kasbahs and ksours (fortified villages) dot the oases in various stages of crumbling disrepair.

Gateway to the region is the workaday French-era town of Ouarzazate, a convenient staging post for side-trips to the spectacular kasbahs of Aït Benhaddou, as well as points east (Dades Valley) and further south. Beyond Ouarzazate, the road runs south-east through Adgz and along the fertile Drâa Valley to Zagora, another functional colonial settlement, and then on to the small settlement of M'hamid, close to the Algerian border at the very end of the road, and the jumping off point for expeditions into the great dunes of the Sahara itself.

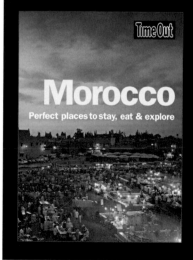
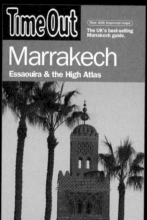

Explore

Ouarzazate (pronounced 'wa-zah-zaat') sits at an important stragetic crossroads where the Dades and Drâa valleys fork off from the High Atlas route, and where the route de Taroudant winds in from the west. The River Drâa begins where the Oued Dadès, Oued Mellah and other streams come together at Ouarzazate, and theoretically it runs all the way to the Atlantic Ocean, some 750 kilometres distant, although the last time it actually managed that feat was in 1989. More usually, it vanishes into the sand near M'Hamid, the town that marks the end of the Drâa Valley route, some ten kilometres short of the Algerian border.

OUARZAZATE

This functional town was founded by the French in 1928 as a regional capital and Foreign Legion outpost and has little in the way of traditional sights, although its size and location as gateway to the Sahara means that if you're travelling in the south you're almost bound to end up spending a night here sooner or later. Nowadays, the town is best known for its cinematic connections, which date back to when David Lean shot some of *Lawrence of Arabia* around here. Bertolucci's *The Sheltering Sky*, Martin Scorsese's *Kundun* and Ridley Scott's *Gladiator* and *Kingdom of Heaven* have been among the many other films to make use of the area's needle-sharp light, cheap labour and variety of mountain and desert locations.

The mid 18th-century **Taouirt Kasbah**, at the eastern end of town, is Ouarzazate's one historical sight and the only thing remaining from before the Protectorate. More interesting is the still occupied section of the kasbah beyond: a picturesque little tangle of alleyways and courtyards entered through a separate entrance some 50 metres east along the main road, it's difficult to get in without acquiring a small entourage of local kids and would-be guides en route.

Some ten kilometres south of Ouazarzate is the well-preserved Glaoui kasbah at **Tiffoultoute** (open 8am-7pm daily; admission 10dh), dramatically located between the river and a palmeraie. The kasbah is open for visits, and is also home to a restaurant that is popular with tour groups. To reach the Tiffoultoute, head out of town on the Zagora road then follow the sign to the right of the petrol station.

The Atlas Corporation Studios

024 88 21 66/www.atlastudios.com. Open 8am-6pm daily. Admission 30dh.

Seven kilometres west of town on the Marrakech road, the Atlas Studios were built in the early 1980s and can be toured when there's no filming. Attractions include the Tibetan monastery built for *Kundun* (complete with polystyrene stupa), and the Caesar's Palace and Karnac Temple sets from the *Asterix* movie, as well as a fake World War II fighter plane used in *Jewel of the Nile*. Some 500m further along the road, the CLA Studios (024 88 20 53/www.clastudios.com, open 8-11am, 2-5pm daily; admission 30dh), built in 2004, are less interesting, though the Jerusalem set used in the *Kingdom of Heaven* is worth a look.

Musée du Cinema de Ouarzazate

Open 8am-7pm daily. Admission 30dh.

Opposite the Taouirt Kasbah (*see below*), the recently opened Musée du Cinema de Ouarzazate is home to an array of carefully reconstructed film sets used in assorted obscure movies shot between 1999 and 2003 and includes fake gothic cloisters, a Roman-style throne room and senate, and an 'Assyrian' boudoir, along with assorted props and posters. It's not quite as interesting as the town's genuine film studios (*see above*), but is nicely put together, and has a certain surreal charm.

Taouirt Kasbah

Open 8am-6pm daily. Admission 10dh.

During the 1930s, when the Glaoua dynasty were in their prime, this was one of the largest kasbahs in the area, housing many of the clan's lesser-known members, plus hundreds of servants and slaves. Much of the kasbah has now been patched up under UNESCO auspices; the heavily restored section of the kasbah facing the main road is what gets shown to visitors, although there's not much to see beyond a few rather lifeless courtyards and corridors hosting crafts shops and galleries.

AÏT BENHADDOU

Some 30 kilometres west of Ouarzazate, and nine kilometres north of the main Marrakech road, the fortified kasbahs of Aït Benhaddou are some of the best preserved and most striking in southern Morocco. Like Ouarzazate, the village boasts a healthy roster of cinematic credits, ranging from David Lean's *Lawrence of Arabia*, through Robert Aldrich's *Sodom and Gomorrah* and Franco Zeffirelli's *Jesus of Nazareth* to Ridley Scott's *Gladiator*. Despite the interest of film-makers and tourists, however, Aït Benhaddou has suffered a long and irreversible decline since its days as an important staging post on the old Saharan caravan route. Much of the old village is now uninhabited, and lies under the protection of UNESCO.

The road brings you into the new village on the far side of the river, where you'll find a cluster of hotels, cafés and souvenir shops, along with probably a coach party or two swiftly passing through. In spring it can be necessary to paddle (or occasionally wade) through water across the ford. Locals will inevitably appear to guide you over the stepping stones or through the passages and stairways of the old village, entrance to which costs 10dh.

There's another striking kasbah, this one dating from the 17th century, six kilometres up the road at Tamdaght, also often used as a film location. You can look around but it's not in very good condition and there's little to see inside.

THE DRAA VALLEY

Immediately south of Ouarzazate the road climbs over a sequence of breathtakingly bleak flatlands of brown rubble, stretching as far as the eye can see, before winding up through the layered rock formations of the Jebel Sarho to the 1,600-metre Tizi-n-Tinififft pass.

On the other side of the pass, **Agdz** is a small market town with a Thursday souk and an increasing number of upmarket accommodation options. There are also a couple of nearby kasbahs worth checking out. The most striking are those at **Tamnougalk** and **Timiderte**. Tamnougalk is just north of the Zagora road roughly six kilometres past Agdz; the more palatial Glaoui kasbah of Timiderte lies in the opposite direction, around ten kilometres south of the main road.

Agdz is where the Drâa Valley oasis begins. For the next 100 kilometres, the Zagora road rolls past a long verdant strip cut into the desert, offering a memorably beautiful drive past endless palm groves and crumbling kasbahs. Every last scrap of fertile land is planted to grow olives, lemons, oranges, almonds, cereals and, most of all, dates, which are the valley's principal

Ouarzazate & Drâa Valley

Historic sites
● ● ● ● ○

Art & architecture
● ● ○ ○ ○

Hotels
● ● ● ● ○

Eating & drinking
● ● ● ○ ○

Scenery
● ● ● ● ●

Outdoor activities
● ● ● ● ○

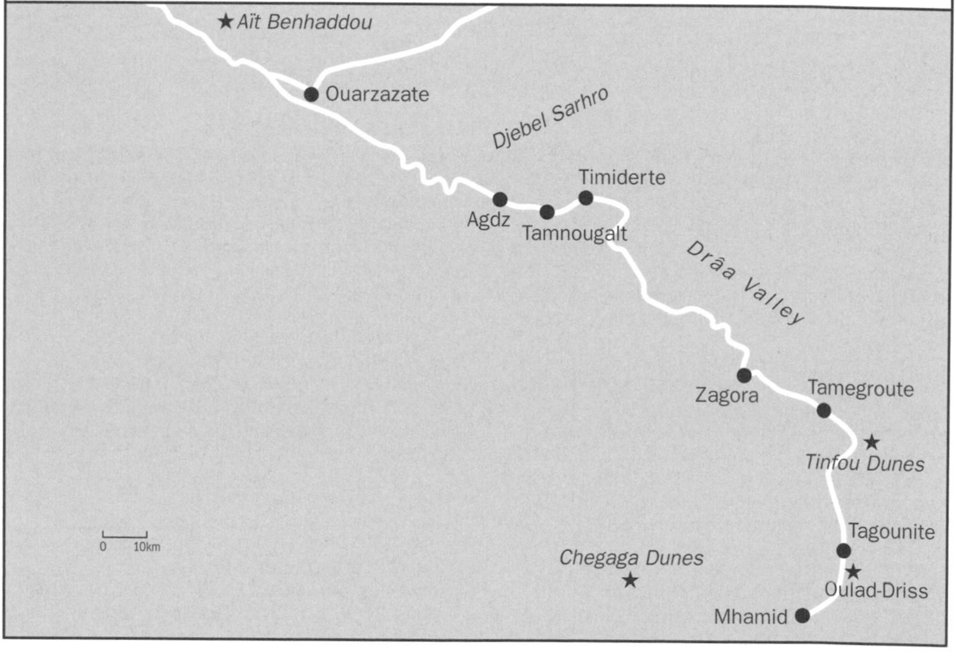

★ Aït Benhaddou

● Ouarzazate

Djebel Sarhro

Timiderte

Agdz
Tamnougalt

Drâa Valley

Zagora

Tamegroute

★ Tinfou Dunes

0   10km

Tagounite

Chegaga Dunes
★

★ Oulad-Driss

Mhamid ●

crop. Dates like lots of water and are sweetest and plumpest where it is hottest. A Moroccan saying has it that date palms have 'their heads in fire and their feet in water'. Dense with such trees, the Drâa Valley produces some of the finest dates in North Africa. Local children can often be seen standing by the road trying to sell boxes of them to passing motorists.

ZAGORA

Like Ouarzazate, present-day Zagora is a colonial creation, built by the French as a garrison and administrative centre. But the oasis has been inhabited for millennia. There's an 11th-century Almoravid fortress, built to guard the Sahara trade route, on top of Jebel Zagora at the end of town. And the Saadians would set out from around here at the beginning of the 16th century to conquer first Taroudant, then the rest of Morocco.

This trading history is acknowledged in the town's famous sign that shows a camel train and the legend 'Timbuktu, 52 days', which stands just behind the Hotel la Palmeraie on the roundabout at the western end of Boulevard Mohammed V (an older and more colourful sign was taken down a few years back, although local souvenir merchants still sell postcards and paintings of it).

There's a large souk on Wednesdays and Sundays, at which the biggest section is given over to dates, compressed and packed into plastic sacks. Common types include the small, black *bousthami* and the light, olive-coloured *bouzeki*. But the sweet *boufeggou* date, whose sugar content delays decomposition, is the most important – highly nutritious and edible for up to four years if dried properly.

There's not much else going on in Zagora proper and it isn't the friendliest of towns. Expect a fair bit of hassle from locals in search of a buck. Over the river, the adjacent hamlet of **Amezrou** is more interesting. The palmeraie is wonderfully dense and lush here, and crossed by paths that afford a good stroll. Amezrou is also known as the 'Kasbah des Juifs', although only a small section was actually inhabited by Jews, until they left for Israel in the 1960s. Any local will guide you round the kasbah, which has underground passageways that are still partially inhabited.

TAMEGROUTE AND TINFOU

Around 18 kilometres south of Zagora, the town of Tamegroute has long been an important religious centre. Its green-roofed *zaouia* (shrine) was founded in the 17th century and is headquarters of the Naciri Islamic brotherhood whose leaders, known as 'peacemakers of the desert' have traditionally been called upon to settle disputes between tribes or rival traders. The main thing to see is the wonderful **library** (open 8am-noon, 3-6pm daily, 20dh donation), up a side street on the left of the main road.

It was once much larger but there are still 4,000 volumes, carefully stored in glass-fronted cases, including an 11th-century gazelle-skin Qur'an as well as old books from as far afield as Egypt and Mali.

Back by the minaret, there's also a cloistered courtyard that acts as a sanctuary for the infirm or mentally ill. People huddle in blankets, waiting for miracles or donations, or just for the next square meal. Around the corner on the left as you head south is a clutch of pottery shops selling cups, plates and tagines in the distinctive green glaze native to Tamegroute. The same glaze is used for the roof tiles on the nearby *zaouia*, as well as on mosques and royal buildings throughout Morocco.

About five kilometres south of Tamegroute, the village of Tinfou is home to an isolated patch of authentic Saharan sand dunes. They're only the size of a few football pitches, and you'll be sharing this Saharan experience with any number of tour groups, camel touts and kids trying to sell you animals made out of clay or palm leaves, but if you're not going all the way down to M'Hamid, this will be your only glimpse of desert sands.

ON TO M'HAMID

Beyond Tamegroute the road narrows and runs through mostly arid landscape for the next 70 kilometres, crossing the barren Jbel Bani before coming back into oasis country at Tagounite. Before M'Hamid it's worth stopping off to see the small, private **museum** (open 8am-6pm daily, donation 15dh) in **Ouled Driss**. Follow the 'Musée' sign from the main road and a guide will pick you up. It's a beautiful 17th-century Berber house, once owned by the village chief, containing exhibits of costumes, jewellery and tools.

M'Hamid is a tiny town that really does feel like the end of the line, fighting a losing battle against the sand. The locals, many of whom are Sahrawi, will stare like they've never seen a tourist before – although the entire town seems to be involved in the camel-trekking business. You'll be beating away touts from the various agencies as soon as you step out of the car. There are impressive dunes to explore hereabout. Those at **Erg Lehoudi**, eight kilometres north of town, reach heights of 100 metres and are easily accessible, albeit usually busy with tourists and touts. Alternatively, head out to the much more remote, 300-metre-high dunes at **Chigaga**, 60 kilometres distant, a two-hour trip by four-wheel-drive.

Eat

Relais de Saint Exupéry
Ouarzazate *13 Boulevard Abdellah, Quartier El-Qods (024 88 77 79/www.relaissaintexupery.com). Open 1-3pm, 7.30-10pm daily. ££££. French/Moroccan*

Top: Draa Valley.
Bottom: sand dunes at Tinfou.

Tucked away on the very edge of Ouarzazate, this rather upmarket French restaurant is one of the town's most surprising discoveries, with a formal but friendly atmosphere in an elegant setting, the dining room embellished with a colourful display of aviation-themed pictures and posters. The menu offers a good selection of Moroccan and European dishes, with a range of five-course fixed menus centred on excellent and authentic Moroccan standards (pastillas, tagines, tangias), as well as European classics like tournedos Rossini, entrecôte steak and Norwegian salmon, and a few cheaper pasta options. To reach the restaurant, leave Ouarzazate on the Skoura road. Turn left at the last roundabout, and the restaurant is immediately to the left.

Restaurant Dmitri
Ouarzazate 22 Boulevard Mohamed V (024 88 73 46). Open noon-3pm, 7.30-10pm daily. ££. Moroccan/international.
Founded in 1928, the same year as Ouarzazate, this famous old restaurant also served at various times as the town's first petrol station, first telephone bureau and first transport office. It retains the quietly elegant air of a good provincial French restaurant, with neatly starched white tablecloths and walls plastered with assorted film memorabilia inside and a pleasant terrace overlooking the street outside. Food is an eclectic mix of Moroccan and European, including no fewer than eight types of tagine, along with the other Moroccan dishes, such as tangias and pastillas, supplemented with a few French and Greek dishes, salads and pastas. There's a good wine list and the beer is refreshingly cheap.

Stay

Ouarzazate and the Drâa Valley boast plenty of memorable places to stay, with dozens of beautifully restored traditional riads and hotels set in old kasbahs, as well as a fair number of modern hotels built in traditional styles. Many are the creations of expat French and Spanish owners who have taken a shine to life on the edge of the Sahara.

Auberge Restaurant Jardin Chez Ali
Zagora Avenue de l'Atlas Zaouiate El-Baraka (024 84 62 58/www.chezali.prophp.org). £.
One of the region's longest-established and most appealing budget options, Chez Ali offers spacious and comfortable en-suite rooms (some with air-conditioning) at bargain rates, while staff can also fix you up with a range of inexpensive desert excursions. The main draw, however, is the spectacularly lush garden restaurant, with fresh Moroccan cuisine (although the menu is a bit limited) served at tables set out on the lawns between a verdant riot of trees, flowering shrubs and great clumps of purple bougainvillea.

Le Berbère Palace
Ouarzazate Quartier Mansour Eddahbi (024 88 31 05/www.palaces-traditions.com). ££££.

The place the stars stay when they come here to film, this sumptuous five-star is the pick of Ouarzazate's upmarket hotels. Sprawling faux-kasbahesque buildings are set amid extensive palm-studded grounds, dotted with huge Egyptian-style statues and other props, which – aptly – lend the feel of a film set. Rooms, with all the expected accoutrements, are spacious and colourfully furnished. Amenities include Moroccan, international and Italian restaurants (the latter embellished with film posters and signed photos of the stars), as well as a comfy bar, heated pool, hammam, gym, Jacuzzi, massage room and sauna.

Dar Azawad
M'Hamid Douar Ouled Driss (024 84 87 30/www.darazawad.com). ££.
French-owned maison d'hôte among the palms about four kilometres west of M'Hamid along the main road to Zagora. There are 15 cool and tasteful bungalow rooms in the walled grounds here, furnished with Moroccan fabrics and artefacts, as well as simpler and cheaper tented rooms with en-suite showers. There's also a pool with bar, a hammam, dining room and a good French-Moroccan kitchen. Owner Vincent Jacquet creates a good atmosphere.

Dar Daif
6km SE of Ouarzazate 024 85 42 32/www.dardaif.ma. ££.
Signposted off the road to Zagora, on the very edge of Ouarzazate, this stylish little maison d'hôte occupies a traditional pisé building set around a lovely tree- and flower-filled courtyard, with shady terrace seating and a small swimming pool. Inside, the hotel bursts with colour, with virtually every surface smothered in an eye-catching array of rugs, wall hangings, Moroccan lamps and old paintings, both in the cosy little public lounges and in the comfortably equipped rooms. There's also a pretty little hammam, a massage room, and fine views from the roof terrace over the surrounding village – taking in everything from the storks nesting in the towers of the nearby mosque to the distant pink sprawl of Ouarzazate.

Dar Kamar
Ouarzazate 45 Kasbah Taourirt (024 88 87 33/www.darkamar.com). ££.
Half the fun of Dar Kamar is just finding the place, buried amid a labyrinthine tangle of little alleyways in the middle of the Kasbah Taourirt. Once inside, you'll discover one of southern Morocco's most appealing traditional riads, full of old-world atmosphere, but with a luxurious contemporary twist. Air-conditioned rooms are decorated with brightly coloured cushions, African silk bedspreads and enough Moroccan artefacts to fill a small handicrafts shop. Upstairs there are memorable kasbah views from the roof terrace and a neat little tented bar and restaurant.

Dar Mouna
Aït Benhaddou 028 84 30 54/www.darmouna.com. ££.
Given that there's nowhere to sleep in the old village of Aït Benhaddou itself, a stay at Dar Mouna is the next best thing. The atmospheric pisé building, arranged around a

traditional interior courtyard and airwell, has bags of old-fashioned rustic charm, with simple rooms kitted out with Berber rugs and bedspreads. All come with en-suite bathroom and air-conditioning; the more expensive ones also have stunning views of the kasbahs of Aït Benhaddou, as does the spacious upstairs terrace. There's also a small swimming pool, a diminutive hammam and a homely little restaurant.

Dar Qamar
Agdz *024 84 37 84/www.locsudmaroc.com. ££.*
Occupying an old, single-storey pisé house, the French-owned 'House of the Moon' offers a low-key retreat in a tranquil setting on the edge of Agdz (signposted 1.5km from Agdz town square), complete with intimate gardens and a decent-sized pool. The traditional building has been given a discreet modern makeover, with a cosy lounge and rustic little restaurant enlivened with eye-catching contemporary artwork, and the addition of a jacuzzi and hammam. Rooms are simple but comfortable, and all come with air-conditioning and en-suite bathrooms.

Dar Raha
Zagora *Amezrou (024 84 69 93/ http://darraha.free.fr). £.*
Simplicity and authenticity are the keynotes at this French-owned *maison d'hôte* on the edge of Zagora, set in a pair of traditional pisé buildings, decorated entirely with locally produced rugs, fabrics and artefacts. There are just nine rooms, all sharing (extremely clean) communal bathrooms. Upstairs the rooftop terrace provides superb views over the palmeraie and crumbling rooftops of the surrounding village. Moroccophiles will enjoy the extensive library full of local-interest books, as well as insightful tours of the nearby Amezrou kasbah with the hotel's owner and local history buff Antoine Bouillon. Excellent value.

Kasbah Azul
2.5km N of Agdz *024 84 39 31/www.kasbah azul.com. ££.*
Hidden away at the end of a very bumpy little track, the recently opened Kasbah Azul, under combined French-Moroccan ownership, is a haven of peace and understated luxury in a building that seamlessly combines traditional kasbah style with soothing modern comfort. The seven rooms (all with air-conditioning) are bright, light and very comfortable, simply but attractively decorated with bright rugs and fabrics. Public areas are enlivened with *objets d'art* and contemporary paintings. There's a cosy little library and lounge, and a good-sized pool in the attractive gardens.

Kasbah Ellouze
4km N of Aït Benhaddou *Tamdaght (024 89 04 59/ www.kasbahellouze.com). ££.*
Tucked away in the back alleys of the atmospheric village of Tamdaght (and thus well away from the passing coach parties), Kasbah Ellouze offers a homely mix of traditional style and contemporary creature comforts in a peaceful and secluded rural setting. The hotel occupies a modern building constructed in traditional pisé style, with simple,

stylish but traditionally furnished air-conditioned rooms. There's a cosy little restaurant, which has been plastered with photos of jazz notables by the music-loving French owner, and a series of delectably shady terraces with superb views of the local palmeraie, mountains and the eye-catching kasbah.

Mercure Ouarzazate
Ouarzazate *Avenue Moulay Rachid (024 89 91 00/ www.mercure.com). ££.*
This suave modern hotel – one of the Mercure chain – is housed in an appealing contemporary take on the region's traditional pisé architecture. Low-rise adobe and stone buildings sit in a prime position on a bluff above Ouarzazate, with superb bird's-eye views over the kasbah and valley below. Rooms are arranged around a pair of courtyards and are attractively furnished in bright colours. All have air-conditioning, TV, minibar, phone and safe. Amenities include hammam and massage rooms, a spacious bar and a chic restaurant, cunningly built beneath one side of the hotel pool, so you can tuck into your food while looking up at your fellow guests splashing around in the waters above. It's a good alternative to the riad experience.

Palais Asmaa
Zagora *Amezrou (024 84 75 55/www.asmaa-zagora.com). ££.*
A pair of nodding camel statues and a huge, floridly tiled doorway set the tone for this large, kitsch Moroccan-themed four-star hotel. It's far from authentic, of course, but there's something appealing about its palatial chintziness, with flamboyant tiled and carved marble decorations covering virtually every surface, plus fountains, chandeliers and traditional Berber artefacts galore. Facilities include an attractively decorated bar and restaurant, extensive gardens and perhaps the biggest pool in southern Morocco. Rooms are a tad humdrum compared to the glitzy public areas, but perfectly comfortable. Nearby is the slightly more modest sister hotel, the Kasbah Asmaa, with a delightful garden.

Riad Lamane
Zagora *Amezrou (024 84 83 88/www.riadlamane.com). ££.*
Set in a gorgeous location amid Zagora's shady palmeraie, the Riad Lamane occupies a traditional pisé building enlivened with kitsch modern touches, backing on to lush gardens with a small pool, a pair of attractive restaurants and a quaint African-themed bar. Most of the accommodation is in a series of spacious, cool and bright bungalows arranged around the gardens, enlivened with quirky decorative touches and eye-catching colour schemes. There are also a couple of less appealing rooms in the main building, as well as some rather gloomy tents.

Riad 'Le Sauvage Noble'
7km NW of Zagora *Ouarzazate road (024 83 80 72/ www.sauvage-noble.org). £.*
An attractive riad occupying a meticulously restored old kasbah centred around a picture-perfect airwell and

Hotel Kasbah Asmaa.

Auberge Restaurant Jardin Chez Ali.

fountain. All rooms are individually designed. Those downstairs are exquisitely decorated, though rather small, and perhaps nicer to look at than to stay in; rooms upstairs are bigger, brighter and altogether more comfortable. There's a nice little garden and tiny pool out the back, and marvellous views over the palmeraie and surrounding kasbahs from the rooftop terrace. Welcoming owner Abdellah Naji runs desert excursions, and profits from the hotel help fund various local community projects in the surrounding village.

Au Reve Berbère

4km SE of Ouarzazate *Douar Tajda (073 26 18 95/www.reve-berbere.com).* £.

Tucked away in a newly restored traditional building on a sidestreet four kilometres from the centre of Ouarzazate (the road leading to Dar Daif, *see p277*), this simple little French-owned guesthouse offers a friendly and low-key retreat in a slightly down-at-heel but interesting local neighbourhood. Decorated in vivid colours, the guesthouse is more Moroccan funk than Berber dream, with just six rooms (all with shared bathroom) decorated with bright batik wall hangings and arranged around a small courtyard-cum-interior garden that is painted in vivid strains of yellow and blue, with floor cushions to lounge about on. There's also a pretty little restaurant serving decent and authentic Berber cuisine prepared by a local cook from the village, and the owners are happy to arrange desert safaris and other excursions.

Rose Noir

Ouarzazate *Quartier de la Mosquée, Kasbah Taourirt (024 88 20 16/aubergelarosenoire@yahoo.fr).* ££.

Tucked away in the deepest reaches of the Kasbah Taourirt, this atmospheric but unpretentious *maison d'hôte* feels more like a family homestay than a hotel, with a welcoming and sociable atmosphere – albeit not as peaceful as other places in town (and the adjacent mosque doesn't help either). The building itself has bags of unadulterated kasbah character, and rooms are spacious and comfortably furnished in traditional style, though not quite as polished as other places in town – the Chambre Bleu and the Chambre Berbère are the nicest.

Villa Zagora

Zagora *Amezrou (024 84 60 93/www.mavilla ausahara.com).* £.

With just five rooms and a low-key and homely atmosphere, a stay at this French-owned *maison d'hôte* is more like borrowing a friend's very well-equipped Moroccan villa rather than spending time in a conventional hotel. Built in traditional style in 2000, the villa has an engagingly unpretentious but lived-in feel, with cheerful contemporary artworks on the walls and shelves of dog-eared books to browse through. Bedrooms are pleasantly light and spacious, with simple, attractively rustic decor, while there's a lush flower-filled garden to relax in, complete with a lovely little terrace and a small pool. One of the best bargains in the south at current rates.

Factfile

When to go

Not surprisingly, Ouarzazate and the surrounding countryside can get swelteringly hot in summer, with daytime temperatures climbing up into the 30s between late May and late September (and approaching 40°C in July and August). Daytime temperatures during the remainder of the year are pleasantly mild, although the thermometer can fall to 0°C during winter nights. The other thing to bear in mind is that the major road into the region, the N9 from Marrakech, crosses some of the highest mountains in the country and is often closed due to heavy snowfall for days at a time between November and April.

Getting there and around

There are daily flights to Casablanca from Taourirt Airport, 2km (1.25 miles) north of Ouarzazate, with Royal Air Maroc; otherwise, the nearest airport is in Marrakech, a four- to five-hour drive away on the well maintained N9 national highway.

Getting around is easiest by private car: the main roads are well maintained and traffic light. Many visitors hire a car in Marrakech, although there are also numerous car-hire agencies in Ouarzazate, mostly along avenue Mohammed V

and on place du 3 Mars, including Avis, Budget and Hertz, as well as various local agencies. The journey down the Drâa Valley from Ouarzazate to Zagora takes around 3-4 hours; it takes around 5-6 hours to reach M'Hamid. There are also around eight bus services daily from Marrakech to Ouarzazate, and less frequent departures on from Ouarzazate to M'Hamid. Regular grands taxis also run between all the major towns.

Tourist information

Ouarzazate Délégation Régionale du Tourism, Avenue Mohammed V, opposite the post office (024 88 24 85). Open 8.30am-4.30pm Mon–Fri.

You will probably find, though, that staff in your hotel are more able to help you.

Internet

Many of the hotels and *maisons d'hôte* featured in the listings above offer internet access to guests. If not, your choices are limited to a small number of rather hit-and-miss internet bureaux in Ouarzazate (mostly towards the west end of Rue du Marché) and Zagora (mostly along Boulevard Mohammed). Rates at these places are usually around 10dh per hour.

Clockwise from top left:
Ksar Ouled Abdelhalim;
Kasbah Mohayut;
Auberge Kasbah
Derkaoua (left); Auberge
du Sud; Erg Chebbi.

The Tafilelt Oasis & Merzouga

Once, the Tafilelt Oasis was the most important area south of the Atlas. Here stood the medieval city of Sijilmassa, a political and cultural centre at the nexus of the desert trade routes, raking in gold from across the Sahara. And it was from here that the Alaouites, three centuries ago, sallied forth to become the dynasty that still rules Morocco today. Sijilmassa sank into the sand long ago: the region stopped being the centre of anything and instead became the end of the line – literally, with the Algerian border to the south and east. Hints of former glories remain, though, in the form of decaying kasbahs and ancient palm groves, and a certain indefinable brooding quality.

Today it's the natural landscape that draws visitors. South of these haunted houses – and the modern settlements of Erfoud and Rissani – lie the haunting dunes of Erg Chebbi. Close to the settlement of Merzouga, these are 200 square kilometres of the sort of desert that you might have suspected existed only in the imagination. Nothing can quite prepare you for the precise beauty of the sand, its colours shifting from pink to gold against a backdrop of a clear blue sky, or particularly vivid at dawn or sunset. They are one of the great sights of Morocco, and today they're a tourist attraction, with hotels edging their western border. But while the sands are not deserted, they are plenty big enough to feel lost in, to experience the solitude and wonder at the silence.

Explore

This is not the most densely populated region on earth and most travellers who come this far carry straight on past Erfoud and Rissani to Merzouga and the dunes of Erg Chebbi. This should be your plan too. But Rissani is worth spending some time in, either coming or going, and there is life to the south of Merzouga too.

ERFOUD

Erfoud is a mostly French-built administrative town that, on account of having the most mod cons within striking distance of the photogenic Erg Chebbi dunes, also has connections with the film business. It's a desultory sort of place – a frontier town with a gridlike street pattern and ideas above its station. But it's where you'll find essential facilities like banks and a pharmacy, and there's a Sunday souk and an October date festival.

The one unique local item is a kind of fossil-rich black marble that is polished up and used for tabletops and bar counters. By another process, the stone is sculpted to bring the fossils into relief on everything from ashtrays to washbasins. The results are usually quite kitsch.

RISSANI

Around 20 kilometres south of Erfoud, Rissani is an untidy village with a small modern central core, and *ksour* (fortified tribal village) and kasbahs

(fortified family mansions) scattered throughout its extensive palmeraie. This is the home town of the Alaouite dynasty, which started feeling expansive in the early 17th century and had taken power by 1664.

Before that it was the site of Sijilmassa (*see p287*), founded in the mid eighth century by Berber heretics. At the heart of such a fertile oasis, and at the nexus of trade routes connecting West Africa to Morocco and Europe – and Morocco to the rest of North Africa and the Middle East – Sijilmassa quickly became a great trading centre and dominated the South for five centuries. The place was never the same after the Portuguese opened up maritime routes to sub-Saharan Africa, and Sijilmassa fell into decay long ago. Such ruins as there are can be found on the north side of Rissani, near the outlying hamlet of El-Mansouria, where a gate known locally as the Bab Errih probably dates from the Merenid period. (You can ask for directions at the nearby Hotel Kasbah Asmaa, three kilometres towards Erfoud.) The other faint traces of Sijilmassa are really only of academic interest. A few archaeological finds are on display at the small and not very interesting museum of the **Centre d'Étude et de Recherches Alaouite** (055 77 03 05, open 8.30am-6.30pm Mon-Fri) on the north side of Rissani's main square – basically a handful of dusty pots. It also hosts temporary exhibitions.

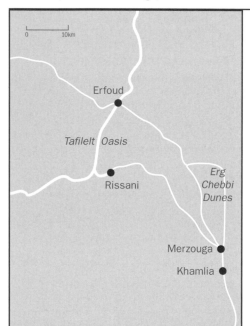

Tafilelt Oasis & Merzouga

Historic sites

● ● ● ● ●

Art & architecture

● ● ● ● ●

Hotels

● ● ● ● ○

Eating & drinking

● ● ○ ○ ○

Scenery

● ● ● ● ●

Outdoor activities

● ● ● ● ○

The ancestors of the current ruling Alaouite dynasty in Morocco settled in the region in the 13th century. Off the road running towards Merzouga, just after the village peters out into the desert, there are signposts directing you to the **Mausoleum of Moulay Ali Cherif**, founder of the dynasty, who was buried here in 1640. It's a modern building, an older one having been destroyed by flash flooding in the mid 1950s, but entrance is forbidden to non-Muslims.

Beyond the mausoleum is a signposted turn on to the **Circuit Touristique**, a 21-kilometre loop around the *ksour* and kasbahs of the palmeraie. The first point of interest is the 19th-century **Ksar Akbar**, once used to house disgraced members of the Alaouite family. About two kilometres further along the route is the grand **Ksar Ouled Abdelhalim**, built for Moulay Hassan's brother around the turn of the 20th century and touted as the 'Alhambra of the Tafilelt'. Its remains include imposing towers, cloistered courtyards and ornate gateways that succeed in giving a flavour of the *ksar*'s former grandeur. The whole circuit takes in a number of other kasbahs and *ksours* – some in an advanced state of erosion, others still housing a substantial part of Rissani's population.

> ## "A shallow seasonal lake sometimes attracts large flocks of pink flamingos – a particularly exotic sight out here in the arid wilderness."

Back downtown, Rissani has a lively souk on Sunday, Tuesday and Thursday, drawing people from all over the area to buy and sell everything from dates to doorknobs. There's also an animal market behind it, with donkeys, sheep and camels on sale. Souk days are good for people-watching, and there are some strategically placed cafés with terraces, but after that, once you've done the boring museum there's not much else to see.

MERZOUGA

Until recently the road ran out at Rissani and proceeding to Merzouga and the dunes of Erg Chebbi involved setting off across 30 kilometres of piste. Now there's good paved road to Merzouga village and beyond to Taouz near the Algerian border.

There's nothing much at Merzouga itself but squat, flat-roofed houses, a few general stores, some extremely basic café-hotels, and a couple of carpet dealers. The real attraction here are the dunes looming over to the east of the road and to the north of the village. About 27 kilometres from north to south and eight kilometres from east to west, Erg Chebbi is a huge, shifting expanse of pink sand that looks exactly how the desert always looks in the movies – probably because many of them were shot right here. But the celluloid image doesn't quite prepare you for their other-worldly dramatic beauty: the sheer expanse stretching to the horizon, the colours mutating with the changing light, the chiselled peaks and swerving contours.

But it's not the world's quietest piece of desert. This area has long been a big tourist attraction. Around two dozen hotels nudge up to the western edge of the sands, and in the late afternoon there are both tourists and locals running around on quads and motorbikes, as well as camel-trekking trains setting off to overnight at the small oasis that lies out of sight among the dunes. If you are on your own overnight camel trek, ask your guides to turn off the generator after you have finished dinner, so you can hear the silence while gazing into the clearest night sky you've ever seen.

Camels aren't the only wildlife here. Birders should look out for Egyptian nightjars, fulvous chatterers and blue-cheeked bee-eaters. Best of all, however, is when there's been enough rainfall for a shallow seasonal lake to appear to the north-west of the village, usually in late spring, which sometimes attracts large flocks of pink flamingos – a particularly exotic sight out here in the arid wilderness.

SOUTH OF MERZOUGA

The road from Rissani continues all the way to Taouz. About eight kilometres south of Merzouga is a gnawa village called **Khamlia**, populated by the Berber-speaking descendants of black African slaves. The sun-blasted scattering of poor, flat-roofed pisé houses feels like it could have been lifted whole from the other side of the Sahara. As with gnawa everywhere, music is one of the locals' main pursuits and there are several family bands here. You can sometimes find them playing at the village's small cultural centre, or you can locate the house of the Zaid family on Khamlia's south-east side. Go in, say hello, and settle on cushions in the room to the left. Someone will bring you mint tea, and then musicians in white robes will appear to play and dance – drummers, castanet players and a guy on a *gimbri*. It's excellent entertainment. Tip them 50dh or buy their CD.

Sixteen kilometres further on, past salt flats and dry lake beds, is the village of **Taouz**. It's little more than a military outpost by the Algerian border, but if you like being stared at then this is the place.

Stay & eat

Erfoud has a clutch of old-school four- and five-star hotels, suitable for housing film crews and correspondingly overpriced. We wouldn't particularly recommend staying in Rissani, and there aren't many eating options there either, though on market days you'll find a tagine or two on sale around the colonnaded souk.

There are hotels dotted all along the western fringes of the Erg Chebbi dunes, and getting to these involves a rattle across bumpy piste from the road between Rissani and Merzouga (the more northerly ones are further from the road). The road from Rissani to Merzouga is a little over 40 kilometres; for hotels in this area we have included approximate distances from Rissani to the turn-offs for the hotels, as that is the direction from which you will probably be driving (even though many hotels are closer to Merzouga). Remember that you then need to add on the journey across the piste to your hotel. Individual establishments are well signposted.

The only electricity comes from generators, so expect no power late at night or in the middle of the day. All the hotels are half-board, which makes sense around here as there isn't anywhere else to eat.

If you are interested in a camel trek, your hotel will certainly be able to help (as will more or less anyone you come across in this region, see also p292).

Auberge Dar Al Janoub

30km SE of Rissani *Merzouga, off Rissani–Merzouga road, GPS: N 31° 07.36.3 – W 04° 00.49.7 (035 57 78 52/068 471 516/www.dareljanoub.com). ££.*
Just a kilometre off the Merzouga road, at the foot of the dunes, Auberge Dar Al Janoub is an Italian-owned hotel that successfully combines Latin design aesthetics with the colours and materials of Morocco. Sophistication is not something one would expect in the middle of the desert, but here it is, albeit in a form calculated to ensure peace and tranquillity. Four of the 21 guest rooms have views of the dunes. The rest are set around a shady terrace beside the swimming pool. Spotlessly clean, all rooms have air-conditioning and en suite bathrooms. The restaurant serves good Moroccan and international food. Of course, you're not here just to look at the desert but to get into it, and the Auberge can arrange a night sleeping under the stars, with camels to get you there and dinner provided.

Auberge du Sud

34km SE of Rissani *Merzouga, off Rissani–Merzouga road, GPS: N 31° 12.63 – W 04° 01.45 (061 21 61 66/ www.aubergedusud.com). £.*
If you're looking for somewhere a little less expensive, then the Auberge du Sud, something of a desert institution after 20 years in business, is probably a good bet. It's invariably buzzing (with people rather than flies, we hasten to add), which ensures a good audience for the nightly entertainments. The cheap rooms are comfortable, though without frills. The owner has let his fancy run a little wild in some of the more expensive suites: try the 'pottery room', with bed posts, seat legs and shower head made out of pots, and a clay bowl light switch. All rooms have showers and a private terrace where you can sleep under the stars, and most come with air-conditioning, meaning you can retreat indoors should a night outside not prove quite as romantic as you hoped. Nights can be organised in the dunes in a luxury tented camp. The only real downside is the lack of a swimming pool, though one is planned for summer 2009…inshallah.

> **"Sophistication is not something one would expect in the middle of the desert, but here it is, albeit in a form calculated to ensure peace and tranquillity."**

Auberge Kasbah Derkaoua

23 km SE of Erfoud *Erfoud, GPS: N 31° 17.23 – W 04° 05.31 (025 57 71 40/www.aubergederkaoua.com). Closed Jan, June-Aug. ££.*
The Auberge Kasbah Derkaoua, the northernmost hotel along the fringes of the sand and reachable from Erfoud on the R702 as well as the Rissani–Merzouga road (turnoff is 12km from Rissani), was the first in these parts, established in the late 1980s, and it remains one of the best places to stay, particularly for families. Set in its own small oasis, there's lots of space for children to run around, and sufficient shade to stop them overheating. There is an assortment of rooms and bungalows, a bar and restaurant, a swimming pool, tennis court, and its own desert encampment not far away. As with most of the area's hotels, accommodation is half board only, and the food is excellent. There's the usual French-Moroccan cuisine, but also some welcome changes to the usual desert fare: spring rolls with vegetables and cheese followed by tagine with pear, say, and raisins and crème caramel for dessert. It's possible for non-residents to eat in the restaurant, although it's best to book in advance. When it's warm enough, dinner is taken on the candlelit terrace. Wine and alcohol are also served from

Queen of the south

Looking at the dusty, down-at-heel backwater that is today's Rissani, it's hard to imagine that this was once the site of one of the Maghreb's major political and cultural centres. Like Fès and Marrakech, Sijilmassa was an entrepôt town at the northern end of one of the great trans-Saharan trade routes. It was founded in 757 between the Oueds (rivers) Ziz and Rheris. Efficient organisation of water resources enabled the development of a logistics hub capable of hosting and provisioning caravans consisting of thousands of camels and hundreds of traders. By the ninth century, while Europe was still emerging from the Dark Ages, Sijilmassa was already a cosmopolitan city of several hundred thousand.

Traders would trek 20 days across the desert to Taghaza, in what is now Mali, and exchange weapons, fabrics and spices for salt. They'd then trek another 40 days to Timbuktu and trade the salt for gold and slaves. Maybe half or two-thirds of the latter would survive the pitiless trek back across the Sahara.

Sijilmassa grew fat on the proceeds, with lush gardens and grand mansions, busy markets and landmark mosques, counting houses and brokerages, and a mint that produced the coinage for most of North Africa. It was reckoned to take half a day to walk from one end of town to the other. Ibn Battuta described it as 'a very beautiful place, with an abundance of dates'.

Wealth did not buy stability, however. Founded by Muslim heretics, Sijilmassa was tussled over by the Fatimids of Ifriqiya and the Umayyads of Cordoba throughout the tenth century, overrun by the Almoravids in the 11th, sacked by the Zayyanids in the 13th, and destroyed all over again in 1363. In the 15th century it was the source of uprising that toppled the Saadians and established the Alaouite dynasty that still rules Morocco today.

But all this conflict was bad for business, and it was a decaying Sijilmassa that the Alaouites restored in the 17th century. The town was then destroyed one last time by the Aït Atta tribe in 1818. Today there is nothing but some shapeless, unedifying ruins to the west of Rissani (see p284). The lone archway, known to the locals as Bab Errih and probably dating from the Merenid period, is the only piece of the once-eminent Sijilmassa that hasn't melted back into the desert.

Clockwise from top left:
Nasser Palace (2);
Kanz Erremal;
Auberge Kasbah
Derkaoua;
Kanz Erremal; Auberge
Kasbah Derkaoua.

the bar. You'll sometimes hear the hotel referred to as Chez Michel, after the now deceased original owner.

Kanz Erremal
30km SE of Rissani *Merzouga, off Rissani–Merzouga road, GPS N 31° 07.76.5 – W 04° 00.76.9 (035 57 84 82/www.kanzerremal.com). ££.*
A chic and stylish desert retreat. The modern building is designed in traditional, indigenous kasbah style, with added mod cons. Decoration makes judicious use of local artefacts to help put together a design-savvy look. Rooms are a little small compared with the overall grandeur of the place, but they look good, are painted in strong southern Moroccan colours, and are all en suite, with air-conditioning. Once ensconced, take tea on the large terrace at the back, which looks out over the dunes, and watch the camel herders tending their charges. There's also a pristine pool to while away the hotter hours of the day. The hotel can arrange airport transfers, guided 4x4 excursions, camel rides and overnight stays in tents among the dunes.

"Take tea on the large terrace at the back, looking out over the dunes, and watch the camel herders tending their charges."

Kasbah Mohayut
30km SE of Rissani *Merzouga, off Rissani–Merzouga road (066 03 91 85/www.mohayut.com). £.*
Like other Erg Chebbi hotels, Kasbah Mohayut is built and decorated in local style, and furnished with local artefacts. Where Kasbah Mohayut scores, though, is in the personal touch of owner Moha. Born and raised in Merzouga, with years of experience in the tourist industry, he gives the auberge its particular and notable warmth. Most guests are independent travellers. The air-conditioned guest rooms are all different and, natch, decorated in bright desert colours. And after a hard day watching the sun shift across the dunes the hotel provides many different areas in which to relax, with the poolside terrace being a particularly good spot for lunch under the shade of olive trees. The food itself is rather special – very fresh salad and tasty tagines. For those who simply cannot bear being parted from the modern world, the internet is available at the reception.

Kasbah Xaluca
5km N of Erfoud *Erfoud–Errachidia road, GPS: N 31° 29.20.8 – W 04° 12.78.4 (035 57 84 50/www.xaluca.com). £.*
A few kilometres to the north of Erfoud is the Spanish-owned Kasbah Xaluca, a walled enclosure built around a glamorous, palm-lined central pool. Guest rooms – there are bungalows and suites – have lots of mod cons, including air-conditioning, and are decorated with hangings, rugs and so on. Bathrooms come with the sculpted fossil fittings that the town of Erfoud is known for. There's a tennis court and indoor football pitch. The hotel is popular with large groups and as a result there's every kind of excursion, trek, rental, hike, adventure and experience on offer. The Xaluca chain also owns a hotel in the Erg Chebbi area. the Kasbah Tombouctou Merzouga.

Nasser Palace
35km SE of Rissani *Merzouga, off Rissani–Merzouga road, GPS: N 31° 08.39.9 – W 04° 01.35.6 (070 78 00 28/066 03 91 94/www.nasserpalace.com). £.*
Just five kilometres north of Merzouga, Nasser Palace is well signposted down a two-kilometre track off the main road. Moroccan run, it's a good budget option, offering cheap rooms that are clean, comfortable and traditionally decorated, and a laid-back atmosphere. Camping is also available in a tent in the grounds. Most of the action takes place around the large swimming pool in the open courtyard of this riad hotel. There is a dining room with a log fire for cosy nights in when nights are cold – and they do get cold in the desert – and a hammam, plus Jacuzzi and massage facilities on site.

Factfile

When to go
As one would expect, temperatures rise to uncomfortable levels during the summer. Winter nights can get very chilly in the desert, although daytimes are usually sunny. Spring and autumn are ideal times to visit.

Getting there & around
You can get to the Tafilelt Oasis and the dunes of Erg Chebbi by road from the Dadès Valley via the turn-off at Tinejdad. Driving to or from the Drâa Valley there's a road that runs east–west through the empty quarter south of the Jebel Sarho, connecting with the Drâa Valley between Agdz and Zagora.

Buses run from Tinehrir to Tinejdad, and from Tinejdad to Erfoud, but you will not be able to do much without your own transport.

Tourist information
Your best bet is to ask for information in your hotel.

Internet
There are several internet cafés in Rissani, and some hotels have internet access.

Need to Know

ACCOMMODATION

CAMPING
Campingo www.campingo.com

RIADS
Fez Riads 00 212 35 63 77 13/
www.fez-riads.com
Hip Marrakech 8816 7065/
www.hipmarrakech.com
TM Nights 00 212 68 76 01 24/
www.tmexperience.com

AIRLINES

Air France www.airfrance.com
Atlas-blue www.atlas-blue.com
British Airways 0870 850 9850/www.ba.com
EasyJet www.easyjet.com
Iberia www.iberia.com
Royal Air Maroc www.royalairmaroc.com
Ryanair www.ryanair.com

DRIVING

A car can be useful for trips out of the major cities. In cities you are better to rely on taxis, which are cheap and plentiful.

Vehicles drive on the right in Morocco. The French rule of giving priority to traffic from the right is observed at roundabouts and junctions: in other words cars coming on to a roundabout have priority over those already on it. Speed limits are 40km/hr (25mph) in urban areas, 100km/hr (62mph) on main roads, 120km/hr (74mph) on autoroutes.

There are on-the-spot fines for speeding and other traffic offences. It is compulsory to wear seatbelts. Be very wary when driving at night as cyclists and moped riders often have no lights. Neither do sheep, goats and pedestrians, and street lighting can be poor. In the case of an accident, report to the nearest *gendarmerie* o obtain a written report, otherwise insurance will be invalid.

CAR HIRE
To hire a car, you must be over 21, have a full current driving licence and carry a passport or national identity card. Rental isn't cheap; daily rates with a local agency start at about 400dh (around £25/$50 at the time of writing) for a Fiat Palio, Citroen Saxo or Peugeot 205 with unlimited mileage.

A Toyota Corolla kicks in at about 700dh (£44/$86) per day, a Toyota Avensis at 950dh (£60/£118). At the internationals like Avis, Budget or Hertz, expect to pay about 25 per cent more.

The drawback with many of the local hire firms is the back-up service – cars may be ancient and unreliable, breakdown support lacking and replacement vehicles may not always be forthcoming.

Be aware that payments made in Morocco by credit card often incur an additional five per cent fee. This is one of several reasons why it works out cheaper to arrange your car rental in advance through the travel agent booking your flight or via the internet.

The major companies allow you to rent a car in one city and return it in another. Almost all agencies will deliver cars to your hotel and arrange pick-up at no extra charge but this service must be booked in advance. If you are heading south over the mountains, remember that you are responsible for any damage if you take a car off-road or along unsuitable tracks. Four-wheel drives, such as Toyota Landcruisers, are available from most hire companies and start at around 1,200dh (£75/$147) per day.

Marrakech car-hire company offices
Always Car 15 rue Imam Chafi, Kawkab Centre, Guéliz (061 19 31 29).
Always can organise anything from a two-door Fiat to a 4x4 to a minibus. Also has offices in Casablanca and Agadir, so cars can be dropped off there. English-speaking drivers also available.
Avis 137 avenue Mohammed V, Guéliz (024 43 25 25/www.avis.com/avisrak@iam.net).
Other locations: Aéroport Marrakech Menara (024 43 12 65
Budget 68 boulevard Mohammed Zerktouni, Guéliz (024 43 11 80/www.budgetrentacar.com). Other locations: Aéroport Marrakech Menara (024 43 88 75).
Concorde Cars 154 avenue Mohammed V, Guéliz (024 43 11 16/fconcordecar@iam.ma).
Europcar 63 boulevard Mohammed Zerktouni, Guéliz (024 43 12 28/www.europcar.com).

Other locations: Aéroport Marrakech Menara (024 43 77 18). Open to meet incoming flights.
Fathi Cars 183 avenue Mohammed V, Guéliz (024 43 17 63).
Hertz 154 avenue Mohammed V, Guéliz (024 43 13 94/www.hertz.com).
Other locations: Aéroport Marrakech Menara (024 44 72 30). Club Med (061 36 75 37).
Majestic Locations 21 rue Tarek Ibn Ziad, Guéliz (024 43 65 00/majesticloc@yahoo.fr).
Sublime Car Rental 1422 Zarktouni Bouakaz M'hamid (044 42 03 87).

DRUGS

Morocco is the world's largest cannabis producer. Discreet use is tolerated and a significant minority still consume the stuff.

However, Moroccan law maintains stiff penalties for sale or consumption, so be careful. Some dealers double as police informers, angling for a share of the *baksheesh* you'll later pay to buy yourself out of trouble.

There are 60 or so Europeans in Moroccan jails and nearly all of them have been banged up for cannabis-related offences. To reduce the risk of joining them, follow these guidelines:
• Avoid street dealers. If you don't know any locals, the best bet is a younger souk stallholder who might have a bit under the counter. Don't ask. Wait for their approach.
• Never buy more than a small amount for personal use, and don't travel with any in your possession.

ELECTRICITY

Morocco operates on 220V AC. Plugs are of the European two-pin variety. If you forget to bring an adapter, they're available from electrical shops for around 25dh. Visitors from the USA will need to bring a transformer if they intend to use appliances from home.

EMBASSIES & CONSULATES

Australia
See Canada.

Canada
Canadian Embassy 13 rue Jaafar Es Sadiq, Agdal, Rabat (037 68 74 00/www.rabat.gc.ca). Also offers consular assistance to Australians.

France
French Consulate 1 rue Ibn Khaldun, Medina, Marrakech (024 38 82 00/www.consulfrance-ma.org).

French Embassy 3, rue Sahnoun, Agdal, Rabat (037 68 97 00).

Ireland
See UK.

New Zealand
See UK.

South Africa
South African Consulate 34, Rue des Saadiens in Hassan, Rabat (037 70 67 60/037 70 67 56/www.morocco.com/destinations/rabat).

UK
British Consulates in the following cities also handle Irish and New Zealand consular affairs (www.britain.org.ma/consular/services.html).
Agadir British Honorary Consulate, Complet Tour, 26 Avenue Hassan II, Immeuble Oumlil – 3eme étage (028 84 04 69).
Marrakech Residence Taib, 55 Boulevard Zerktouni, Gueliz (024 42 08 46/024 43 60 78).
Rabat 17 boulevard de la Tour Hassan (037 72 96 961).
Tangier Trafalgar House, 9 rue Amerique du Sud, Tangier 90000 BP 1203 (039 93 69 39/40/email: uktanger2@menara.ma).
British Embassy 28 avenue S.A.R. Sidi Mohammed Souissi, Rabat (037 63 33 33/email rabat.consular@fco.gov.uk).

US
US Consulates
Casablanca: 8 boulevard Moulay Youssef (022 26 45 50).
Rabat: 2 avenue de Marrakech, Rabat (037 76 22 65).
US Embassy 2 avenue de Mohamed El Fassi, Rabat (037 762 265/www.usembassy.ma).

EMERGENCIES

Fire service 15. **Police** 19.

GLOSSARY

ARCHITECTURE
bab gate
dar house
fundouk medieval merchants' inn arranged around a central courtyard with stabling on the gound floor, sleeping quarters above hammam traditional bathhouse
kasbah traditional Berber fortress/palace
koubba domed tomb

ksour traditional fortified village
mashrabiya fretworked wooden screens traditionally used for windows
Mauresque French colonial version of neo-Moorish architecture
méchouar parade ground
medersa Quranic school
muqarna Moorish ceiling ornamentation resembling stalactites
pisé mud reinforced with straw and lime, a primary building material.
riad house with a central courtyard garden
tadelakt moisture-resistant polished plaster wall surface
zaouia shrine of a holy man, usually also doubling as a theology school
zelije mosaic tilework typical of Moorish decoration

CULTURE

babouche traditional leather slippers, typically yellow
baksheesh a tip or kickback
baraka blessings
ben son of (also spelled ibn)
Berber the indigenous tribes people of southern Morocco
gnawa semi-mystical brotherhood of muscians descended from black African slaves. Also the name of the music they play
djellaba traditional men's robe
kif the local marijuana, cultivated extensively in **mellah** traditional Jewish quarter
muezzin the man who makes the call to prayer
oud musical instrument, like a lute
oued wadi or dried river bed
sidi saint

FOOD

briouates little envelopes of paper-thin *ouarka* (filo) pastry wrapped around ground meat, rice or cheese and deep fried
couscous coarse-ground semolina flour. Also the name of the cooked dish
harira vegetable soup
pastilla ouarka (filo) pastry typically filled with a mixture of shredded pigeon, almonds and spices, dusted with icing sugar and cinnamon
tagine slow-cooked stew of meat (usually lamb or chicken) and/or vegetables. Also the name of the conically lidded dish it's cooked in

HEALTH

Morocco has no reciprocal health care agreements with other countries, so taking out your own medical insurance is advisable. Travellers commonly complain of stomach upsets, but this is more often due to the change in diet than food poisoning. Bring along anti-diarrhoeal capsules, such as Imodium, and avoid tap water: bottled water is inexpensive and available at all restaurants and cafés. Should you become ill, be warned: the Moroccan healthcare system is ropey. While good doctors can be found and pharmacies are surprisingly well stocked and knowledgeably staffed, for anyone afflicted with serious illness the best route to take is the one leading straight to the airport and home.

PHARMACIES

Pharmacies are clearly marked with a green cross and/or green crescent. There's at least one in every neighbourhood. The drugs may have strange names, but staff can usually translate. Most pharmacies are open 9am to 6-7pm Monday to Friday. Some may also open on Saturday mornings or afternoons. When closed, each pharmacy should display a list of alternative pharmacies open after hours.

ID

You are meant to carry ID at all times. Moroccans have identity cards but a passport is fine for foreign visitors, or better still, a photocopy, so you can leave the original at the hotel. Valid ID is essential when checking into a hotel, hiring a car, changing or paying with travellers' cheques (and sometimes just changing foreign currency) and collecting poste restante.

MONEY

Local currency is the Moroccan dirham, abbreviated dh (in this book) and sometimes MDH, or MAD. Small change is always useful for things like tips and taxi fares and should be hoarded.

If you want to exchange dirhams back to a hard currency you may be asked to show the exchange receipts from when you converted into dirhams – this is because banks will only allow you to change back up to half the amount of Moroccan currency originally purchased.

ATMS

Cashpoints, or *guichets automatiques*, are common in most Moroccan towns and cities, and it's perfectly possible to travel on plastic – although it's always wise to carry at least a couple of days' 'survival money' in cash. Most banks set a daily withdrawal limit of 2,000dh (currently around £120) on ATM withdrawals. If you need more, go to an exchange bureau with your card and passport and get a cash advance. Beware of Monday mornings; machines are often empty.

BUREAUX DE CHANGE

Almost all banks have a bureau de change counter, as do most major hotels of three stars and up. The exchange rate is set by the Bank of Morocco and is uniform. No commission is charged. When changing money you will usually be asked to show your passport.

CREDIT CARDS

MasterCard and Visa are widely accepted at shops, restaurants and hotels; American Express less so. Places that accept AmEx often add five per cent to cover the cost of the transaction. It's wise to carry cash back-up because management will often claim that the machine is 'broken' or that your card won't go through – they aren't keen on the delay in payment that comes with credit cards. Credit-card fraud is also a problem in Morocco, so keep all receipts to check against your statement. Chip and PIN has yet to reach Morocco.

Lost/stolen credit cards

All lines of the companies listed below have English-speaking staff and are open 24hrs daily. **American Express** 00 973 256 834, **Barclaycard** 00 44 1604 230 230, **Diners Club** 022 99 455/00 44 1252 513 500, **MasterCard** 00 1636 722 7111, **Maestro** 00 870 000459.

OPENING HOURS

Opening times listed in this book should be taken more as guidelines than gospel (many places close in the afternoon for a siesta, which is not always reflected in the times we have given). Note that hours vary in summer (from around 15 June to the end of September) and during Ramadan (see below), when businesses open and close later.

Banks are open 8.30-11.30am, 2.30 3.30pm Mon-Fri.

PERSONAL SHOPPER

Laetitia Trouillet 074 21 72 28/www.lalla.fr. Runs a personal shopping service in Marrakech.

PUBLIC HOLIDAYS

Religious holidays occupy two or three days and if these happen to fall midweek then the government commonly extends the holiday to cover the whole working week. Morocco's six secular holidays occupy a day each. Banks, offices and civil service institutions close, but many shops stay open and public transport runs as usual.

NATIONAL HOLIDAYS

New Year's Day 1 January. **Labour Day** (Fête du Travail) 1 May. **Feast of the Throne** (Fête du Trône) 30 July. **Allegiance Day** 14 August. **Day of the Green March** (Marche Vert), commemorating the retaking of Spanish-held Saharan territories 6 November. **Independence Day** 18 November.

RAMADAN & ISLAMIC HOLIDAYS

On the Islamic calendar, **Ramadan** is the most significant event and the one that has the greatest impact on the visitor. This is the Muslim month of fasting. Many Moroccans abstain from food, drink and cigarettes between sunrise and sunset. Many cafés and restaurants will close during the day. It's only polite not to flaunt your non-participation by smoking or eating in the street. Ramadan nights are some of the busiest of the year as, come sundown, eateries are packed with large groups communally breaking their fast, a meal known as iftar. Jemaa El Fna gets particularly wild.

The end of Ramadan is marked by the two-day feast of **Eid al-Fitr** ('the small feast'). A few months later the feast of **Eid al-Adha** ('the festival of sacrifice') commemorates Abraham's sacrifice of a ram instead of his son. It's not a good time for sheep as every family that can afford to emulates the patriarch's deed by slaughtering an animal.

	2008	2009	2010
Ramadan	2 Sept	22 Aug	11 Aug
Eid al-Fitr	2 Oct	21 Sept	9 Sept
Eid al-Adha	9 Dec	28 Nov	16 Nov
Moharram	10 Jan	29 Dec	7 Dec
Mouloud	20 Mar	9 Mar	26 Feb

Note that these dates are approximate as the exact start of the celebrations depends on the sighting of the full moon.

TELEPHONES

DIALLING & CODES

To call abroad dial 00, then the country code followed by the telephone number. When calling within Morocco you need to dial the three-digit area code even if you are calling from the same area. For instance, if you are making a local call within Marrakech, you must still dial 024.
• Mobiles begin with the prefix 06 or 07 or 01.
• The Morocco country code is 212.

Area codes
Casablanca 022. **Essaouira** 024. **Fes** 035. **Marrakech** 024. **Ouarzazate & the south** 024. **Rabat/Tangier** 037.

TIME

Morocco follows GMT all year round (it's on the same time as Britain and Ireland in winter but an hour behind during British Summer Time, from late March to late October).

TIPPING

Tipping is expected in cafés and restaurants (round up the bill or add 10-15 per cent), by guides and porters, and by anyone else that renders you any sort of small service. Five or ten dirhams is sufficient. It is not necessary to tip taxi drivers, who can just be content with overcharging.

TOILETS

Public toilets are a rarity – use the facilities when in bars, hotels and restaurants. They're usually decent enough (and occasionally stunning). It's a good idea to carry tissues as toilet paper is not always available; most people use the water hose to sluice themselves clean. The wastebasket beside the toilet is for used tissues. At cafés the toilet attendant expects a few dirhams as a tip; it's bad form not to oblige.

TOUR COMPANIES

Best of Morocco 01380 828 533/ www.morocco-travel.com
Rediscover 01989 730 552/ www.rediscover.co.uk
Destination Evasion 00 2112 024 44 73 75/ www.destination-evasion.com
Carrier 0161 491 7650/www.carrier.co.uk
Naturally Morocco 01239 710 814/ www.naturallymorocco.co.uk/ ≈
Tribes Travel www.tribes.co.uk/01728 685 971
Mad about Morocco www.madabout morocco.com/+212 764 68553

ACTIVITY HOLIDAYS

Point 101 www.point101.com/artholidays
Photography course in Marrakech.
Best of Morocco www.morocco-travel.com/morocco
Specialist trips including cookery, stargazing, bird-watching and trekking.
Travellers Tales www.travellerstales.org
Travel writing and photography.

CULINARY COURSES

Best of Morocco www.morocco-travel.com/morocco/Cookery/
See also p51 **How to make a Fassi feast**.

ECO TOURS

Naturally Morocco www.naturallymorocco.co.uk
Eco-tourism.

HIKING/BIKING/DRIVING

Responsible Travel www.responsibletravel.com
Trekking and camping in the Sahara.
Best of Morocco www.morocco-travel.com/morocco
Organises cross-country safaris, camel treks, and walking holidays.

TOURIST OFFICE

Moroccan National Tourist Office
www.visitmorocco.org

INTERNATIONAL OFFICES

London 205 Regent Street, W1R 7DE (+44 20 7437 0073).
New York 20 East 46th Street, suite 1201, 10017 (+1 212 55 72 520).

TRAINS

ONCF 024 44 77 68/www.oncf.org.ma

VISAS & IMMIGRATION

All visitors to Morocco need a passport to enter (it should be valid for at least six months beyond the date of entry). No visas are required for nationals of Australia, Britain, Canada, Ireland, New Zealand, the US and most EU countries. If in doubt check with your local Moroccan embassy. Foreigners can stay in Morocco for three months from the time of entry. Extensions require applying for an official residence permit – a tedious procedure. For a simpler option, leave the country for a few days and re-enter, gaining a new three-month stamp.

WOMEN

Though Marrakech is a Muslim country, the dress code for women is not strict – with a few provisos. Leave the minis and micros behind. Shorts are out too. Wear trousers or dresses and skirts that reach the knee or lower. In conservative areas it's a good idea to keep shoulders covered too.

In touristy areas such as Marrakech, you may get hit on, so avoid direct eye contact and don't smile at men. Ignore come-ons or obnoxious comments. If a man is persistent, raise your voice so others can hear; someone may intervene on your behalf.

Festivals

A more comprehensive list of festivals can be found at www.morocco.com/culture/celebrations or www.moroccofestivals.co.uk.

JANUARY

Marrakech
Marrakech Marathon
www.marathon-marrakech.com

FEBRUARY

Marrakech
Dakka Marrakchia Festival
An annual festival of traditional Marrakechi music.
www.morocco.com/blog/dakka-marrakchia-festival-a-musical-celebration

APRIL

Meknès
Moussem Sidi Ben Aissa
Spectacular two-festival honouring local saint Sidi Ben Aissa. Expect jousting, music and dancing.
www.moroccofestivals.co.uk/other.html

Essaouira
Alizés Musical Spring Festival
A festival of classical music, with a touch of jazz.
www.moroccofestivals.co.uk/alizes_musical_spring.html

MAY

Tangier
Tanjazz Music Festival
Jazz events in May and June each year.
www.tanjazz.com

JUNE

Essaouira
Festival d'Essaouira
Four days and nights of gnawa, world music and jazz, as performers from around the world join the musicians of Morocco's gnawa brotherhood.
www.festival-gnaoua.net

Fès
Festival of World Sacred Music
International event with artists as diverse as Jessye Norman and the Qawwali Sufi of Pakistan.
www.fesfestival.com

JULY

Chefchaouen
Festival Alegria
Annual celebration of traditional music and arts.
www.alegriafestival.com/039 986 147

Marrakech
National Festival of Popular Arts
A five-day celebration of Morocco's arts.
www.marrakechfestival.com

AUGUST

Asilah
International Arts Festival
This annual cultural festival turns the town into an art gallery, with paintings on the city walls.
www.morocco.com/sights-activities

SEPTEMBER

Moulay Idriss
Moussem Moulay Idriss
Morocco's biggest moussem.
www.worldeventsguide.com.

Imilchil
Marriage Festival
This huge Berber food and supplies market is also a 'marriage market', with music and dancing, where young people can check each other out.
www.whatsonwhen.com

Tissa
Horse Festival
Equine competitions, plus music and dancing – all in honour of a 15th-century saint.
www.morocco.com/blog/the-traditional-tissa-horse-festival

OCTOBER

Tangier
Festival National du Film
www.ccm.ma

NOVEMBER

Marrakech
Marrakech International Film Festival
www.festival-marrakech.com

Advertisers' Index

Please refer to relevant sections for contact details

Editor's Picks

FIVE-STAR DESTINATIONS

Each destination in the book is rated by a series of categories. Here are the top performers in each:

ART & ARCHITECTURE

Chefchaouen p208-p219
Essaouira p180-p197
Fès p46-63
Meknès p110-p123

EATING & DRINKING

Fès p46-p63
Marrakech p64-p109

HISTORIC SITES

Fès p46-p63
Meknès p110-p123

HOTELS

Essaouira p180-p197
Marrakech p64-p109

OUTDOOR ACTIVITIES

Agadir to Sidi Ifni p154-p167
Ameln Valley & Tafraoute p16-p23
Essaouira p180-p197
Middle Atlas p255-p267
Toubkal Atlas p237-p247

SCENERY

Agadir to Sidi Ifni p154-p167
Ameln Valley & Tafraoute p16-p23
Dadès Valley & the Gorges, The p248-p257
El-Jadida, Oualidia & Azzemour p198-p205
Ouarzazate & the Drâa Valley p270-p281
Tafilelt Oasis & Merzouga, The p282-p289
Taza & Around p24-29
Toubkal Atlas p237-p247

SHOPPING

Fès p46-p63
Marrakech p64-p109

ACCOMMODATION

LAP OF LUXURY

Berbère Palace, La, Ouarzazate p278
Dar Ahlam, Skoura, The Dadès Valley & the Gorges p254
Dar Mimosas, Essaouira p193
Dar Zemora, Marrakech p95
Deux Tours, Les, Marrakech p98
Jardins de las Medina, Les, Marrakech p95
Jnane Tamsna, Marrakech p95
Kasbah Tamadot, Asni, Toubkal Atlas p247
Ksar Char-Bagh, Marrakech p98
Riad Fernatchi, Marrakech p101
Sultana, La, Oualidia p205

EXPENSIVE

Dar Beida, Essaouira p193
Hôtel Gazelle d'Or, Taroudant p226
Kasbah du Toubkal, Imlil, Toubkal Atlas p247
Riad Azama, Azemmour p205
Riad Enija, Marrakech p98
Riad Fès, Fès p63
Riu Tikida, Agadir p165

MID-RANGE

Casa Hassan, Chefchaouen p216
Casa Lalla, Marrakech p92
Dar Kamar, Ouarzazate p277
Dar l'Oussia, Essaouira p193
Dar Roumana, Fès p60
Dar Seffarine, Fès p60
Dar Walili, Asilah p177
Hôtel Nord Pinus, Tangier p148
Jardins de la Koutoubia, Marrakech p95
Kasbah Ait Ben Moro, Skoura, The Dadès Valley & the Gorges p257
Riad al Bartel, Fès p60
Riad Magi, Marrakech p101
Trois Chameaux, Les, Mirleft, Agadir to Sidi Ifni p167

BUDGET BEDS

Abertih, Mirleft, Agadir to Sidi Ifni p164
Auberge Restaurant Chez Ali, Zagora, The Dadès Valley & the Gorges p278
Beau Rivage, Essaouira p193
Dar Mounir, Chefchaouen p216

ARTS & ARCHITECTURE

FOOD & DRINK

SHOPPING

CERAMICS
Art Naji, Fès p59
Chez Aicha, Essaouira p190
Palais Damasquini, Meknès p117

LEATHER GOODS
Atika, Marrakech p86
Chez Said, Marrakech p86
Ouchen Mohammed, Essaouira p193

SOUVENIRS
Afalkay Art, Essaouira p190
Boutique Bel Hadj, Marrakech p86
Centre Artisanal, Marrakech p86
Maison d'Argent, Rabat p130

TEXTILES
Akbar Delights, Marrakech p85
Ali Baba, Taroudant p226
Art des Vilies Imperiale, L', Meknès p117
Atelier des Soeurs Franciscaines, Broderie &
  Tissage Berbères, Midelt & Around p263
Atelier Moro, Marrakech p85
Bazaar Mehdi, Essaouira p190
Bazar du Sud, Marrakech p86
Comptoir de L'Artisanat, Rabat p130
Dyers' souk, Fès p54
Textile souk, Chefchaouen p215
Tinerhir medina, The Dadès Valley
  & the Gorges p253

MIND & BODY

HAMMAMS
Dar Karma, Marrakech p95
Deux Tours, Les, Marrakech p08
Jardins de la Medina, Les, Marrakech p95
Maison Anglaise, La, Taroudant p224
Villa Maroc, Essaouira p197

NATURE

BIRD WATCHING
Merzouga p285
Middle Atlas p255-p263
Oualidia p201

GARDENS
Agdal Gardens, Marrakech p75
Boujiloud Gardens, Fès p56
Majorelle Gardens, Marrakech p79
Mamounia Gardens, Marrakech p70
Menara Gardens, Marrakech p80
Nectarome, Toubkal Atlas p241
Sources de Lalla Mimouna, Tinejdad,
  The Dadès Valley & the Gorges p253

SCENERY

COAST
Agadir to Sidi Ifni p154-p167
Asilah & Around p168-p179
Casablanca p32-p45
El-Jadida, Oualidia & Azzemour p198-p205
Essaouira p180-p197
Rabat & Salé p124-p133
Tetouan & Around p230-p235

DESERT
Ouarzazate & the Drâa Valley p270-p281
The Tafilelt Oasis & Merzouga p282-p289

MOUNTAINS
Ameln Valley & Tafraoute p16-p23
The Dadès Valley & the Gorges
  p248-p257
Middle Atlas p255-p267
Ouarzazate &the Drâa Valley p270-p281
Taza & Around p24-p29
Tetouan & Around p230-p235
Toubkal Atlas p237-p247

NATIONAL PARKS
Ifrane National Park, Middle Atlas p260
Parc National du Tazekka, Taza & Around p27
Souss Massa National Park,
  Agadir to Sidi Ifni p159

OUTDOOR ACTIVITIES

HIKING & BIKING
Ameln Valley & Tafraoute p16-p23
The Dadès Valley & the Gorges p250
Toubkal Atlas p238-p247

SKIING
Toubkal Atlas p238-p247

SURFING & WINDSURFING
Agadir to Sidi Ifni p154-p167
El-Jadida, Oualidia & Azzemour p198-p205
Essaouira p186

SIGHTS

KASBAHS

Amridil, The Dadès Valley & the Gorges p250
Chefchaouan, p211
Kasbah & Musée d'Al-Kasbah, Tangiers p139
Kasbah des Oudayas, Rabat & Salé p126
Taouirt Kasbah, Ouarzazate & the Drâa Valley
  p273

MISCELLANEOUS

American Legation, Tangier p139
Atelier des Soeurs Franciscaines, Broderie
  & Tissage Berbères, Midelt & Around,
  Middle Atlas p263
Ben Youssef Medersa, Marrakech p73
Chellah, Rabat p127
Cinemathèque de Tangier, Tangier p146
Fondation Lorin, Tangier p139
Granaries, Meknès p113
Koubba El-Badiyin, Marrakech p73
Koubbet Es-Soufara & the underground storage,
  Meknès p113
Maison Tiskiwin, Marrakech p77
Mausoleum of Moulay Ismail, Meknès p113
Medersa Bou Inania, Fès p53
Saadian Tombs, Marrakech p77
St Andrew's Church, Tangier p141
Théâtre de la Kasbah, Chefchaouen p216
Tour Hassan & Mausoleum de Mohammed V, La,
  Rabat p127

MOSQUES

Andalous Mosque, Fès p54
Grand Mosque & Bou Inania Medersa,
  Meknès p114
Hassan II Mosque, Casablanca p36
Karaouiyine Mosque & Library, Fès p53
Koutoubia Mosque, Marrakech p69
Spanish Mosque, Chefchaouen p212
Tin Mal, Tin Mal, Toubkal Atlas p242
Tour Hassan & Mausoleum de Mohammed V, La
  Rabat p127

MUSEUMS

Dar Si Said Museum, Marrakech p77
Musée Dar Batha, Fès p53
Musée Dar Jamai, Meknès p114
Musée de Judaisme Marocain, Casablanca p37
Musée des Oasis, Tinejdad, The Dadès
  Valley & the Gorges p254
Musée du Marrakech, Marrakech p73
Musée Maroc Belghazi, Fès p53
Musée National des Bijoux, Rabat p127
Musée Nejjarine des Arts et Métiers
  du Bois, Fès p54

PALACES

Badii Palace, Marrakech p75
Bahia Palace, Marrakech p76
Palais des Idrissides, Meknès p114
Palais Glaoui, Fès p54
Palais Raissouli, Asilah p173
Palais Royal, Rabat p129

SOUKS

Essaouira p185
Fès p53
Marrakech p70
Taroudant p226

SYNAGOGUES

Essaouira p185
Synagogue Rabbi Shlomo Ibn Danan, Fès p54

TANNERIES

Fès p54
Marrakech p75

TOURS

Camel tours, Tafilelt Oasis & Merzouga p282-p289
Restoration tours, Fès p55

GOING OUT

CLUBS

Amstrong Legend, Casablanca p41
Black House, Casablanca p42
Dawliz Le, Casablanca p42
Hôtel Transatlantique, Meknès p118
Kazbar, Casablanca p42
Pacha, Marrakech p92
Palais Jad Mahal, Marrakech p92
Petit Roche, Le, Casablanca p42
Thêatro, Marrakech p92

COCKTAILS

Bar Al Mandar, Fès p59
Kechmara, Marrakech p92
Riad Fès, Fès p60

LIVE ENTERTAINMENT

Amstrong Legend, Casablanca p41
Camping Fès, Fès p60
Comptoir, Marrakech p91
Hôtel Transatlantique, Casablanca p45
Jardin Ziryab, Chefchaouen p212
Khamlia, The Tafilelt Oasis & Merzouga p285
Palais La Medina, Fès p59
Tricam's, Le, Tangier p146